Palgrave Studies in Classical Liberalism

Series Editors
David Hardwick
Vancouver, BC, Canada

Leslie Marsh
Department of Pathology and Laboratory Medicine,
Faculty of Medicine
University of British Columbia
Vancouver, BC, Canada

This series offers a forum to writers concerned that the central presuppositions of the liberal tradition have been severely corroded, neglected, or misappropriated by overly rationalistic and constructivist approaches.

The hardest-won achievement of the liberal tradition has been the wrestling of epistemic independence from overwhelming concentrations of power, monopolies and capricious zealotries. The very precondition of knowledge is the exploitation of the epistemic virtues accorded by society's situated and distributed manifold of spontaneous orders, the DNA of the modern civil condition.

With the confluence of interest in situated and distributed liberalism emanating from the Scottish tradition, Austrian and behavioral economics, non-Cartesian philosophy and moral psychology, the editors are soliciting proposals that speak to this multidisciplinary constituency. Sole or joint authorship submissions are welcome as are edited collections, broadly theoretical or topical in nature.

More information about this series at
http://www.palgrave.com/gp/series/15722

Walter E. Block

Property Rights

The Argument for Privatization

palgrave
macmillan

Walter E. Block
Loyola University
New Orleans, LA, USA

Palgrave Studies in Classical Liberalism
ISBN 978-3-030-28352-0 ISBN 978-3-030-28353-7 (eBook)
https://doi.org/10.1007/978-3-030-28353-7

This Palgrave Macmillan imprint is published by the registered company Springer Nature Switzerland AG.
The registered company address is: Gewerbestrasse 11, 6330 Cham, Switzerland

Foreword

Dr. Walter Block is one of the most impressive, and productive, students of my late friend and advisor Murray Rothbard. Like Murray, and myself, Dr. Block's work is rooted in Austrian Economics as taught by the man I consider the greatest thinker of the twentieth century, Ludwig Von Mises. In *Private Property Rights*, Dr. Block applies his mastery of Austrian economics to explain why private property rights must be respected if we are to obtain economic prosperity, individual liberty, and a civilized social order. Even more importantly, Dr. Block exposes the fallacies in the arguments of those who oppose private property rights.

Perhaps the most useful service Dr. Block performs is his analysis of the fallacies that cause some non-Misesian libertarians to take positions undermining private property and a free society. Hopefully, Dr. Block's arguments will cause these well-meaning but misguided libertarians to reexamine and ultimately adopt the Misesian paradigm.

One of the most impressive aspects of this book is Dr. Block's demonstration that respecting private property rights helps resolve areas of social conflicts. For example, if the government controls schools, then there will inevitably be quarrels about how the students shall dress, what they should read, what shall be taught, and how the institution should deal with other controversial issues. But when parents control education, then students can receive an education that reflects their needs and the wishes of their parents.

Even those who disagree with some of Dr. Block's conclusions will benefit from studying this publication. Buy this book, and an extra copy for a friend with a thirst for an exhilarating intellectual adventure encompassing the sort of legal theory, economics, history, and political philosophy that we must adopt if we are to have a truly free society.

Former U.S. Congressman (R, Texas) Dr. Ron Paul

Contents

List of Tables

Introduction

Private property rights are the bedrock not only of the economy but of civilization itself. They may not be a sufficient condition to justice and prosperity, but they are certainly a necessary condition. And yet private property rights have been widely denigrated not only by economists and philosophers characterized as of the left but of the right as well. This book presents a radical and unflinching defense of private property rights and a critique of its intellectual enemies.

New Orleans, 2019 Walter E. Block

Part I

Philosophy

1

Property and Exploitation

1. Property Rights

Whenever one says "I own a house," what one normally means is: I have the right to determine how that particular resource—described in objective, physical terms—is to be employed; I am free to employ it for any purpose whatsoever, provided that in so doing I do not impair the physical integrity of resources owned by others; I am likewise entitled to expect that the physical integrity of my resource, my house, remains unaffected by the actions others perform with the physical resources at their disposal. Property rights, then, are commonly conceived of as extending to specific, physical objects. These objects are economic goods and hence have value; otherwise, no one would claim them. Yet it is not to the value attached to a specific resource that property rights extend, but rather exclusively to the physical integrity of such a good. I do not own the value of my house. I own a physically specified house, and I have the right to expect that others will not physically damage it.

W. E. Block, *Property Rights*, Palgrave Studies in Classical Liberalism,
https://doi.org/10.1007/978-3-030-28353-7_1

2. Physical Property, Yes; Values, No

Plausible as this theory of property is,[1] in much of contemporary political economy and philosophy, confusion abounds on the issue of whether property rights concern the value of physical things or, instead, it is the physical things themselves which are of value.[2] It is thus necessary to clarify why the common notion of property rights as extending exclusively to physical things is indeed correct, and why the notion of property rights in values is flawed.

First, it should be noted that these theories are incompatible with each other. It is easily recognized that every action of a person may alter the value (or price) of another person's property. If A enters the labor or the marriage market, this may impair B's value in these markets. And if A changes his relative evaluation of beer and bread, or if A decides to become a brewer or a baker himself, this may change the property values of the—other—brewers and bakers. According to the view that value-impairments constitute rights violations, it follows that A's actions may represent punishable offenses. Yet if A is guilty, then B and the brewers or bakers in turn must be entitled to defend themselves against A's actions. Their right to defend themselves can only consist in their (or their agent) being permitted to physically attack or restrict A and his property: B must be entitled to physically bar A from entering the

[1] See, for instance, Armen Alchian, Economic Forces at Work, Indianapolis: Liberty Fund, 1977, pp. 131–132; notes Alchian: "although private property rights protect private property from physical changes chosen by other people, no immunity is implied for the exchange value of one's property … Private property, as I understand it, does not imply that a person may use his property in any way he sees fit so long as no one else is 'hurt.' Instead, it seems to mean the right to use goods (or to transfer that right) in any way the owner wishes to long as the physical attributes or uses of all other people's private property is unaffected. And that leaves plenty of room for disturbance and alienation of affections of other people."

[2] The idea of property-in-values underlies, for instance, John Rawls' "difference principle," that is, the rule that all inequalities among people have to be expected to be to everyone's advantage—regardless of how they have come about (Rawls, A Theory of Justice, Cambridge: Harvard University Press, 1971, p. 60, pp. 75f, p. 83); and also Robert Nozick's claim that a "dominant protection agency" has the right to outlaw competitors regardless of their actual behavior, and his related claim that "non-productive exchanges," in which one party would be better off if the other did not exist, may be outlawed—again regardless of whether or not such an exchange involved any physical invasion (Nozick, Anarchy, State, and Utopia, New York: Basic Books, 1974, pp. 55f, pp. 83–86).

labor or marriage market; and the brewers or bakers must be allowed to physically hinder A from spending his own money as he pleases, for example, from using his own possessions for the operation of a brewery or bakery. Based on this theory, the physical damaging or restricting of another person's property use obviously cannot be said to constitute a rights violation. Rather, physical attacks and physical restrictions on the use of private property then have to be classified as lawful defenses. On the other hand, suppose that physical attacks and physical property restrictions constitute rights violations. Then B and brewers or bakers are not allowed to defend themselves against A's actions. For A's actions—his entering the labor or marriage market, his changed evaluation of beer and bread, and his opening of a brewery or bakery—affects neither B's bodily integrity nor the physical integrity of other brewers' or bakers' property. If they engage in physical resistance against A's actions nonetheless, then the right to defense rests with A. In this case, however, it cannot be considered a rights violation that a person's actions impair the value of another person's property. No other, third alternative exists.

These two theories of property are not only incompatible, however. The alternative view—that a person may own the value (or price) or scarce physical goods—is also "praxeologically" impossible[3]; that is, it is a theory that we cannot put into effect even if we wanted to; as well, it is as argumentatively indefensible. For while every person can, in principle, have control over whether or not his actions cause the physical attributes of other persons' property to change, control over whether or not his actions affect the value of other people's property rests with other people and their evaluations. Consequently, it would be impossible to ever know in advance if one's planned actions were permitted or not. One would have to interrogate the entire population to make sure that one's planned actions would not impair the value of anybody else's property; as well,

[3] On the concept of "praxeology," and the systematic reconstruction of economic theory as a "logic of action," see Ludwig von Mises, Human Action. A Treatise on Economics, New Haven: Yale University Press, 1949 (3rd ed. Chicago: Regnery, 1966); idem, Theory and History: An Interpretation of Social and Economic Evolution, New Haven: Yale University Press, 1957 (reprint: Auburn University, Alabama: The Ludwig von Mises Institute, 1985).

one would have to reach a universal agreement on who was permitted to do what, with which goods.

Mankind would be long dead before this was ever accomplished. Hence, the theory breaks down as nonoperational. Moreover, the proposition that a person may own the value of a physical thing involves an internal contradiction. For simply in order to propose this theory it would have to be presupposed that its proponent is allowed to act.

He must do so prior (and simultaneously) to making his proposition or seeking agreement for his proposal regarding how to protect property values from value-intrusive actions. He cannot wait, and suspend acting, until an agreement is reached; rather, he must be permitted to employ at least his own physical body (and its standing room) immediately.

Otherwise he could not even make his proposal. Yet if one is permitted to assert a proposition—and no one could deny this without falling into a contradiction—then this is possible only because there exist objective (physical) borders of property. Every person can recognize these borders as such on his own, without having to agree first with anyone else with respect to one's subjective system of values and evaluations. Prior to even beginning the intellectual endeavor of proposing property theories, then, as its very own praxeological foundation, there must be an acting (e.g., speaking) man, defined in terms of physical or human resources. Value of utility considerations, agreements, or contracts—all things that contemporary political philosophers and economists typically regard as fundamental to their various theories of justice or property—already presupposes the existence of physically independent decision-making units. Also presupposed is a description of these units in terms of a person's property relations to definite physical resources—otherwise there would be no one to value or agree on anything, and nothing on which to agree or about which to make contracts. Anyone proposing anything other than a theory of property in physically defined resources would contradict the content of his proposition merely by making it. He could not even open his mouth if his theory were correct; and the fact that he does open it disproves his claim.[4]

---

[4] See also Hans-Hermann Hoppe, A Theory of Socialism and Capitalism, Boston: Kluwer Academic Publishers, 1989, ch. 7; idem, The Economics and Ethics of Private Property, Boston: Kluwer

3. Exploitation

The notion of property in values is praxeologically impossible (nonoperational) if formulated as a theory of justice, that is, as a system of rules that applies universally to each and every person alike. It becomes operational if—and only if—it is employed instead as a theory of exploitation. It is at least logically coherent as a system of rules that privileges one person or group of persons at the expense of another, underprivileged person or group. No one could act, if everyone owned the value attached to what he regarded as his.

Acting is possible, however, if B owns the value of the resources presently at his disposal and is entitled to determine what others, A, may or may not do with resources they control so as to not impair his, B's, property values. This would perforce include A's compensatory delivery to B of resources presently possessed by A. On the other hand, A is then entitled to own neither the value nor the physical integrity of his possessions and has no claim against B except that B allows him to do anything as long as it is to B's advantage.

Although praxeologically possible, such a system of rules does not even qualify as a potential human ethic, because it fails to meet the universalizability criterion. By adopting this system, two distinct classes of persons are created—super-humans or exploiters such as B, and sub-humans or the exploited such as A—to whom different "law" applies. Accordingly, it fails from the outset as a universal, human ethic. It is not—not even in principle—universally acceptable and thus cannot qualify as law. In order to be considered lawful, a rule must apply universally, for everyone equally. The idea of property in values, then, is not only praxeologically impossible—if universalized—but also inhumane—if not universalized.

Academic Publishers, 1993, part II; idem, 'Man, Economy, and Liberty,' Review of Austrian Economics, Vol. 4, 1990, esp. pp. 260–263. Hoppe, Hans-Hermann, Democracy – The God that Failed: The Economics and Politics of Monarchy, Democracy, and Natural Order, Rutgers University, N.J.: Transaction Publishers, 2001.

4. Examples

From this conclusion far-reaching consequences follow: (1) Discrimination; (2) defamation and libel suits; (3) comparable worth, parity, and affirmative action policies; and (4) the notorious "ex-lover seeks compensation for no longer being loved" suits would then have to be regarded as scandalous if at times amusing perversions of law and justice. Likewise, institutions such as (5) licensing laws; (6) zoning regulations; (7) anti-trust laws; and (8) insider trading laws represent legal outgrowths of the property-in-values theory.

Ultimately, they all involve restricting A's control over specified resources by correspondingly expanding B's control over them. This holds true even though A had not physically damaged, and was not in the process of physically damaging, any of B's possessions in doing whatever A wants to do with the means presently at this own disposal. B's claim against A is based not on physical losses caused by A, but rests solely on B's assumption that A's actions, unless restricted, impose a value loss on him. In this theory B owns the value of his property and hence is entitled to reassure his value-integrity by imposing physical restrictions on A's actions. One party seeks material compensation from another for the crime of non-material value damages suffered from having one's expectations regarding another's actions disappointed. Disappointed hopes, of which life offers an unlimited supply, are used by one person as a justification for trying to physically enrich himself at the expense of another.

Let us now illustrate the exploitative character of each of these legal practices in some more detail.

4.1. Discrimination

Strictly speaking discrimination is the refusal to deal with, trade with, live next to, buy from, sell to, engage in any commercial or non-commercial activity whatsoever, with another person. In discriminating against B, A undoubtedly reduces B's economic well-being, compared to what it would have been had A not so discriminated.[5] The value of B's physical

[5] A reduces his own wealth, too, apart from the psychic income gains that accrue to him, which is the reason he indulges his preferences in this manner.

property, as well as his "human capital,"[6] falls below the level otherwise attainable. Nevertheless, since B can only own his person plus his physical property, he can have no just claim against A for shunning him.

There exists a categorical distinction between physical invasion and the refusal to deal with, or discrimination.[7] A's actions are that of a boycott and do not constitute physical intrusion. But many commentators, unfortunately, fail to make this vital distinction. All too often it is thought, for example, that rape and discrimination against women are on a continuum. Or that lynching blacks is different only in degree to ignoring them. But a moment's reflection will show that these activities are night and day compared to each other. The physical assault of B on A (as "retaliation" against A's prior discriminatory action) always involves losses in value terms. But it also robs A temporarily or permanently of the very means to recover such losses. In contrast, while discrimination may likewise be unpleasant, in leaving B's physical possessions unimpaired, it strictly limits B's value losses. For example, if no one will hire ugly women to be secretaries, the wages they command will tend to decline. But at lower compensation levels, these females—their physical integrity and hence their job skills being unimpaired—will become more of a bargain in the labor market. This, presumably, will counter the negative effect of the initial discrimination. They will not be consigned to unemployment, the first result, but will rather find jobs, albeit at lower wages than absent discrimination. However, once on the payroll, they will be able to demonstrate their "true" productivity (perhaps even in excess of that of their more beauteous competitors) and can in this way recoup at least in part their initial salary losses. In sharp contrast, had physical invasion been directed against them (or, as a retaliatory action, against their more beautiful competitors), none of these ameliorative reactions could have come into play.[8]

---

[6] Gary Becker, Human Capital, New York: National Bureau of Economic Research, 1964.

[7] See Walter Block, 'The Economics of Discrimination,' The Journal of Business Ethics, Vol. 11, 1992, pp. 241–254.

[8] One must also distinguish between discrimination on the part of a private property owner and that engaged in by the State. In the former case, as we have seen, the law of private property assures that value losses may be recovered by the "victim." But this does not apply when government engages in discriminatory behavior. If the civil service shuns ugly secretaries, their wages will fall as a result. But this will not make them more attractive to the bureaucracy, since their access to

4.2. Defamation and Libel

Most commentators have argued that one has a legitimate ownership right to one's reputation. But this is not so. For the simple reason that one's reputation consists of the thoughts of other people.[9] That is, A's reputation consists solely of the thoughts of B, C, D, and B's reputation of those of A, C, D, and so on. But since no one can own the thoughts of other people, one cannot, paradoxically, own one's own reputation.

While there can be no universal right to one's reputation, and libel and defamation do not constitute exploitation per se, the right of a person to engage in libelous or defamatory action is not unrestricted. For while everyone has an unrestricted right concerning his thoughts, the right of free speech is not absolute. For example, no one has the right to tell another person "unless you hand over to me your wallet, I'll shoot you." This sort of speech would be strictly forbidden in a private property society. It is a threat to engage in initiatory violence. As well, no one, including any of my detractors, has a right to come to my living room to give me a speech or tell me what he thinks about me and when I tell him to leave object on the ground of his right to freedom of speech. A trespasser has no free speech rights whatsoever—on my property. Free speech rights, so called, are really but an instance of private property rights. I can say anything I want on my property and so can anyone else, including any libelous person, on his own property.

4.3. Comparative Worth and Parity Policies

Most advocates of Equal Pay for Equal Work (EPFEW) or of Equal Pay for Work of Equal Value (EPFWOEV) legislation maintain that these enactments are necessary in order to combat employer discrimination

---

coercive levies from the citizenry (e.g., taxes) shield them from any concern for profit. To the extent that the government engages in discrimination, then, the victims are in a far worse position than when this occurs in the private sector.

[9] See Murray N. Rothbard, Power and Market: Government and the Economy, Menlo Park, Cal.: Institute for Humane Studies, 1970; idem, For a New Liberty, Macmillan: New York, 1973; idem, The Ethics of Liberty, Humanities Press: Atlantic Highlands, N.J., 1982; see also Walter Block, Defending the Undefendable, New York: Fleet Press, 1976.

between males and females. Even were this the case, there would be nothing that should be legally untoward in such a situation, for women own only their labor power, not the price placed upon it by others. Did they but have a right to the latter, as we have seen, it would be impossible for anyone at all to engage in human action, lest they advertently or inadvertently impact on the value of any women's effort.

But it is not at all the case that women earn less than men due to employer discrimination. On the contrary, this state of affairs is due to the asymmetrical effects of marriage: it enhances male wages and reduces that of females. Due to unequal responsibilities in the average family for child care, shopping, cleaning, laundering, cooking, and a whole host of other such activities, the average wife earns only some 40% of her husband's salary. In contrast, there is no pay gap at all between females and males who have never been touched by the institution of marriage; the salaries of the never married are virtually identical. The much noted and reviled by feminists income ratio of 60%–75% is actually an amalgam of the experiences of these two very different groups of people.[10]

Contrary to the views of feminists, private property and markets are the institution, par excellence, which assures not only EPFEW, but EPFWOEV as well. Suppose, for example, that a man and a woman had equal productivity of $20/hour and that the man were paid this amount of compensation.[11]

[10] See Thomas Sowell, Race and Economics, New York: Morrow, 1983. See also Walter Block, 'Economic Intervention, Discrimination, and Unforeseen Consequences,' in: Walter Block/Michael Walker, eds., Discrimination, Affirmative Action and Equal Opportunity, Vancouver: Fraser Institute, 1982, pp. 101–125; idem, Focus on Employment Equity: A Critique of the Abella Royal Commission on Equality in Employment (with Michael Walker), Vancouver: Fraser Institute, 1985; Michael Levin, Feminism and Freedom, New Brunswick, N.J.: Transaction Books, 1987. Epstein, Richard A., Forbidden Grounds: The Case against Employment Discrimination Laws, Cambridge: Harvard University Press, 1992.

[11] That wages tend to equal productivity levels is one of the best established propositions in all of economics. This result can be illustrated in our example. If the man's productivity is $20 and his wage is higher than that, say, $25, the firm employing him will lose $5/hour. If they persist in this behavior, and especially if they apply it to other workers as well, they will go bankrupt. On the other hand, if the wage is below this level, say at $12, then a profit opportunity of $8 exists. Any competitor would be glad to woo these workers away from his present employer for, say, $12.25. But if one company offers that amount, another will up the ante to $12.50. Where will this bidding process end? As close to the productivity level of $20 as search and transportation costs will allow.

Suppose further that the women were paid only $12, 60% of the male wage, exemplifying the supposedly discriminatory "pay gap." This would set up the same irresistible profit opportunities as in the case of the male paid less than his productivity level. Any "male chauvinist" employer who hired the man at $20, rather than the equally productive woman at $12, would place himself at a serious competitive disadvantage. He would be a prime candidate for bankruptcy.

EPFEW and EPFWOEV, then, equate wages between equally productive males and females. The reason women earn only some 60% of what males do is because, on average (due, perhaps largely, to marriage asymmetries), they are only 60% as productive. So EPFEW and EPFWOEV have already been attained on the market. There is no discriminatory wage gap. But this is not at all what the advocates of pay "equity" demand. Their view, predicated on the notion that people have a right not merely to their own persons and property but to the value thereof, is in effect that males and females should receive the same compensation, despite differences in productivity. Imagine that their wish were granted. That is, suppose that the law requires a male with productivity of $20, and a female with productivity of $12, both to be paid the former amount. Now, incentives will all be turned around. Instead of having a financial interest in hiring the woman, the firm now will be led "as if by an invisible hand" to avoid her at all costs. The result will be greatly enhanced unemployment rates for women, a result which obtains whenever the legal system artificially prices factors of production out of the market.

4.4. Affirmative Love

Most people can see through lawsuits seeking damage for alienation of affection. These are properly regarded as a scandal and a disgrace. People cannot own the love of others. The very notion is contradictory; true affection must be given voluntarily, while ownership implies the right to take it from another person, whether or not he is willing to bestow it. So these suits, too, are an instance of the confusion over physical ownership vs. property in values. An ex-lover seeking financial compensation from her no longer amorous suitor is really asserting that she has the right to control his feelings. If this were true his ownership right over his person would be null and void, since he could not even choose the object of his desires.

4.5. Licensing Laws

This legislation is an attempt to restrict the actions of others so that the value of one's own property can be enhanced or stabilized. If entry into the industry of potential competitors can be precluded, one's wealth increases. Naturally, this motivation is disguised, hidden behind a plethora of "public interest" billingsgate. Accordingly, taxi license holders wax eloquent about the reduced traffic congestion afforded by this system, and members of the American Medical Association take pride in the enhanced quality of medical services thus engendered. But this is empty rhetoric. Taxi cab medallions sell for many thousands of dollars, attesting to the value of government-imposed monopoly, not to the ease of traffic flows. And the salary levels achieved by doctors have little to do with the nation's health; if anything, the very opposite is true.[12] For example, consider the Viennese doctors—the best in the world at that time—who came to the United States to escape the ravages of National-Socialism in the 1930s. It was no coincidence that the AMA did everything in its power to hinder the process whereby they could practice their profession. They insisted on loyalty oaths, but this had nothing to do with patient care. They compelled familiarity with the English language—as if there were no German-speaking sick people or translators. They demanded residence periods, as if these were anything but a blatant attempt to forestall unwanted competition.[13]

But licensing laws do not even go far enough if the values of taxis, medical equipment, and skills are to be maintained and enhanced. Strictly speaking, there should also be requirements on the demand side as well.

---

[12] See Milton Friedman, Capitalism and Freedom, Chicago: University of Chicago Press, 1962, ch. 9; Ronald Hamowy, Canadian Medicine: A Study in Restricted Entry, Vancouver: Fraser Institute, 1984. Henderson, David R., The Joy of Freedom: An Economist's Odyssey, Financial Times, Prentice Hall, 2001, ch. 15.

[13] A similar situation took place with regard to Cuban doctors who fled Castro. The AMA placed obstacles in their way of attempting to practice medicine in the United States as well.

That is, the temporarily unemployed cabbies should be able to commandeer the man on the street, force him into the taxi, and drive him, if need be right back to the point of embarkation, so as to maintain revenues. And if ever revenues decline, doctors ought to be allowed to inflict diseases on innocent people—so that they can charge them for cures. After all, according to the property-in-values theory, people who do not get sick, and/or refuse to ride around in taxis, are really stealing from doctors and cabbies, respectively.

4.6. Zoning

Who has not yielded to the temptation—at least in thought—of wishing to maintain, if not upgrade the value of his real estate holdings? One way to do this is through entrepreneurial action (including insurance). A person purchases a home in a large-scale condominium development, for instance, where all owners are precluded from any activity (painting a house with polka dots, ripping it down, and putting in a cement factory) which might conceivably lower property values. Alternatively, a restrictive covenant can be signed with neighbors to the same end. But this costs money, time, and effort. There are "transactions" costs involved. Frequently it is much easier to rely on the political process. If a law is passed requiring a minimum one-acre lot size for single family dwellings, hordes of "undesirables" can be kept out. For the only chance of the poor successfully bidding against wealthy people is in the form of multiple dwelling units. They can "gang up" on the rich by more intensive land settlement. But if this is precluded by zoning laws, that option is not available to them. Better yet, inaugurate the no growth philosophy, ostensibly for environmental ends; this obstructs any new building, for whatever purpose, the better to maintain property values. Why rely on an "imperfect" market when legislative enactments can attain such ends?[14]

City planners (who owe employment to the existence of zoning laws) argue that this system keeps "incompatible" land uses separated from one another. But private property rights can achieve the same ends, without

[14] See William Tucker, The Excluded Americans: Homelessness and Housing Policy, Chicago: Regnery-Gateway, 1990.

the use of force and compulsion.[15] The reason filling stations do not locate in cul-de-sacs is that there is too little traffic to support them there. Likewise, cement factories are prohibited by marketplace considerations from setting up shop in downtown areas. High real estate prices relegate them to the periphery. When land use bureaucrats err, they do so on a colossal, city-wide scale. They lose millions for the citizenry but not a penny of their own personal funds. The benefits of marketplace zoning, as is illustrated most drastically by the failure of the Soviet economic system, is that private investors, who risk their own money, tend to be more careful with it. The drawbacks of central planning apply to cities as well as to countries.

4.7. Anti-trust

Anti-trust laws serve many purposes. From the point of view of the expert in law and economics, for instance, they function as a full employment bill, calling forth millions of hours of highly paid expert testimony. From the perspective of the neo-classical economist it furnishes an opportunity to demonstrate manual dexterity with average and marginal cost and revenue curves, "dead weight losses" and "resource misallocations," the better to dazzle naive students. For the political ideologue, the theory of monopoly, upon which anti-trust laws are based, provides the "scientific legitimation" for the permanency of so-called market failures; it is a stick which can be used to beat up on the private property (capitalist) system.

For our purposes, anti-trust laws illustrate yet another instance of defining property in terms of values, not physical criteria. If company A sells a better product, or the same one at a lower price, how does it "hurt" its competitors? Only in value terms, not physical ones. As in the case of witch craft, or heresy during the period of the inquisition, there is no defense against the charge of monopoly. Promotion of consumer welfare is no defense; indeed, it is part of the indictment. Selling at a price lower than competitors' is prima facie evidence of cutthroat competition; selling at a higher price indicates monopolistic profiteering; selling at the

[15] See Bernard Siegan, Land Use without Zoning, New York: Lexington, 1972.

same price as everyone else is evidence of collusion. Since there is no fourth alternative, any firm is theoretically guilty as charged, no matter what its behavior. Similarly with quantity sold. Too much is pre-emptive, too little is monopolistic withholding, and the same as others is collusive dividing up of the market. Heads the anti-trust division and the Federal Trade Commission win; tails, the business concern loses.[16]

4.8. Insider Trading

The last instance of the property-in-values theory we shall discuss are laws prohibiting "insider trading." The complaint on the part of the advocates of such laws is that the knowledge possessed by someone, when acted upon in a commercial matter, is a violation of the rights of others. Previously we had asserted that "no one could act, if everyone owned the value attached to what he regarded as his." With insider trading we see a paradigm case of this.[17]

The legally established contention here is that a knowledgeable state of mind can convert what would otherwise be a legitimate purchase of stock into an illegitimate one, provided that the information relied upon is not homogeneously spread throughout the population. Since it never is, virtually any commercial activity with regard to stocks and bonds can be deemed unlawful. The situation is indeed worse than that. A rigorous pursuit of the "logic" of insider trading prohibitions could potentially be used to preclude any market transaction.

Did a woman buy an umbrella because she heard a newscast that if would rain tomorrow? Unless everyone turned into the same weather program, and listened as attentively as did she, this would give her an unfair advantage over other people. And what of the person who attended horrors! a course on the case and feeding of stocks and bonds? Such

[16] See Anderson, William, Walter Block, Thomas J. DiLorenzo, Ilana Mercer, Leon Snyman and Christopher Westley, 'The Microsoft Corporation in Collision with Antitrust Law,' The Journal of Social, Political and Economic Studies, Vol. 26, No. 1, Winter 2001, pp. 287–302.

[17] See Henry A. Manne, Insider Trading and the Stock Market, New York: Free Press, 1966; idem, 'In Defense of Insider Trading,' Harvard Business Review, 113, Nov./Dec. 1966. See also Walter Block and Robert McGee, 'Information, Privilege, Opportunity and Insider Trading,' Northern Illinois Law Review, December 1989, Vol. 10, No. 1, pp. 1–35.

studies would surely give the student an "inside track" vis-à-vis those who had not attended the lectures. If the crime of excessive information[18] can be applied to umbrellas and stocks and bonds, it can be applied to anything: to real estate, to amenities, to human capital, to factors of production. Moreover, this doctrine calls into question the acquisition of any knowledge (unless, of course, it is evenly spread throughout the entire world community). Those particularly at risk include doctors, lawyers, economists, college professors, Nobel Prize winners.

[18] Another 'market failure' beloved by interventionists is 'lack of perfect information.' Let's see if we have this straight. Too little information is no good, because it violates the requirement of perfect information. Too much information is problematic, because it is incompatible with the strictures against insider trading. How about 'the same amount of information as everyone else?' Aha. A lacunae in the theory. So far, to the best of knowledge of the present authors, this state of affairs has not been subjected to legal prohibition. But who knows? A theoretical breakthrough may be lurking in these intellectual thickets.

2

The Moral Dimensions of Poverty, Entitlements, and Theft

The Ideal World

For the limited government, free enterprise-oriented classical liberal, there is only one type of entitlement the citizen may properly receive from the state: security of his person and property. This entitlement entails an army to protect him from foreign despots, a police force to shield him from domestic villains, and a court system to determine who is and who is not an initiator of violence against another person or his property. Any and all other entitlements are illegitimate—at least from the perspective of this economic philosophy.[1] One defense of this limited notion of government is that entitlement programs[2] are counterproductive,

[1] Observe that this conclusion is similar—but not precisely equal—to the vision of appropriate entitlements as provided for in the US Constitution. There, in addition to the aforementioned courts, armies, and police, the citizen is also entitled to a post office and other public enterprises. These services and institutions would be strictly prohibited under a libertarian limited government vision, the model we shall assume for the purpose of this chapter.

[2] Now and henceforth, we use the term "entitlement program" to refer to other initiatives of the state over and above armies, courts, and police. These latter three we characterize not as entitlement programs, which are always illegitimate uses of government force, but as the sole legitimate functions of government. For a critique of this limited government philosophy from within libertarianism, see Bruce L. Benson, The Enterprise of Law: Justice Without the State (San Francisco: Pacific

W. E. Block, *Property Rights*, Palgrave Studies in Classical Liberalism,
https://doi.org/10.1007/978-3-030-28353-7_2

which means they actually hurt their presumptively intended beneficiaries.

The list of such instances is long and woeful. Perhaps the most egregious is the welfare program Aid to Families with Dependent Children (AFDC). Originally introduced as a means of helping the needy,[3] AFDC has instead promoted dependency, eviscerated personal ambition, and created whole generations of unwanted and often abused children.[4] These

---

Research Institute, 1990); "The Impetus for Recognizing Private Property and Adopting Ethical Behavior in a Market Economy: Natural Law, Government Law, or Evolving Self-Interest," The Review of Austrian Economics 6, 2 (1993): 43–80; "Customary Law as a Social Contract: International Commercial Law," Constitutional Political Economy 2 (1992): 1–27; "An Evolutionary Contractarian View of Primitive Law: The Institutions and Incentives Arising under Customary Indian Law," The Review of Austrian Economics 5, 1 (1991): 41–65; "Enforcement of Private Property Rights in Primitive Societies: Law Without Government," The Journal of Libertarian Studies IX, 1 (Winter 1989): 1–26; "Legal Evolution in Primitive Societies," Journal of Institutional and Theoretical Economics 144 (1988): 772– 88; "The Lost Victim and Other Failures of the Public Law Experiment," Harvard Journal of Law and Public Policy 9 (1986): 399–427; Anthony De Jasay, The State (Oxford: Basil Blackwell, 1985); David Friedman, The Machinery of Freedom: Guide to a Radical Capitalism, 2nd ed. (La Salle, Ill.: Open Court, 1989); "Private Creation and Enforcement of Law: A Historical Case," Journal of Legal Studies 8 (1979): 399–415; Hans-Hermann Hoppe, The Economics and Ethics of Private Property: Studies in Political Economy and Philosophy (Boston: Kluwer, 1993): "The Economics and Sociology of Taxation," in Taxation: An Austrian View, ed. L. Rockwell (Boston: Dordrecht, 1992); A Theory of Socialism and Capitalism: Economies, Polities, and Ethics (Boston: Kluwer, 1989); David Osterfeld, "Anarchism and the Public Goods Issue: Law, Courts, and the Police," The Journal of Libertarian Studies 9, 1 (Winter 1989): 47–68; Joseph R. Peden, "Property Rights in Celtic Irish Law," The Journal of Libertarian Studies 1, 2 (Spring 1977): 81–96; Murray N. Rothbard, For a New Liberty (New York: Macmillan, 1973); Power and Market: Government and the Economy (Menlo Park, Calif.: Institute for Humane Studies, 1970); The Ethics of Liberty (Atlantic Highlands, N.H.: Humanities Press, 1982); Lysander Spooner, No Treason (Larkspur, Co.: Tannehill, Morris, and Linda, 1966 [1870]); The Market for Liberty (New York: Laissez-Faire Books, 1984); William C. Woolridge, Uncle Sam the Monopoly Man (New Rochelle, N.Y.: Arlington House, 1970).

[3] For an alternative Marxist perspective, one which analyzes welfare as enabling capitalists to control labor markets, see Piven and Cloward, 1971.

[4] See Thomas Sowell, The Vision of the Anointed (New York: Basic Books, 1995); Race and Economics (New York: Longman, 1975); Ethnic America (New York: Basic Books, 1981); The Economics and Politics of Race: An International Perspective (New York: Morrow, 1983); A Conflict of Visions: Ideological Origins of Political Struggles (New York: Morrow, 1987); Race and Culture: A World View (New York: Basic Books, 1994); Charles Murray, Losing Ground: American Social Policy from 1950 to 1980 (New York: Basic Books, 1984); In Pursuit: Of Happiness and Good Government (New York: Simon & Schuster, 1990); Walter F. Williams, "Good Intentions—Bad Results: The Economic Pastoral and America's Disadvantaged," Notre Dame Journal of Law, Ethics, and Public Policy 2, 1 (1985): 179–99; Gary M. Anderson, "Welfare Programs in the Rent Seeking Society," Southern Economic Journal 54 (1987): 377–86; Martin Anderson, Welfare: The

children, in turn, often graduate to a life of crime and continue the practice of raising still other children of the same ilk.[5] The reason for this is not difficult to discern: supply curves slope in an upward direction; the more one pays for an item, the more of it is called forth in the market. Welfare is the offer of money for people who are poor. The more money offered for this purpose, the more incentive people have to change their behavior to be eligible for these funds, which is not to say that a Bill Gates or a Donald Trump will be attracted to this lifestyle. But there are always people on the margin, teetering on the edge, where, on one side, lies the (lower) middle class life of honesty and probity, and, on the other, the underclass of dissolution. In their precarious position on the fence they are particularly vulnerable to a slight push in either direction. AFDC provides that impetus, and it is all in the wrong direction—for our society in general, as well as for the particular people involved.[6]

Then there is the issue of public housing. Originally based on similar benevolent motives,[7] this attempt to help the poor, too, has instead boomeranged into disaster. The Cabrini Green projects in Chicago are world famous for feces and urine in the (often nonfunctioning) elevators, ripped out light bulbs, boarded up windows, crime, gangs, drugs, and other accouterments of a return to barbarism. The Pruitt-Igoe homes in Saint Louis were so uncivilized that they had to be bombed, not by terrorists,[8] but by the government housing authority charged with their upkeep and maintenance.

The cause of this dissolution is not hard to understand. Socialist to the core, the governments involved with these entitlements precluded commercial establishments such as stores, banks, and restaurants from these environs. But without the pedestrian traffic of shoppers, people living in

---

Political Economy of Welfare Reform in the United States (Stanford: Hoover Institution Press, 1978); Marvin Olasky, The Tragedy of American Compassion (Chicago: Regnery Gateway, 1992).

[5] Observe how the illegitimate entitlement of the dole is incompatible with the legitimate state function provided by the courts, armies, and police. One protects person and property from attack; the other exacerbates these problems.

[6] Anderson, "Welfare Programs in the Rent Seeking Society."

[7] Of course, as the old adage goes, "The road to hell is paved with good intentions."

[8] This is a debatable point.

the apartments above are less likely to keep their "eyes on the street."[9] This, in turn, leads to increased crime rates as criminals prefer to ply their trade without witnesses. Tipper income cut-offs are generally used by bureaucrats to determine eligibility for public housing. Thus when a poor tenant family surpasses a certain level of income, it is booted out of its accommodation. One can easily appreciate the disincentive effects here. Worse yet, those who prosper, and then are forced to leave, are the most successful among the inhabitants. They are the natural neighborhood leaders, typically adult males, who are desperately needed to serve as role models for teenagers. In this situation, the cream rises to the top, and then is skimmed off, leaving a helpless and victimized mass of people in its wake.

Another criticism of entitlements is that they have perverse income effect.[10] While most people see transfers as helping the poor at the expense of the rich, in fact, an inordinate number go to (sectors of the) middle class and the rich.[11] Listed under this rubric are farm subsidies (which go mainly to large-scale agri-business), bailouts for big business (Lockheed, Chrysler), rescues for the banks (e.g., the billions spent to undergird the Mexican peso), protective tariffs (which benefit domestic manufacturers while despoiling local consumers and third world industry), minimum wages (which oppress poor, unskilled minority group workers to further aggrandize rich, well-organized labor unions).[12] It is not without good reason that such recipients have been well and truly castigated as "corporate welfare bums."

If we have learned anything from the Public Choice School[13] it is that the more well-off are able to assert their will not only in the private but

---

[9] Jane Jacobs, The Death and Life of Great American Cities (New York: Vintage, 1989).

[10] This phraseology is particularly unfortunate because it implies that while there is something perverse about robbing the poor to enrich the wealthy, no such opprobrium applies to stealing from the rich and giving their money to the poor. However, at least for the classical liberal, theft is theft, no matter what the income status is of the victim or the recipient of the stolen goods.

[11] Terry Anderson and P. J. Hill, The Birth of the Transfer Society (Lanham, Md.: University Press of America, 1989).

[12] This is perhaps the most egregious and deceitful entitlement plan in that all experts know full well the effects of minimum wages on the poor. See Walter F. Williams, The State Against Blacks (New York: McGraw-Hill, 1982).

[13] Thomas J. DiLorenzo, "Competition and Political Entrepreneurship: Austrian Insights into Public Choice Theory," The Review of Austrian Economics 2 (1988): 59–71; James M. Buchanan, Cost and Choice: An Inquiry into Economic Theory (Chicago: Markham, 1969); James

also in the public sector. It should not occasion much surprise that this also holds true with regard to transfers. The rich are simply too well organized to allow a system of subsidies to function contrary to their own best interests.

A further difficulty with government largesse with taxpayers' money is that it engenders the idea that these funds come as a matter of right. The so-called welfare rights movement is only the tip of the iceberg. People now believe that they have the "right" to such diverse benefits as social security, education, food stamps, workers compensation, unemployment insurance, to mention only a few. But how can two separate people have the right to one and the same thing? How is it possible for both the rightful owner (the one who earned the money through voluntary market activity), as well as for the recipients of all these programs, to have a right to this wealth? This is impossible, since, if properly construed, there can be no such thing as a conflict in rights.

Adherents of entitlements often argue that these programs came about as a result of democratic institutions. Duly constituted politicians, who derive their authority from the electorate, inaugurated them. They, in turn, appointed bureaucrats and administrators who received a warrant for their subsequent actions indirectly from the voters through Congress and the President. Entitlements, then, are justified as part and parcel of our democracy.

While this may sound reasonable, in my opinion, it fails utterly. The argument is a variation on legal positivism, the claim that the law is always just, since it can trace its beginnings back to a majority vote. Why is a forced transfer of money rendered any less of a theft because more than half the voters supported it? Suppose two hoodlums break into my apartment and are walking off with my television set. When I object that they are stealing my property, they agree to hold a referendum on the issue. One of them (a philosophical robber) says, "How many object to

M. Buchanan and Gordon Tullock, The Calculus of Consent: Logical Foundations of Constitutional Democracy (Ann Arbor: University of Michigan Press, 1971); Robert Lloyd and Joseph P. McGarrity, "A Profit Analysis of the Senate Vote on Gramm-Rudman," Public Choice 85 (November 1995): 81–90; Kevin B. Grier and Joseph P. McGarrity, "The Effect of Macroeconomic Fluctuations on the Electoral Fortunes of House Incumbents," Journal of Law and Economics XLI (April 1993): 143–61; James M. Buchanan, Robert D. Tollison, and Gordon Tullock, eds., Toward a Theory of the Rent-Seeking Society (College Station: Texas A&M University Press, 1980).

us taking Block's television set?" Whereupon I raise my hand. He then asks, "How many favor this action?" and the two thieves register their approval. Does this veneer of democracy legitimize their act of theft? Hardly. Nor can it be objected that in the case of the United States—unlike the democratic robbers—we had all agreed beforehand to be bound by the results of elections because of the Constitution. In point of fact, no one ever signed any such agreement.[14] Hitler, to cite one extreme case, came to power as the result of an exercise of the ballot. Does this fact alone legitimize all his political acts? Certainly not. But if not, how can mere democracy justify the US government forcibly transferring money from some to give to others?

In addition to harming the poor both directly (e.g., welfare creates dependency) and indirectly (elements[15] of the middle class and the rich attain the lion's share of the wealth) these entitlements are immoral. We have focused thus far on the harm to the supposed beneficiaries of these programs. But no discussion of the moral dimensions of poverty and entitlements can ignore the fact that these initiatives are financed by coercive tax levies. The money to pay for welfare, public housing, and other such transfers is taken from innocent taxpayers at gunpoint. If the sole justification for the limited state is to protect the person and property of

[14] Nor can our agreement to abide by majority rule be predicated on the fact that we continue to reside in the United States. Some might argue, "If you do not like the way we run things here, you are always free to leave. Since you choose to stay, this indicates your willingness to be bound by electoral processes." As Spooner (Spooner, Lysander. 1870 [1973] No Treason No. VI: The Constitution of No Authority at 15, in No Treason: The Constitution of No Authority and A Letter to Thomas F. Bayard. Ralph Myles Publisher 1966 [1870]), makes clear, many present residents can trace their property titles, in an unbroken chain, back to a time before the birth of our nation. The government, presumably, is set up to safeguard our property. How, then, can such people be told to leave if they do not support democratic conclusions?

[15] It is impossible for the entire middle and upper classes to benefit at the expense of the poor. By definition, the poor have little that can be taken from them. The former cannot exploit them to a great degree since "you can't get blood out of a stone." But different categories of the rich and middle classes most certainly enrich themselves at the expense of other members of society. Agricultural subsidies, for example, benefit wealthy and middle class farmers. The same is true for tobacco subsidies, automobile subsidies, subsidies to scientific research and development, and so forth. When all of the taxes and subsidies are taken into account, there are only two possibilities: (1) everyone ends up with exactly what he had before, rendering the whole process absurd and nugatory; or (2) there are winners and losers. The contention here is that elements of the rich and middle class are the main beneficiaries, not the poor. See Franz Oppenheimer, The State (New York: Free Life Editions, 1975 [1914]).

the citizen, then these entitlements must be seen as a contradiction or violation of that principle. The point is, if we are to undertake a thorough moral analysis of entitlements, we must not constrict the scope of our deliberations merely to the recipients. Even on the unwarranted assumption that the people who receive these monies actually benefit from them, the transfers cannot be morally sanctioned because they violate the rights of those who made the contributions.

The Real World

So far we have discussed the ideal classical liberal world in which entitlements would be entirely absent.[16] In the real world, however, such programs are all too common, which furnishes us with the opportunity to engage in further analysis. To wit, *given* the fact that entitlement programs exist, how should the moral agent act in regard to them?

One possibility, which is the simplest and perhaps the most emotionally satisfying response, is that they simply be ignored.[17] After all, if these initiatives are unjust, what could be more appropriate than remaining detached from them? But there are problems with this view. Superficially, such a course of action is highly impractical. If a person was to eschew benefiting from any government expenditures or to refrain from taking part in any welfare or public housing programs, this would mean that

[16] In the economic literature there are numerous attempts to justify entitlements. For a criticism of these attempts, see Robert McGee, "Mergers and Acquisitions: An Economic and Legal Analysis," Creighton Law Review 22, 3 (1938): 665–93; Jack High, "Bork's Paradox: Static Versus Dynamic Efficiency in Antitrust Analysis," Contemporary Policy Issues 3 (1984–1985): 21– 34; Walter Block, "Total Repeal of Anti-Trust Legislation: A Critique of Bork, Brozen, and Posner," The Review of Austrian Economics 8, 1 (1994): 1–64; Fred McChesney, "Antitrust and Regulation: Chicago's Contradictory Views," Cato Journal 10 (1991): 775–98; Hoppe, A Theory of Socialism and Capitalism; "Fallacies of the Public Goods Theory and the Production of Security," The Journal of Libertarian Studies IX, 1 (Winter 1989): 27–46; Jeffrey Rogers Hummell, "National Goods Versus Public Goods: Defense, Disarmament, and Free Riders," The Review of Austrian Economics 4 (1990): 88–122; Walter Block, "Public Goods and Externalities: The Case of Roads," The Journal of Libertarian Studies 7, 1 (Spring 1983): 1–33; David Osterfeld, "Anarchism and the Public Goods Issue: Law, Courts, and the Police," The Journal of Libertarian Studies 9, 1 (Winter 1989): 47–68; Robert Nozick, Anarchy, State and Utopia (New York: Basic Books, 1974).

[17] By stipulation, we cannot ignore paying for these programs since they are foisted on us. But there is no law compelling us to take part in them as *recipients*.

citizens could not use the post office, streets, roads, highways, lighthouses, schools, libraries, museums, symphony halls, and so forth. Life under such conditions might not approach Hobbes's description of society as "nasty, brutish, and short," but would come too close for comfort and an important part of life would be impoverished.

Another possibility is that participation in entitlement programs is a matter of mere pragmatism unworthy of moral analysis. More important, it might be argued, is that classical liberal principles simply do not mandate avoiding governmental largesse. For advocates of strictly limited government, too, have been forced to finance these entitlements. If they avail themselves of the benefits thereto, their actions can be interpreted as merely seizing (the use of) their own money back and not as theft.

Contrary to this simplistic solution, the problem with entitlements is *the whole process* of government seizing our wealth and giving it to others. Since we are all victims *and* beneficiaries of this game, the whole process of forcing the entire society to pay for things its members are unwilling to finance themselves is morally objectionable. In isolation, then, it is not improper for people to seek to recover the taxes that have been levied against them.

Who, then, should accept government entitlements? To what extent should this be occurring in society? To answer the first question, we must avail ourselves of libertarian class theory.[18] Suppose, for instance, there were a classical liberal Nuremberg Trial, the purpose of which was to discern who was guilty for perpetuating the welfare state entitlement system. Would everyone be responsible, since, willy-nilly, all people (excluding a few hermits) participate in it? No. As we have seen, it is morally justified for at least some people to get their own money back. Instead, the answer is given that the ruling class is guilty for perpetuating the entitlement system.[19] Members of this class are considered to be in violation of the

---

[18] Murray N. Rothbard and Jerome Tucille, eds., Left and Right: Selected Essays, 1954–1965 (New York: Arno Press, 1972); Rothbard, For a New Liberty; Hans-Hermann Hoppe, "Marxist and Austrian Class Analysis," in Marxism: Economics, Religion, Politics, and Philosophy, ed. Yuri Maltsev (Boston: Dordrecht, 1992).

[19] Marxists have given ruling class theory, as they have everything else they have touched, a bad name. In their view, to employ someone is to exploit him, and thus to be a member of the ruling class. For a critique of this viewpoint, see Eugen von Böhm-Bawerk, Capital and Interest, trans.

strictures of free enterprise. But who are members of the ruling class? How can they be distinguished from other people, all of whom accept government transfers?

First of all, the distinction is based on whether a person actively works to support, aid, and abet the entitlement system, or works to dismantle it.[20] As a first approximation, the former at least potentially qualify for ruling class status, the latter do not, but this is only a presumption. It can be defeated on several grounds. Take, for example, the issue of free speech. In a free society, anyone can say nearly anything he pleases.[21] Mere verbal support of entitlements will not suffice. Another exception is for low-level administrators. Not every mail carrier, or typist in the social security administration, would be deemed to be in violation of libertarian law.

Standard protocol in war may shed some light on these deliberations. Typically in war the officers of the defeated army are found guilty; by contrast, the enlisted men, who were usually drafted in any case, are incorporated into the victors' army, and subsequently treated as relative equals with the other soldiers. Likely to be in the dock, then, are the politicians who enacted entitlement legislation, and the senior bureaucrats who carry it out. The senior bureaucrats would be equivalent to the officers in our model. Furthermore, all those involved at any level in impermissible activities would be forced to defend their actions. Candidates for this category might include the East German soldiers who shot their

George D. Hunke and Hans F. Sennholz (South Holland, Ill.: Libertarian Press, 1959 [1884]), particularly Part I, Chapter XII, "Exploitation Theory of Socialism-Communism."

[20] Conservatives often ridicule the notion of ruling class. While their criticisms do indeed refute the Marxist version, they leave libertarians unscathed. Consider the following statement by Horowitz (David Horowitz, "Clarence Page's Race Problem and Mine," Heterodoxy (May/June 1996): 6.): "The very phrase 'institutional racism' is, of course, of leftist provenance. It is also a totalitarian term. Like 'ruling class' it refers to an abstraction, not a responsible individual being. You are a class enemy (or in this case a race enemy) not because of anything you actually think or do, but 'objectively'—because you are situated in a structure of power that gives you (white skin) privilege." This author is clearly denigrating Marxist ruling class theory but not the libertarian variety. For in the latter case, it is one's actions and not status that is responsible for membership in the ruling class. For classical liberals, it is not sufficient (nor, even strictly speaking, necessary) to be rich to be included in this category. All one need do is engage in theft, which is certainly something a person of any background can actually do.

[21] Hitler himself may have never directly or personally killed a single Jew but he gave the orders to do so. Commands of this sort must be distinguished from free speech, at the very least, on the ground that the former implies physical threat while the latter does not.

compatriots fleeing to the West or, to a lesser extent, our own police force who systematically violate civil rights.

According to the philosophy of classical liberalism, it is to members of the ruling class that we owe the forced transfer society and who alone would be ineligible from receiving entitlement benefits. All others would not be precluded from accepting government grants on moral grounds.

An immediate objection might be registered to this scenario. According to this analysis, then, the welfare mother will still receive her benefits. She, after all, is a poor candidate for membership in the ruling class. I concede that this conclusion may seem paradoxical coming from a perspective that condemns welfare root and branch. If the logic of the case leads in this direction, then it really does not matter whether it is counterintuitive. The point is, given that there are entitlement programs, anyone who is not a member of the ruling class can possibly (but is not required to) make a moral claim to the existing benefit. While there is no justification, in my estimation, for entitlement benefits in the first place, the fact that they exist in the real world places no ethical barrier against the aggrieved making use of them.

Reparations

While reparations and entitlements share some characteristics—both are payments from one party to another—there is a gigantic moral chasm between the two. Entitlements, as we have seen, amount to no less than theft. Parties of the first part, taxpayers, are forced by law to subsidize parties of the second part, welfare recipients, corporate welfare bums, and agri-business. Reparations, by contrast, are the opposite of theft because they attempt to undo the effects of stealing by returning property to its rightful owner. Indeed, a large part of libertarian punishment theory is predicated upon restitution.[22]

---

[22] Randy Barnett, "Pursuing Justice in a Free Society, Part One: Power vs. Liberty," Criminal Justice Ethics 4 (1985): 50–72; The Structure of Liberty: Justice and the Rule of Law (Oxford: Clarendon Press, 1998); Randy Barnett and John Hagel, eds., Assessing the Criminal (Cambridge, MA: Ballinger, 1977); Hoppe, The Economics and Ethics of Private Property; Rothbard, For a New Liberty, op cit.

But can entitlements such as welfare not be justified on the ground that they are an implicit form of reparation? After all, AFDC recipients are poor; the taxpayers, on average, are certainly richer than those at the lowest income brackets. The problem with this line of reasoning is that mere wealth does not imply theft. Mere poverty does not imply victimization by robbers since people can become rich without stealing and poor without being pilfered. It is only vulgar Marxism to contend that the rich are rich because the poor are poor. Who, after all, did Ray Kroc, Steve Jobs, or Bill Gates rob? The millions of dollars of new wealth they created simply did not exist before them, nor, by definition, did anyone rob a starving group of Stone Age tribesman who were suddenly discovered in Africa or South America. No one denies that robbery can sometimes be a sufficient condition for wealth, but it is certainly not a necessary one as implied by this argument.

But what about slavery? Indeed, this institution amounted to theft of labor (and much more, of course). Therefore, a classical liberal perspective certainly could justify reparations in the case of slavery.[23] However, if the payments are to be morally enacted, several conditions must be met. First, if there is any case for reparations, these should come from guilty parties, not from the entire citizenry through the tax system. To make all citizens pay for the crimes of a few would be to extend—not diminish—the effects of robbery. Second, if the reparations are for an act that took place many years ago, a direct link between the historical victims and the present recipients must be forged. For example, although virtually all slaves in the United States were black, and many present welfare recipients are of the same race, not all of the latter can trace their roots to the former. That is, many present African Americans are the children not of

---

[23] Curiously, several classical liberal writers have rejected the notion of reparations. They did so not for slavery, but for land theft perpetrated on the peasants by the conquistadors in Latin and South America, a case certainly analogous to slavery. Included here are Milton Friedman, David Friedman, Walter Berns, and Edmund Opitz. See Walter Block, Geoffrey Brennan, and Kenneth Elzinga, eds., Morality of the Market: Religious and Economic Perspectives (Vancouver, B.C.: The Fraser Institute, 1985), 495–508. For a response to the anti-reparation position, see Walter Block and Guillermo Yeatts, "The Economics and Ethics of Land Reform: A Critique of the Pontifical Council for Justice and Peace's Toward a Better Distribution of Land: The Challenge of Agrarian Reform," Journal of Natural Resources and Environmental Law 15, 1 (1999–2000): 37–69; and Walter Block, "On Reparations to Blacks for Slavery," Human Rights Review, Vol. 3, No. 4, July–September, pp. 53–73.

slaves, but of people who came to this country after 1865, from Africa, from the Caribbean, and so forth. Third, for historical cases, a close connection between the guilty and those called upon to make the payments must be established. Most important, in all such cases, we must cleave mightily to the basic legal axiom: "Possession is nine-tenths of the law." That is, the presumption must always be that the present owner is the rightful owner. It is the burden of the one who would upset property titles to prove beyond a reasonable doubt that reparation is justified.

In the case of slavery, these somewhat stringent conditions can conceivably be met.[24] It is common knowledge that plantations throughout the old Confederacy were established with slave labor. When the Civil War ended, if more complete justice were to have taken place, the slaves would not merely have been freed. The lands they had been forced to cultivate would have been given to them and would not have remained in the hands of their former owners. Full compensation might even have contemplated enslaving these former masters to the newly freed slaves—a sort of poetic justice.

Unfortunately, in the modern era, those slaveholders are beyond reach of the civil authorities. But the plantations, houses, farms, and the wealth that was left to their progeny, which should have been given to the newly freed slaves, are still in existence and now owned by the great-grandchildren of the slave masters. If any present black person can prove family connection with a slave who endured forced labor at a specific plantation, he should be given that property. If there is more than one claim to the property, then it should be divided equally among all legitimate claimants.

One objection to this modest proposal is that to enact this idea would be to punish the grandchild for the sins of the grandparent. But this is simply not true. To take away a farm from a white person in Alabama and give it to an African American person is, in some sense, to "punish" the former. But this is not really true—the white relative should not have been given the farm in the first place. The reparation is merely the return of stolen property to the heir of the rightful owner. If my grandfather

[24] This lends support to Malcolm X's claim for reparations to blacks. See Malcolm X, Malcolm X Speaks: Selected Speeches and Statements, ed. George Breitman (New York: Merit Publishers, 1965).

stole your grandfather's ring and then gave it to me, I am not the rightful owner of the ring even though I have possession of it. On the contrary, *you* are the rightful owner. If justice is to prevail, I must turn it over to you. I will not have been punished, only made to do what returning stolen property implies.

Another objection to reparations is that there should be statute of limitations on past crimes. The enslavement of blacks by white Americans, or of biblical Jews by Egyptians, land theft from the Indians, the seizing of Japanese American property during World War II, Arab-Israeli land conflict, and the latifundia are lost in the winds of time and should remain so. But why should there be any statute of limitations on justice. Suppose that we know A stole X from S, and then gave it to his progeny, a, and we also know of b, the latter's grandchild. Surely justice requires that we right this wrong, even if it is an ancient one.[25]

Finally, there are legitimate concerns about fairness. How do we know the reparations are actually justified, when the theft took place so long ago? At this point, the classical liberal conditions come back to the forefront of discussion. Possession is nine-tenths of the law and the burden of proof is always on those who seek to overturn present property titles. If the robbery took place in biblical times, or before there was a written language, then, to that extent, it is exceedingly unlikely that anyone can prove anything. This stricture lends a conservative element to the reparation proceedings. Reparations are very different from entitlements. When properly construed, they amount to no more and no less than a return of stolen property; however, by contrast, entitlements constitute the theft of legitimately owned property.

[25] To be sure, there are practical objections to reparations. Enacting them is certain to create hard feelings and to rekindle ancient animosities. But we are concerned here with justice not practicality. We are analyzing payments from a moral point of view and not necessarily from a practical one. In any case, a large part of the present conflict is due to occurrences that took place a long time ago. It is possible that reparations might also reduce hard feelings and not exacerbate them.

3

Ona'ah

Ona'ah is a Talmudic prohibition against charging "excessive" prices, and earning "exorbitant" profits.[1] Specifically, in order to comply with this law, prices are to be at such a level that profits are no higher than 16%.[2]

The problem with all such controls is that prices (e.g., rates of exchange between two goods, or one good and money) have a crucial role to play in an economy. It is no exaggeration that they are the only way a large-scale society can function. Indeed, the sole alternative to prices is central planning.[3] Happily, ever since the unraveling of the Soviet Union, most people are properly suspicious of government intervention into the economy.[4]

---

[1] The literal translation of the law into English is as follows: "the law of mispricing" (Wilson, R. 1997, "Comparative religious thought on economic behavior and financial transactions," *The Journal of the Association of Christian Economists*, No. 23, August, p. 1); "price fraud" (Warhaftig, n.d.).

[2] Is there some reason for 16%, as opposed to 15% or 17%? If so, what is it?

[3] Most modern economies, of course, are "mixed," in the sense that some prices are controlled and others not.

[4] For earlier critics of Soviet-style economics, see Bauer, P.T. and Yamey, B.S. (1957), The Economics of Underdeveloped Countries, University of Chicago Press, Chicago, IL.; Boettke, P.J. (1993), Why Perestroika Failed: The Politics and Economics of Socialist Transformation, Routledge, London; Mises, Ludwig von, Socialism, Indianapolis: Liberty Fund, 1981 (1969); Mises, Ludwig

W. E. Block, *Property Rights*, Palgrave Studies in Classical Liberalism,
https://doi.org/10.1007/978-3-030-28353-7_3

Suppose that for some reason there is a surplus of carpenters and a shortage of plumbers. The way the price system handles such a challenge is simplicity itself. The wages of carpenters falls, and that of plumbers rises. This leads people who have or can attain both skills to switch from the former to the latter. Similarly, if there is a great demand for carrots and small demand for corn relative to supply, the price of the former will rise and of the latter will fall. This will again tend to lead entrepreneurs, as if by an "invisible hand,"[5] to tailor their offerings to the wishes of consumers. The higher price of carrots will call forth more of this vegetable, and the lower price of corn will reduce incentives to bring that product to market, at least on the part of all those who attempt to maximize their returns. As for those who ignore these market signals, other things equal they will become bankrupt. It is in this way that a decentralized market can function in a rational manner without any central direction at all. This may not seem important to all, but it has great importance for our welfare; no less than the feeding, clothing, and sheltering of the human race is at stake.

Controls, of course, prohibit the movement of prices (without government permission). But by the time the bureaucrats merely discern the difficulties in relative supply of carpenters and plumbers, or corn and carrots, to say nothing of the hundreds of thousands of other items in a modern economy, there is no possibility of rectifying matters and attaining a smoothly functioning economy.[6]

---

von. [1957] 1985. Theory and History: An Interpretation of Social and Economic Evolution, New Haven: Yale University Press, 1957 (reprint: Auburn University, Alabama: The Ludwig von Mises Institute, 1985).

[5] By this terminology Smith meant to indicate God's role in economics; Smith, Adam. 1776/1979. An Inquiry into the Nature and Causes of the Wealth of Nations, Indianapolis, IN: Liberty Fund.

[6] On this see Hayek, F.A. (1945), "The use of knowledge in society", 35 American Economic Review, Vol. 35, pp. 519–25; Hayek, F.A. (1948), "Socialist calculation I, II, & III", Individualism and Economic Order, University of Chicago Press, Chicago, IL. For an even more radical claim, that it is not merely the information that is lacking for the central planners, but that even if they had it they still could not function due to lack of appraisement, see Mises, Ludwig von, Socialism, Indianapolis: Liberty Fund, 1981 (1969); Mises, Ludwig von. [1949] 1966. Human Action. A Treatise on Economics, New Haven: Yale University Press, 1949 (3rd ed. Chicago: Regnery, 1966); Mises, Ludwig von. [1957] 1985. Theory and History: An Interpretation of Social and Economic Evolution, New Haven: Yale University Press, 1957 (reprint: Auburn University, Alabama: The Ludwig von Mises Institute, 1985); Salerno, J.T. (1990), "Ludwig von Mises as social rationalist", Review of Austrian Economics, Vol. 4, pp. 26–54; Salerno, J.T. (1992), "Mises and Hayek

In this regard ona'ah is not a total disaster. Instead of preventing such price changes, it merely retards them. This Hebraic law allows only those changes at which profits are still held below 16% per year. If resources can be fully allocated by, say, a price change yielding only a 10% profit on employees or commodities, then ona'ah will have no explicit deleterious effect on the economy. In a stable economy,[7] with little call for the beneficent intermediation of changing prices in order to allocate resources, this law, conceivably, would do little harm. But in a modern economy, replete with inventions, innovations, a computer revolution, immigration, trade, discoveries, quick and massive changes in tastes, and so on, the economic arteriosclerosis engendered by ona'ah might be serious indeed.

Fraud

Let us now address an interpretation of ona'ah according to which what is being banned is not earning profits greater than 16%, but rather fraud.[8] Posit the following scenario: a man walks into a restaurant, and orders a sandwich, French fries, and a coke without looking at the menu. He expects to pay about $10, based on his experience of prices in that neighborhood, and on his estimate of the quality of this particular eating establishment. Were the bill presented to him $8, he would feel he had a bargain; were it $12, he would be surprised, but would not think of his experience as in any way remarkable. Were it $16 he might feel victimized by sharp practice, but would still pay without protest. The quality of food does vary after all, different establishments have different costs, and,

de-homogenized", Review of Austrian Economics, Vol. 6, No. 2, pp. 113–46; Salerno, J. (1995), "A final word: calculation, knowledge and appraisement", Review of Austrian Economics, Vol. 9 No. 1, pp. 141–2.

[7] An ancient one, of the sort which occurred when this law was first promulgated. Leviticus was written sometime in 1400 BC; the actual date varies between different authorities; see: http//www.carm.org/bible/biblewhen.htm.

[8] For one scholar who has interpreted *Ona'ah* in this way as pure fraud see, Zvi Weiss who states: "The halacha states that if I *explicitly* tell someone that I am overcharging what I am selling (or that I am offering an artificially low price for what I am buying), then there is no prohibition of *Ona'ah*. This would seem to make clear that *Ona'ah* is strongly based upon issues of value and *deception*." Mail Jewish Mailing List, Volume 16 Number 5; Produced: Mon Oct 24 22:53:39 1994. http://www.ottmall.com/mj_ht_arch/v16/mj_v16i05.html.

then, there is always "location, location, location." All of this might account for a price variation of as much as, say, the 100% differential between $8 and $16.

In the event, however, the man is presented with a bill for $500.[9] Now this is a horse of an entirely different color. It seems reasonable to adopt a "reasonable man" standard in cases of this sort.[10] On the basis of any such test $500 would presumably be ruled out of court. Here the ona'ah rule would be a reasonable one.

Suppose now a slightly different scenario. Again the man orders his meal, but this time the waiter cautions him: "You know, the cost of the food you just ordered is $500.00. Are you sure you want it? Let me see the color of your money or a credit card first." If the reach of ona'ah is limited to fraud, there can be no question of that taking place in this second scenario. The diner knows full well the rate of exchange of money for lunch.

But ona'ah still applies.[11] Even though this law combats fraud, it is by no means limited to that task.[12] That is, according to this law, the $500

---

[9] This article was written in 1999. There is no doubt, given government inflationism, that in a few years hence $500 for such a meal will not raise any eyebrows. The present writer, in his youth, was accustomed to paying for a sandwich, fries and a coke in the neighborhood of $0.50.

[10] The bill might have specified $5000, $50,000, $500,000, and so on, or perhaps even indentured servitude for life.

[11] See Warhaftig (n.d.).

[12] In a similar vein, anti-trust law also proscribes fraud, but does much more. For a critique of the non-fraud combating aspects of anti-trust, see Armentano, Dominick T. 1972. The Myths of Antitrust, New Rochelle, N.Y.: Arlington House; Armentano, Dominick T. 1982. Antitrust and Monopoly: Anatomy of a Policy Failure, New York: Wiley; Armentano, Dominick T. 1999. Antitrust: The Case for Repeal. Revised 2nd ed., Auburn AL: Mises Institute; Armstrong, Don, Competition vs. Monopoly, Vancouver: The Fraser Institute, 1982; Block, Walter E. 1977. "Austrian Monopoly Theory – a Critique," The Journal of Libertarian Studies, Vol. I, No. 4, Fall, pp. 271–279; Block, Walter E. 1982. Amending the Combines Investigation Act, Vancouver: The Fraser Institute; Block, Walter E. 1994. "Total Repeal of Anti-trust Legislation: A Critique of Bork, Brozen and Posner, Review of Austrian Economics, Vol. 8, No. 1, pp. 35–70; Boudreaux, Donald J., and DiLorenzo, Thomas J. 1992. "The Protectionist Roots of Antitrust," Review of Austrian Economics, Vol. 6, No. 2, pp. 81–96; DiLorenzo, Thomas J. 1996. "The Myth of Natural Monopoly," Review of Austrian Economics, Vol. 9, No. 2, pp. 43–58; http://www.mises.org/journals/rae/pdf/rae9_2_3.pdf; High, Jack. 1984–1985. "Bork's Paradox: Static vs Dynamic Efficiency in Antitrust Analysis," Contemporary Policy Issues, Vol. 3, pp. 21–34; McChesney, Fred. 1991. "Antitrust and Regulation: Chicago's Contradictory Views," Cato Journal, Vol. 10; Rothbard, Murray N. (2004 [1962]). Man, Economy and State, Auburn AL: Ludwig von Mises Institute, Scholar's Edition; Shugart II, William F. 1987. "Don't Revise the Clayton Act, Scrap It!," 6 Cato

price tag would be unenforceable even if the customer agreed to it.[13] This seems like a "capitalistic act between consenting adults" (Nozick, 1974). Why might the law of ona'ah oppose such a contract?

In order to see this we ask, Why would a person consent to pay $500 for a meal, given that it is widely available in the neighborhood for prices ranging from $8 to $16?

One possibility is that he is so rich that "money is no object to him." Yes, he could avail himself of an equally good and far cheaper meal, but in order to do that he would have to invest in a walk of five minutes, and perhaps it is raining. Saving some $500 doesn't seem worthwhile to him, given the amount of effort he must expend.

Why should the restaurateur obey the law under such circumstances, other than for the fact that it indeed is the law? There is certainly no fraud, nor anything which can be called "exploitation."

Another possibility is that the diner is simply unaware of what is being charged elsewhere.[14] He would vastly prefer to pay, say, $10, but does not know of any such opportunity; he only reluctantly consents to the $500.

This scenario depicts tourist-like (to the extent we can give this example any credibility) behavior. The man is unwilling to engage in any research (e.g., comparative shopping) since he intends soon to leave the area, and will not in the future benefit from such an investigation. That is to say, his search would not be economically warranted. The law of ona'ah may thus be economically inefficient, in that it will compel the restaurateur to in effect do this search in behalf of the customer (by telling him of other prices in the neighborhood) even though, by stipulation, this was inefficient since it can be capitalized only over a very short period of time.

If not economic inefficiency, there is but one other interpretation: ona'ah violates the commandment against theft. For it is forcing the

---

Journal, 925; Smith, Jr., Fred L. 1983. "Why not Abolish Antitrust?," Regulation, Jan-Feb, 23; http://cei.org/op-eds-and-articles/why-not-abolish-antitrust.

[13] And not only unenforceable; presumably, the law would have some teeth (I need some info on this), and penalties would be imposed upon the restaurateur.

[14] According to folklore, there was a case in the 1990s, possibly apocryphal, where a taxicab driver charged a foreign customer some $5000 to take him from JFK Airport to downtown Manhattan If true, this would certainly be a violation of the *Ona'ah* proscription.

owner of the restaurant to give something of value (information about local prices) to all his customers, for free. But information is a valuable economic commodity, just like cars, sandwiches, and soft drinks. If the diner walked out of his establishment without paying, we would have no difficulty in labeling that as stealing. Why, then, not, also, when the diner walks out without paying for the information?[15]

Profit

I buy a quart of orange juice under ordinary circumstances. It will take me perhaps a week to consumer this beverage, since I drink only a small glass of it each day. The cost is $2 per quart. I value it at $2.20. (I *had* to value it at a level greater than its cost, or I would not have made the purchase.) I earn a profit of $.20, or 10% on the price tag. I am within the bounds of ona'ah.

The next time I go to the store to buy orange juice, I have just finished running the marathon. This time, I value it at $100, so desperate am I for liquid refreshment. I will drink it all in one fell swoop, immediately. I value it at $100, so desperate am I for a taste. That is, this is the top price I *would* have paid. But the cost is still $2. (The store owner is much too busy to monitor my desires for his products, and, in any case, had he charged me anywhere near the $100 I would have been willing to pay, I would simply make my purchase at a neighboring grocery.) Now, however, I am making a vast and exorbitant profit from my transaction,[16] to wit, 100 – 2 = $98. Surely, I am transgressing against the law of ona'ah. If I want to be obedient to this law, I cannot purchase the orange juice until my need or desire for it has returned to normal levels. If I *always* register such a strong consumer surplus from this product, I can never purchase it.

---

[15] What price would this information have? The restaurateur, by his actions, does not wish to make it available to the tourist customer. If he did, he could have charged $10. The only price he would in effect agree to is $500 - $10 = $490. But this would have been attained without the charade of information selling, merely by a direct charge of $500 for the meal.

[16] This is called "consumer's surplus" by economists.

The implicit premise of ona'ah is that if the profiteer is not engaging in fraud, he is then exploiting his trading partner. It seems difficult to sustain such a charge in the present case. How have I harmed the grocer, merely by taking such pleasure in what he sells me?

I am walking in the dessert one day and see a sparkling stone on the ground. I bend down to pick it up and lo and behold it is a diamond, worth $100,000. The cost of my labor is insignificant. It took all of two seconds to acquire this jewel. I calculate that my labor is worth $60 per hour, or $1 per minute. The total cost to me of engaging in this labor is thus about three cents. If I sell this diamond for its market value, my profit rate will be enormous. If I wish to live up to the rule of ona'ah, I must either keep the diamond for myself, or give it away as a gift, or sell it for no more than four cents.

The implicit premise of ona'ah is that if the profiteer is not engaging in fraud, he is then guilty of exploitation. But why is it wrong to sell a diamond for its market value?

In the diamond and orange juice cases, only one party to each of these commercial arrangements is in violation of ona'ah: the seller in the former, and the buyer in the latter. It is possible, however, for *both* parties to a deal to disobey this regulation.

For example, if the diamond of our example is sold for $100,000, to a billionaire, who values it at $1,000,000, perhaps for sentimental reasons. Then, each of the two parties to the arrangement gains an enormous amount, but would have to cease and desist, for they would be acting incompatibly with ona'ah.

Actually, the situation is worse, far worse, for this curious doctrine. For profit transcends mere monetary or trade arrangements. We need not limit our purview to the world of commerce. A happily married husband and wife[17] might each treasure each other inordinately. Compared to the cost to each of them in setting up and continuing this relationship, their gains are astronomical. This may be all well and good for the institution of marriage, but it leaves ona'ah mortally wounded.

Strictly speaking, profit is the difference in how a man evaluates the world if he makes choice A vs. B, where option B is the next best

[17] Or two very good friends.

opportunity known to him. Suppose that A is the decision to go to school, get a good job, get married, have children, while B entails dropping out of school, engaging in criminal activity, and joining the drug culture. In most calculations, A would be vastly superior to B. Thus, the profit[18] of this course of action would be enormous. If so, it would be proscribed by ona'ah.

Are we to give up highly profitable personal or commercial relationships because they do not square with ona'ah? Or, should we, rather, rethink this curious enactment? The latter seems by far[19] the better choice.

[18] A non-economist would place quotation marks around these words. I do not.

[19] But not too far, lest we in contemplating it be found guilty of a violation of the very law under discussion.

Part II

Libertarian Property Rights Theory

4

Hayek's Road to Serfdom

The work of Hayek, in contrast with the Marxist-Socialist-Interventionist-Galbraithian paradigm that held sway in the mid-twentieth century, appears as a beacon for free enterprise amid a sea of totalitarianism. When considered in comparison to the writings against which he contended, Hayek's was a lonely voice, crying in the wilderness for freedom; he stood, like the Dutch boy, with his finger in the dike of onrushing statism.[1] But if one weighs his output against that of free enterprise advocates who came later,[2] or, better yet, against an ideal of laissez-faire capitalism, then one must categorize Hayek as lukewarm, at best, in his support of this

[1] This may be a bit too strong, since there were other voices, alongside that of Hayek, who championed much the same philosophy, and did it more consistently. Preeminent among these must of course be Mises. For a study of the American "Old Right" tradition, see Justin Raimondo, Reclaiming the American Right (Burlingame, Calif.: Center for Libertarian Studies, 1993).

[2] Cf. Murray N. Rothbard, "Law, Property Rights, and Air Pollution," Cato Journal 2, no. 1 (Spring 1982), reprinted in Walter Block, ed., Economics and the Environment: A Reconciliation (Vancouver: Fraser Institute, 1990); Hans-Hermann Hoppe, A Theory of Socialism and Capitalism: Economics, Politics and Ethics (Boston: Kluwer, 1989); Hans-Hermann Hoppe, The Economics and Ethics of Private Property: Studies in Political Economy and Philosophy (Boston: Kluwer, 1993).

W. E. Block, *Property Rights*, Palgrave Studies in Classical Liberalism,
https://doi.org/10.1007/978-3-030-28353-7_4

system.[3] This is a rather surprising thesis, even a paradoxical one, in view of the fact that 1994 was the 50th anniversary of Hayek's *Road to Serfdom*,[4] a book widely (and accurately!) credited with turning away from socialism the political thinking of an entire generation.[5] It is therefore incumbent upon an author, such as myself, who makes such a claim, to offer evidence in support of it.[6] Let us consider the record.

Road to Serfdom

It cannot be denied that this book was a war cry against central planning. However, in making the case against socialism, Hayek was led into making all sort of compromises with what otherwise appeared to be his own philosophical perspective—so much so, that if a system was erected on the basis of them, it would not differ too sharply from what this author explicitly opposed.

First of all, one searches in vain for a *principle*, such as the non-aggression axiom of libertarianism,[7] which would serve as a rudder with

---

[3] John Gray, "F.A. Hayek on Liberty and Tradition," Journal of Libertarian Studies 4, no. 2 (Spring 1980): 119–37; Arthur M. Diamond, "F.A. Hayek on Constructivism and Ethics," Journal of Libertarian Studies 4, no. 4 (Fall 1980): 353–66; Roger Arnold, "Hayek and Institutional Evolution," Journal of Libertarian Studies 4, no. 4 (Fall 1980): 341–52.

[4] Friedrich A. Hayek, The Road To Serfdom (Chicago: University of Chicago Press, 1944).

[5] Perhaps, though, the fact that Keynes lavishly praised this book should have given us pause for thought. See Diamond, "F.A. Hayek on Constructivism and Ethics," p. 353.

[6] I write this with not a few misgivings. Hayek was always exceedingly kind to me, both personally and in writing; for example, see his forward to Walter Block, Defending the Undefendable (New York: Fox and Wilkes, [1976] 1991). In criticizing him now, part of me feels as if I am "biting the hand that fed me." The reason I finally decided to take pen to hand on this topic is that I feel I owe Hayek my best thoughts; it would seem a dishonesty, and a renunciation of the scholarship for which he stood all of his life, to "pull punches" out of considerations of friendship. We all, that is, the best of us, encourage our students to be critical about our own viewpoints, Hayek no less than anyone else. It is in this spirit, then, that I take up the arduous task of criticism. For a contrasting view of Hayek, see Peter J. Boettke, "Hayek's The Road to Serfdom Revisited: Government Failure in the Argument Against Socialism," Eastern Economic Journal 21, No. 1 (Winter 1995): 7–26; and also Peter J. Boettke, "The Theory of Spontaneous Order and Cultural Evolution in the Social Theory of F. A. Hayek," Cultural Dynamics 3, np. 1 (1990): 61–83.

[7] Cf. Murray N. Rothbard, The Ethics of Liberty (Atlantic Highlands, N.J.: Humanities Press 1982); Hoppe, A Theory of Socialism and Capitalism; Hoppe, Economics and Ethics; Anthony de Jasay, The State (Oxford: Basil Blackwell, 1985).

which to steer the ship of political-economic philosophy. As a matter of fact, Hayek specifically renounces the *possibility* of a principle: "There is nothing in the basic principles of liberalism to make it a stationary creed; there are no hard-and-fast rules fixed once and for all." Not only is there no principle, he specifically singles out free enterprise as precisely the *wrong* path: "Probably nothing has done so much harm to the liberal cause as the wooden insistence of some liberals on certain rough rules of thumb, above all the principle of laissez faire."[8] Lacking such an axiom[9] or postulate, Hayek needlessly weakens his case for the market.[10]

At one point, perhaps unconsciously, he even adopts the mindset of precisely the people he is ostensibly criticizing. He states:

> The attitude of the liberal toward society is like that of the gardener who tends a plant and, in order to create the conditions most favorable to its growth, must know as much as possible about its structure and the way it functions.[11]

But what is this if not the central-planning mentality? People are like chess pieces, to be moved around the board at the behest of the relatively all-knowing chess master. It seems to have escaped Hayek that his goals may be different from theirs. This may well be the perspective taken on by a Hayek-type liberal, but things are very different for the classical liberal, the one who advocates economic freedom. For the latter, people are not at all like vegetables, or inanimate chess pieces. On the contrary, they are adult human beings with goals and desires of their own, which must be respected.

---

[8] Hayek, The Road to Serfdom, p. 17.

[9] We consider below, and reject, the hard-and-fast principle adumbrated in Friedrich A. Hayek, The Constitution of Liberty (Chicago: Henry Regnery, 1960), pp. 397–411.

[10] Take, for example, his reiteration (The Road to Serfdom, pp. 3, 5, 8) that it is "largely people of good will" who are responsible for the slide into socialism in North America and Western Europe. As a rhetorical device, this is unexceptionable. How better to convince a largely hostile audience of the error of their ways than by first complimenting them? But a strong case can be made for the very opposite contention. Cf. Helmut Schoeck, Envy: A Theory of Social Behavior (New York: Harcourt Brace & World, 1966); and Walter Block, "Socialist Psychology: Values and Motivations," Cultural Dynamics 5, no. 3 (1992): 260–86.

[11] Hayek, The Road to Serfdom, p. 18.

Money

Now to specifics. Hayek calls for exceptions to the rule of laissez-faire capitalism with regard to "handling of the monetary system." Later, he reiterates this Keynesian point: "There is ... the supremely important problem of combating general fluctuations of economic activity and the recurrent waves of large-scale unemployment which accompany them."[12] But why should the macro monetary and fiscal systems be given over to the tender mercies of the government? There is good and sufficient reason to believe that state control has led at different times to the very destabilization, inflation, depression, and self-aggrandizement that Hayek incorrectly assumes is a result of the operation of the market.[13] Can it be said that these two cited works post-dated *The Road to Serfdom*, and that as a result Hayek could be excused for not being aware of them? Not a bit of it, for Mises made many of the same points, and this work was published long before the publication of Hayek's.[14] Mises was Hayek's mentor and teacher; Hayek could not possibly have been ignorant of this tome. Furthermore, Hayek's own writings demonstrated precisely how government monetary policy leads to temporal misallocations of investment (e.g., to depressions).[15] Paradoxically, our author has himself made significant contributions to the Austrian theory of the business cycle, which convincingly demonstrates the imprudence of granting to the state expansionary monetary power. The Hayek of 1944, then, stands condemned by the Hayek of 1931 and 1933.

---

[12] Hayek, The Road to Serfdom, p. 18.

[13] Milton Friedman and Anna J. Schwartz, A Monetary History of the U.S., 1867–1960 (New York: National Bureau of Economic Research, 1963); Murray N. Rothbard, America's Great Depression (Kansas City: Sheed and Ward, 1975).

[14] Ludwig von Mises, The Theory of Money and Credit (New York: The Foundation for Economic Education, [1912] 1971).

[15] Friedrich A. Hayek, Monetary Theory and the Trade Cycle (New York: Kelley, [1933] 1966); Friedrich A. Hayek, Prices and Production (London: Routledge, 1931).

Hours of Work

In chapter 3 of *The Road to Serfdom*, Hayek makes further concessions to socialism. He starts off this discussion ominously by warning against "a dogmatic laissez-faire attitude." And what roles does he assign the state? One of them is "to limit working hours."[16] But this is a violation of basic rights. Surely consenting adults have a right to contract with one another for a mutually agreeable work week. If this amounts to 50, or 100, or even 150 hours per week, it should be no one else's business. Further, this socialist policy is a recipe for disaster. Interventionists of all stripes try to take credit for the decline in the length of the work day. In their view, rapacious capitalists would never have allowed labor output to decline to a daily eight hours had this decision been left up to them. Were it not for the benevolent effects of compulsory legislation, this could not have occurred. Had the government not mandated this situation, we would still, even nowadays, be working 14-hour days. But logic and common sense are incompatible with this thesis. The reason we work fewer hours than our great-great-grandfathers is that improved technology and skills have so enhanced productivity that we have taken part of the increase in the form of enhanced leisure. There is compelling evidence that legal enactments in and of themselves cannot bring about any such state of affairs. Suppose, then, that the government had limited the work week to 40 hours, but did this in a century when, because of extreme poverty, labor typically lasted twice that duration. Instead of increasing leisure, such an enactment would amount to a death warrant for millions of people who were unable to keep body and soul together in so few hours. How, then, to account for the "success" of hours legislation? After all, nothing like this occurred in our history. The answer is simple: as productivity boosts allowed us to work for fewer hours, the government declared that the new levels would be required by law. Some observers, such as Hayek, were misled by this state of affairs into thinking that the law actually *caused* the fall in work effort. In fact, labor legislation only took credit for a situation which was already occurring anyway, and would have continued to occur even in the absence of such legislation.

[16] Hayek, The Road to Serfdom, p. 37.

Welfare for All

Continues our author, "nor is the preservation of competition incompatible with an extensive system of social services."[17] Later he states: "There is no reason why in a society which has reached the general level of wealth which ours has attained … security against severe physical privation the certainty of a given minimum of sustenance … should not be guaranteed to all without endangering general freedom … There can be no doubt that some minimum of food, shelter and clothing, sufficient to preserve health and the capacity to work, can be assured to everybody."[18]

But this is highly problematic, again, on both moral and pragmatic grounds. With regard to the former, the only justified transfer of funds between one citizen and another is based on voluntarism. That is, if a church, or the Salvation Army, or the Shriners gives money to the poor, it is based on non-compulsory contributions. In contrast, a system of social services, let alone "an extensive" one, can only be financed through the force implicit in the tax-subsidy system. As for the effects, they have been little short of disastrous.[19] Disrespect for law and order, teenage pregnancy, crime, the break-up of the family, and even the failure of the family to form in the first place have all been the results of this policy. To be sure, the worst excesses of the welfare system were not at all apparent at the time of Hayek's writing. However, he is widely thought of as an advocate of capitalism, and this is but one more in a long list of counterexamples to that thesis. As for Hayek's contention that we can engage in activities of this sort on a massive scale without endangering freedom, there is little reason to be optimistic. With large-scale welfare has come the welfare-rights movement; the rent-seeking society we have become as a result has endangered freedom if only because of the sheer size of governmental budgets. As state expenditure has catapulted its way toward 50% of the GNP, it has become a real question as to whether we still live in the free society.

[17] Hayek, The Road to Serfdom, p. 37.

[18] Hayek, The Road to Serfdom, p. 120.

[19] See Charles Murray, Losing Ground: American Social Policy from 1950 to 1980 (New York: Basic Books, 1984).

Saving the Market

There is a long history of intellectual attempts to defend the practice of "saving the market" or "promoting competition" by urging government intervention to this end. Hayek, unfortunately, joins this tradition in calling for the state to "make competition as effective and beneficial as possible—and to supplement it where, and only where, it cannot be made effective."[20] To be sure, he tries to distance his position from that of the socialists by making the following distinction:

> What I mean by "competitive order" is almost the opposite of what is often called 'ordered competition.' The purpose of a competitive order is to make competition work; that of so called 'ordered competition,' almost always to restrict the effectiveness of competition.[21]

But this is a distinction without a real difference. In *both* cases the government will not leave the marketplace to its own devices; in *both* cases the public sector is impinging on the private; in *both* cases the proponents of these schemes, Hayek as well as the avowed central planners, *say* they are urging intervention in order to improve things. The Hayekian position is tantamount to asking the fox to guard the chicken coop, or trying to put out a fire by pouring oil on it. Foxes and chickens, oil and water, have different and contradictory underlying principles. It is to the advantage of the fox to attack; of the chicken to defend (or be defended by the farmer). Oil feeds a fire; water puts it out. In like manner, the market and government are also organized upon different incompatible principles. In the former case, mutual agreement is the watchword; in the latter, the use of force. Now it would be one thing if Hayek were to limit his defense of state action to: "prevention of violence and fraud … (and) the protection of certain rights, such as property and the enforcement of contracts."[22] A case can conceivably be made that here the two institutions are complementary, not incompatible. But Hayek goes much further than this.

---

[20] Hayek, Individualism and Economic Order (Chicago: Regnery, 1972), p. 110.

[21] Hayek (1972), p. 111.

[22] Hayek (1972), pp. 110–11.

I submit that these are not the views of a defender of the free enterprise system. This is not to say that there were no sentiments compatible with capitalism expressed in this interview. For example, Hayek did come out foursquare against parity prices for farmers and tariffs.[23] Or am I being too harsh with the co-winner of the 1974 Nobel Prize in economics? After all, Hayek did most of his work during the years when socialism was in the ascendancy, morally, intellectually, and spiritually. Maybe his many compromises with socialism and central planning were the best that could be expected in this era. This is a tempting hypothesis. After all, I take no pleasure in pointing out the clay feet here. For a long time, until I read him more carefully, I too considered Hayek one of the champions of free enterprise. Unfortunately, it will not suffice. There were many other authors writing at about the same time, several of whom wrote even before Hayek, when the prospects for liberty were, if anything, even worse. Consider the works of Ayn Rand, Henry Hazlitt, Ludwig von Mises, Lysander Spooner, Leonard Read, Benjamin Tucker. These scholars made far fewer compromises with state intervention into the economy than Hayek did. Thus, it is problematic to resort to the epoch in which he wrote as an explanation for Hayek's interventionistic views. The long and the short of it is that he was a rather weak and conflicted supporter of the market—one who for some reason was widely interpreted as a staunch and radical proponent of economic freedom.

Conclusion

There is little doubt that Hayek deserves his reputation as a defender of economic freedom—but only compared to his contemporaries who, with only a few honorable exceptions, were almost totally immersed in interventionistic philosophy. However, when compared either to some ideal standard, or to numerous modern commentators, it is clear that Hayek falls short of a clear unambiguous advocate of the free marketplace.

---

[23] Hayek, Hayek on Hayek, p. 115.

5

Block vs. Friedman on Hayek

When I first received Milton Friedman's letter in response to my article "Hayek's Road to Serfdom"[1] I did not realize it would lead to more. Over the past few years I have shared these letters with several colleagues, friends, and students. However, such are his fame and accomplishments that I thought these back-and-forth letters might be of interest to a wider audience of the *Journal of Libertarian Studies* (*JLS*) readers.

Letter 1

December 17, 1997

Dear Walter:

Having just read your piece on Hayek—a piece written by a fanatic, not by a reasonable man—I have but one question I want to ask you. Please specify for me in not more than two brief paragraphs how you perceive a feasible transition in a non-gradual way from the present state of affairs to your ideal, justified state of affairs. Have you ever thought

[1] Chapter 4 in the present book.

W. E. Block, *Property Rights*, Palgrave Studies in Classical Liberalism,
https://doi.org/10.1007/978-3-030-28353-7_5

seriously about the problem of transition? It is long past time that you should do so.

Sincerely yours,

Milton

Letter 2

January 9, 1998

Dear Milton:

Thanks for your letter of December 17, 1997. I'm sorry you think my article on Hayek fanatical, not reasonable. I reread it, and I can't understand your opposition to it. All I did was show many, many instances where Hayek's views were incompatible with a defense of free enterprise. If you could share with me what you see as my errors in this (e.g., I have wrongly defined free enterprise; Hayek really did not deviate from these principles at all; or as much as I claim; it is inappropriate to set this task for myself) I would greatly appreciate it. Hayek has a reputation as a free-market advocate, and I thought it reasonable to test this against the facts.

I can't see how you can be unhappy with my citation of your book (Friedman 1963). I was making the point that based on your research, the great depression was not a market phenomenon, but rather due to governmental (central banking) failures. Surely I have not misconstrued your work?

Nor can I understand the transition from my criticism of Hayek to my views on transition from our present state of affairs to an ideal one. Nevertheless, since you ask it of me, I will try to answer.

If we are ever to move from our present mixed economy to a very much more free one, I don't think it can be done non-gradually.

After all, it took us (at least in the U.S.) dozens of decades to go from relative freedom to the semi-socialism we now have. Why should the way back be more abrupt? I at least think it unlikely.

However, if it were to occur, and this is a big *if*, the only way I could conceive of it happening is under the aegis of a very powerful spokesman for liberty. He would have to have the eloquence of a Ronald Reagan, and the passion for justice and economic sophistication of a person such as yourself. If I could combine the two of your best relevant traits, that is, somehow get you to be president for eight years, I think we'd have a pretty non-gradual change. I can just see you putting Ward Connolly in charge of Equal Opportunity, Walter Williams as Labor Secretary, myself in charge of HUD, David Henderson in Commerce, Tom Sowell as Education Secretary, etc. etc., and you telling us you'll fire us if our departments are not ended within one year. You would then pull out of Nafta and WTO and instead unilaterally declare free trade with all nations. You would end the minimum wage, rent control, the Wagner Act and all those other regulations—not gradually, but abruptly. Taxes would quickly fall from some 50 % of GDP to, say, 10 %. This is the stuff of dreams, unfortunately.

You talk of "feasible," and this is hardly feasible. There would be too much opposition. You would never be elected. If you were, and you started to dismantle government, you would be impeached. The only way this could work is if the mass of citizens, or at least some critical number less than 50 % (say 35 % and the two opposition parties were divided—this, in my opinion, is why Canada was able to join Nafta) were appreciative of free enterprise. And how can that happen? Why, in the way all of us folks are working, and dedicating our careers: teaching at a university, publishing articles and books, giving speeches, etc. Your own efforts, for example, in trying to attain drug legalization are a case in point and an example for all of us.

I have tried to answer your query, at least as it is written. I've passed "two brief paragraphs" but so far at least I am being reasonably concise. However, I feel that while I have answered the "letter" of your question, I have not yet even touched its "spirit."

Reading between the lines, I think you are really asking me to defend my opposition to such activities with which you have become prominently associated such as educational vouchers, flexible exchange rates, opposition to the gold standard, the voluntary military (during the Viet Nam war), the negative income tax. We also disagree as to whether we should privatize all roads and highways, have tradable emissions rights for pollution or ITQs for fish, eliminate the fed and central banking (as opposed to adopting the "3 %" rule), totally eliminate antitrust, just to name a few. Needless to say, were I to even summarize my opposition to all of these, I could hardly be brief.

However, let me just say that none of this has anything to do with the transition period to freedom, about which you explicitly ask. I guess what I'm trying to say is that we are aiming at (slightly) different goals, mine more extreme than yours, but I don't see that we have any real disagreement as to means. At least, I have never read anything of yours (and I think I've read virtually everything you have ever written) on the subject of transitions with which I disagree.

I don't favor picking up the gun and shooting bureaucrats and politicians. I don't favor violent revolution. On the contrary, at least in this regard, I have modeled my career after your own: education, writing, speaking, publishing, etc. (I don't compare myself with you as far as *success* in these endeavors is concerned; I only say that I am trying to the best of my abilities to emulate you.)

Let me take another hack at this. Consider education for a moment. I think educational vouchers are a moral and economic disaster. I totally oppose them. They remind me of nothing so much as market socialism. What, then, is my "transition plan" for education? It is simply to do what you have tried to do for drugs, or rent control, or minimum wages: educate people against them. In your magnificent "Roofs or Ceilings"[2] you don't call for any "voucher" plan, or transition period. No. You just forthrightly make the case against rent control, and advocate *nothing* at all in its place, except, of course, an end to controls and a free market in rental housing.

This sounds reasonable to me, and not at all fanatical. Why does the case reverse itself when I apply to education the very (lack of?) "transition" plan that you yourself apply to rent control? What is fanatical about making the case against public education, and advocating privatization, with no halfway house of vouchers in this direction? (I don't believe that vouchers are even a tiny step in the right direction, but that is a topic for another day. But do I have to be fanatical to entertain this belief?)

[2] Friedman, Milton, and George J. Stigler. 1946. Roofs or Ceilings?: The Current Housing Problem. Irvington-on-Hudson: N.Y.: Foundation for Economic Education. Reprinted in Rent Control: Myths and Realities. Walter Block and Edgar Olsen, eds. Vancouver, B.C.: Fraser Institute, 1981. This is an article which every intro student of mine has read.

I am sorry I was not as brief as you asked. But I could not do justice to your questions in any shorter space. I am honored that you would criticize my views, and would be delighted if you replied to this letter.

Best regards,

Walter

Letter 3

March 13, 1998

Dear Walter:

I appreciate the lengthy reply you sent to my earlier letter as well as the e-mail I got about the same subject.

There are two different things you and I have written about. One is about an ideal society. The other, that I and to a far lesser extent you have written about, is how, given the imperfect world as it is, we can adopt changes that will make it better and will move us in the direction of that ideal society. My problem with your writing and the respect in which it is fanatical is that you treat Hayek as if every sentence he wrote was devoted to specifying the ideal world. You do not recognize that most of the time he is talking not about that ideal world where he and you would very largely agree, but about how we can move the existing world in the direction we want to go even if it be only a small step in that direction.

Your attempt to answer my question referring to a non-gradual transition brings out clearly that you recognize that a non-gradual transition is hard to conceive, that any transition will certainly be gradual, will consist of a great many small measures. There may be some cases, as was the case with rent control, where it is possible to go all the way in one fell swoop, but there are other cases, as I believe in education, where you cannot at the moment hope to go all the way—not only because of political feasibility but because of commitments made by the community and expectations that have led to irrevocable actions—but you can hope to move in the right direction. I realize that in this case you do not agree with me that vouchers would be a step in the right direction and obviously I can well be wrong about that. But my ultimate goal is to have a situation in which parents are fully responsible for schooling their own children and in which the government is not involved in education.

Today the government is involved in administering education as well as financing it. It seems to me that it is a step in the right direction to limit its role to financing and eliminate its role as an administrator. Indeed, it seems to me that that will set up forces which will tend to further reduction in the role of the state. And, most important, I do not regard myself as being in any way a traitor to my basic values when I propose and discuss such changes in existing circumstances, though I may of course in a particular case misjudge how such a change would work.

Similarly, most of the items for which you criticize Hayek are cases in which he is discussing changes that would improve the present situation but would still leave us far from utopia. Your tone is that of a theologian examining scripture, not a social scientist tackling existing institutions to improve them, or an open-minded analyst of partial improvements. You treat Hayek as if he didn't understand the simple largely *a priori* principles of economic analysis that constitute your armory. Truth to tell, he was trying to analyze a far more complex reality than you are prepared to admit exists. There are indeed market failures, externalities, conflicts of "ultimate" values, ruled out by logic but not by imperfect human understanding.

Every question does not have a simple logical answer.

I believe those of us who want to move to an ideal world have an obligation to concern ourselves with the current problems and with the problem of transition from this world to that. I believe Hayek has been a great force for good and has done a great deal to promote an appreciation of the role of markets in a free society. He deserves better than your self-satisfied diatribe.

Sincerely yours,
Milton

Letter 4

April 10, 1998

Dear Milton:

Thanks for your letter of March 13, 1998.

I had never before read Hayek's *Road to Serfdom* (1944) with the question in the back of my mind: is he advocating something about the ideal world, or, about "how we can move the existing world in the direction we want to go even if it be only a small step in that direction."

Thanks to your letter, I have made good this oversight of mine.

Unhappily for your thesis, however, I can find no evidence that he ever makes practical suggestions for moving us, however marginally, in the ideal direction. On the contrary, a fair reading of this book, in my opinion, shows him talking about ends, not means.

Let us consider the evidence (all unidentified page numbers refer to *The Road to Serfdom*):

"The attitude of the liberal [that's how Hayek categorizes his own position] toward society is like that of the gardener who tends a plant and, in order to create the conditions most favorable to its growth, must know as much as possible about its structure and the way it functions" (p. 18).

This, as far as I am concerned, talks about goals, not movement toward them. Unhappily this is the leftish goal of central planning, not that of *laissez-faire*, which he explicitly disavows (p. 17).

Hayek (p. 37) calls upon the government "to limit working hours." There is no way to construe this as a movement toward a free society. On the contrary, this is a *per se* violation of liberty, with no gains in freedom anywhere on the horizon.

He calls for welfare for the poor (pp. 37 and 120). But this is not in the context of compromise; giving up some liberty here, in order to attain it elsewhere. This is not one step back in order to attain two steps forward. This advocacy of welfare is clearly the way Hayek sees the *ideal* society. Say what you will about it, it cannot be reconciled with the libertarian worldview.

Hayek (p. 38) favors government action in cases of neighborhood effects or externalities. Now I know that you agree with him on this. But this is irrelevant to our present disagreement. To reiterate, we are not now discussing the parameters of the ideal society. You are claiming, and I am denying, that Hayek is advocating these policies as a step in the right direction. I am claiming, and you are denying, that in his ideal society, governments would act so as to overcome neighborhood effects. I have read this page of *The Road to Serfdom* several times.[3] I cannot for the life of me understand how you could see in it anything related to marginal changes.

I cite a paragraph from *The Road to Serfdom* on page 333 of my "Hayek's Road to Serfdom" article.[4] Hayek (pp. 120–21) calls for governmental health and accident insurance. I admit it is somewhat of a low blow to tie this in with the Clintons' attempt to further socialize medical care, but the shoe sure fits. In any case, I see nothing in Hayek's statement which supports your view that he advocated this as a means toward freedom. In my reading, this is part and parcel of Hayek's ideal society.

Aha! One point for your side! Although, strictly speaking, this does not really apply since it did not occur in *The Road to Serfdom*, I am willing to concede that to you when it comes to rent control Hayek is trying to move us toward the free society, which, for all of us, consists of one in which rent control is totally eliminated. I think he is tragically mistaken in taking this moderate position on the elimination of rent control, but that is another matter. (I note that in your letter you agree with my assessment: "There may be some cases, as was the case with rent control, where it is possible to go all the way in one fell swoop.")

Last point. On antitrust (p. 49). Hayek thinks this law is compatible with the free society. The fact that I do not is irrelevant. Again, the point is that he does not advocate antitrust law as a means toward the free or ideal society. He sees this as part and parcel of it.

I am sorry to go on so long about this, but I thought it appropriate to marshal the evidence. How else can we decide whether you or I are correct on this?

In your third paragraph you note that whether school vouchers will actually bring us closer to the free society is a complex issue. I certainly agree. But, strictly speaking, this is not apropos of our disagreement over Hayek. He doesn't talk about educational or any other kind of vouchers. Nor, with the exception of rent control, does he talk about *any* transitions from our present society to a more free one. Thus, I can't see my way clear

---

[3] I cite a paragraph from *The Road to Serfdom* on page 333 of my "Hayek's Road to Serfdom" article.

[4] Now Chap. 4 of the present book.

to agreeing with you that my "tone is that of a theologian examining scripture."

Hayek and I are both discussing the ideal society. Surely it is permissible for me to point out that there is a vast discrepancy between the ideal society Hayek actually advocates, and the one for which he is typically credited. Surely, to do so is not necessarily to be "fanatical."

In your second paragraph you state that I "treat Hayek as if every sentence he wrote was devoted to specifying the ideal world."

Yes, I do, at least as far as *The Road to Serfdom* is concerned. (Again, his concern for rent control transitions came from a different book.) You state: "most of the time (Hayek) is talking not about the ideal world … but about how we can move the existing world in the direction we want to go." If this is true, then you should be able to find many, many cases where he talks about transitions. There is a simple way to settle this dispute: just cite a few of them. Even if you can find them, however, this is still not a valid criticism of my article. For I was attacking Hayek not for his views of the transition (if you can find any) but for his notion of the ideal society.

You raise a fascinating point about whether you are "a traitor to (your) basic values" when you advocate such things as educational vouchers. I think that "traitor" is far too harsh. To me, this word implies a knowing renunciation of your goals, a lying superficial public acceptance of them, while behind the scenes working to undermine them. Utter nonsense, in the present case.

However, I do think it can be fairly said that educational vouchers are logically incompatible with the free society, and, given that your basic values are those of economic liberty, that your advocacy of them is inconsistent with this goal.

You say "Today the government is involved in administering education as well as financing it. It seems to me that it is a step in the right direction to limit its role to financing and eliminate its role as an administrator."

Let us test the logical consistency of this statement by applying it to several other cases:

Right now the U.S. government is involved in administering the Post Office as well as financing it. In Canada this applies to radio and television (the Canadian Broadcasting Corporation), to airlines (Air Canada) and to the oil industry (Petro Canada). Previously, coal mines were financed, owned, and operated by the British government. In India, this applies to such things as steel mills. In Italy, to autos (Fiat). And this of course is but the tip of the iceberg.

Is it really a step in the right direction to limit the role of all these governments to financing and only to eliminate their role as administrators? Suppose I were to argue that the U.S., Canada, England, India, and Italy should continue to finance these myriad industries, but not directly administer them. This sounds to me like nothing but economic fascism, the economic system employed by Nazi Germany, and Mussolini's Italy. In these cases, there was a thin veneer of private property rights, but the underlying economic reality was one of government control. Surely, this is not something that the libertarian in the U.S. can advocate as a step in the right direction, although, I concede to you, that possibly a libertarian now living in Cuba or North Korea might claim that it is a step in the right direction.

Further, I question whether a libertarian, even in such countries, could consistently advocate it, whether or not it is a step in the right direction from something worse.

Let me make this point in a far more radical way. The Nazis both administered and financed concentration camps for Jews, Gypsies, and other unfortunates. Surely no one whose basic values were centered on liberty could advocate that the Nazis give up administering these camps, but *keep* on financing them, supporting private efforts along these lines.

Now the obvious objection is that concentration camps of this sort are intrinsically evil, while education, post offices, broadcasting, airlines, oil, coal, autos, etc., are not. However, for the libertarian, it is wrong for the government to engage itself in these industries, through *either* finance or administration, since it does so through the use of coercive force, and we want to minimize such activities.

Therefore, while the libertarian may of course consistently with his principles advocate elimination of government administration of these industries, he may not counsel continued financing, in my opinion.

It is also interesting to explore the disagreement you have with Hayek regarding rent control. In your view, we should eliminate these regulations in "one fell swoop." Hayek demurs. It seems to me that your difference with him is your view that "*it is possible to go all the way* in one fell swoop." That is, you believe, and he does not, that it is politically possible to rid ourselves of rent controls at once.

Presumably, if the two of you switched views on this (e.g., you now took on his assessment that it is not politically feasible to eradicate rent control all at once, and he, yours, that it is) then he would advocate doing just that, and you would champion his public policy recommendation, that rent control be eliminated slowly, in stages.

William Hutt wrote a magnificent little book on just this topic called *Politically Impossible…?*[5] What I learned from him is that specialization and the division of labor applies, also, to public policy recommendations. That is, as libertarians, we must (logically) stick to advocating the ideal solution. We must leave it to others to determine what is or is not politically feasible. The reason I think you are inconsistent with (not traitorous toward) your basic values is that you are trying to straddle two incompatible horses: libertarianism on the one hand, and political feasibility analysis on the other.

According to my understanding, did you but share Hayek's assessment of the (in)feasibility of totally eliminating rent control in one shot, you would not have advocated this. Instead, you would have joined him in favoring its gradual phasing out. And this, as I see it, would be incompatible with your basic values of economic freedom.

Let me end with one last radical (hopefully not fanatical) analogy. During the 1850s in the U.S., the radical abolitionists advocated the total, complete, and immediate cessation of slavery. At that time, this goal was politically infeasible. The radicals knew this full well, and yet they continued their efforts as if this was irrelevant. Well, it *was* irrelevant to their basic values; they *had* to regard the political feasibility of implementing their goals as irrelevant, if they were to act in a consistent basis with them.

Extrapolating from your views on educational vouchers, you would not have been a radical abolitionist. Instead, you would have advocated some sort of compromise, or what you saw as a marginal improvement. You would have wanted to "move the existing world in the direction we

[5] Hutt, William H. 1971. Politically Impossible…? London: Institute of Economic Affairs.

want to go even if it be only a small step in that direction." In doing so, you would have been incompatible with your basic values, just as is the case with your present advocacy of educational vouchers.

There is nothing I enjoy more than drag out knock down debates about issues such as these, that I consider to be of utmost importance. I am honored that you should be willing to engage in such with me.

Best regards,
Walter

Letter 5

April 24, 1998

Dear Walter:

I believe you have completely misread *The Road to Serfdom*. It is not in any way whatsoever a statement of what Hayek regards as the ideal society though it does contain statements that bear on that issue. Remember *The Road to Serfdom* is dedicated to the socialists of all parties. It was written in a period when the ideas of economic freedom, the ideas of libertarianism, were regarded as extreme views held by very few people; the great bulk of the intellectual community rejected them completely and was rather taken by the notion of scientific central planning. Hayek wrote a book trying to persuade people of that kind that they might be mistaken and trying to persuade them to consider alternatives. Accordingly, his aim is to be as persuasive as possible on what he regards as the key central issues.

For example, you say that "Hayek (p. 37) calls upon the government 'to limit working hours'." You have not read that correctly. He is not calling upon the government to do that. He is saying instead something very different. Read the fuller quotation: "Though all such controls of the methods of production impose extra costs, they may be well worthwhile … To limit working hours … is fully compatible with the preservation of competition. The only question here is whether in the particular instance the advantages gained are greater than the social costs which they impose."

That is not a recommendation to limit working hours. It is simply saying to the people he is addressing, "Look, we don't have to argue about such issues as whether to limit working hours. We want to argue on more important issues, on how we preserve competition, and lots of the things that you people may want to do could be done without destroying competition and while maintaining a very, very large degree of individual freedom.

At repeated points the same situation arises. Hayek is trying to say, "How big a concession can I make to you people so that I won't completely alienate you? I want to attack you on the grounds that I regard as absolutely key and essential," and there he does a very good job.

On a different level having to do with your differences with me as well as with Hayek, neither he nor I is a libertarian in the sense in which you are a libertarian. Neither he nor I believe that you can have zero government. Take in particular the point you raise about his statement on page 120 about providing a basic minimum level of living. I favored that in *Capitalism and Freedom*[6] when I proposed substituting the negative income tax for a whole present collection of welfare measures. I believe there is an enormous difference between a situation in which 90% of the people are willing to tax themselves to help the bottom 10% and a situation in which the middle 80% of the people tax the top 10% ostensibly to help the bottom 10% but probably in fact to tax both ends of the scale to help themselves.

I agree with Hayek that "some minimum of food, shelter, and clothing … can be assured to everybody." He would have agreed with me that taxation for the purpose of redistribution is wrong.

I think you ought to be a little careful about your last radical analogy, namely the elimination of slavery. I do not know whether you have read the book *Emancipating Slaves, Enslaving Free Men: A History of the American Civil War* by Jeffrey Hummel[7] on Lincoln and the Civil War. Hummel is a libertarian closer to you than he is to me, but he believes that Lincoln did a great deal of harm rather than good by forcing the Civil War to keep the country together, that the outcome may have been the elimination of slavery, but not without an enormous and perhaps unjustifiable cost.

---

[6] Friedman, Milton. 1962 [1996]. Capitalism and Freedom, Chicago: University of Chicago Press.

[7] Hummel, Jeffrey Rogers. 1996. Emancipating Slaves, Enslaving Free Men: A History of the American Civil War. Chicago: Open Court.

Incidentally, with respect to rent control, you are right. If I had thought it was politically feasible to take several steps but not to go all the way, I would have said I would like to go all the way but unfortunately we can't so let's do what we can, just as now I have written that I would like to eliminate our present tax system, I would like to replace our present tax system with a simple flat-rate tax, but that is not going to be politically feasible and so let's do those incremental changes which we can. I do not regard it as in any way incompatible with my basic values, contrary to your view, to let my actions depend on the circumstances and the possibilities. On the contrary, I believe it would be incompatible with my basic values to insist that, unless I can achieve my ultimate objective, I am going to pick up my marbles and go home.

Sincerely yours,

Milton

Letter 6

May 13, 1998

Dear Milton:

Thanks for your letter of April 24, 1998. Let me reply to your points in the order you make them.

1. Context

I must once again beg to differ with your interpretation of our debate. I pretty much know the context in which Hayek was writing. I fully agree with your assessment that Hayek wrote in a situation in which socialist ideas were very much more in the ascendency than they are now. (By the way, this is thanks to people such as, preeminently, yourself and Hayek and a mere handful of others who carried the torch in the previous generation. Now, thanks again to this small number of people, for example, who started the Mont Pelerin Society, thousands of their students, or students of students, amongst whom I count myself, have taken up this battle.) I agree with you that Hayek was trying to present his case in a way which would be as attractive to the socialists as possible, without giving away the store. Without, that is, compromising with his own (presumptive) ideology of free enterprise.

My complaint against Hayek is that he gave too much away in his attempt to defang the socialists. Were I to have been writing in the early 1940s (I was born in 1941, by the way), and I wanted to change their minds, I would have tried to show how free enterprise *helps* the poor, and that government regulations (e.g., rent control, minimum wage, working hour limitations, occupational licensure, unions, welfare, centrally planned money, etc., etc.) although ostensibly enacted with this end in mind, actually have the very opposite effect. Hayek, in contrast, tried to do this, but in his attempt conceded far too much of a role for government, in my opinion. In my footnote one I noted that there were others writing at this time, particularly Mises, who also wanted to show the socialists the error of this way but did so without making the numerous concessions made by Hayek.

2. Misconstrual of Limiting Working Hours

Let us consider a specific case in point, the limitation of working hours. In your letter of April 24, 1998 you attribute to me the view that "Hayek (p. 37) calls upon the government 'to limit working hours'." This is roughly correct, but not precisely so. What I in fact said (Block 1996, p. 330) was "And what roles does he (Hayek) assign the state? One of them is 'to limit working hours'." Now I admit that there is not very much difference between the point I actually made and the one you attribute to me, but it is important.

You are quite correct to point out the context in which Hayek was saying this, namely, his previous sentence: "Though all such controls of the methods or production impose extra costs … they may be well worthwhile." No, Hayek is not assigning to government the role to limit working hours. But I didn't say that he was (although you attributed to me this claim). I said only that Hayek was assigning to government the role of deciding *whether or not* to limit working hours. And this, precisely, is what he does do. That is, for Hayek, the decision of whether or not to limit working hours is one which is to be taken by the state. If they act wisely (ha, ha) they will do so when the costs of the limitation are more than offset by the gains, thereby; when these gains are less than the costs, on the other hand, otherwise (ha, ha) government will not limit working hours.

But in either case, for Hayek, it is the government which should decide whether or not to limit working hours. Do you not agree with me, given these points, that Hayek is assigning to the state the role of "limiting working hours," or not, depending upon its empirical assessment of the costs and benefits? Again, I am not now claiming, nor did I in my article, that for Hayek the state *must* limit hours (the view you mistakenly attribute to me) only that it *can*, if it thinks this is beneficial, on net. But surely to do this is to assign to the state the *role* (e.g., the responsibility) of possibly limiting working hours.

3. What Was Hayek Trying to Say and Why?

Why did Hayek write as he did? There are several hypotheses. One is that he was a lone voice crying out in the socialist wilderness; he couldn't be too radical since he would be ignored, summarily dismissed, etc. I have rejected this in my footnote one and in my last paragraph on the ground that there were dozens of other people writing from a free-market perspective in those days who were far more radical and consistent advocates of free enterprise than was Hayek. To the extent that this was true it is hardly complimentary to Hayek. Rather, it perceives him as a person with more than a little bit of moral cowardice.

A second view is that Hayek was in effect a politician, or mediator, or conciliator; he was trying to save the socialists from the error of their ways, and hit upon compromise as the best means to this end. You state in this regard: "Hayek is trying to say, 'How big a concession can I make to you people so that I won't completely alienate you? I want to attack you on the grounds that I regard as absolutely key and essential," and there he does a very good job'."

In my view, the second hypothesis has far more of the truth than the first. My objection to it is not that it is not true, but that it is (almost) despicable. Let me not be misinterpreted on this. I do not at all think that to try to convert socialists to the one true path (I can't help sounding like the "fanatic" you call me in your letter of December 17, 1997; I really do think that free enterprise is the only one true path in all of political economy) is despicable. I would only use such a characterization for doing this by purposefully lying about the free market philosophy, or recklessly disregarding it.

What would you think of me trying to convert you to orthodox Judaism by telling you that under this philosophy it is all right to eat pork, work on the Shabbat, etc.? Surely, this would not be a "good job" from the perspective of the Hasidim; rather, it would be a betrayal. Well, I feel that Hayek betrayed the philosophy of libertarianism with his numerous concessions. Please read again the transcript of Hayek's 1945 radio interview with Krueger and Merriam, two University of Chicago professors who were avowed socialists, and tell me it does not make you sick to your stomach.

Here is but one tidbit:

Krueger: "Is a minimum-wage law permissible?"

Hayek: "A general, flat minimum-wage law for all industry is permissible…" (Hayek 1994, p. 112).

4. Anarchism

Yes, I happen to be an anarchist libertarian (along with your son David; do you think of his views as "fanatical" on this score?) and, yes, "neither [Hayek] nor [you] is a libertarian in this sense." But nothing in my article turned on the complete absence of government. In my article, I did not at all criticize him for finding a small limited role for government (e.g., courts, armies, and police). On the contrary, I criticized him for compromising all over the place on everything else under the sun.

5. Negative Income Tax

I think that the best way to provide "a basic minimum level of living" for the poor is to establish the free enterprise system, not a negative income tax nor any other form of coercive welfare. If I were placed behind a Rawlsian "veil of ignorance" and told I would have grandchildren who might be poor, and I wanted to protect their lives, I would surely pick capitalism, not a welfare state, as their best protection.

I really am completely unable to make sense of the statement "there is an enormous difference between a situation in which 90 percent of the people are willing to tax themselves to help the bottom 10 percent, and a situation in which the middle 80 percent of the people tax the top 10 percent ostensibly to help the bottom 10 percent but probably in fact to tax both ends of the scale to help themselves."

As far as I am concerned, as a libertarian (whether of the anarchist or limited government variety, it matters not one whit), a tax is a tax is a tax and they all amount to theft (that is, when their purpose is to redistribute money from *anyone* to *anyone* else, and is not confined, at least for the limited government libertarian, to financing the legitimate roles of government such as courts, armies, and police). Ten percent, 80%, 90%, none of this matters; it is all coercive.

Moreover, how can people be "willing" to tax themselves? This, it seems to me, is no less than a logical contradiction. Take the case you favor, where the richest 90% pay taxes to subsidize the poorest 10%. If the 90% are "willing," there is no tax at all! Rather, there are voluntary payments, e.g., charity.

On the other hand, if there is a tax, this constitutes a refutation of the claim that it is voluntary. If it is so voluntary, why the need for compulsion? Of course, you answered this, at least to your own satisfaction, in *Capitalism and Freedom* (p. 191):

"It can be argued that private charity is insufficient because the benefits from it accrue to people other than those who make the gifts—again, a neighborhood effect. I am distressed by the sight of poverty; I am benefited by its alleviation; but I am benefited equally whether I or someone else pays for its alleviation; the benefits of other people's charity therefore partly accrue to me. To put it differently, we might all of us be willing to contribute to the relief of poverty, *provided* everyone else did."

But I find this intellectually incoherent. First, this really doesn't answer the question. Even if, somehow, welfare redistributionism could be justified on this ground, it still can't turn a coercive tax into a voluntary "willing" payment. You just can't square the circle.

Second, suppose that there are some of us in the 90% who are not distressed by the sight of poverty. On the contrary, they relish this. How can forcing such misanthropes to contribute taxes for the alleviation of poverty help *them*? Obviously, it cannot. Rather, it hurts them. Nor can we conclude that the external economy benefits to most rich people (in the top 90%) will outweigh the losses to the few misanthropes in this group without engaging in illicit interpersonal comparisons of utility.

Third, suppose that all of us in the top 90% of the income distribution are indeed "distressed by the sight of poverty." Why, then, not consider poverty as an external diseconomy? That is, instead of subsidizing the poor out of their poverty (assuming that this could work) why not penalize them for it? Surely, this is the tack that most economists (well, the Pigouvian ones, if not the Coasean ones) take with regard to, say, prostitution, drugs, air and water pollution, etc.

If the negative income tax cannot be justified on *any* libertarian grounds, in and of itself, can it at least be defended as an improvement on welfare with an implicit 100% marginal tax rate on earned income by welfare recipients? At first blush, it can be. You elsewhere make much of the fact that such a marginal tax rate has serious and negative implications for recipients' incentives. And, of course, you are correct in this.

However, do you not concede the fact that there are always some people on the margin between going on welfare and not going on welfare, and that any efficiency improvement in welfare, such as the negative income tax, will induce more of them to apply for the dole? If so, it is then very difficult to say whether this is a move in the direction of liberty or not. Yes, welfare is perhaps more efficient, at least in some sense; but, as a result, there are more welfare recipients. No clear gain for liberty here.

6. Slavery and the Civil War

In my last letter to you (of April 10, 1998) I stated that were you to cleave to your views on school vouchers, you would not have been a radical abolitionist of slavery; rather, you would have been a gradualist. I take the former, not the latter, to be the only position consistent with libertarianism. Yes, I have read Jeff Hummel's book on the Civil War. And, yes, certainly, his libertarianism is closer to mine than it is to yours.

However, nowhere in his book do I find any attack on radical abolitionism of slavery. Things are very much to the contrary. For example, he attacks Lincoln, and defends the radical abolitionists in ringing terms:

"Conventional wisdom often contrasts wild eyed intransigent and fanatical abolitionists with a moderate, temporizing and humane Abraham Lincoln. Yet … the radical abolitionists never proposed extinguishing slavery in a war of self immolation … The Civil War directly resulted from Lincoln's policy of political compromise, as harnessed in the interests of the nation-State, and not from the ideological radicalism of principled abolitionists." (Hummel 1996, p. 365)

I fail to see how your side of our debate can take much comfort from Jeff.

Let me say once again in closing, at the risk of being repetitive, that I regard it as an honor that you would take the time to engage me in a discussion of these very important ideas. We don't see eye to eye on the substantive issues, but if I treat students of mine who disagree with me half as courteously, intensively and fulsomely as you do me, I shall be delighted with myself.

Best regards,

Walter

Letter 7

June 6, 1998

Dear Walter:

I enclose a copy of a page from a recent *Far Eastern Economic Review*.[8] I wonder why you believe that Hayek is on that page and not "others writing at this time who also wanted to show the socialists the error of this ways, but did so without making the numerous concessions made by Hayek."

More generally, you are a fanatic who finds it absolutely impossible to understand the thinking of anybody other than himself. It is time to close our discussion.

Cordially,
Milton

Letter 8

June 21, 1998

Dear Milton:

Thanks for your letter of June 6, 1998. You once again call me a "fanatic" and say that "It is time to close our discussion." As for the latter, this seems unfair to me, in that you had the first word in this interchange (your letter to me of December 17, 1997). That being the case, it seems only proper that I should have the last word. Hence, this letter.

If "fanatical" means being consistent with my principles (in this case, free enterprise), then, yes, I plead guilty. I base my political philosophy on the nonaggression axiom of libertarianism, and *nothing* in my writings is incompatible with that. If fanatical means unwilling to consider both sides of a debate, unwilling to see clearly what my opponent is saying, misrepresenting the views of my intellectual adversaries (e.g., attacking straw men), then I plead innocent. Certainly, I didn't do it in this case; that is, I criticized Hayek for positions he actually took, not that I falsely attributed to him.

My Merriam-Webster dictionary defines fanatic as "moved by excessive enthusiasm" and "moved by intense uncritical devotion." I don't know about "excessive," but I am certainly enthusiastic about the concept of

[8] "Hayek's Children: An Idea Grows in China," the editorial from the *Far Eastern Economic Review* of May 14, 1998.

liberty. But if I am a fanatic in this regard, then so are you, in that you are one of the most enthusiastic people I have ever met concerning the ideas of liberty. When you were in Vancouver, and I was shepherding you around, I saw you time and again engage waiters, cameramen, producers of tv shows, electricians, etc., in issues of political economy.

Needless to say, Milton, I mean this as a sincere compliment to you. Would that I shall always keep in me a level of enthusiasm which has fueled your intellectual life. I'm not sure I care for "devotion," something which seems more religious than secular to me. As for "uncritical," surely the very reverse is the case, and I can cite no better authority on this than you, yourself. This whole dialogue began with your dismissal of my piece on Hayek; and you were unhappy with me for being too *critical* of him, not *uncritical*.

I tried to do Hayek the honor of treating his writings seriously, unlike those who have uncritically accepted whatever he said because, after all, it came from the pen of Hayek. The Chinese scholars who are now discovering him can perhaps be excused for seeing in him a pure vision of free enterprise. They know no better. They have probably never been confronted with any more radical defense of markets than Hayek's. But what can be said for those of us in the west who are, or could be, or should be familiar with less compromising advocates of capitalism such as Mises, Rothbard, Rand, Hoppe, Spooner, Oppenheimer, and still prefer the likes of Hayek? I suppose the best that can be said of them is that they are *not* "fanatics."

Too bad for them.

I am sorry you do not choose to continue this dialogue with me. I felt sure I could eventually convince you that the libertarian nonaggression axiom was the only worthwhile basic premise in political economy, and that its logical implications lead to a far more radical version of *laissez-faire* than the one envisioned by Hayek. (Heck, on my good days, I feel I can convince everyone of this.)

I am honored that you have chosen me as a debating partner to the degree you have. I have bragged to my children of this, and my grandchildren one day, hopefully, will know of it too. I shall be even more honored if you should change your mind and decide to continue it with me, until neither of us has anything more to say to each other on these topics. I would relish exploring differences between us on school vouchers, the negative income tax, the neighborhood effects argument, the fed, the gold standard, government itself, the voluntary military, flexible exchange rates, Austrian economics, and much more.

Even though you see me as a fanatic, I persist in thinking of you as my intellectual parent. (Officially, perhaps, you are my intellectual grandparent, because Gary Becker was your student, and my teacher at Columbia.) Paradoxically, because of your career (during which, on numerous occasions, I expect, you have been called a fanatic) my own views are seen by many as less fanatical than would otherwise have been the case.

Best regards as always,

Walter

P.S. I think a more accurate assessment of me than "fanatical," from your own point of view, would be "extremist." To that, I gladly plead guilty. In any version of the political economic spectrum, my views place me further to the extreme than do yours place you. But I wonder in this connection how you would evaluate the perspective of your son David? After all, he and I share an "extremist" vision of free-market anarchism, while you favor government, albeit a limited one. Just out of curiosity, would you place David and I in the same category as far as extremism or fanaticism is concerned?

6

Pipes on Property and Freedom

Every once in a while a book comes along which bodes well to explain, expound upon, and, most importantly, defend and justify that much maligned institution—private property rights—but which turns out, in the end, to be a disappointment. Two years ago it was Bethell's *The Noblest Triumph*[1] that took on this role. This time around it would appear to be the turn of Pipes's *Property and Freedom*[2] that fails to meet our hopes and expectations.

Although I have come to "bury, not praise" this book for its deviations from the philosophy of private property it ostensibly defends, I must start out on a positive note, because however flawed, Pipes does

The author wishes to thank Ilana Mercer for editorial assistance.

[1] Bethell, Tom, The Noblest Triumph: Property and Prosperity Through the Ages, New York: St. Martin's Press, 1998. For a critique see Block, Walter, "Review Essay of Bethell, Tom, The Noblest Triumph: Property and Prosperity Through the Ages, New York: St. Martin's Press, 1998," in The Quarterly Journal of Austrian Economics, Vol. 2, No. 3, Fall 1999, pp. 65–84. Pipes (p. 286) is a supporter of the Bethell book, stating that the latter has "convincingly presented … the close relationship between property and prosperity."

[2] Pipes, Richard, Property and Freedom: The story of how through the centuries private ownership has promoted liberty and the rule of law, New York: Knopf, 2000.

W. E. Block, *Property Rights*, Palgrave Studies in Classical Liberalism,
https://doi.org/10.1007/978-3-030-28353-7_6

make a contribution to our appreciation for private property. It cannot be denied that the book starts out on a high plain. Certainly, he is correct in locating the difficulties suffered by both Russia and later the USSR in terms of the lack of appreciation for private property endemic in that society. And what could be more uplifting than to be told, with clarity and passion, that property rights promote stability, constrain the powers of government, enable people to capture the fruits of their own labor, enhance economic efficiency, and promote an individual's sense of self-worth (Pipes, p. 4)? Also to be admired is his careful exegesis of the views on property of such philosophers as Plato, Aristotle, Ovid, Augustine, Aquinas, More, Spinoza, Bodin, Grotius, Seneca, Hobbes, Locke, Hume, Rousseau, Proudhon, Marx, Engels, Mil, Boas, Rawls, Fromm, Condorcet, and many more. This is a tour de force of the history of philosophy.

Nor is this book at all behindhand in stressing the importance of possessiveness in animals, children, primitive peoples, hunters, and gatherers, in antiquity, under feudalism, in medieval days, in accounting for the range and depth of property in human civilization. His history of property in England is alone more than worth the price of admission.

As a historian of property, throughout the centuries and all around the world, Pipes is exemplary. And this goes, in spades, for his criticism of how property is treated under both communism and fascism. It is only his economic and political understanding of the concept—particularly in regard to the welfare state—with which I wish to quarrel.

Here, Pipes's treatment can only be considered problematic. Consider his views on the New Deal in general, and such measures as the Social Security Act of 1935 and the Fair Labor Standards Act of 1938: "These measures belatedly guaranteed Americans the kind of social benefits that the Germans and English had taken for granted for decades. They were certainly needed" (p. 241). This is neither the time nor the place for a full-scale critique of the New Deal; suffice it at this point to state that these legislative initiatives were if anything the very antithesis of private property rights.

Or consider this statement (Pipes, p. 287): "The symbiotic relationship between property and freedom does not preclude the state from imposing reasonable restraints on the uses made of objects owned, or ensuring the basic living standards of the neediest strata of the population. Clearly, one cannot allow property rights to serve as a license for … ignoring the fundamental needs of the unemployed, sick, and aged. Hardly anyone contests this proposition today: even Frederick (*sic*) Hayek, an implacable foe of state intervention in the economy, agreed that the state has the duty to ensure for all citizens 'a minimum of food, shelter and clothing, sufficient to preserve health and the capacity to work." Pipes cites Hayek's *Road to Serfdom*[3] in this regard. But there are difficulties here. First and foremost, the Pipes book is presumably one in *favor* of private property rights. How can this possibly be squared with the forced taking of the wealth of some citizens, in order to give it to others? Would not private charity be a way of helping the poor far more in keeping with the presumed goal of this book?[4] Second, Pipes employs the argument from authority, an informal fallacy in logic. "Even Hayek says" is not a coherent argument; it is the substitute for such. And third, it is simply not true that Hayek is "an implacable foe of state intervention in the economy," no matter how widespread is this fallacious rumor. Very much to the contrary, he makes room for all sorts of government interventions, and violations of property rights.[5]

Perhaps realizing something of the intellectual quagmire into which he has just jumped, Pipes (p. 287) attempts to pull back from the precipice with the following: "But to say this is not to grant the state the authority to use the powers at its disposal to interfere with the freedom of contract, to redistribute wealth, or to compel one part of the population to bear the cost of the self-defined 'rights' of special constituencies. Limitations on the use of property imposed for public good should surely be interpreted as 'takings' and adequately compensated." But like the tar baby, this only gets him deeper into the pit.[6]

---

[3] Hayek, Friedrich A., The Road To Serfdom, The University of Chicago Press, Chicago, 1944.

[4] Olasky, Marvin, The Tragedy of American Compassion, Chicago: Regnery Gateway, 1992; Hughes, Mark D., "Middle Class Windfalls and the Poverty of the Welfare State," The Philanthropist, (Winter 1991); Vol. 10, No. 4, pp. 3–24; Hughes, Mark D., "Counterpoint: A Response to Bennett and DiLorenzo's Unfair Competition Thesis," The Philanthropist, (Fall 1990); Vol. 9, No. 3, pp. 43–56. Beito, David T., From Mutual Aid to the Welfare State: Fraternal Societies and Social Services, 1890–1967, Chapel Hill: University of North Carolina Press, 2000.

[5] See on this "Hayek's Road to Serfdom," Journal of Libertarian Studies: An Interdisciplinary Review, Vol. 12, No. 2, Fall 1996, pp. 327–350.

[6] I couldn't help mixing my metaphors. Please excuse me. At least this is not a violation of property rights.

Pipes has just finished, a la Hayek, justifying the welfare system.[7] He now contradicts himself by asserting that "this is not to grant the state the authority … to redistribute wealth." What else *but* a wealth redistribution scheme does this author think the welfare system is? Welfare, further, is the very paradigm case of compelling "one part of the population to bear the cost of the self-defined 'rights' of special constituencies." In this case, the special constituencies are the poor. And as for "rights," Pipes (pp. 288–289) is on record as *opposing* "printing press rights" and "class rights," even going so far as to cite libertarians Ayn Rand and Henri LePage to this effect. The point is, there is simply no such thing as a "right" to the wealth of other people, the premise underlying the forced transfer of income from the rest of the population to the poverty stricken.[8] It is one thing to contradict oneself in a large book in widely dispersed sections of it, or in other writings, but here the inconsistency appears on the very same and contiguous pages. Nor will compensation for "takings" avail this author much in the way of mitigation. First, a "taking" is the equivalent of theft, surely incompatible with a regime of private property rights. Second, where does Pipes think the government will get the money with which to compensate the people from whom it just "took"? Surely, apart from inflating the currency a bit more (e.g., counterfeiting) the only way would be to "take" from still others in the form of taxation (borrowing is only deferred taxation). Third, if these takings are "adequately compensated," what is the *point* of stealing? Surely, adequate compensation in this context implies that which the *robber* determines it to be. Were it to satisfy the property owner, there would be no reason for the "taking" in the first place; an ordinary purchase would suffice. Suppose you own a car, and I "take" it from you, offering compensation of $10, which I deem adequate. This is indistinguishable from a theft of the value of the automobile minus the $10. On the other

[7] For a devastating critique, see Murray, Charles, Losing Ground: American Social Policy from 1950 to 1980, New York: Basic Books, 1984.

[8] Pipes cannot plead ignorance of the distinction between the legitimate "negative" rights not to be molested or victimized by theft, on the one hand, and the so called "positive" rights to food, clothing, and shelter at other people's expense, as he discusses these, correctly, on pp. 245–247. (For more on this see Rothbard, Murray N., "Isaiah Berlin on Negative Freedom," in The Ethics of Liberty, New York: New York University Press, 1998.) Pipes understands this, full well, in "theory," but is unable or unwilling to apply these insights to the welfare state.

hand, suppose you place a value of $10,000 on your vehicle, and I "take" it, while giving you precisely this amount of money. Then, there is no difference between this and an ordinary purchase. Pipes cannot be allowed to have it both ways: either compensation for a "taking" is adequate in the mind of the original owner, in which it is not a taking, or it is inadequate in his view, in which case it is downright theft. And fourth what is it with this "public good" business? Surely, if there is anything such as the "public good," a dubious proposal on its face, it consists of nothing more and nothing less than the *protection* of property rights (to persons as well as physical objects), not the denigration of them as urged by Pipes with his advocacy of welfare state socialism. Pipes (p. 289) explicitly rejects "group rights rather than individual rights" but is not the right to welfare a "group right"?

Pipes's views of the relationship between democracy and coercion are also somewhat suspect. He (p. 291) approvingly cites Hayek to the effect that "the functions of the State (should be) limited to fields where real agreement among a majority could be achieved." He (ibid.) then goes on to declaim: "This reasoning explains why government interference in the life of the citizenry even for benevolent purposes endangers liberty: it posits a consensus which does not exist and hence requires coercion." But the implication of this is that if but majority consensus *could* be achieved, why, then, state action would *not* be coercive, and nothing could be further from the truth. For take a case where a democratically elected government pursued policies that were popular with the majority: the Nazi persecution of the Jews. Were he to carry forth on the logic of his own premises, Pipes would have to deny that the Holocaust was coercive, since "real agreement among a majority (was) achieved" here; a consensus on this policy *did* exist. The point is, there can be such a thing as the tyranny of the majority. Democracy is hardly a guarantee of the respect for private property rights in persons and things.

Nor need we accept Pipes's contention that the welfare system evidences "benevolent purposes." Suppose five robbers break into the home of a family of four people. As they are about to leave with the owners' possessions, the latter object, on the ground of private property rights. The criminals, being of a philosophical bent, are willing to engage in dialogue with their victims. Under the influence of Pipes they are willing to hold a democratic referendum on the issue of whether or not it is justified for them to "take" the family's household goods. The vote proves conclusive: five in favor (the thieves) and four against (the family members.) Would it make any difference if thereupon the gang stated that it was their intention to distribute their ill-gotten gains to the poor, and thus their motives were "benevolent"? Not at all. Theft is theft, and there is no benevolence to it at all.

Let us end on a sad note for Pipes's comprehension of the doctrine of private property rights. I quote him in full on this, one, so that there be no possible misunderstanding, and two, the better to ferret out his errors and expose them. He (p. 253) states:

> The government is not the only entity restricting property rights to real estate. Guilty also are private associations of homeowners which arrogate to themselves quasi-governmental functions. Such associations, set up by developers to administer condominia, cooperative apartments, and single-family planned units, have grown from fewer than 500 in 1964 to 150,000 in 1992; their rules and regulations affect an estimated 32 million people. The objective of these associations is to protect property values of a community by imposing strict guidelines concerning the appearance and use of real estate. Paradoxically, by protecting the values of the community's housing they infringe on the property rights of owners. Many of the restrictions are proper and sensible. But some communities go to extremes: they may forbid the growing of vegetables or the installation of air conditioners, limit visits by grandchildren, regulate the color of curtains, prohibit the home delivery of newspapers or the display of the American flag. etc., etc. Failure to abide by the community's rules and regulations can lead to the imposition of fines. Although in theory membership in such regulated communities is voluntary, many families have no choice but to buy into them because of price, location, or some other compelling factor. And once they do so, they lose a great deal of freedom and even privacy.

It is hard to know where to begin, there are so many mischievous errors packed into so small a space.[9] The core fallacy is that ownership of prop-

[9] For another statement along these lines see Holcombe, Randall G., The Economic Foundations of Government, New York: New York University Press, 1994. For a rebuttal, see Block, Walter,

erty under such restrictive covenants is somehow coercive, as if people are forced against their will into making condominium purchases. If a man can be "compelled" to buy a coop apartment because of "price or location" then there is no hope for any of us, since the same can be said of *every* possible purchase of *anything*. That is, everything that anyone takes into ownership through commercial means has some sort of price and is located somewhere or other. We must conclude that this consideration, contrary to Pipes, is entirely insufficient to establish coercion. Further, it matters not one whit what specific rules are imposed upon owners; as long as they agree to them, and are not initially mislead through fraud, there is no violation of property rights. It doesn't matter if I agree to do something truly demeaning; for example, push a peanut with my nose down the street, wearing a propeller beanie. As long as I *consent* to be bound by such rules, there is nothing amiss, as far as private property is concerned.[10] Nor can we accept Pipes's distinction between "sensible infringements" upon rights, and those which "go to extremes." One man's extreme is another's moderation. In the event, all such contracts must necessarily be mutually beneficial in the ex ante sense. Were they not expected to generate benefits, they would hardly be entered into in the first place. Based on the statistics supplied by Pipes himself, they must be very successful, too, in the ex post sense.

In conclusion, while this author does support private property rights, his analysis is vitiated somewhat by a welter of mistakes and confusions. Perhaps a better title for the book would have been "One Cheer for Private Property Rights."

"National Defense and the Theory of Externalities, Public Goods and Clubs," Hoppe, Hans-Hermann, ed., Explorations in the Theory and History of Security Production, forthcoming.

[10] Under voluntary sado-masochism, people assent to being whipped. Should such a person be allowed to accuse the sadist of assault and battery? No more than should one boxer be allowed to sue another for punching him. When you enter the boxing ring, you *agree* to being hit (above the belt). Under Pipes's dispensation, there could be no such contracts, a violation of liberty if ever there was one.

7

Bethell on Property and Prosperity

Introduction

There once was a little girl with a curl. According to the nursery rhyme, "when she was good, she was very, very good; when she was bad, she was horrid."

Much the same can be said about this book.

What are the very, very good parts? It is a thorough, lively, and almost encyclopedic defense of private property rights. In this benighted age, there are not too many of those around. Ranging far and wide, Bethell shows the benefits of private property throughout history and in virtually every corner of the globe. He demonstrates how the institutions of private property can solve environmental problems, were responsible for the success of the industrial revolution in England, and how the lack of them accounted for the failures of the USSR, feudalism, and the third world. His explanation of the Irish famine is alone worth far more than the price of admission. Standing head and shoulders over many purely economic defenses of this institution, Bethel's book also demonstrates the virtues of property rights on political and moral grounds.

W. E. Block, *Property Rights*, Palgrave Studies in Classical Liberalism,
https://doi.org/10.1007/978-3-030-28353-7_7

The horrid part of the book is that its case in favor of private property rights makes needless compromises; it is hemmed in by a welter of caveats, restrictions, exceptions, and provisos. In the light of these, a better title for it might have been "Two cheers for private property rights," or "A semi noble triumph: limited property rights and prosperity through the ages." Before exploring this contention, a bit of background.

Background

Private property rights (including self-ownership rights) may be articulated on three basic levels: logic; justice, and economic efficiency.

The first point is that it is self-contradictory to try to *deny* the concept of private property rights. For the denier must use, at least, his vocal chords, chest cavity, and so on, and have a place to stand (Hoppe, 1993). If there are to be no private property rights, whence came the critic into legitimate possession of the wherewithal necessary to make his very objection?

Second, justice. Without such rights, there can be no justice (Rothbard, 1982b). For justice, at least in the realm of law, consists of no more and no less than ensuring that owners of personal and physical property are allowed full use of them; injustice, in contrast, is limited to a denial of such a state of affairs. There is no injustice that cannot be reduced to a violation of private property rights.[1]

Third, economic efficiency. Even Chicagoans such as Bethell can be trusted on this one, for the most part. Our author, for example, weighs in heavily with his attacks on central planning (142),[2] foreign aid (208–215), welfare (164), "social justice" (162–168), uncompensated "takings" (181), land use regulations (182), support of the industrial revolution (87–91), and privatizing universities (180). He knows, and tells us in loving detail, that those countries which have relied upon private property

[1] Again, I am limiting this to the legal realm. If I make a promise to you, but then break it, this might well be "unjust." But since this does not involve an uninvited border crossing, or the initiation of violence, it is not taken cognizance of by the libertarian legal system as "unjust."

[2] All otherwise unidentified page citations such as this refer to the Bethell book.

to a greater degree than others have also been more prosperous (12, 28, 337–338).

Bethell, moreover, correctly identifies the various aspects of private property as "the rights to use the thing and to exclude others from doing so, to alter its physical configuration, to enjoy its fruits, including its income, and, not least, to transfer the title of ownership to another" (19). This means, or at least it should mean, that the owner should be allowed by law to do *whatever* he wishes with his legitimately held property, provided *only* that he does not thereby violate the equally valid private property rights of others.

Anarchism

There are several key implications of a fearless and thorough analysis of private property rights, however, on which Bethell fears to tread. One of them is anarchism.[3] Why anarchism? Why, that is, is the existence of a compulsory government the enemy of private property rights? States do two things which take them out of the realm of free markets based upon private property rights. First, they *compel* allegiance to themselves.[4] They *demand* that all people within a given geographical area subscribe to their system of laws, and pay taxes for this privilege. But Bethell just got finished saying that private property confers "the rights to use the thing and to exclude others from doing so." If so, then the individual surely has the right to *exclude the government* from the use of his property, without permission.[5] Second, a state demands a *monopoly* of power within "its" geographical area. That is, it will use force to crush any private agency daring

[3] I would not bring up this issue in a review of a book ostensibly on private property rights if not for his gratuitous attack on statelessness (339).

[4] All throughout his book, Bethell waxes indignant about the use of force and compulsion as the enemy of freedom, liberty, and private property rights. (See, for example, 76, 84, 137, 192.) Why does this well-justified antipathy not apply to the government?

[5] If, of course, the person *agrees* to deal with a protection agency, and pay it fees for protection, judiciary and other such services, then this is a private defense firm, not a government at all. See on this Hoppe, 1993, Rothbard, 1982, Friedman, 1989, Spooner, [1870] 1966.

to set itself up in competition with it, offering police, judicial, and other services.[6]

And what is Bethell's take on all of this? He (339) asserts: "In most places and times (it) is obviously not true (that) … anarchy begets efficiency. There has been plenty of unproductive anarchy in the world. One only has to think, recently, of Haiti, Sudan and Somalia. Nothing good has come of the institutional near vacuum in these countries."[7]

This is a bit of a departure for those who oppose the fully free society. For it concedes that at *some* times and *some* places society managed to function without the state.[8] But if we define anarchy as places without governments, and we define governments as the agencies with a legal right to impose violence on their subjects, then whatever else occurred in Haiti, Sudan, and Somalia, it wasn't anarchy. For there were well-organized gangs (e.g., governments) in each of these places, demanding tribute, and fighting others who made similar impositions. Absence of government means absence of government, whether well-established ones, or fly-by-nights.[9]

Emergencies

Nor is this merely a dispute over formal anarchism. Bethell makes excuses for governmental activity all throughout his book; preeminently, he makes exceptions to the rights of private property for "emergencies." For example, he (322) states: "The common law has long held that people

---

[6] In the view of Bethell (25), "some goods are naturally managed by the states—those that are needed to provide for the common defense, for example, or for administering justice and enforcing the law. Such goods are natural monopolies."

[7] Elsewhere, Bethell (12) equates anarchy with, of all things, "tyranny."

[8] Surely, the present situation of anarchy between the some 200 presently constituted nations of the world would have to be opposed by anti-anarchists such as Bethell. This logically implies that he favors a one world government (with China and India, the most populous countries, together controlling global politics). If not, and I suspect not, then this author must rescind his opposition to anarchism.

[9] As Spooner ([1870] 1966) shows, the only difference between a gang and a government is better public relations on the part of the latter.

may be entitled to trespass on others' rights in emergencies. And no doubt … (p)roperty rights should give ground when time is short."[10]

But one man's "emergency" is just another man's violations of private property rights. Bethell is fully aware of just how subjective things can be when he (very perceptively) attacks Demsetz (1967) for overlooking subjectivism (47), but when it comes to making exceptions for governments to violate private property rights for this reason, he appears to lose sight of his own insight.

Nor can any reasonably well-informed man be unaware of the fact that there are always "emergencies." Consider that spate of advertisements inviting charity abroad: "Here is little Maria. She will soon die of lack of food. You can send her $15 per month, or turn the page" (paraphrase). As I write this, the peril of Yugoslavian refugees, many of them children, are there for all the world to see on television.

Bethellnomics would appear to imply that all bets are off, private property wise, while there is an "emergency" anywhere in the world. For if emergencies justify governmental violation of property rights, and there are always emergencies somewhere in the world, even in each country, then statist depredations on our sacred rights of private and personal property are *always* justified. This is a *defense* of our "noblest triumph"?

But we don't have to reach far and wide for a refutation of this Bethellian decline into socialism. He stands condemned on the basis of his own words. For in his well-taken critique of zoning and urban renewal as an affront to private property, he objects to the use of "the legislature's 'police power'—its authority to act on behalf of the public safety, health and morals" (297). But what more is this "police power," that he objects to in the context of zoning and urban renewal, than the self-same governmental power to act in "emergencies."

---

[10] Bethell (9) also sees "private property (as) a compromise between our desire for unrestricted liberty and the recognition that others have similar desires and rights." But this is a very perverse way to interpret "liberty." Liberty, used in this context, is a synonym for "license," for the right of the individual to do whatever he wants to do, even if it violates the equal liberties of others. Who, with this definition, could favor liberty? Who could be a libertarian? Surely, a more reasonable definition of liberty (utilized in this review) is the right to do with your own property whatever it is you wish, provided only that this doesn't interfere with anyone else's similar liberty. Nor is Bethell's dismissal of libertarianism only implicit. On the contrary, he (25) goes so far as to characterize this philosophy, along with Marxism, of all things, as "dogma."

Communalism

Another problem with our author's vision of private property arises with regard to communalism. He states (25): "Broadly speaking, there are three configurations of property rights: private, communal and state." This is entirely erroneous. The truth of the matter is that there are but *two* divisions of property: just and unjust. Into the former category are placed *both* private, for example, individual, and private, for example, communal.[11] Why? Because, as even Bethell acknowledges, legitimately held property is based on initial (86) homesteading (Locke, 1960) and lawful title transfer.[12] If I homestead some land, or purchase it from the legitimate owner with money I have earned honestly, and then farm it by myself, Bethell will support me. But, if I turn around and share it with a bunch of communitarians, as did Robert Owen, I will get the back of the hand from Bethell. Our author goes so far as to link Owen with, of all people, the leaders of the USSR. He does this, implicitly, by considering the two in one section of his book. Section V is entitled "The New Man," and has but two chapters in it: 7, devoted to "Robert Owen's Trinity of Evils," and 8, to "The Soviet Experiment." He does this explicitly with the following statement (127): "In 1816, Owen opened his Institute for the Formation of Character, more or less anticipating Soviet developments 100 years later." More or less anticipating? The Soviets killed tens of millions of people, violating property rights in the person on a truly gargantuan scale (Conquest, 1986, 1990); as well, under forced collectivization, and the expropriation of practically all goods, houses, factories, means of production, these brutes violated the rights over physical property to a tremendous extent. Owen, in contrast, not only murdered no one, he engaged in his communalist experiments with his own money; he was joined in them by willing collaborators. Even Bethell admits (125) that Owen "spent his own money on the cause in which he so firmly believed."[13]

[11] Into the latter go *both* kinds of stolen property, individual, for example, stolen by a single robber, and communal, stolen by gangs, whether "private" or governmental.

[12] In this context Bethell could well have cited Nozick (1974), but did not.

[13] Bethell (132) further states: "Owen … proposed that the Harmonites should form themselves into a Community of Equality right away, with the property—his property! to be shared in common" (emphasis added).

There is nothing intrinsically wrong with communalism. Yes, when combined with force, it is a particularly evil brew.[14] But take away the coercion, and it is rendered powerless, even, sometimes, beneficial. It is the same with practically anything. For example, there is nothing wrong with pizza. But if everyone were forced to eat this foodstuff, every meal, every day, numerous deaths would no doubt ensue, perhaps, even, who knows, equivalent to the loss of life which resulted from forced communism. Does this mean we should oppose pizza (communism)? Not a bit of it; only when imposed through force.

Yes, yes, Owen's New Lanark and New Harmony communes didn't work in the sense that they only lasted for a few years. But no less is true of thousands of business firms which go bankrupt after a similar period of time. Would Bethell wish to condemn the latter in the manner he does the former? Soviets indeed!

Bethell can perhaps be interpreted as being on firmer ground in his discussion of the evils of communalism with regard to the Plymouth experience. After all, at least some people died; not of Soviet proportions, but there were a few. But even here, Bethell's conflation of coercion and communalism does him in. For what was wrong with Pilgrim economics was *not* that "it sets up a system of rewards and punishments that puts the welfare of the community on a collision course with human nature" (31). Rather, the problem was that this system of communism was done on a *coercive* basis.[15] Had this not been the case, had the Pilgrims been perfectly free to arrange economic matters on an individual basis, then, one of two things would have happened. Either they would have come to their senses and substituted private individual property for private communal property, given that the former was not successful. Or, and this is a very big or indeed, they would have stuck to their guns, gone down starving as they did, and we would have been forced to interpret this situation as one where they all preferred death rather than the "dishonor" of not living communally. How else could such a situation possibly be analyzed, again, on the assumption that all involved were consenting adults?

---

[14] Bethell recognizes the evils of initiatory force in the context of foreign aid and planning, but not when it comes to voluntary communal property (192).

[15] Bethell (35) describes the economic system as the "Crown-devised policy of joint possession" (emphasis added).

But is communism of the voluntary variety always unsuccessful? Not at all, as even Bethell himself admits. For example, he acknowledges that this is indeed the system which most families utilize. As well, religious orders and organizations such as monasteries, nunneries, Hutterites, and Jesuits live by the maxim, "from each according to his ability, to each according to his need." Yet, such is our author's visceral and Chicagoesque antipathy to allowing people to be free to choose their own paths in life, that he still cannot give up his opposition to capitalist acts between consenting adults of a socialistic variety. This sounds like a contradiction in terms, but only because Bethell cannot discern what system is the real enemy of the free society.

Consider, then, the following chart:

	Socialism	Capitalism
Coercive	A	B
Voluntary	C	D

Here, A stands for coercive socialism of the Soviet variety, and C depicts voluntary socialism of the kibbutz, commune, family, religious order, or Owen's New Harmony. D represents laissez faire capitalism, where all economic action is based on legitimate private property rights and voluntary contract, while B features the veneer of capitalism and private firms, but these are hedged in with a welter of government interferences with the market. Examples are Hitler's Germany, Italian fascism, and, of course, the present economic system of the United States.

Most commentators, Bethell specifically included, think that the crucial debate in political economy is between socialism and capitalism. This, in our terms, would place A and C on one side of the barricades, and B and D on the other. Nothing, however, could be further from the truth. In actual point of fact, the real contending parties are A and B vs. C and D. It is not socialism vs. capitalism, but, rather, a purely voluntary system which allows full sway to the choices of the owners of private property, whether they wish to use their holdings individually or communally it matters not one whit, vis-à-vis a coercive system where some people dictate how others can use their property rights, and again, it matters little whether there is a superficial coating of "capitalism" or "socialism" to which lip service is given.

Bethell misconstrues the enemy of freedom. He thinks it includes C, which is why he takes off after poor inoffensive Owen.[16] Our author offers half a dozen ad hoc defenses of his thesis, concerning the size of the commune, its religiosity, familial relations, and so on. All of this is totally beside the point. In other words, were communalism per se a violation of property rights, then these things wouldn't matter at all. That these considerations actually do matter, are even crucial, only underscores the point that the commune is fully compatible with property rights.

Consider Bethell's "analysis" of sharing restaurant checks (44): "When property is communally owned, there is no 'mine' or 'thine' by intention. Everything is 'ours.' This is likely to create dissension, as it did at Plymouth Colony. The lack of ratio between effort and reward 'was thought injustice.' Such an outcome may be expected when members have rights to equal shares in the product of a community. Those who contribute little will enjoy a free ride at the expense of those who work hard. We recognize the free-rider problem, even if we don't know its name. A group dividing the check equally at a restaurant will encounter it. Those ordering expensive items will come out ahead. Separate checks are the solution—the equivalent of privatization."

But suppose a group of friends at a restaurant reject Bethell's advice. Are they guilty of a private property rights violation? Not even this author, presumably, would go that far. For these people have every right to share the check precisely as they wish. This is hardly the opposite of privatization; rather, it is the *embodiment* of the free society, in microcosm. Each of the diners decides this for himself; they all agree to allow "free riders" on a unanimous basis.

With this analysis Bethell has ceased being a commentator on political economy; he has taken on the role of the managerial consultant. He is *advising* people not to split restaurant checks, not to join communes, and so on. But what business is it of his *how* people enjoy their private property rights? As a presumed advocate of this system, he is supposed to be neutral on such issues. That he is far from neutral about them only lessens the more his claim to be a defender of our "Noblest Triumph."

[16] Inoffensive, that is, in what he *did*, not necessarily what he *advocated*.

Market Failure

But this is not the end of the mischief caused by his mistaken analysis. Because of it, Bethell is also led into the trap of accepting the doctrine of "market failure," at least when it comes to so-called free riders,[17] non-excludability, tragedy of the commons and public goods.[18]

The free-rider "problem" comes about, it is alleged by most mainstream economists, when all the benefits of an act cannot be confined to those who undertake their costs. Free riders, beneficiaries who do not pay their own way, cannot be excluded from the enjoyment thereof. Therefore, either the act will not be carried out at all, or there will be an underinvestment in it, at least compared to the situation where this problem does not arise. And what does our free enterpriser Bethell add to this? He (50) asserts that this problem "may be insoluble, in which case government action may be called for." Surely this deserves to rank among the all-time malapropisms. If the free riding problem is truly "insoluble," how on earth are government bureaucrats going to solve it? Do they have magical powers?

The government "solution," of course, is to *force* the recalcitrant non-paying beneficiaries to cough up their "fair share" of the costs through taxation. But this opens up a Pandora's box of difficulties. For one thing, how do we *know* that the free rider really benefits?

The most typical illustrative example is national defense. It is argued that we "all" benefit from the army, navy, marines, and so on, in that they protect us against invasions from foreigners.[19] Says Bethell (51):

> Because a national defense system will protect those who don't pay for it, a privately financed defense system will immediately run into the free rider

[17] It is no exaggeration to say that complaints about free riders form the core of Bethell's "defense" of private property rights. He mentions them often: (31–32, 42, 44, 46, 49, 51, 54, 137, 157, 167, 268, 323).

[18] Market failure doctrine leads a long and not very savory life in the history of economic thought. In addition to the three mentioned in the text other major accusations against the free market include monopoly, inequitable distribution of income, slow growth, and unequal information. For critiques of this doctrine see Hoppe (1993), Hummel (1990), and Rothbard (1962).

[19] The US government has some 800 military bases located in roughly 130 different countries, and is engaged in approximately a half dozen separate "hot" wars.

problem. As a matter of both justice and practical politics, therefore, the government intervenes and taxes are levied from all to pay for such goods.

But what of the pacifist? Can Bethell and the other advocates of this view seriously maintain that pacifists such as the Amish "benefit" from expenditures on military hardware, even in their own view?[20] According to the old adage, "One man's meat is another man's poison." Precisely. Bethell, again, superbly wielded this subjectivist concept in his (47) critique of Demsetz (1967), only four pages earlier. Strange that he forgets all about it at this juncture.

Further, if the government levies coercive taxes[21] on those unwilling to pay for defense, it will be doing to these hapless individuals exactly the opposite of what it is purporting to do for them. That is, the whole point of the exercise is presumably to *protect* the citizenry. This can hardly be done when, at the outset, the state initiates the very violence against them from which it is supposed, according to the theory, to be *saving* them.

Nor is it entirely outside the realm of the possible to exclude at least some of those who refuse to pay for service. All the government (or the private defense agency) need do is issue placards to its clients. Those without them, whether on their persons or their property, will be "fair game" for criminals, whether domestic or foreign. They would have to make their own private arrangement for protection, on the assumption they were not pacifists.

It is possible, too, to apply a reductio ad absurdum to this entire line of argument. If Bethell can assert, in the face of pacifists,[22] that *everyone* benefits from national defense, then I can claim, with equal justification, that we all gain from the things *I* enjoy, such as handball, chess, karate, libertarianism, Austrian economics, and baroque music. All people, whether they know it or not, benefit from these avocations, not only directly, themselves, but even when others engage in them. This is because their practice makes people "better persons," and this, in turn, "spills over," even to those "refusenicks" who do not directly participate.

---

[20] See on this Rothbard (1962, pp. 883–890).

[21] And what other kind of taxation is there?

[22] As well as traitors.

Therefore, I confidently assert, there is less than an optimal amount of investment in these things[23]; government must subsidize all those involved in these pursuits. The point is, by use of this "logic," anyone can prove anything he wants.

Particularly disappointing[24] is Bethell's defense of highway socialism[25]: for example, his support for governmental, as opposed to privatized,[26] vehicular thoroughfares. In his view (51):

> Road building has with reason been a government activity for a long time, mainly because the cost of collecting fees from road users has been high. The private purchase of right of way also runs into the problem that hold-outs can command monopoly prices. But digital technology is reducing the cost of collecting tolls, and if, in the years ahead, clogged freeways are not cleared by user fees (collected by road scanners 'reading' prepaid magnetic strips and deducting a toll) then ideology will surely have trumped technology.

This simply will not do. Private roads, too, have been around for a "long time." Among the first highways in the United States were built by private turnpike companies. The reason for their failure had little or nothing to do with the costs of collection being "high." Rather, it was due to the fact that governments, the self-styled protectors of private property, refused to safeguard the toll houses of these corporations from physical attack.[27] Digital technology, universal product codes, have been in

---

[23] Soap, too, by the way.

[24] See on this Block (1979, 1980, 1983a, 1983b, 1996b); Block and Block (1996); Cadin and Block (1997); Gunderson (1989); Klein (1990); Klein, Majewski, and Baer (1993a, 1993b); Klein and Fielding (1992, 1993a, 1993b); Roth (1966, 1967, 1987); Rothbard (1973), Woolridge (1970).

[25] Hopefully the context here, as well as in the case of "water socialism," below, will make clear that we are referring to coercive, and not voluntary, socialism.

[26] Another self-contradiction. When it comes to Robert Owen, or "the tragedy of the commons," or, for goodness sake, friends splitting restaurant checks, Bethell is adamantly in favor of "privatization." Why not, then, real privatization in the case of streets and highways?

[27] Demsetz (1967) would likely claim that it was too *expensive* for the government to do so. This presumes that the state can discern just which enterprises it is appropriate to shield, and which not. But this is unconvincing. A police presence, in any case, was not required at every toll gate, any more than a cop is needed at each store. It would have sufficed had government merely threatened to punish toll booth violators, should they be apprehended, the same sort of offer presumably made to every other property owner.

operation in grocery stores, pharmacies, supermarkets, railroads, and so on, for some three decades now; only very recently has the government bestirred itself sufficiently to utilize these breakthroughs on the nation's highways. And when they do, for Bethell this is only a reason for allowing *government*-managed highways to reduce traffic congestion, not for full privatization.

Worst of all, under statist management, some 40,000 people per year lose their lives due to traffic accidents. Instead of accepting responsibility for this carnage, apologists for highway socialism are apt to blame it on speed, drunken driving, poor weather conditions, and a whole host of other reasons, none of them having to do with government management. But it is the failure of the statist highway managers to *deal* with these phenomena, not they, themselves, which is ultimately responsible for the massive fatalities.[28] We must realize that the same folks who bring us such great efficiency in the post office are also responsible for managing roads and streets. In any case, why a defense of government highways in a book devoted to private property?

And what of "rights of way" and "holdouts"? Bethell is off base on these considerations, too. In the United States there is a long history of private ownership of railroads. These, like roads, are very long thin enterprises. If rights of way were not a sufficient reason for governmental trains, they are not, either, for highways. As to "holdouts," these are precisely the people a book devoted to the Noblest Triumph ought to be *defending*, not denigrating. For holdouts are private property owners, going about their business, refusing to sell to developers. In any case, there are many ways to deal with "holdouts." One can build a road around, under, or over them (Block and Block, 1998). Ironically, Bethell himself touches upon yet another commercial technique in this regard: options. Only two pages after the above quote (53) he mentions these, but only in the context of land assembly for Disney World in Florida. He doesn't seem aware of the fact that the private street builder, too, can avail himself of this course of action.[29]

[28] In like manner, we do not blame the bullet, but the gunman, for the murder. Similarly, the restaurant *manager* is the ultimate cause of business failure, not the proximate causes of poor service, bad food, dirty floors, and so on. It is the manager's job to improve these conditions.

[29] Consider the strategy of the highway owner who wants to build between points A and B. All he need do is to buy option to purchase land along five or six alternative routes. Only when he has a

Law and Economics

Coase is the litmus test for anyone who wants to be considered a defender of private property rights. Bethell passes this test, although not with flying colors; rather, just barely. But he does pass, and this is an exceedingly rigorous test, at least for those with strong Chicagoesque tendencies, such as our author.

What are the specifics? Coase (1960) took the economics profession by storm. The most heavily cited article of all time,[30] it launched the *Journal of Law and Economics*, which, in turn, became a mainstay of the new subdiscipline, law, and economics. The essence of Coase's message had to do with the real-world positive transactions costs. Here, property under dispute (and this would mean *all* property, once Coaseanism became the law of the land) should be given *not* to its rightful owner (indeed, the idea of rightful ownership, justice, etc., has no place in the Chicagoesque philosophy), who had either homesteaded it or purchased it from a person who had mixed his labor with the land (Locke, 1960; Rothbard, 1982b; Hoppe, 1993; Nozick, 1974). Rather, wait for this, the property should be given to that party who, in the judges' opinion, would make best use of it in the future and in that way maximize total wealth.

Suppose I were to "steal" your wallet (it is now necessary to affix quotation marks to this word, since its meaning changes violently in the Coasean world). The old fashioned (pre-Coase) judge would inquire into the *past history* of this item. Were your credit cards and pictures of you and your family in it, and did this wallet have a bill of sale with your name on it, that would pretty much be the end of the matter. I would be the thief, you the rightful owner. However, for the judge under the baleful influence of Coase, the past would be *irrelevant*. Sunken costs, after all, hold no sway for the economist. On the contrary, the judicial inquiry would turn on the *future*. If I could prove I would make better use of the wallet and its contents than you (I would use it for good wealth-

complete set of options for any one of them—with no holdouts—does he exercise his option and actually purchase the land.

[30] According to Cheung (1983, p. 20) between 1966 and 1980 it had garnered some 700 citations; cited in Bethell (315).

maximizing purposes, you are a ne'er do well who will waste the money on wine, women, and song), then I would become the "legitimate" owner, that is, until someone else who could use it even more efficiently than I came and relieved me of it.

But this is not yet the bottom of the barrel as far as Coase and the "law and economics" movement are concerned. To add insult to injury to this thorough going attack on private property rights, the members of this school of thought saw themselves, and were widely perceived as, not critics of capitalism, but supporters. This is surely intolerable. It is one thing for a Proudhon, or a Marx, or a Stalin, to attack free enterprise. It is quite another, and altogether far more problematic, for those who march under the flag of the marketplace to be its most serious detractors.

Bethell, to his credit, sees through this scam. He replies to this radical attack on the institution of private property rights (318): "Justice itself should be subordinated to efficiency—to economics." Characterizing this as a (319) "strange doctrine," our author (318) sharply rebukes Posner (1986), a leading Coasean, for the facile equation of justice and economic efficiency. He continues (320):

> The claim that 'inefficient situations sometimes exist within a private property system, thanks to high transactions costs, seemed (in Coase's initial formulation) to legitimize the rearrangement of all property rights by efficiency experts … It would render all property insecure and destroy the entire basis of the free market system: exchange by consent. Thus, an exercise that began with Coase weakening the Pigovian rationale for government intervention went on to raise the possibility of a far more serious intervention.

Further, Bethell (321) approvingly and correctly cites Simpson's (1996, p. 91) characterization of the Coasean system as "the end of the right of private property." Our author (321–322) is highly critical of Posner's (1986, pp. 128–129) analysis of *Ploof v Putnam* (1908) on the ground that the latter resorts to illegitimate interpersonal comparisons of utility.[31]

[31] This is somewhat marred by Bethell's own transgressions in this regard (320): "the level of inefficiency resulting from marginal impositions upon neighbors has never been established in practice. But it is surely low." Low? How do we know this? How *can* we know this? Low, compared to what?

And yet, and yet. Despite the foregoing, Bethell's dismissal of Coaseanism is not at all an unambiguous one. His blistering attacks on this system are marred by an admixture of actual praise. For example, he (315) states: "The Journal of Law and Economics ... was intended as an alternative to the strongly statist tendency of economics departments at that time." How can it be *anti*-statist to undermine private property rights? And again (316–317):

> The Coase theorem drew attention to one of the key contentions in this book: that transferable (exchangeable) property rights are the key to economic efficiency, to amity between neighbors and to peaceful relations in society more generally. Coase's insight has since been reformulated as one of the most basic principles of economics: When goods are owned in a well defined way, and the rights to them are exchangeable, they will be purchased by those who value them most highly.

Well defined? How can property be well defined if ownership is based not on past considerations but on future ones? As Bethell has himself shown us, well definedness and property rights, for Coase, are antithetical. On the contrary, Coaseanism is the paradigm case of *ill*-defined property rights. Yet another evidence of equivocation: Bethell (319–320) cites as critics of Coaseanism only the likes of Horwitz (1980), Leff (1974), Dworkin (1977), and Simpson (1996), few of them, with the possible exception of the latter, as thorough going in their rejection of this system as the libertarian Austrians.[32] For Bethell, it is almost as if there are only critics of Coaseanism in economics only from the left, not the right.

Bethell sees the flaws in Coase, but lets him off easily, certainly, compared to how he treats Marx and Proudhon. But the latter two proudly wore their (coercive!) socialist garb. Not so, Coase and Posner, and their ilk. One interpretation of this might be that on an intellectual plane Bethell sees through this Chicago attack on property rights. But he is

[32] On this see Block (1977, 1995b, 1996a), Cordato (1989, 1992a, 1992b), Krecke (1992), North (1990, 1992), Rothbard (1990).

himself so much a part of this movement that he cannot quite bring himself to as harsh a judgment as might be warranted.

Hayek as Libertarian

Hayek (1944) is characterized by Bethell (147) as "a strong defender of private property." By no stretch of the imagination is this true. Very much to the contrary, Hayek makes dozens of exceptions to the free enterprise system. These include "an extensive system of social services" (Block 1996c, p. 331), government "health and accident insurance" (Block 1996c, p. 337), opposition to "the immediate abolition of rent control," (Block 1996c, p. 339), maximum hours legislation (Block 1996c, p. 346), minimum wages laws (Block 1996c, p. 347), and TVA (Block 1996c, p. 347).

There are some who defend Hayek on the ground that his views must be taken in context; that, apart from Mises, he was the strongest defender of private property in the decades in which he did most of his writing, and thus deserved to be categorized as a staunch defender of private property rights even though he was in effect no such thing. But this defense simply will not do. There were plenty of far more radical supporters of free enterprise than Hayek during the 1930s–1950s: Ayn Rand, Henry Hazlitt, Albert J. Nock, Garet Garrett, Frank Chodorov, Robert LeFevre, Henry George, H.L. Mencken, Baldy Harper, Leonard Read, W.H. Hutt, Bruno Leoni, Benjamin Anderson, John V. Van Sickle, Wilhelm Ropke, Lionel Robbins, Peter Bauer, Isabel Patterson. And why limit our perusal to only these decades? Benjamin Tucker and Lysander Spooner wrote long before Hayek on matters of political economy, and they were far more radical libertarians than he.

Further, why should context matter? Let us suppose, just for argument's sake, that Hayek was the second most (to Mises) libertarian writer in this era. Why does that make him a "a strong defender of private property," as Bethell asserts? On the contrary, he could still be the very weak proponent of private property rights that he actually was. If Michael Jordan and I are playing one-on-one basketball, I am the second best basketball player on that court. But this does not mean I am a very good one.

Hayek as Austrian Economist

Bethell swallows whole the Hayek analysis of the failure of the Soviet Union. This view focused almost entirely on the inability of the central planners to obtain accurate information about the economy. First of all, much of it consisted of the knowledge of entrepreneur's specific to time and place; for example, the reliability and skills of various workers, the quickest way from this point to that, the honesty of merchants, the location of inputs, and so on. None of this was readily quantifiable. Even and to the extent that it was, there would still be the difficulty of informational overload. Says Bethell (142) in this regard:

> The problem can be appreciated by thinking about getting a message into the Oval Office. Speech writers in the White House itself cannot easily do it. They can pass on their brilliant ideas to the chief of staff—who might not think them so brilliant. He has other messages to deliver, and the president is busy.[33] Most messages must be excluded. A whole White House bureaucracy has already been established to decide which things are urgent, which things can wait.
>
> But in a planned economy, the planners were supposed to control minute details of faraway events. If a deputy commissar in Omsk needed Moscow's permission to switch a consignment of harvesters from one destination to another, he could wait—and ruin the harvest by abiding by the law.

In taking this stance, however, Bethell ignores the far more radical perspective of Mises. Worse, he claims (144) that Mises' "more detailed criticism of planning ... was really a variant of the problem of information."

This is entirely fallacious. Mises (1966, 1969) went so far as to demonstrate that *even if* this knowledge problem could be solved the central planners would *still* face insuperable barriers. The real difficulty, for Mises was one of *appraisement* and rational *calculation*, not the relatively superficial one of knowledge. Forget about information pertaining to manufactures, and also consumer desires. Without meaningful market prices,

---

[33] This line, I take it, was written before the advent of Monica-gate. Either that, or Bethell, was too much "above the fray" to take note of it. I am not.

based on the value appraisal of thousands of entrepreneurs, the economic dictator wouldn't know whether it was more efficient to build his limousine, yacht, or palace out of gold, silver, copper, brick, wood, plastic, or whatever,[34] let alone how to deal with the myriad of other decisions made in an economy greater than the size of the Swiss Family Robinson.

Land Reform

It is practically a shibboleth on the right that land reform is a pact with the devil, a plot to undermine private property rights. Bethell certainly conforms to this pattern.

At a superficial level, evidence certainly abounds in support of this contention. All we need do is keep those blinkers on, look only at a narrow realm of all possible land reforms, and this conclusion ineluctably follows. Bethell (203–221) treats us to a survey of this policy as practiced in numerous countries all around the world. One error of his is to treat as "successful" all cases where the expropriation was "peaceful" (206). What happened to justice? Merely because an act does not call forth outrage and resistance hardly renders it just.

A more basic methodological mistake is to treat all such transfers of property as if they were intrinsically a limitation on the rights of private property (209) and never an instance of their implementation and protection. What raises Bethell's ire is land reform as an "immunization" (208) against Communism. Well and good for him. If the only way to deflect this tyrannical system is to engage in land theft on a massive scale, perhaps there is not that much difference between the cure and the disease.

However, land reform can also, upon occasion, be properly interpreted not as an attack on the rights of private property, but as their main bulwark. Suppose A steals a farm from B, and then deeds it over to his son A', whereupon, in due course, the grandson A" inherits it from his father A'. Now, along comes B", the grandson of the victim, and demands the

[34] For the definitive rejection of Hayek, in favor of Mises, see Salerno (1992). More generally, for the de-homogenization literature on Hayek and Mises, pointing to the serious differences between them, and to the inferiority of the former vis-à-vis the latter, see Salerno (1990, 1995) and Block and Garschina (1995a).

return of this stolen property, for example, land reform of a justified, that is, libertarian variety.

How is Bethell to reply? That all forced transfers of land are per se improper? But this would grant a stamp of approval to theft. If the robber or his heirs cannot be forced to disgorge their ill-gotten gains, this is a direct and utter *violation* of property rights. Nor need this insight be confined to land. If it is true in that case, why not also for stolen cars, jewelry, money, television sets, and so on. If we generalize, that will mean the absolute end to all private property.

We need not be so theoretical. There are plenty of cases where land reform would *support* the rights of private property, not impair them. For example, consider the fall of the Berlin Wall, and the end of the Soviet Union. There are now behind the ex–Iron Curtain thousands of acres of land, not to mention factories, houses, and so on, which are occupied by people who cannot be considered their rightful owners, nor their heirs. Clearly, it would be just, it would be an implication of private property rights, if these people were forced to vacate these premises, and cede them to those from whom they were initially stolen by the Communists. One day, too, North Korea and Cuba will end their sorrowful decades-long experiment with Communism and the same will apply there.

There are also cases closer to home. When the slaves were freed at the end of the Civil War, there was one very serious oversight: they were not compensated for the labor which had been in effect stolen from them. To wit, they had poured out their "blood, sweat and tears" on those plantations, which were kept by their masters, and handed down to their own children. It would certainly be consistent with private property rights, not a denigration of them, that this acreage be given over to the grandchildren of the slaves.[35] Of course, not any black person will do as a candidate for land reform below the Mason Dixon line. The burden of proof always rests with he who would overturn otherwise presumably legitimate property titles. This is why the reductio about overturning property theft from medieval or Roman times, to say nothing about cave man days, simply doesn't work. This libertarian version of property title trans-

[35] For a debate between Milton Friedman, David Friedman, Paul Heyne, who took, roughly, the Bethell position on land reform, vs. myself, see Block, Brennan, and Elzinga (1985, pp. 495–510).

fer is naturally "conservative." The further back in time you go, the harder it is to prove theft; and this is to say nothing of the absence of a written language and records.

But, at least, contrary to Bethell, this perspective does not entirely close down the possibility of land reform that actually promotes private property rights.

Tradable Emissions Rights

Bethell (52) supports a tradable emissions right system, and goes so far as to characterize this as a "property mechanism." He states: "Air pollution can be controlled by giving emission permits to smokestack industries within a given air basin, and allowing these permits to be traded voluntarily."

This certainly fits well within the Chicago philosophy, but whatever such a scheme is, it is *not* compatible with property rights. Actually, it resembles nothing so much as the "market" socialist plan of Tito's Yugoslavia.

For pollution is a trespass. It is an uninvited border crossing of smoke particles, soot, or ground up and pulverized garbage. If this is not a violation of private property rights, something about which the author of the Noblest Triumph could well be expected to object, then nothing is. But instead of calling for a ban on it, Bethell falls in with the compromisers, and advocates a system where polluters are allowed to engage in their nefarious activities, but only to a limited extent, covered with a veneer of rhetoric about a "property mechanism," as opposed to a property *right* to be free of invasions.[36] Bethell's colleague at the Hoover Institution, Anderson (1989, p. 19) is far more attuned to the essence of private property; here is his analysis of pollution:

> We have tried many remedies in the past. We have tried to dissuade polluters with fines, with government programs whereby all pay to clean up the

[36] For a defense against the argument that an outright ban on pollution would mean the end of industry and thus civilization, see McGee and Block (1994) and Rothbard (1990).

garbage produced by the few, with a myriad of detailed regulations to control the degree of pollution. Now some even seriously propose that we should have economic incentives, to charge polluters a fee for polluting—and the more they pollute the more they pay. But that is just like taxing burglars as an economic incentive to deter people from stealing your property, and just as unconscionable.

The only effective way to eliminate serious pollution is to treat it for what it is—garbage. Just as one does not have the right to drop a bag of garbage on his neighbor's lawn, so does one not have the right to place any garbage in the air or the water or the earth, if it in any way violates the property rights of others.

What we need are tougher clearer environmental laws that are enforced—not with economic incentives but with jail terms.

Fish Quota

Based on his analysis of depleting fish stocks due to the tragedy of the ocean commons (52), Bethell also supports marketable "fishing quotas," the water-based analogue to tradable emissions rights. These would give each boat owner the right to capture "a certain percentage of the overall permitted catch."

This would indeed address the "tragedy of the commons." This tragedy, however, springs *not* from communalism, but rather from coercion. To wit, governments so far refuse to recognize private property rights in bodies of water.

The problem with fish quotas is that the government still administers this system, and sets the overall level of the catch. The oceans still remain a no man's land as far as real private property rights are concerned. Why recommend a system with such an admixture of central planning? Why not go all the way toward a radical private property stance and call for the privatization of oceans, rivers, lakes, streams, and seas[37] as well? Why this utter and total cave-in to the forces of water socialism?

---

[37] And while we're at it, the Arctic and Antarctica also, to say nothing of the moon, Mars, Venus, and land on still other planets. Should socialism or capitalism be the order of the day regarding the frontiers of the earth and the heavenly bodies? Reading in between the lines of Bethell, the former is implied.

This is truly a radical departure, at least in today's anti–property right context. The problem is that this book was supposed to help change all that; instead, it accepts the very philosophy it is presumed by most reviewers to be challenging.[38]

It cannot be denied that there are many and serious obstacles to ocean privatization. But chief among them is the refusal of analysts such as Bethell to apply to the seas the private property rights lessons we have achieved at such great expense on land.

For example, it will be argued by the Demsetz's (1967) of the world that it is *costly* to entertain property rights in water, and until and unless these expenses sharply decline, this proposal is a chimera. Bethell (47), to his great credit, has rejected this argument on grounds of subjectivity. But there is more to be said against it. Of course there are conceptual, philosophical, practical, technological, and legal problems associated with ending the tragedy of the commons on the oceans, which have been so far enforced by the world's governments. How can fences be built to demarcate an owner's property from that of his neighbors? What to do about wandering fish stocks which do not respect lines "drawn" in the water? How about sharks and other predators? Will different people own different levels of the ocean, for example, surface transport, mid-level fishing, and mining at the ocean floor or below? How will homesteading work in an arena in which it has not yet been tried?

This is not the time or place to even begin to give definitive answers to these questions.[39] Suffice it to say that these are challenges of degree, not kind: there is not a one of them that has not been dealt with on the land. For example, before there was barbed wire, there were "human fences" (e.g., cowboys)[40] and cattle branding; neither buffalo nor cows respect property lines drawn in the sand; sharks are merely wolves and cougars without feet; there are disputes, and resolutions, to conflicting demands on the land for low-flying planes, farming, and mining.

The bottom line, though, is that it is in a book of this sort that we would expect if not progress on these issues, then at least an acknowledg-

[38] Solomon (1999, pp. 43–47), for example, entitles his review "A Paean to Property."

[39] For an attempt, see Block (1992).

[40] See Anderson and Leal (1991).

ment that private property can at least potentially play a role in this sphere. After all, the ocean, which comprises some 75% of the surface of the planet, probably accounts for less than 1% of global GDP. This is surely a way to promote "prosperity through property," the subtitle of this book.

Conclusion

In summary, this is a frustrating volume; it is close to libertarianism and Austrianism in many ways, yet doesn't quite make it.

Am I being unfair in characterizing Bethell as a "Chicagoan"? After all, there is not a good word from him on school vouchers, government money, anti-trust, volunteer militaries to fight unjust wars, flexible exchange rates, negative income taxes, withholding taxes, and all the rest of the panoply of socialism emanating from this school of thought. Moreover, he does frontally attack stalwarts of the Chicago-inspired law and economics movement such as Coase, Posner, and Demsetz, even though, as we have seen, he pulls his punches. Perhaps most significantly, he avoids the facile Chicagoite equation of justice and efficiency.

On the other hand, he uncritically favors Public Choice (282),[41] dismisses philosophical anarchism, sees "monopoly" as compatible with free markets (51), buys into the public goods and free-rider "market failure" arguments, ignores the contributions of libertarians such as Rothbard[42] and Hoppe who have devoted their entire careers to the defense of private property rights, takes the Hayek side vis-à-vis Mises regarding central planning, accepts water and highway socialism, misunderstands communalism, and favors tradable emissions rights.

[41] For libertarian criticisms, see Rothbard (Logic of Action) and DiLorenzo and Block (forthcoming).

[42] To not even cite Rothbard once in his entire book is indeed a remarkable oversight. And this for two reasons: one public, the other private. The public reason is that Rothbard is the most eminent economist to have made private property rights the bedrock of his philosophy. Why Bethell should totally ignore him is a puzzle on this ground alone. Second, I have in my hand a letter to me dated August 30, 1991, where this author asks my opinion of writings of Rothbard (a two-page, single-spaced letter addressed to Bethell, dated June 14, 1991), David Friedman, and Paul Heyne, material from all three which would later be incorporated into his book. Bethell mentions the latter two, but not the former.

At the end of the day, the best way to characterize him might be as a wannabe libertarian, or as a particularly good Chicagoan, or maybe even as a hybrid libertarian conservative.

The problem with Bethell, from my perspective, is that this is such a hard-hitting book, so sound as we have seen in many ways, that it is likely to become the canonical text of private property rights. Then, libertarians and Austrians shall be faced with the charge from critics of property, "Even Bethell concedes … Even Bethell allows."[43] Libertarians and Austrians, in contrast, must be extremists or just plain wrong. No greater error could be committed.

References

Anderson, Martin. 1989. "Pollution." The Christian Science Monitor (January). Reprinted in Block, ed. 1990.

Anderson, Terry L., and Donald R. Leal. 1991. Free Market Environmentalism. San Francisco: Pacific Research Institute.

Block, Walter. 1979. "Free Market Transportation: Denationalizing the Roads." Journal of Libertarian Studies 3(2): 209–38.

Block, Walter. 1980. "Congestion and Road Pricing." Journal of Libertarian Studies 4(3): 299–330.

Block, Walter. 1983a. "Public Goods and Externalities: The Case of Roads." Journal of Libertarian Studies 7(1): 1–34.

Block, Walter. 1983b. "Theories of Highway Safety." Transportation Research Record #912: 7–10.

Block, Walter. 1992. "Institutions, Property Rights and Externalities: The Case of Water Quality." Agriculture and Water Quality: Proceedings of an Interdisciplinary Symposium. Murray H. Miller, et al., eds. Guelph Centre for Soil and Water Conservation. University of Guelph Press, pp. 191–208.

Block, Walter. 1996a. "O.J.'s Defense: A Reductio Ad Absurdum of the Economics of Ronald Coase and Richard Posner." European Journal of Law and Economics 3: 265–86.

[43] Bethell (141) reports that something of this sort has occurred with "Mr. Friedman, the American expert," whose imprimatur was used to support the accuracy of Soviet economic statistics in the 1930s.

Block, Walter. 1996b. "Road Socialism." International Journal of Value-Based Management 9: 195–207.
Block, Walter. 1996c. "Hayek's Road to Serfdom." Journal of Libertarian Studies 12(2): 327–50.
Block, Walter, and Matthew Block. 1998. "Roads, Bridges, Sunlight, and Private-Property Rights: Reply to Gordon Tullock." Journal des Économistes et Des études Humaines 7(2/3): 315–26.
Block, Walter, Geoffrey Brennan, and Kenneth Elzinga, eds. 1985. Morality of the Market: Religious and Economic Perspectives. Vancouver, BC: Fraser Institute.
Block, Walter, and Kenneth M. Garschina. 1995. "Hayek, Business Cycles and Fractional Reserve Banking: Continuing the De-Homogenization Process." Review of Austrian Economics 9(1): 77–94.
Cadin, Michelle, and Walter Block. 1997. "Privatize the Public Highway System." The Freeman 47(2): 96–97.
Cheung, Steven N.S. 1983. "The Contractual Nature of the Firm." Journal of Law and Economics. 26(April).
Coase, Ronald H. 1960. "The Problem of Social Cost." Journal of Law and Economics 3: 1–44.
Conquest, Robert. 1986. The Harvest of Sorrow. NY: Oxford University Press.
Conquest, Robert. 1990. The Great Terror. Edmonton, Alberta: Edmonton University Press.
Cordato, Roy E. 1989. "Subjective Value, Time Passage, and the Economics of Harmful Effects." Hamline Law Review 12(2): 229–44.
Cordato, Roy E. 1992a. "Knowledge Problems and the Problem of Social Cost." Journal of the History of Economic Thought, 14(Fall).
Cordato, Roy E. 1992b. Welfare Economics and Externalities in an Open-Ended Universe: A Modern Austrian Perspective. Boston: Kluwer.
Demsetz, Harold. 1967. "Toward a Theory of Property Rights." American Economic Review (57): 347–59.
DiLorenzo, Thomas J., and Walter Block. Forthcoming. "Critique of the Public Choice Perspective of the State."
Dworkin, Ronald. 1977. Taking Rights Seriously. Cambridge, MA: Harvard University Press.
Friedman, David. 1989. The Machinery of Freedom: Guide to a Radical Capitalism. 2nd Ed. LaSalle, IL: Open Court.
Gunderson, Gerald. 1989. "Privatization and the 19th-Century Turnpike." Cato Journal 9(1): 191–200.
Hayek, F.A. 1944. The Road To Serfdom. Chicago: University of Chicago Press.

Hoppe, Hans-Hermann. 1993. The Economics and Ethics of Private Property: Studies in Political Economy and Philosophy. Boston: Kluwer.

Horwitz, Morton. 1980. "Law and Economics: Science or Politics?" Hofstra Law Review 8: 905.

Hummel, Jeffrey Rogers. 1990. "National Goods Versus Public Goods: Defense, Disarmament, and Free Riders." Review of Austrian Economics 4: 88–122.

Klein, Dan. 1990. "The Voluntary Provision of Public Goods? The Turnpike Companies of Early America." Economic Inquiry (October): 788–812.

Klein, Dan, and G.J. Fielding. 1992. "Private Toll Roads: Learning from the Nineteenth Century." Transportation Quarterly (July): 321–41.

Klein, Dan, and G.J. Fielding. 1993a. "How to Franchise Highways." Journal of Transport Economics and Policy (May): 113–30. Review Essay 83.

Klein, Dan, and G.J. Fielding. 1993b. "High Occupancy–Toll Lanes: Phasing in Congestion Pricing a Lane at a Time." Policy Study No. 170. Reason Foundation.

Klein, Dan, J. Majewski, and C. Baer. 1993a. "Economy, Community and the Law: The Turnpike Movement in New York 1797–1845. Journal of Economic History (March): 106–22.

Klein, Dan, J. Majewski, and C. Baer. 1993b. "From Trunk to Branch: Toll Roads in New York, 1800–1860." Essays in Economic and Business History: pp. 191–209.

Krecke, Elisabeth. 1992. "Law and the Market Order: An Austrian Critique of the Economic Analysis of Law." Paper presented at the Ludwig von Mises Institute's Tenth Anniversary Conference.

Leff, Arthur Allen. 1974. "Economic Analysis of Law: Some Realism about Nominalism." Virginia Law Review 60: 451.

Locke, John. 1960. An Essay Concerning the True Origin, Extent and End of Civil Government. Vol. 5. In Two Treatises of Government. P. Laslett, ed. Cambridge: Cambridge University Press.

McGee, Robert, and Walter Block. 1994. "Pollution Trading Permits as a Form of Market Socialism, and the Search for a Real Market Solution to Environmental Pollution." Fordham University Law and Environmental Journal 4(1): 51–77.

North, Gary. 1990. Tools of Dominion: The Case Laws of Exodus. Tyler, TX: Institute for Christian Economics.

North, Gary. 1992. The Coase Theorem. Tyler, TX: Institute for Christian Economics.

Nozick, Robert. 1974. Anarchy, State and Utopia. New York: Basic Books.

Posner, Richard A. 1986. Economic Analysis of Law. 3rd ed. Boston: Little Brown.
Roth, Gabriel. 1966. A Self-financing Road System. London: Institute of Economic Affairs.
Roth, Gabriel. 1967. Paying for Roads: The Economics of Traffic Congestion. Middlesex, England: Penguin.
Roth, Gabriel. 1987. The Private Provision of Public Services in Developing Countries. Oxford: Oxford University Press.
Rothbard, Murray N. 1962. Man, Economy, and State. Los Angeles: Nash.
Rothbard, Murray N. 1973. For a New Liberty. New York: Macmillan.
Rothbard, Murray N. 1982b. The Ethics of Liberty. Atlantic Highlands, NJ: Humanities Press.
Salerno, Joseph T. 1990. "Ludwig von Mises as Social Rationalist." Review of Austrian Economics, 4: 26–54.
Salerno, Joseph T. 1992. "Mises and Hayek Dehomogenized." Review of Austrian Economics 6(2): 113–46.
Simpson, A.W.B. 1996. "Coase v. Pigou Reexamined." Journal of Legal Studies 25(1): 53–97.
Solomon, Martin M. 1999. "A Paean to Property." Liberty (June): 43–47.
Spooner, Lysander. [1870] 1966. No Treason. Larkspur, CO: Pine Tree Press.
Woolridge, William C. 1970. Uncle Sam the Monopoly Man. New Rochelle, NY: Arlington House.

8

Radical Privatization and Other Libertarian Conundrums

A conundrum is a seeming logical contradiction, one that can actually be solved, or resolved. Perhaps the most famous example in theology is the following challenge: can God create a stone so big that even He cannot lift it. Either way, the case for religion loses out, at least at first glance. If God *can* create such a big stone, all well and good for Him; however, then, as He cannot also lift it, there can be no such thing as a Higher Power. On the other hand, if God is *unable* to create so heavy an object, then the case for belief in Him is dashed from the very start. For He cannot be truly omnipotent, since here is something He cannot do.

The solution to the conundrum is to realize that the act "create so heavy a stone it cannot be lifted" does not refer to anything in the world, or to anything, for that matter, which *could* exist in reality. The concept itself is an inner self-contradiction. It is as if we are castigating the Supreme Being for being unable to create a square circle. The point is, the phrase "square circle" consists of two terms, each of them meaningful in isolation; but when they are juxtaposed in this manner, they *cannot* refer to anything coherent. By making this claim, the skeptic is not really pointing to anything that God cannot create. There is no such thing as a

W. E. Block, *Property Rights*, Palgrave Studies in Classical Liberalism,
https://doi.org/10.1007/978-3-030-28353-7_8

square circle. This being the case, it is no failure of God's that he cannot create one. The skeptic is, in effect, only talking gibberish.[1]

I. Libertarianism

As I am about to introduce several conundrums aimed at undermining libertarianism, it might not be inappropriate to first briefly review that political economic philosophy.

The basic axiom of libertarianism is the non-aggression principle: a man may do whatever he wants with his own body and legitimately owned property, as long as he does not thereby threaten, or actually invade the person or property of anyone else. Thus, suicide and narcotic drug use are legal in this system, but murder, rape, and theft are not. Legitimately owned property begins with the man's body, and radiates out, in effect, to all un-owned parts of nature, through homesteading. A man mixes his labor with a forest; cuts down some trees; cultivates, sows, and reaps a crop; and thereby becomes the owner of that land. Other sources of legitimate holdings are voluntary trade with other consenting adults, gifts, gambling. As long as wealth is achieved through any of these non-invasive processes, it is legitimate.

Libertarianism is limited to *political* philosophy; it does not include ethics. It takes no view whatsoever as to the *morality* of pornography, prostitution, homosexuality, gambling, drugs, and so on. It states only that, given that these acts take place between consenting adults, they should not be proscribed by law. When prohibited they are *victimless* crimes, and thus should be legalized.

The libertarian is not a pacifist. He believes that uninvited border crossings against other people and their property are illegitimate, but allows for the use of physical force, only, however, in the case of self-defense. But these invasions must be *physical*, not merely mental or spiritual. Rape, murder, arson, pick-pocketing, and kidnapping are all, properly, crimes, because they interfere with other people's holdings.

[1] The critique of the argument presented in the text, of course, cannot prove that God exists. Only that this particular refutation has failed.

Fraud may only be a "white collar" crime, but it is a crime nonetheless. Even though it may not be brutal like assault and battery, it alienates property from victims against their will. Rape, too, need not always be physically vicious. To a third party, it might be indistinguishable from voluntary sex. But as long as the woman is engaging in the act against her will, it is a crime.[2]

In sharp contrast, such things as teasing, imposing psychological harm, libel, slander,[3] blackmail,[4] insider trading,[5] teasing, and (racial, sexual, and other) discrimination[6] do not constitute invasive violence. Hence, even though they may be immoral, they would not be considered illegal.

Even more narrowly, libertarianism may properly be construed *solely* as a theory of punishment. *If* someone uses coercion, then it is proper to utilize physical force against him, with the goal of rectifying the injustice, compensating the victim, as much as possible.[7]

A side order claim of libertarianism, something not intrinsic to it, is that it will in some sense lead to the "greatest happiness for the greatest number of people." In other words, this philosophy claims a compatibility with utilitarianism.

But not a direct one. Were libertarianism a mere branch of utilitarianism,[8] it would ask of every contemplated action in order to

[2] Suppose a starving woman agrees to sexual congress only in order to feed herself and her children. Is this coercive, and thus tantamount to rape? If her customer put her in this precarious position in the first place, then and only then is this so. Not because of the sexual act, but because of the initial theft. If on the other hand this customer was in no way responsible for her plight, then the trade of sexual services for money is not equivalent to rape. Indeed, the customer is the *benefactor* to the woman, as he saves her and her children from starvation. She, of course, benefits him as well; this should be no surprise, as all trade is mutually beneficial.

[3] Rothbard (1973), Block (1976/1991).

[4] Block (1986, 1997), Rothbard (1962).

[5] Manne (1966a, 1966b), McGee and Block (1989).

[6] Block and Williams (1981), Block and Walker (1982), Block (1992), Epstein (1992), Levin (1984, 1987, 1997).

[7] Rothbard (1982), Barnett and Hagel (1977), King (1980), Kinsella (1997, 1996a, b spring and fall, 1992).

[8] There are two main branches of utilitarianism: act utilitarianism and rule utilitarianism. In the former case, that act which brings about the most utility is to be preferred. In the latter case, behavior is judged on the basis of whether or not it is compatible with a rule that, if followed, maximizes utility. See on this Mill (1957, 1971).

determine its legitimacy, not whether it constitutes an invasion of person or property, but rather whether it will maximize utility.[9]

That there is nevertheless an important connection is a pretty reasonable claim. For with invasions or uninvited border crossings ruled out, the only thing left is voluntary interaction. These can be of two sorts: trade or gifts; but both enhance utility.

In the first case, buying, selling, renting, bartering, hiring, both parties must gain utility at least in the ex ante sense, otherwise, why would they agree to take part in the commercial interaction? If I give you $5 for your pen, it must be that I value the writing implement more than the money, and that your preferences are the reverse. We each gain the difference to us between the lower value we give up and the higher one we attain. Now it may be that you really like your pen more than $5, but want to get on my good side and value the money I give you *plus* my good will more highly than the pen. All we as third parties can know is that there is *something* about the trade that promotes your utility; otherwise, you would not agree to do it. And likewise for me.

Charity, too, is part and parcel of the free society. It, too, is mutually beneficial. The donor benefits from the improved well-being of the recipient, as well as from the satisfaction of helping the less fortunate. And the donee, by accepting this largess, demonstrates that he, too, gains from this interaction.

In sharp contrast, the relation between the government and the people is highly problematic. The state forces the people to pay taxes against their will,[10] and refuses to allow us to make other arrangements for our own protection.[11] At best the government is a necessary evil. At worst it is a fraudulent gang of murderers and thieves.[12]

---

[9] This is problematic on its face since how can any third party ever accurately observe whether utility rises or falls. For a libertarian perspective on utilitarianism, see Rothbard (1982, 1977).

[10] They have *not* given prior assent to this contractually; the brute fact of the matter is that in reality, either no one, or very few, have ever signed a constitution. Nor do we demonstrate our agreement to be bound by a government by continuing to live under its rule. According to the consent theory of the state, we came first, before the government. *We* don't have to leave if we don't like it; rather, *they* do.

[11] On this see Rothbard (1973, 1982), Hoppe (1989, 1992, 1993), and Benson (1989a, 1989b, 1990).

[12] See Rothbard (1973, 1982) and Spooner (1870).

II. The Martians

This challenge is an attempt not to frontally attack libertarianism, but only to show it as totally and irredeemably incompatible with utilitarianism.

Here, the "Martians," an all-powerful, but evil, group of beings, beam down a message to an entirely libertarian earth: "Kill innocent person Joe, or we will blow up your entire planet."

But killing an innocent person is the paradigm case of illegitimate behavior under libertarianism. There is (usually) nothing more important to a person than his own life.[13] If murder isn't incompatible with this philosophy, then nothing is. On the other hand, blowing up the entire earth does not appear to be too compatible with utilitarianism. "Justice though the heavens fall" may make a good libertarian motto, but it is hard to square this with the maximization of human well-being.

There is a way out of this conundrum for the libertarian who wants to maintain ties with utilitarianism. Strictly speaking, one might argue, libertarianism is *not* incompatible with murder. This is because libertarianism is a theory of punishment, not proper behavior. The libertarian qua libertarian, then, does *not* say, "Don't murder." He only says, "If you murder, you should be punished."

Thus, when the Martians beam down their message, it is entirely possible that a utilitarian-libertarian, call him Pete, will kill Joe, and then, after a ticker parade in his honor organized by utilitarians (since he saved the earth and everyone on it from total destruction), will turn himself in for the punishment due to murderers. In this way we can maintain both libertarianism (the murderer is properly punished) and utilitarianism (the planet is saved).

But we speak too soon. For no sooner do the Martians get wind of our intended doings than they beam down a second message: "If you harm a hair on the head of Pete, much less impose upon him the libertarian punishment for murder (of Joe), We Will Kill You All."[14]

---

[13] Exceptions sometimes include children, a loved one, or a principle or a philosophy. That is, sometimes people are willing to sacrifice themselves for values they hold higher than even their own life.

[14] I owe this addition to the traditional "Martian" critique of libertarianism to Matthew Block.

Those Martians are a nasty lot. Not only do they utter all sort of threats,[15] they are actually launching a reasonably good menace to cut asunder libertarianism and utilitarianism.

The problem is, the critic bodes *too* well to attain this goal. *Of course*, if we endow the Martians with God (well, Devil) like qualities, and set Him forth with the sole mission of severing the connection between libertarianism and utilitarianism, He can do it. But this is not really legitimate. It is eerily far too reminiscent of asking God to square the circle, or create an all too heavy rock. It shows, only, that if we pack enough premises into a syllogism, we can call into question practically *anything*, up to and including the libertarian claim that its system will benefit mankind.

God, by definition, can do pretty much anything He wants (apart from creating contradictions in terms, for these are not real things that can be made, or even fail to be made). For example, He can, presumably, make water run uphill, make wood rust, and create water out of other elements than hydrogen and oxygen. If He can do all that, it should come as no surprise that he can also eliminate the utilitarian benefits of libertarianism.[16]

It is thus difficult not to notice how far removed from reality does the "Martian" critic have to go in order to sunder the philosophies of utilitarianism and libertarianism. A more "realistic" example along these lines is the case where a terrorist has planted a bomb that can blow up the whole city on a moment's notice. Fortunately, the authorities have under their control the young son of the terrorist, of whom he is very fond. So much so that if they threaten to torture or kill the boy, his father will cease and desist from his evil designs. Unfortunately, at least for the lives of the citizens, the authorities happen to be libertarians. If we interpret libertarianism as being incompatible with torturing the boy, its claim to

[15] Prohibited by libertarian law.

[16] One conclusion which can be drawn from this is that the connection between libertarianism and utilitarianism is not an apodictic or necessary one; rather, it is contingent and empirical. That is, the claim that libertarianism leads to the greatest happiness for the greatest number is akin to the claim that water runs downhill and that water consists of oxygen and hydrogen. It is *not* in the same synthetic a priori category as the statements "Square circles are impossible," "minimum wage legislation leads to unemployment," and "free trade benefits mankind." On this see Hoppe (1988, 1991, 1995).

maximize happiness for the greatest number of people is cast into doubt. For then the terrorist will carry out his nefarious deed. On the other hand, given that libertarianism, strictly and narrowly construed, does not forbid killing the innocent, but only requires that such a person be duly punished, its claim to promote utility can still be maintained.

The difference between the terrorist and the Martians is that the latter are assumed to be all knowing, while the former, a "real" person, is not. Thus, we can out maneuver the terrorist, not the aliens. That is, we can play a tape where a child actor screams as if tortured. A person can threaten to kill the boy, and even actually do it, and we need not fear a second "message" from the terrorist that if we punish this killer, he'll blow up the city. We can always promise him we won't, and then do so, later, after he is captured, squaring ourselves with the requirements of libertarianism.[17,18] This option is simply not available to us with the Martians.

III. Unanimity[19]

For libertarians, the illegitimacy of the state rests squarely on the fact that "the consent of the governed" is no more than a myth (Spooner, 1870). Well, what if, just suppose, that the scenario depicted in civics classes were correct. That is, we posit that there was a time, during the formation of the country, when the entire populace, all of them, every last person, *did* sign the constitutional contract. It was a unanimous agreement, binding all to all. And not only that. Let us also presume that this was true of every nation on earth, the totalitarian ones, the democracies, the monarchies,[20] all of them. Further, while we are supposing, let us concede the fact that all of these countries, unified into a completely voluntary

[17] Surely we owe no debt of truthfulness to would-be mad bombers, at least qua libertarians.

[18] Of course, if we lie to the mad bomber, and word of this gets out, our options become more truncated with regard to the *next* terrorist.

[19] I owe this example to Patrick English.

[20] For an argument that monarchy is a superior form of government when compared to democracy, see Hoppe (2001).

World Government, had homesteaded *every square inch of the earth's surface*. (If we can posit Martians, we can certainly give credence to this scenario, if only for argument's sake.)

Now this world need not be a libertarian one. Indeed, we posit that it is not. All we need do in order to attack libertarian premises is to assume that the World Government was formed, initially, under *premises* required by the libertarian philosophy. Namely, that it was the *voluntary* formation of a state. Once in effect, it could take any measures supported by a majority. After all, if libertarianism can support (the legalization of!) voluntary sado-masochism, or "murder parks" (where people may shoot one another, provided only that all of them had agreed to take part in this game, and there are thick walls so that no outsiders are shot), then certainly they may unanimously and voluntarily set up a government which is less than libertarian. As long as it was set up in a manner totally consistent with libertarianism, no adherent of this philosophy can logically object to the results.

Under these circumstances does it not follow that freedom will be *reduced* by libertarianism? For consider the position of a new world citizen, or, rather, a person of, say, age 21, who is now being considered for citizenship. This person is offered a stark choice indeed: join us in our mixed economy world (similar, by the way, to what obtains today in reality), or die. Since we, all together, legitimately own the entire world (this ownership was established through the libertarian process of homesteading), he has no right to exist on it without our permission. To do so is to engage in trespass, which is legitimately a crime even under libertarianism.

If newcomers must either embrace the mixed economy (or Marxism, or feminism, or whatever the majority wants), or die, this, to say the very least, doesn't bode too well for libertarianism claim to be compatible with freedom. An unfree society brought about solely in conformity with libertarianism[21] is surely a major flaw in this philosophy.

There are several ways to reply to this challenge.

---

[21] This is very similar to Nozick's (1974) claim that the state can arise out of a totally justified libertarian process. For critiques, see Barnett (1977), Childs (1977), Evers (1977), Rothbard (1977), and Sanders (1977).

1. It Is Rather Unrealistic

When as few as five friends get together for dinner and a movie (leaving 5 × 5 = 25 different combinations for those two events, if everyone has his choice and each has different preference for both), it is rare that all will be fully satisfied. To think that *all* of the people in the world at any one time would unanimously agree to be bound by the majority vote of all of them on *anything* beggars the imagination.

This, it must be confessed, is not much of a response, since this particular critic of libertarianism is certainly prepared to admit as much. His is more of a theoretical than a practical critique of this philosophy.

2. Inalienability

There are some libertarians who maintain that as the will is inalienable, no one should be forced to uphold any such contract, if he later changes his mind. In effect, to do so is to demand specific performance, and this is akin to slavery (Barnett, 1998).

Says Rothbard (1982, pp. 134–135) in this regard:

> the only valid transfer of title of ownership in the free society is the case where the property is, in fact and in the nature of man, <u>alienable</u> by man. All physical property owned by a person is alienable, i.e., in natural fact it can be given or transferred to the ownership and control of another party. I can give away or sell to another person my shoes, my house, my car, my money, etc. But there are certain vital things which, in natural fact and in the nature of man, are <u>in</u>alienable, i.e., they <u>cannot</u> in fact be alienated, even voluntarily Specifically, a person cannot alienate his <u>will</u> more particularly his control over his own mind and body. Each man has control over his own mind and body. Each man has control over his own will and person, and he is, if you wish, "stuck" with that inherent and inalienable ownership. Since his will and control over his own person are inalienable, then so also are his <u>rights</u> to control that person and will. That is the ground for the famous position of the Declaration of Independence that man's natural rights are inalienable; that is, they cannot be surrendered, <u>even</u> if the person wishes to do so. …

Hence, the unenforceability, in libertarian theory, of voluntary slave contracts.

I find this argument not fully persuasive.[22] If contracts can be set aside, the whole foundation of the private property free enterprise libertarian society will tend to crumble. When a man signs a contract he is bound by its provisions. In the adult world, at least, there are no "backsies." All contracts give up something in return for something else. Once they are signed, the thing given up is now the property of the grantee. To nullify the agreement, then, is to steal the latter's property. To do this really would be to contradict libertarianism.

Yes, one may agree with Rothbard that it is impossible to alienate the will. One (logically) cannot force someone else to do something he wishes not to do, and still have it be a voluntary act. But this is a (correct) positive statement, not a normative one. As such, it cannot really contradict libertarian premises, which are normative. All that is demanded by strict contractarians such as myself is not the alienation of the will, but rather that it be legal to physically force the signer of the contract to live up to its provisions. Thus, I see little hope in saving the day for libertarianism by allowing citizens to renounce their contractual obligations. To do so would be to contradict the basic premise of this philosophy.

Rothbard (ibid.) continues his analysis:

> Suppose that Smith makes the following agreement with the Jones Corporation: that Smith, for the rest of his life, will obey all orders, under whatever conditions, that the Jones Corporation wishes to lay down. Now, in libertarian theory there is nothing to prevent Smith from making this agreement, and from serving the Jones Corporation and from obeying the latter's orders indefinitely. The problem comes when, at some later date, Smith changes his mind and decides to leave. Shall he be held to his former voluntary promise? Our contention—and one which is fortunately upheld under present law—is that Smith's promise was not a valid (i.e., not an enforceable) contract. There is no transfer of title in Smith's agreement because Smith's control over his own body and will are <u>inalienable</u>. Since that control <u>cannot</u> be alienated, the agreement was not a valid contract,

[22] See Block (1999, forthcoming a, b, c, d).

> and therefore should not be enforceable. Smith's agreement was a mere promise, which it might be held he is morally obligated to keep, but which should not be legally obligatory.

The difficulty here is that while it may be readily conceded that a man necessarily has control over his *will*, this certainly does not apply to his *body*, as slavery, imprisonment, kidnapping, rape, murder, and so on eloquently attest. The point is, libertarian advocates of contract obligations such as myself do not maintain that the *will* must be turned over to the (voluntary) slave-owner, only that this should apply to the *body*. Hence, the courts should determine that when Smith runs away from the justifiable control of the Jones Corporation, he is in effect stealing a valuable piece of property belonging to the latter. Smith can keep his will, but he is still guilty of being a robber (of Jones's property, e.g., Smith himself). What he cannot keep, under libertarian law in my view, is his body. That being the case, it is the obligation of the court to turn over the runaway slave Smith back to the proper *physical* control of Jones.

3. This Scenario Is Incompatible with the Nature of Physical Reality

A weakness of the critical scenario is that it requires that *all* land be owned by the political collective. If there are significant, not to say large, tracts of space still available, the choice for the man coming of age is not to join or die. He now has the option of moving to an un-owned area.

At present there are vast parts of the earth's surface that have *not* been homesteaded. The high mountains in many countries, the Sahara, and deserts in Australia and other continents, the tundra in Canada, Russia, the Antarctic. And this is to say nothing of the oceans, seas, lakes, and rivers of the world, both on the surface and underwater. As well, our homesteading on the land (apart from mineral exploration and mining) has barely even begun to scratch the surface.

It cannot be denied that these lands are now *claimed* by various countries. However, mere claim is insufficient under the libertarian legal code. For legitimate ownership—whether of land or water—the would-be owner must mix his labor with it.

The point is, with modern technology, it would be impossible at this time for the political collective to legitimately own the entire globe, surface and subsurface. Therefore, this scenario would fail to overturn libertarianism even had there once been a unanimous agreement for a world government.

Suppose, however, that another few centuries pass; that the economic system adopted by the world government is so interventionistic that no progress can occur; that in the year 2525 there will truly be no space on the earth or in it that has not been already (legitimately) homesteaded. Would this critical scenario *then* suffice to embarrass libertarianism?

Not a bit of it. For then there will be the moon, Mars, Venus, the asteroids, and other heavenly bodies. Those who turn 21 years of age and are asked to join the world government would still have an option other than death. They could migrate to these other places. (Presumably, interplanetary travel will then be so cheap as to be able to accommodate youngsters whose only savings is based on the type of part-time work that many reaching their years of majority will have undertaken.)

The reason the critique fails is that in any even slightly realistic scenario the very technology that will allow for more and more thorough homesteading (thus precluding new adults from setting up shop for themselves) will *also* enable them to move to further and further away far-off destinations.

There is no reason that this process would not continue indefinitely. So that at no epoch would it be true that unanimous agreement to a constitutional contract, a phenomenon consistent with libertarianism, lead to people being forced to join the resultant collective against their will, something inconsistent with this philosophy.

IV. Flagpole Sitter[23]

A man is standing at the edge of his balcony on the 45th floor of a high-rise apartment building. He teeters over the side and drops to the 25th floor. There, fortunately, he is able to grab hold of a flagpole, jutting out

[23] I owe this example to Bill Bradford.

from the building. He would like nothing so much as to be able to inch his way down onto the 25th-story balcony, go inside that apartment, leave it for the hall, and take the elevator back up to his own apartment.

Unhappily, the owner of the 25-floor apartment, and of the flagpole to which he is precariously holding, comes out on the deck with a shotgun and demands that he respect private property rights and let go, thus dropping to his death.

Liberty magazine took a poll of its mostly libertarian readers, asking how many of them would comply with this request and drop to their deaths. Very few agreed that they would. The implication drawn from this survey is that libertarianism is a rather weak philosophy, impossible to put into effect under such circumstances, and certainly incompatible with the promotion of utilitarianism.

There are several possible rejoinders to this attack.

1. Internalization of the Externalities

Since there is one owner of the building, and he is a profit maximizer, he might well anticipate such a situation.[24] If he did, he would make it a condition of tenancy such that the flagpole owner would have to save the life of the hanger on.

But this is to evade the point of the criticism. Presumably, it could be refashioned in such a way as to obviate this reply.

2. Illicit Question

It is an illicit question to ask a libertarian, qua libertarian, if he would continue to hang on to or let go of the flagpole. Remember, libertarian is a very limited political philosophy. Essentially, it asks only one question and gives only one answer. The question: under what conditions is the use of or threat of physical force justified? The answer: only in response or in reaction to the prior use of such force. The only germane question

[24] One such incident in the entire world is all it would take, appropriately publicized, as it would be.

raised by this scenario is what to do with the homeowner if he shoots the flagpole sitter, or, forces him to drop to his death under the threat of the gun.

3. Clear Answer

Looked at in this way, the answer is clear. The owner of the flagpole is totally within his rights to defend his property, both the flagpole and his apartment. It might be *nice* if he allowed the person in this precarious position to scurry back to safety, but he is by no means required to do so under the libertarian law code.

What, then, of the greatest good for the greatest number? Isn't the insistence on private property rights at variance with that goal? Yes, to be sure, in this one case, on the assumption that the flagpole sitter is entirely innocent and means the property owner no harm. But how can we be sure of that? Suppose the owner is a frail old man, and the flagpole sitter a young strong one. Suppose the latter will victimize the former if allowed access to the apartment. Then, the implications for utilitarianism are not at all so clearly in against the flagpole owner.

The problem with the scenario as stated is that it takes place all from the point of view of the flagpole sitter. When once we look at matters from the perspective of the property owner the anti-libertarian conclusion drawn by the critic no longer seems so obvious.

As a matter of general principle, it is pretty certain that more lives will be saved, and happiness enhanced, by allowing property rights to be upheld than from the opposite alternative. What we have here is rule utilitarianism, not act utilitarianism: act according to a rule such that if followed by all would maximize utility.

If the general rule were that all strangers could always have access to private property, there is little doubt that there would be far more murders and rapes than under the rule of the sanctity of property rights. Nor is it plausible to entertain the rule that except in cases of emergency, property rights must prevail. Who can tell what is an emergency? One person's emergency is another person's carelessness. Who gets to determine whether it is an emergency, or a ruse to penetrate into another's domicile? Under the property rights rule, it is the owner who makes this determination. In the critic's scenario, this would be decided by the person in difficulties. But if so, then anyone could claim any trouble he wished, and we would be back in the situation where murderers and rapists could venture at will.[25]

V. Conclusion

If a philosophy such as libertarianism is worth defending, it is worth defending not (only) against straw men, but also in the face of truly powerful challenges. In this chapter we have attempted to deal with three criticisms of libertarianism that are a bit off the beaten philosophical path: the Martians, the flagpole, and the unanimous supported but evil monopolistic world government. How well we have acquitted this task is for others to say. But it cannot be maintained that in our defense of libertarianism we have confined ourselves to weak arguments. If even these cannot be shown to topple the edifice of this philosophy, then our exercise will have rendered it that much more the stronger.

References

Barnett, Randy E., The Structure of Liberty: Justice and the Rule of Law. Oxford: Clarendon Press, 1998.
Barnett, Randy, and Hagel, John, eds., Assessing the Criminal. Cambridge MA: Ballinger, 1977.
Barnett, Randy, 1977, "Whither Anarchy? Has Robert Nozick Justified the State?," The Journal of Libertarian Studies, Vol. 1, No. 1, Winter, pp. 15–22.
Benson, Bruce L., The Enterprise of Law: Justice Without the State. San Francisco: Pacific Research Institute for Public Policy, 1990.
Benson, Bruce L., "The Spontaneous Evolution of Commercial Law," Southern Economic Journal, 55: 644–661, 1989a.

[25] The author is grateful for the financial and moral support of David Kennedy and Tony Sullivan of the Earhart Foundation. Without friends such as these, his task would have been a far more arduous one.

Benson, Bruce L., 1989b, Enforcement of Private Property Rights in Primitive Societies: Law Without Government," The Journal of Libertarian Studies, Vol. IX, No. 1, Winter, pp. 1–26.

Block, Walter, "The Economics of Discrimination," The Journal of Business Ethics, Vol. 11, 1992, pp. 241–254.

Block, Walter and Walker, Michael A., eds., Discrimination, Affirmative Action and Equal Opportunity. Vancouver: The Fraser Institute, 1982.

Block, Walter and Walter Williams, 1981, "Male-Female Earnings Differentials: A Critical Reappraisal," Journal of Labor Research, 2(2): 383–388.

Block, Walter, Defending the Undefendable. New York: Fleet Press, 1976, Fox and Wilkes, 1991.

Block, Walter, "Market Inalienability Once Again: Reply to Radin," Thomas Jefferson Law Journal, Vol. 22, No. 1, Fall 1999, pp. 37–88.

Block, Walter, "Toward a Libertarian Theory of Inalienability: A Critique of Rothbard, Barnett, Gordon, Smith, Kinsella and Epstein," Journal of Libertarian Studies, forthcoming-a.

Block, Walter, "Alienability, Inalienability, Paternalism and the Law: Reply to Kronman," American Journal of Criminal Law, forthcoming-b.

Block, Walter, "Epstein on Alienation: A Rejoinder," forthcoming-c.

Block, Walter, "Kuflik on Inalienability: A Rejoinder," forthcoming-d.

Block, Walter, "The Case for De-Criminalizing Blackmail: A Reply to Lindgren and Campbell," Western State University Law Review, Vol. 24, No. 2, Spring, 1997, pp. 225–246.

Block, Walter, "Trading Money for Silence," University of Hawaii Law Review, Vol. 8, No. 1, Spring 1986, pp. 57–73.

Childs, Roy A., Jr., 1977, "The invisible hand strikes back," The Journal of Libertarian Studies, Vol. 1, No. 1, Winter, pp. 23–34.

Epstein, Richard A., Forbidden Grounds: The Case Against Employment Discrimination Laws. Cambridge: Harvard University Press, 1992.

Evers, Williamson M., 1977, "Toward a reformulation of the law of contracts," The Journal of Libertarian Studies, Vol. 1, No. 1, Winter, pp. 3–14.

Hoppe, Hans-Hermann, Democracy, the God that Failed: The Economics and Politics of Monarchy, Democracy and Natural Order, New Brunswick, N.J. Transaction Publishers, 2001.

Hoppe, Hans-Hermann, Praxeology and Economic Science. Auburn, AL: Mises Institute, Auburn University, 1988.

Hoppe, Hans-Hermann (1995), Economic Science and the Austrian Method. Auburn, AL: The Mises Institute.

Hoppe, Hans-Hermann, A Theory of Socialism and Capitalism: Economics, Politics and Ethics. Boston: Dordrecht, 1989.
Hoppe, Hans-Hermann, The Economics and Ethics of Private Property: Studies in Political Economy and Philosophy. Boston: Kluwer, 1993.
Hoppe, Hans-Hermann, "Austrian Rationalism in the Age of the Decline of Positivism," Ebeling, R., ed., Austrian Economics: Perspectives on the Past and Prospects for the Future. Hillsdale, MI: Hillsdale College Press, 1991.
Hoppe, Hans-Hermann, "The Economics and Sociology of Taxation," Rockwell. L., ed., Taxation: An Austrian View. Boston: Dordrecht, 1992.
King, J. Charles, A Rationale for Punishment, 4 J. Libertarian Stud. 151, 154 (1980).
Kinsella, Stephan N., "A Libertarian Theory of Punishment and Rights," (volume) 30 Loy. L.A. L. Rev. 607 45 (1997).
Kinsella, Stephan N., "New Rationalist Directions in Libertarian Rights Theory," 12:2 J. Libertarian Studies 313 26 (Fall 1996a).
Kinsella, Stephan N., "Punishment and Proportionality: The Estoppel Approach," 12:1 J. Libertarian Studies 51 (Spring 1996b).
Kinsella, Stephan N., "Estoppel: A New Justification for Individual Rights," Reason Papers No. 17 (Fall 1992), p. 61.
Levin, Michael, "Comparable Worth: The Feminist Road to Socialism," Commentary, September 1984.
Levin, Michael, Feminism and Freedom. New York: Transaction Books, 1987.
Levin, Michael, Why Race Matters. Westport, CT: Praeger, 1997.
Manne, Henry A., "In Defense of Insider Trading," Harvard Business Review, 113, Nov/Dec 1966a.
Manne, Henry A., Insider Trading and the Stock Market. New York: The Free Press, 1966b.
McGee, Robert W., and Block, Walter, "Information, Privilege, Opportunity and Insider Trading," Northern Illinois University Law Review, December 1989, Vol. 10, No. 1, pp. 1–35.
Mill, John Stuart, Utilitarianism: With Critical Essays, Samuel Gorowitz, ed. New York: Bobbs-Merrill, 1971.
Mill, John Stuart, Utilitarianism, New York: The Library of Liberal Arts, no. 1, 1957.
Nozick, Robert, Anarchy, State and Utopia. New York: Basic Books, 1974.
Rothbard, Murray N., Man, Economy and State. Los Angeles, Nash, 1962.
Rothbard, Murray N., For a New Liberty. New York: Macmillan, 1973.
Rothbard, Murray N., The Ethics of Liberty. Atlantic Highlands, NJ: Humanities Press, 1982.

Rothbard, Murray N., 1977, "Robert Nozick and the immaculate conception of the state, The Journal of Libertarian Studies, Vol. 1, No. 1, Winter, pp. 45–58.
Sanders, John T., 1977, "The free market model versus Government: a reply to Nozick," The Journal of Libertarian Studies, Vol. 1, No. 1, Winter, pp. 35–44.
Spooner, Lysander. 1870. No Treason: The Constitution of No Authority and A Letter to Thomas F. Bayard, Larkspur, Colorado: Rampart College; http://jim.com/treason.htm.

9

Prices and Location: A Geographical and Economic Analysis

Economics is concerned with prices, profits, and incentives; geography with spatial considerations; political philosophy of law with the normative question of what should constitute proper legislation in the free society. The overlap of the three gives rise to the interdisciplinary field of political economic geography (Block and Block, 2000).

Nowhere is there a more appropriate subject matter for this field than in the area of real estate law. In this chapter I attempt to analyze from this perspective the Amsterdam Houses, a public housing project located on the west side of Manhattan, immediately between the Trump Place Towers and the Tischman building and West End Towers to the west, and the Lincoln Center complex to the east. For those unfamiliar with New York City real estate markets, this is some of the most valuable territory on the entire planet.

The inhabitants of Amsterdam Houses are poor, mainly black, with many on the welfare dole. Their neighbors, in the surrounding high-rise luxury buildings, are anything but. Rarely is such a phenomenon found, except on the periphery of rich and poor neighborhoods. But this housing project is located in roughly the center of one of the most luxurious areas in the world. Here is a comment on this strange and unlikely

W. E. Block, *Property Rights*, Palgrave Studies in Classical Liberalism,
https://doi.org/10.1007/978-3-030-28353-7_9

juxtaposition from the perspective of the tenants of Amsterdam Houses: "For better and worse, affluence surrounds a housing project: As Trump and Tischman build towers, poor neighbors get a chance to move up" (Wall Street Journal, 10/9/00, p. 1). According to this author, in some respects there were improvements in their lot in life: employment opportunities as maids, grocery clerks, increased, as did the safety of the neighborhood. In other ways, for example, envy of the rich, the very opposite occurred.

But the real story is that in a free society, it is unlikely in the extreme that such a geographical positioning would have ever occurred. Or if it did, through some accident, it would have been quickly ended. This is because had a group of poor people located in an area which later came into red hot demand, they would tend to be bid out of their premises by attractive competing offers. This is the typical case of urban yuppification, where rich upwardly mobile professional folk buy out the locals and others who have long occupied the area. (When the World's Fair was located in Vancouver, British Columbia, this phenomenon also occurred: hotel owners, looking to cater to the expected crowds of tourists, attempted to purchase many properties in the downtown area, in order to turf out the mainly poor people who had lived there.) Needless to say, strenuous objections to this practice were leveled by socialists. If the poor had been ensconced in a neighborhood of the city suddenly in greater demand as property owners, they would tend to sell at vastly higher prices. (The poor, too, can own property.) Had they been renters, the landlord would likely evict them in favor of tenants who could afford the new higher prices.

Note the effect of this process on the geographical makeup of a city: it tends to bring like into close proximity with like, and to put some distance between those on different places in the economic spectrum. That is, the rich tend to live cheek-by-jowl with others of their income class, and the poor are segregated into their own areas, occupied by other members of this wealth category.

What are the utilitarian benefits of such segregation on the basis of wealth or income? One advantage is that it reduces transactions costs (Coase, 1960). Rich people are more like others of their ilk than they are like the poor (otherwise they would likely be poor), and the same goes for members of the opposite end of the spectrum. But those who come from the same backgrounds have a similar set of values, mores, religions, and so on, and tend to find each other easier to deal with than people with entirely different characteristics. This not only reduces interpersonal strife but also enhances neighborhood cooperation; it promotes "mediating" institutions (see on this Novak, 1978, 1979a, 1979b, 1985, 1986) such as bowling leagues, churches, clubs, and boy scouts.

Another benefit is that the poor have no particular reason for being located in the west side of Manhattan, while the rich certainly do. Specifically, those of the wealthy persuasion are more likely to work in Wall Street, or in other business districts in this borough, than their counterparts at the opposite end of the income distribution. Even if the costs of travel were the same for the wealthy and the impoverished, it would still make sense for the former to be located closer to the center of the city, where their jobs are located, and for the poor to maintain residences in the periphery, since the latter do not work in downtown Manhattan to the same extent. But the costs of travel are highly correlated with hourly earnings. Bus or subway fare is an insignificant proportion of the total; the overwhelming majority of the costs are the opportunities forgone while traveling, namely, the wage that might have been earned during this time. By definition, this is more for those with higher hourly earnings than lower ones. (We abstract from psychic income which could conceivably turn this around upon rare occasions. For more on this see Block, 1977.)

But is this "fair"? Is it not immoral that the poor should be forced to vacate their domiciles in favor of the rich, especially when the latter may have been occupying their residences in these areas for years, even decades? This, at least, is the viewpoint expressed by many who object to the wholesale displacement of the latter by the former, based on what seems to be either a whim, or esoteric and irrelevant economic considerations. "A man's home is his castle" might be their rallying cry—apart from the fact that many of them are staunch feminists and would object to the use of the male pronoun in this sentence (see on this Radin, 1987; for a rejoinder, see Block, 1999)—in this battle against the "evil" real estate developers. (It is difficult to discern why otherwise intelligent people blame the developer for a phenomenon that emanates from underlying economic realities. This is like blaming the messenger for bad news.)

There are several difficulties with this position, however. First, it is simply not true to maintain that the poor are "forced" out of their dwellings. As we have seen, if they are property owners in an area suddenly in greater demand, they leave only because they value the sale price more than their continued occupancy. As the case of the "holdout" exemplifies, the poor property owner can persist in his ownership rights, rejecting any and all financial blandishments to the contrary. In this case, it cannot be denied, the rich all too often resort to extra market techniques for evicting poor homeowners: for example, eminent domain, or expropriation, or so-called urban renewal. However, we are discussing the system of laissez-faire capitalism, and no such forms of legalized theft are compatible with such a system. The classic work on urban renewal is Anderson (1964).

As to the tenant, he is not "forced out" either. Rather, he loses a bidding war for residential space he did not own in the first place. But doesn't the tenant really own, in at least some extended sense, the apartment he occupies? (This perspective has been articulated by Radin, 1986, 1987. For rejoinders see Block, 1999, 2002.) After all, we all commonly refer to it as "his" dwelling.

Suppose there is a restaurant that a poor man has been patronizing for years. Suddenly, this eating place goes "upscale," changes its menu, and doubles its prices. Has this poverty stricken individual been "forced" to seek another establishment? Not at all. Rather, he has made a choice to continue to patronize cheaper eateries. It is precisely the same in the case of the rental unit. The poor tenant is no more forced out of his residence than he was from his restaurant. He has no property rights in either of these cases. Continued patronage of either a restaurant or a dwelling owner's property confers no special privileges upon the customer. In both cases, in all such cases, the truth of the matter is that this consumer has (finally) been outbid by other customers for the good or service in question.

In like manner, it is very dangerous to infer ownership rights from the possessive pronoun. We all commonly refer to "my wife," "my husband," "my tailor," "my customer," "my teacher," "my student," "my job," "my boss," without any claims in the least as to ownership of any of these relationships.

Second, the position of the critics cannot possibly be generalized from food or shelter to all purchases, without embracing the noxious doctrine of absolute and perfect income and wealth equality. The point is, if wealth is to be rendered impotent when it comes to a choice of a place to live, why should not the same apply in all other economic decisions? And if it does, there will be little point in attempting to become wealthy, by, say, refraining from consumption and investing the saved proceeds, or by working harder, or for more hours, or working smarter (e.g., investing in education or training so as to be able to earn more and thus contribute to society to a greater degree). More strictly, this would reduce to zero all selfish motives for acting in such a public-spirited manner. Only benevolence would remain as a motivation toward these ends, surely a weak reed upon which to rest the economic well-being of society. Said Smith (1776, Book I, Chapter II, pp. 26–27): "It is not from the benevolence of the butcher, the brewer, or the baker, that we expect our dinner, but from their regard to their own interest. We address ourselves, not to their humanity but to their self-love, and never talk to them of our necessities but of their advantages." See also Seldon and Harris (1977) on this matter.

Third, there are also problems with a more moderate version of this thesis: allowing prices and considerations of profit to apply to "luxury" goods, such as yachts and jewelry, but not to "necessities," for example, food, clothing, and shelter. One difficulty is that one person's luxury is another's necessity. Goods do not come with such labels affixed to them; rather, these are evaluations placed on them by people, and tastes do differ. Another is that under these conditions, we would soon be awash in "luxuries," while "necessities" would come to be in short supply, as economic incentives became perverse: shifting investment from the latter to the former. Why? If the businessman can earn more profits in jewelry than in milk or apples, he will soon shift interest from the one to the other.

Fourth, this doctrine is subject to yet another reductio. (For a classic articulation of this egalitarian doctrine, see Rawls, 1971; for a refutation, see Nozick, 1974.) If its advocates wish to maintain that any income disparity is illegitimate, then on what basis can they defend differences in the characteristics that account for them in the first place? That is, the antecedents of diversity in wealth (it is interesting to note that the mind-set which opposes diversity in income or wealth very much favors it when it comes to education, or employment, etc., on a racial or sexual basis) consist of mainly intelligence (Herrnstein and Murray, 1994; Levin, 1997) but also of initiative, hard work, artistic or athletic skills, and luck. Further, they are in no logical position to defend human differences in other things that make life enjoyable such as a sense of humor and beauty.

Moreover, they embroil themselves in a logical inconsistency. For it is only as intellectuals that they make these arguments in the first place. But if human beings were leveled down to an amorphous mass, with the intelligence of all pegged at its present average, it is doubtful that anyone would have had the cunning it takes to put forth this argument in the first place. Thus the critics are relying on skills to make their point which they would not be able to call upon were their own wishes carried out.

References

Anderson, Martin. 1964. The Federal Bulldozer, Cambridge, MIT Press.

Block, Walter and Matthew Block. 2000. Toward a Universal Libertarian Theory of Gun (Weapon) Control," Ethics, Place and Environment, 3 (3): 289–298.

Block, Walter. 1977. "Coase and Demsetz on Private Property Rights," The Journal of Libertarian Studies: An Interdisciplinary Review, 1 (2): 111–115. http://www.mises.org/journals/jls/1_2/1_2_4.pdf.

Block, Walter. 1999. "Market Inalienability Once Again: Reply to Radin," Thomas Jefferson Law Journal, 22 (1): 37–88.

Block, Walter. 2002. "A Critique of the Legal and Philosophical Case for Rent Control," Journal of Business Ethics. Forthcoming.

Coase, Ronald. 1960. "The Problem of Social Cost," 3 Journal of Law and Economics: 1–44.

Herrnstein, Richard J., and Murray, Charles. 1994. The Bell Curve: Intelligence and Class Structure in American Life, New York: The Free Press.

Levin, Michael. 1997. Why Race Matters, Westport, CT: Praeger.

Novak, Michael. 1978. The Spirit of Democratic Capitalism, Simon & Schuster, New York, N.Y.

Novak, Michael, ed. 1979a. The Denigration of Capitalism, American Enterprise Institute for Public Policy, Washington, D.C.

Novak, Michael, ed. 1979b. Capitalism and Socialism, American Institute for Public Policy Research, Washington, D.C.

Novak, Michael. 1985. "The Liberal Society as Liberation Theology," Notre Dame Journal of Law, Ethics and Public Policy, Volume 2, No. 1.

Novak, Michael. 1986. Will it Liberate? Questions about Liberation Theology, New York, Paulist Press.

Nozick, Robert. 1974. Anarchy, State and Utopia, New York: Basic Books.

Radin, Margaret Jane. 1987. "Market-Inalienability" Harvard Law Review, 100 (8): 1849–1937.

Radin, Margaret Jane. 1986. "Residential Rent Control," Philosophy and Public Affairs, 15: 350–380.

Rawls, John. 1971. A Theory of Justice, Cambridge: Harvard University Press.

Seldon, Arthur, and Harris, Ralph. 1977. "Not from Benevolence: Twenty Years of Economic Dissent," London, UK: Institute for Economic Affairs.

Smith, Adam. 1776/1979. An Inquiry into the Nature and Causes of the Wealth of Nations, Indianapolis, IN: Liberty Fund.

Part III

Reparations

10

On Reparations to Blacks for Slavery

Introduction

This chapter is an attempt to shed some light on the legitimacy of some recent claims by prominent black leaders and scholars that reparations are owed to members of their race, and should be paid for by the US government out of tax revenues. I shall critically consider in the light of libertarian theory both the views in favor of this position put forth by Robinson[1] and those against it of Horowitz[2]; http://www.salon.com/news/col/horo/2000/05/30/reparations/index.html. See also Myron Magnet, *The Dream and the Nightmare*, New York: Manhattan Institute for Policy Research, especially the chapter "Race and Reparations."

The author wishes to thank Jeff Tucker of the Mises Institute for helpful comments and criticism, and Hannah Block for editing. All errors that remain are the author's alone, of course.

[1] Robinson, Randall, The Debt: What America Owes to Blacks. See also Richard America Paying the Social Debt: What White America Owes Black America.

[2] Horowitz, David, "The latest civil rights disaster: Ten reasons why reparations for slavery are a bad idea for black people—and racist too."

W. E. Block, *Property Rights*, Palgrave Studies in Classical Liberalism,
https://doi.org/10.1007/978-3-030-28353-7_10

Libertarianism

Libertarianism is a political philosophy with private property rights at its core. Its axiom is that physical invasions of persons or property are unjustified,[3] and should be punished. It is based on a variant of Lockean[4] homesteading theory, according to which mixing one's labor with the

[3] On libertarianism, see Anderson, Terry and Hill, P.J., "An American Experiment in Anarcho-Capitalism: the not so Wild, Wild West," Journal of Libertarian Studies Vol. 3, No. 1, 1979, pp. 9–29; Barnett, Randy E., The Structure of Liberty: Justice and the Rule of Law, Oxford: Clarendon Press, 1998; Benson, Bruce L., 1989, Enforcement of Private Property Rights in Primitive Societies: Law Without Government," The Journal of Libertarian Studies, Vol. IX, No. 1, Winter, pp. 1–26; Benson, Bruce L., "The Spontaneous Evolution of Commercial Law," Southern Economic Journal, 55: 644–661, 1989; Benson, Bruce L., The Enterprise of Law: Justice Without the State, San Francisco: Pacific Research Institute for Public Policy, 1990; Cuzán, Alfred G., "Do We Ever Really Get Out of Anarchy?," Journal of Libertarian Studies, Vol. 3, No. 2 (Summer, 1979); De Jasay, Anthony, The State, Oxford: Basil Blackwell, 1985; Friedman, David, The Machinery of Freedom: Guide to a Radical Capitalism, La Salle, IL: Open Court, 2nd ed., 1989; Friedman, David, "Private Creation and Enforcement of Law: A Historical Case," Journal of Legal Studies, 8: 399–415, 1979; Hoppe, Hans-Hermann, A Theory of Socialism and Capitalism: Economics, Politics and Ethics, Boston: Kluwer, 1989; Hoppe, Hans-Hermann, The Economics and Ethics of Private Property: Studies in Political Economy and Philosophy, Boston: Kluwer, 1993; Hoppe, Hans-Hermann, "The Private Production of Defense," Journal of Libertarian Studies, Vol. 14, No. 1, Winter 1998–1999, pp. 27–52; Hummel, Jeffrey Rogers, National Goods Versus Public Goods: Defense, Disarmament, and Free Riders, 4 Rev. Austrian Econ. 88 (1990); Morriss, Andrew P., "Miners, Vigilantes and Cattlemen: Overcoming Free Rider Problems in the Private Provision of Law," Land and Water Law Review, Vol. XXXIII, No, 2, 1998, pp. 581–696; Peden, Joseph R., 1977, "Property rights in Celtic Irish law," The Journal of Libertarian Studies, Vol. 1, No. 2, Spring, pp. 81–96; Rothbard, Murray N., For a New Liberty, Macmillan, New York, 1978; Rothbard, Murray N., The Ethics of Liberty, Humanities Press, Atlantic Highlands, N.J., 1982; Rothbard, Murray N., "Society Without a State." J. R. Pennock and J. W. Chapman (eds.), Anarchism: Nomos XIX. New York: New York University Press, 1978, pp. 191–207; Rothbard, Murray N., Man, Economy and State, Auburn AL: Mises Institute, 1993; Skoble, Aeon J. "The Anarchism Controversy," in Liberty for the 21st Century: Essays in Contemporary Libertarian Thought, eds. Tibor Machan and Douglas Rasmussen, Lanham MD: Rowman and Littlefield, 1995, pp. 77–96; Sechrest, Larry J., "Rand, Anarchy, and Taxes," The Journal of Ayn Rand Studies, Vol. I, No. 1, Fall 1999, pp. 87–105; Spooner, Lysander, No Treason, Larkspur, Colorado, (1870) 1966; Stringham, Edward, "Justice Without Government," Journal of Libertarian Studies, Vol. 14, No. 1, Winter 1998–1999, pp. 53–77; Tinsley, Patrick, "With Liberty and Justice for All: A Case for Private Police," Journal of Libertarian Studies, Vol. 14, No. 1, Winter 1998–1999, pp. 95–100; Tannehill, Morris and Linda, The Market for Liberty, New York: Laissez Faire Books, 1984; Woolridge, William C., Uncle Sam the Monopoly Man, New Rochelle, N.Y.: Arlington House, 1970.

[4] John Locke, *An Essay Concerning the True Original, Extant and End of Civil Government*, in Social Contract 17–18 (E. Barker ed., 1948).

land justifies ownership of it, whether or not Locke's proviso of "enough and as good still being available" is met.

This proviso is all well and good when there are vast lands unsettled, as in the US frontier of historical memory. But what is to be done when virtually all usable land has been taken up? There are only several possibilities. We can resort to government ownership.[5] But why should land socialism[6] work any better than the economic variety? In any case, members of the apparatus of the state, by stipulation, did not mix their labor with the land, or do anything else which would remotely justify their ownership status over it. Why, then, should it be granted? True, the government can auction off the land to the highest bidders, or on a first-come, first-served basis, but why would the owners who eventuate from such a process—initially unjustified—be preferable to those whose

[5] The US Bureau of Land Management's control over much of the land west of the Mississippi has been more of a disaster than anything else. See on this Anderson, Terry L., and Hill, Peter J., "Property Rights as a Common Pool Resource," Bureaucracy vs. Environment: The Environmental Costs of Bureaucratic Governance, John Baden and Richard L. Stroup, eds., Ann Arbor: University of Michigan Press, 1981; Anderson, Terry L., and Leal, Donald R., Free Market Environmentalism, San Francisco: Pacific Research Institute, 1991; Block, Walter, "Ownership will save the environment," New Environment, First Quarter, 1991, 41–43; Block, Walter, "Protection of property rights key to maintaining resources," Environment Policy and Law, Vol. 1, No. 3, June 1990, p. 28; Block, Walter, ed., Economics and the Environment: A Reconciliation, Vancouver: The Fraser Institute, 1990; Block, Walter, "Earning Happiness Through Homesteading Unowned Land: a comment on 'Buying Misery with Federal Land' by Richard Stroup," Journal of Social Political and Economic Studies, Vol. 15, No. 2, Summer 1990, pp. 237–253; Hill, Peter J., and Meiners, Roger E., eds., Who Owns the Environment?, New York: Rowman and Littlefield, 1998; Hoppe, Hans-Hermann, The Economics and Ethics of Private Property: Studies in Political Economy and Philosophy, Boston: Kluwer, 1993; Horwitz, Morton J., The Transformation of American Law: 1780–1860, Cambridge: Harvard University Press, 1977; Margaret N. Maxey and Robert L. Kuhn, eds., Regulatory Reform: New Vision or Old Curse, New York: Praeger, 1985; Rathje, William L., "Rubbish!," Atlantic Monthly, Vol. 264, No. 6, December 1989, pp. 99–109; Ray, Dixie Lee, 1990, Trashing the Planet, Washington D.C.: Regnery Gateway; Rothbard, Murray N., "Law, Property Rights, and Air Pollution," Economics and the Environment: A Reconciliation, Walter Block, ed., Vancouver: The Fraser Institute, 1990; Stroup, Richard L., and John C. Goodman, et al., (1991) Progressive Environmentalism: A Pro-Human, Pro-Science, Pro-Free Enterprise Agenda for Change, Dallas, TX: National Center for Policy Analysis, Task Force Report; Stroup, Richard L., and Baden, John A., "Endowment Areas: A Clearing in the Policy Wilderness," Cato Journal, 2 Winter 1982, pp. 691–708.

[6] The latest managerial failure of the bureaucrats, the US Park Service in this case, has been a forest fire set by the authorities themselves as a preventative; the only difficulty is that it raged out of control, creating millions of dollars of damages. See on this "Los Alamos Under Siege," Newsweek, 5/22/00, p. 35. Were any private enterprise guilty of so massive a blunder, it surely would have become enmeshed in bankruptcy proceedings. But by the very nature of things this fail-safe mechanism is available to markets, not governments.

ownership is based on homesteading? This process would indeed see more money placed into the coffers of the state, but it is easy to make out the case that they already have far too much wealth and control over the economy as it is.[7] The only other candidate is claim theory; ownership, here, is based on a mere affirmation. But this also fails to establish any connection between the owner and that which is owned. In addition, there is the problem of vast over-determination, as anyone would be free to claim anything he wishes.

Alterations in Property Titles

Having established ownership in property, the next step in determining justice in property titles is to outline a theory of how they can legitimately change hands from one person to another. This may be done in any non-invasive manner possible, for example, trade, gifts, inheritance, or gambling, for these are the only options compatible with ownership in the first place.[8] That is, if I give you my ring in exchange for your car, this is logically consistent with property rights; if I merely seize your auto, it is not. Nozick calls this "legitimate title transfer."[9]

It must be emphasized that the key element of libertarian punishment theory[10] is an attempt to make the victim "whole," preeminently by

---

[7] Gwartney, James, Robert Lawson and Walter Block, Economic Freedom of the World, 1975–1995, Vancouver, B.C. Canada: the Fraser Institute, 1996.

[8] Nozick, Robert, Anarchy, State, and Utopia, New York: Basic Books Inc., 1974; N. Stephan Kinsella, "A Theory of Contracts: Binding Promises, Title Transfer, and Inalienability" (paper presented at Auburn, Alabama, April 1999, Ludwig von Mises Institute's Austrian Scholars Conference 5; published version forthcoming.

[9] Nozick, Robert, Anarchy, State, and Utopia, New York: Basic Books Inc., 1974, p. xz.

[10] On libertarian punishment theory, see Barnett, Randy, and Hagel, John, eds., Assessing the Criminal, Cambridge MA: Ballinger, 1977; Block, Walter, "Toward a Libertarian Theory of Guilt and Punishment for the Crime of Statism," Huelsmann, Guido, ed., The Rise and Fall of the State, forthcoming; Block, Walter, "National Defense and the Theory of Externalities, Public Goods and Clubs," Hoppe, Hans-Hermann, ed., Explorations in the Theory and History of Security Production, forthcoming King, J. Charles, A Rationale for Punishment, 4 J. Libertarian Stud. 151, 154 (1980); Kinsella, Stephan N., "A Libertarian Theory of Punishment and Rights," (volume) 30 Loy. L.A. L. Rev. 607–45 (1997); Kinsella, Stephan N., "New Rationalist Directions in Libertarian Rights Theory," 12:2 J. Libertarian Studies 313–26 (Fall 1996); Kinsella, Stephan N., "Punishment

compensating him. While this is never fully possible, the goal is to attain this state of affairs insofar as possible. Crimes, in this perspective, are not committed against some general "society," and the main aspect is not on incarceration, much less reform. Rather, a crime such as assault and battery, murder, and rape is seen as aimed primarily at the victim. Jail, to the extent it arises in a libertarian society, is merely a way of forcing hard labor upon the perpetrator in an attempt to get him to compensate the victim.

Reparation Theory

Justified reparations are nothing more and nothing less than the forced return of stolen property—typically after a significant amount of time has passed. For example, if my grandfather stole a ring from your grandfather, and then bequeathed it to me through the intermediation of my father, then I am, presently, the illegitimate owner of that piece of jewelry. To take the position that reparations are always and forever unjustified is to give an imprimatur to theft, provided a sufficient time period has elapsed. In the just society, your father would have inherited the ring from his own parent, and then given it to you. It is thus not a violation of property rights, but a logical implication of them, to force me to give over this ill-gotten gain to you.[11] "In short, we cannot simply talk of defense of 'property rights' or of 'private property' per se. For if we do so, we are in grave danger of defending the 'property right' of a criminal aggressor—in fact, we logically must do so." Of course, "pos-

---

and Proportionality: The Estoppel Approach," 12:1 J. Libertarian Studies 51 (Spring 1996); Kinsella, Stephan N., "Estoppel: A New Justification for Individual Rights," Reason Papers No. 17 (Fall 1992), p. 61; Kinsella, N. Stephan, "Inalienability and Punishment: A Reply to George Smith," Journal of Libertarian Studies, Vol. 14, No. 1, Winter, 1998–1999, pp. 79–93; Rothbard, Murray N., The Ethics of Liberty, Humanities Press, Atlantic Highlands, N.J., 1982.

[11] States Rothbard, Murray N., The Ethics of Liberty, New York: New York University Press (1998 [1982], pp. 51–52): "Suppose we are walking down the street and we see a man, A, seizing B by the wrist and grabbing B's wristwatch. There is no question that A is here violating both the person and the property of B. Can we then simply infer from this scene that A is a criminal aggressor, and B his innocent victim?"

session is nine tenths of the law." It is not sufficient, on your part, merely to claim that the ring now on my finger is rightfully yours. You must be forthcoming with specific evidence undergirding this demand. A dated picture of your grandfather wearing it, or a bill of sale, would do just fine. Moreover, it is only *I* who owe you this piece of jewelry, not my neighbor or the general taxpayer,[12] and it is owed only to you, not to any person who wants it, or to those of a given race or ethnicity. Further, I am not a criminal for innocently possessing the ring before you came to claim it, but I am guilty of a criminal act once it is proven that the ring was really your grandfather's and I refuse to give it up to you.

Precisely the same analysis applies to slavery. Owning a slave is a crime under libertarian law. The Nuremberg Trials have established the validity of ex post facto law. Those people who owned slaves in the pre–Civil War United States were guilty of the crime of kidnaping, even though such practices were legal at the time. A part of the value of their plantations was based on the forced labor of blacks. Were justice fully done in 1865, these people would have been incarcerated, and that part of the value of their holdings attributable to slave labor would have been turned over to the ex-slaves. Instead, these slave masters kept their freedom, and bequeathed their property to their own children. Their (great)-grandchildren now possess farms which, under a regime of justice, would have never been given to them. Instead, they would have been in the hands of the (great)-grandchildren of slaves. To return these specific lands to those blacks in the present day who can prove their ancestors were forced to work on these plantations is thus to *uphold* private property rights, not to denigrate them.

[12] The freed slaves were presumably promised "40 acres and a mule." If from the slave master, well and good; this is at least an approximation of what they were owed. If this was to have been derived, however, courtesy of the taxpayer, then it would be unjust, since the average citizen was not responsible for slavery. For the view that voting does not make one responsible for the acts of politicians, see Spooner, Lysander, No Treason, Larkspur, Colorado, (1870) 1966.

Horowitz

Horowitz seems to have had a kneejerk reaction to the claims of Jesse Jackson, Conyers, Gates, Randall Robinson, and their confreres.[13] Since they have been wrong in just about everything they have ever said in the areas of economics, politics, discrimination, race relations, ethics, and so on, he presumes that this applies in this case as well.[14] But here, perhaps through sheer good luck, they have finally hit upon a principle compatible with libertarianism and the free society. Because of his inability to discern a pro-free enterprise viewpoint when it comes from so unlikely a quarter, Horowitz is then unable to tax these people with their logical inconsistency; they are Johnny-come-latelies to the banner of capitalism. If they really wish to press their reparations claims, which are based on the doctrine of private property rights (returning possessions to their rightful owners), then they must renounce all of their previous positions which are incompatible with this vision, for example, their support for welfare, unions, government intervention into the economy, regulation, and business nationalization. Alternatively, if they insist on maintaining these spurious views, then upon pain of contradiction, they must withdraw their demand for reparations, based on stolen (labor) property.[15]

Paradoxically, even if Jackson, Conyers, Gates, Robinson, Dorothy Lewis, Hannibal Afrik, Albert Thornton et al. do change their tune on property rights in general, and thus are logically enabled[16] to press for

---

[13] Others who have made similar reparations claims in behalf of blacks include Dorothy Lewis and Hannibal Afrik of the National Coalition of Blacks for Reparations in America, and Albert Thornton, chairman of the political science department at Howard University, a historically black college. See on this The National Post, 6/7/00, p. A3.

[14] I confess this is a very tempting conclusion to draw. Why else do we have induction if not for things just of this sort?

[15] Their probable response to this sally would be to attempt to have their cake and eat it, presumably by claiming that "linear" logic is an invention of dead white males, and doesn't apply to them. It is impossible to take such people seriously. In any case, my argument is with the far more coherent Horowitz, not them. Here, I am only pointing out that Horowitz does not carry forth as fully as he might his attack on these black "scholars," due to his inability to see that for once they are on the side of the angels.

[16] In Kinsella's terminology, they are no longer "estopped" from making these claims. See on this Kinsella, Stephan N., "A Libertarian Theory of Punishment and Rights," (volume) 30 Loy. L.A. L.

reparations, they will derive no great measure of comfort from it, as a practical matter. This is because it is notoriously difficult to trace property titles back in history for any great length of time, particularly if there were no written records kept (as was the case with Indians and other preliterate people).[17] This is why, again only as a practical matter, there are no implications of the libertarian theory of reparations to far-off events such as Mongol hordes and competing claims in Jerusalem from 2000 years ago. Reparations theory comes into its own regarding more recent occurrences such as land stolen in the USSR, Cuba, East Germany, and so on, where scrupulously accurate records are available. Black slavery in the United States occupies an intermediate position; it took place a century and a half ago, and while there were written records, many have been lost in the sands of time. It is only from the position of an all-knowing God that reparations, from as far back in history as you wish to go, written records or no, are relevant to property titles in the present time.

There is another reason black leaders cannot take too much comfort from libertarian reparations theory. Suppose there were 500 slaves on a

Rev. 607–45 (1997); Kinsella, Stephan N., "New Rationalist Directions in Libertarian Rights Theory," 12:2 J. Libertarian Studies 313–26 (Fall 1996); Kinsella, Stephan N., "Punishment and Proportionality: The Estoppel Approach," 12:1 J. Libertarian Studies 51 (Spring 1996); Kinsella, Stephan N., "Estoppel: A New Justification for Individual Rights," Reason Papers No. 17 (Fall 1992), p. 61; Kinsella, N. Stephan, "Inalienability and Punishment: A Reply to George Smith," Journal of Libertarian Studies, Vol. 14, No. 1, Winter, 1998–1999, pp. 79–93.

[17] A court in Canada has ruled that written records are not required for proof of ownership. The recollections of tribal elders will suffice in their stead. Here is the court's finding in *R. v. Van Der Peet*, [1996] 2 S. C. R. 507, a case concerning Indian fishing rights, from the summary: "A court should approach the rules of evidence and interpret the evidence that exists, conscious of the special nature of aboriginal claims and of the evidentiary difficulties in proving a right which originates in times when there were no written records of the practices, customs and traditions and customs engaged in. The courts must not undervalue the evidence presented by aboriginal claimants simply because that evidence does not conform precisely with the evidentiary standards applied in other contexts." This finding played a role in the decision concerning a land reparations case, *Delgamuukw v British Columbia*, [1997] 3 S.C.R. 1010, which cited paragraph #68 of *R. v. Van Der Peet*, [1996] 2 S. C. R. 507, which has been just summarized. To say the least, this determination is not at all compatible with libertarian requirements of proof. For one thing, the testimony may be a lie. For another, it is not disinterested. For a third, it may be honestly believed, but mistaken. This seems to be the conclusion in many cases of recovered memory of girlhood incest charges on the part of adult women. But there is a practical implication as well. If this unwarranted decision were to become a precedent, then, truly, the reductio ad absurdum charge against the libertarian position that it would open the floodgates of land reparations cases back before the beginning of recorded history could then be sustained. But this is only a utilitarian consideration, unworthy, probably, of our attention.

plantation, but the grandchildren of only one of them can be found. They are entitled to split among themselves not all the contributions made by all the slaves, but rather only 1/500th of that, the estimate of the productivity of their own ancestor alone.

Why is this? Would it not be more reasonable to award the children of this one slave the fruits of the labor of all the slaves? At first blush, this is a tenable idea. After all, at the time of the freedom of the slaves, were justice to have reigned at that time, the product of their entire output would have been given to them; none of it at all would have remained in the slave master's hands.[18] And if the ex–slave owner would not have been able to keep any of this property, he would not have been able to hand it down to his own progeny. Instead, it would have been under the control of the ex-slaves, and, with time, wended its way into the hands of blacks now alive.

Although not an altogether unreasonable scenario, it is simply incompatible with libertarian law. This is because we must look at this matter not from the point of view of 1865, and on the assumption that the offspring of all 500 slaves can be found, but rather from the perspective of the case we are assuming; that is, it is now the modern era, almost a century and a half after these historical events have unfolded, and we can demonstrate a connection between only one slave and persons now living. Yes, the property in question, in justice, never should have remained in the hands of the slave master; but it did. He handed it on to his innocent children, and they to theirs. Now, as judges, we are faced with blacks who can trace their roots back to only one of the 500 slaves. Why should they be entitled to land to which they have no connection? The extant owners, at least, are not themselves guilty of any land theft or slave holding, and have established homestead rights to that which they occupy.

Rothbard explains:

> But suppose that Jones[19] is <u>not</u> the criminal, not the man who stole the watch, but that he had inherited or had innocently purchased it form the

[18] He, himself, would have been very seriously punished for the crime of slave holding.

[19] In our context, Jones is the white grandchild of the slave owner, who is now in possession of the property under dispute.

thief. And suppose, of course, that neither the victim nor his heirs can be found.[20] In that case, the disappearance of the victim means that the stolen property comes properly into a state of no-ownership. But we have seen that any good in a state of no-ownership, with no legitimate owner of its title, reverts as legitimate property to the first person to come along and use it, to appropriate this now unowned resource for human use. But this 'first' person is clearly Jones, who has been using it all along. Therefore, we conclude that even though the property was originally stolen, that if the victim or his heirs cannot be found, and if the current possessor was not the actual criminal who stole the property, then title to that property belongs properly, justly, and ethically to its current possessor.

To sum up, for any property currently claimed and used: (a) if we know clearly that there was no criminal origin to its current title, then obviously the current title is legitimate, just and valid; (b) if we don't know whether the current title had any criminal origins but can't find out either way, then the hypothetically 'unowned' property reverts instantaneously and justly to its current possessor; (c) if we do know that the title is originally criminal, but can't find the victim or his heirs, then (c1) if the current title-holder was not the criminal aggressor against the property, then it reverts to him justly as the first owner of a hypothetically unowned property. But (c2) if the current title-holder is himself the criminal or one of the criminals who stole the property, then clearly he is properly to be deprived of it, and it then reverts to the first man who takes it out of its unowned state and appropriates it for his use. And finally, (d) if the current title is the result of crime, and the victim or his heirs can be found, then the title properly reverts immediately to the latter, without compensation to the criminal or to the other holders of the unjust title.[21]

There are three reasons why black leaders[22] should jettison their socialist leanings, and begin to support capitalism. One, it will inure to the

---

[20] Remember, in our example, the 499 victims and their heirs cannot be found.

[21] Rothbard, Murray N., The Ethics of Liberty, Humanities Press, Atlantic Highlands, N.J., 1982, pp. 58–59.

[22] We must never lose sight of the fact that there are *some* black scholars who are avid supporters of free enterprise. Unfortunately, while this honor roll is very distinguished, it is also very short. Among economists it includes Williams, Walter, E., The State Against Blacks, New York, McGraw-Hill, 1982; Williams, Walter E., South Africa's War Against Capitalism, New York: Praeger, 1989; Williams, Walter E., and Walter Block, "Male-Female Earnings Differentials: A Critical Reappraisal," The Journal of Labor Research, Vol. II, No. 2, Fall 1981, pp. 385–388; Sowell,

benefit of their followers right now in ways unrelated to reparations. Two, they will be able to logically maintain their position on reparations as a matter of principle. And three, some few black grandchildren might actually be able to trace their claims back in time to the pre–Civil War era, and thereby obtain some compensation, under libertarian law.

A Critique

In one sense, I have nothing critical to say about Horowitz (2000). He opposes "the idea that taxpayers should pay reparations to black Americans for the damages of slavery and segregation" and so do I. My argument is that no one owes anything to anyone for segregation, since the law of free association guarantees (or should guarantee) that anyone can discriminate against anyone else for any reason, or no reason at all. Second, I maintain that although reparations are indeed owed to some blacks, from some whites, for slavery, all blacks should not be creditors in this regard, nor all (non-black) taxpayers, debtors.

In another sense, I look upon Horowitz (2000) with profound disquiet. For one thing, this essay "proves" far too much; in the view of this writer, there are no blacks at all who are owed reparations from anyone. That is, presumably, the entire concept of reparations for past crimes is somehow invalid, or at least when applied to black slavery in the United States. For another, most of his arguments are contrary to the libertarian doctrine of reparations in general; they are not limited to all blacks being

---

Thomas, The Vision of the Anointed, New York: Basic Books, 1995; Sowell, Thomas, Race and Economics, New York: Longman, 1975; Sowell, Thomas, Patterns of Black Excellence, Washington D.C.: Ethics and Public Policy Center, 1976; Sowell, Thomas, Pink and Brown People, San Francisco: The Hoover Institution Press, 1981; Sowell, Thomas, Ethnic America, New York: Basic Books, 1981; Sowell, Thomas, "Weber and Bakke and the presuppositions of 'Affirmative Action,'" Discrimination, Affirmative Action and Equal Opportunity, Walter Block and Michael Walker, eds., Vancouver: The Fraser Institute, 1982; Sowell, Thomas, The Economics and Politics of Race: An International Perspective, New York, Morrow, 1983; Sowell, Thomas, Civil Rights: Rhetoric or Reality, New York: William Morrow, e1984; Sowell, Thomas, A Conflict of Visions: Ideological Origins of Political Struggles, New York: William Morrow, 1987; Sowell, Thomas, "Preferential Policies," in Thinking About America: The United States in the 1990s, Annelise Anderson and Dennis L. Bark, eds., San Francisco: The Hoover Institution Press, 1988; Sowell, Thomas, Inside American Education: The Decline, the Deception, The Dogmas, New York: The Free Press, 1993; Sowell, Thomas, Race and Culture: A World View, New York: Basic Books, 1994.

owed reparations by all (non-black) taxpayers. As such, Horowitz is arguing against a bunch of philosophically very weak straw men: so-called civil rights leaders such as Rep. John Conyers (D-Mich.), Henry Louis Gates of Harvard, Jesse Jackson, and Randall Robinson, the author of *The Debt: What America Owes to Blacks*. By laying waste to their arguments, he concludes that no reparations are owed in this case, and that is a fallacy.

I do not quarrel in every respect with Horowitz's decision to take these people to task for their many and serious lapses of logic and intellectual coherence. Their views may be dead from the neck up, but they are certainly politically powerful. However, I would not want the impression left that the only arguments for reparations[23] are the ones put forth by these representatives of the "civil rights" establishment. And since Horowitz (2000) argues against *all* reparations for black slavery in the United States, seemingly as a matter of principle, not mere expediency, it is important that a necessary corrective of his views be entertained. Further, he overlooks one important criticism of his opponents that they richly deserve to have rubbed in their faces.

Among the charges made by Horowitz is that the call for reparations for black slavery will negatively "impact on race relations and [lead to] the self-isolation of the African-American community." To my mind, these are purely peripheral issues. In this reply I shall instead focus on whether these claims are *just*. After all, it is entirely possible that to hang an innocent man will have positive effects on race relations and reduce isolation of the black community. Even if this merely utilitarian consideration is true, it is still almost unworthy of consideration. Of far more importance is the *justice*, or lack of same, underlying these claims.

---

[23] For the libertarian case in behalf of reparations, see Block, Walter and Yeatts, Guillermo "Land Reform," University of Kentucky Journal of Natural Resources and Environmental Law, forthcoming; Block, Walter, "Review Essay of Bethell, Tom, The Noblest Triumph: Property and Prosperity Through the Ages, New York: St. Martin's Press, 1998," in The Quarterly Journal of Austrian Economics, Vol. 2, No. 3, Fall 1999, pp. 65–84; Walter Block, David Friedman, Milton Friedman, Philip Wogaman, Kenneth Boulding, Walter Berns, Edmund Opitz, Paul Heyne and Geoffrey Brennan, *Discussion*, in Morality of the Market: Religious and Economic Perspectives, Walter Block, Geoffrey Brennan & Kenneth Elzinga, eds., Fraser Institute: Vancouver, 1985, pp. 495–510; Rothbard, Murray N., The Ethics of Liberty, Humanities Press, Atlantic Highlands, N.J., 1982. Levin, Michael, Why Race Matters: Race Differences and What They Mean, New York: Praeger, 1997, pp. 229–289, opposes reparations to blacks, but not for reasons relevant to our present concerns.

Ten Reasons

Horowitz considers and rejects ten separate claims for reparations. In what follows, I shall comment on each, following his order of presentation.

1. States Horowitz: "Assuming there is actually a debt, it is not at all clear who owes it." Our author is perfectly correct in objecting to the claim made by our friends in the "black studies" departments of our major universities that all Americans owe blacks a debt for slavery. No one living now, clearly, was alive during that unhappy epoch; not everyone in the United States has illegitimately inherited property not properly belonging to their ancestors. But just because not everyone owes blacks for enslaving their forebears does not mean no one does. As we have seen, the present possessors of wealth handed down to them through the generations, emanating from slavery, do indeed owe a debt to those who can prove they are the direct decedents of the slaves involved.

Horowitz argues "It was not whites but black Africans who first enslaved their brothers and sisters. They were abetted by dark-skinned Arabs … who organized the slave trade. Are reparations going to be assessed against the descendants of Africans and Arabs for their role in slavery? There were also 3,000 black slave owners in the antebellum United States. Are reparations to be paid by their descendants too?" He asks these questions as if there were no possible affirmative answers. Slave holding or slave capturing is a crime. This is so regardless of the skin color of masters or victims. Yes, a hundred times yes, if a black person A can prove that money now held by another member of his own black race, B, was inherited improperly by B, and that the grandparents of A were the victims, then this property *should* be transferred from B to A. The races of A and B are strictly irrelevant.

2. It may well be that the socialist black advocates of reparations rely on "the idea that only whites benefited from slavery." As Horowitz avers, this claim "is factually wrong." But this criticism is the reddest of red herrings as far as the libertarian case for reparations is concerned. I might "benefit" in some direct or indirect sense from any number of goings on. For example, if I own a detective agency, then my profits rise with juvenile delinquency rates. But this does not make me responsible for the crime wave in the first place. An orange grower in Florida benefits from a frost which kills this type of fruit in California; but no one is rash enough to blame him for the bad weather on the other side of the country.

In like manner, Horowitz scores heavily against his straw men opponents by noting that "American blacks on average enjoy per capita incomes in the range of 20 to 50 times those of blacks living in any of the African nations from which they were kidnapped," and asks, "What about this benefit of slavery? Are the reparations proponents going to make black descendants of slaves pay themselves for benefiting from the fruits of their ancestors' servitude?" Yes, these are telling arguments against those of Robinson et al. But they are irrelevant to the libertarian case on behalf of returning stolen property to the modern descendants of African slaves. It is not a matter of adding up benefits and costs, and subtracting the one from the other. On the contrary, there are specific people who now own property they should not have inherited. This physical property and land, and it alone, is vulnerable to transfer. Since "benefits" play no role in the justification, the question of comparing those which helped blacks against those which hurt them does not arise.

Suppose a man rapes a woman, and it is later somehow proven that had he not molested her in this way, she would have instead been run over by a bus and killed. Should this fact mitigate the punishment imposed on him? Not a bit of it. He is a rapist, and should be punished to the full extent of the law. It is entirely irrelevant that in some sense blacks gained from their association with whites, through slavery and kidnapping. The enslavers and the kidnapers should still be punished.

3. Horowitz plaintively and very tellingly asks: "Why should the descendants of non-slaveholding whites owe a debt? What about the descendants of the 350,000 Union soldiers who died to free the slaves? They gave their lives. What possible morality would ask them to pay (through their descendants) again?" This is all well and good insofar as is concerned the claim that all (white) Americans owe a debt to blacks. But it does not at all relieve of obligation the descendants of specific white plantation[24] slave owners to give up their ill inherited gains.

[24] There is a temptation to assume that all defendants in black reparations cases would be southerners. This must be resisted. Strictly speaking, of course, slavery took place not only in the South, but in the North as well.

4. Our author in this section makes the point that the children of post-slavery immigrants to the United States owe blacks nothing for the subjugation of their ancestors, since their ancestors had nothing to do with it, and I am entirely in accord with him on this.

5. Not so, unfortunately, with regard to the precedents established by reparations to Jews from Germany and Japanese Americans from the United States. Horowitz rejects these analogies on the entirely spurious ground that "The Jews and Japanese who received reparations were individuals who actually suffered the hurt." But what does it matter whether the payments go to the people actually brutalized, or to their children, who would have, in any case, inherited from them? In taking this position, our author is implicitly arguing that my grandfather owes his grandfather the ring he stole from him, but that when they both die, all bets are off between himself and myself regarding the return of this stolen property. But Horowitz gives no reason for believing that there is some sort of natural statute of limitations for crimes which calls justice to a complete halt when the specific victims and victimizers vanish from the scene.

Horowitz continues: "Jews do not receive reparations from Germany simply because they are Jews. Those who do were corralled into concentration camps and lost immediate family members or personal property. Nor have all Japanese-Americans received payments, but only those whom the government interned in camps and who had their property confiscated." Yes, this argument will suffice against the black "leaders" who argue for compensation for all people of a certain skin color, but it falls by the wayside as far as the more powerful libertarian case is concerned.

6. According to Horowitz, "Behind the reparations arguments lies the unfounded claim that all blacks in America suffer economically from the consequences of slavery." His "exhibit A" to the contrary is the case of wealthy blacks such as Oprah Winfrey. But this is not only insufficient to undermine the libertarian case; it doesn't even lay a glove on the case put forth by Jesse Jackson et al. Even the latter do not claim a transfer of wealth on the ground that blacks are poorer than whites; they do so out of (somewhat misguided) claims of *justice*. Is it not possible that rich people can be oppressed? It seems to be Horowitz's argument that this cannot occur; it deserves to be characterized, and rejected, as the "Oprah

Winfrey fallacy." This is part and parcel of the *left-wing* philosophy which sees the poor as impoverished because of the wealth of the rich,[25] of the view that the well-off cannot, by definition, be victims.

It matters not one whit how affluent is Oprah. If she is the great-granddaughter of a slave who worked on the XYZ plantation in Alabama, and she can prove this, then she is entitled, as a matter of libertarian law, and justice, not welfare statism, to a portion of that which she would have received from her great-grandparents upon their release from bondage, had full justice occurred at that time. Her "extraordinary achievement" does not at all "refute … the reparations argument," contrary to Horowitz. All of his discussion about the prosperous black middle class, and the underclass, and the relative success of "West Indian blacks in America (who) are also descended from slaves," is all beside the point. No one asked how rich were the Japanese Americans who had their property stolen, nor about the wealth of Jews in Germany. This was entirely irrelevant, and properly so. Why is it apropos in the case of blacks?

7. In this section Horowitz argues that black claims will be resented by other ethnic groups. This is but another red herring. We are here concerned with the *justice* of the claim for reparation, not what others will think of it.

8. Horowitz's next sally concerns the "'reparations' to blacks that have already been paid. Since the passage of the Civil Rights Acts and the advent of the Great Society in 1965, trillions of dollars in transfer payments have been made to African Americans, in the form of welfare benefits and racial preferences (in contracts, job placements, and educational admissions)—all under the rationale of redressing historical racial grievances."

This is not at all a bad argument against the case of the left-wing blacks for reparations. After all, they want taxpayers' money, and they have already had quite a bit of that.

However, it will not suffice against the libertarian claim. Yes, there were "transfer payments" galore, but not a penny of this was in the form

[25] Horowitz may have had "second thoughts" about some of his previous political economic philosophy, but, judging from his analytic framework in the present case, there are still vestiges of Marxism infecting his perspective.

of true reparations. This is because the latter can only come *from* the illegitimate holders of what is in effect stolen property, not from entirely innocent taxpayers as a whole, and none of these "transfers" came courtesy of the present owners of plantation grounds and buildings. Further, proper reparations can only go *to* the grandchildren of those were slaves. The welfare system fails as a candidate for reparations on both these grounds. In addition, the so-called Great Society payments actually harmed blacks, rather than help them. As Charles Murray[26] has shown, giving blacks money under provisos which discouraged the formation of their families only undermined their economic and social conditions. The Jews and the Japanese Americans were given reparations with no such strings attached. Why should blacks be any different, were these true reparations? Further, it was not only blacks who suffered from welfare: so did all recipients, of whatever hue.

9. Horowitz is also mistaken with regard to the relevance of "the debt blacks owe to America—to white Americans—for liberating them from slavery." Contrary to this author, the Civil War was *not* fought to end enslavement; it was undertaken in order to quell secession.[27] However, there is no doubt, as our author eloquently attests, that "there never was an anti-slavery movement until white Englishmen and Americans created one." That ought to put quite a spoke in the wheels of those who deride the culture and philosophy of "dead white males." But of what relevance is the fact that *some* whites acted in a manner which greatly benefitted blacks (e.g., the Union soldiers) to the claim that *other* whites (the grandchildren of plantation-owning slave holders) owe them a debt of reparations? Horowitz is free with his condemnation of "racism" against his interlocutors, but here it would appear he is guilty of this himself. That is, whites are not all alike. Some of them owe a debt to blacks for slavery; others actually helped blacks. But the latter only erases the former if, somehow, members of the same race (the white one, in this case) are interchangeable. And I take this implicit claim to be incorrect and objectionably racist.

---

[26] Murray, Charles, Losing Ground: American Social Policy from 1950 to 1980, New York: Basic Books, 1984.

[27] Hummel, Jeffrey Rogers, Emancipating Slaves, Enslaving Free Men: A History of the American Civil War, Chicago: Open Court, 1996.

10. According to Horowitz, "The final and summary reason for rejecting any reparations claim is recognition of the enormous privileges black Americans enjoy as Americans, and therefore of their own stake in America's history, slavery and all."

What are these "privileges"? If they are the ability to participate in a (semi-) free enterprise system, then they are rights, not privileges. If this refers to the disproportionate number of blacks on welfare, or who have benefited from programs such as affirmative action, then these are not privileges either; they are rights violations. In either case, however, how do these benefits relieve the whites who are now in possession of the farm grounds and buildings from their responsibilities to give up their ill-gotten gains?

Our author warns "the African-American community [against] isolat[ing] itself even further from America [for this] would be to embark on a course whose consequences are troublesome even to contemplate. Yet the black community has had a long-running flirtation with separatists and nationalists in its ranks, who must be called what they are: racists who want African-Americans to have no part of America's multiethnic social contract."

But what is so wrong with separatism? If blacks wish to isolate themselves from Horowitz and his ilk, that is, whites, it is their right. Does this author believe in forced integration with unwilling blacks? Are we to have school busing again, only this time with an impetus from a different direction? Will he oppose black secession, if that is what (some) blacks want? And if so, on what ground? Does he not believe in freedom of association, which would allow blacks (or anyone else) to withdraw from unwanted social (or other) contact?

And which "social contract," pray tell, is he referring to? Did anyone ever sign this contract? If not, why is it incumbent upon anyone to respect it? According to libertarian law, the only thing that all people must respect is the persons and property of everyone else. Anything more is made up by Horowitz as he goes along.

Yes, many of the leftists who urge reparations to all blacks from all non-black US taxpayers are admirers of "Fidel Castro, one of the world's longest-surviving and most sadistic dictators." But this does not by one iota denigrate the rights of the black grandchildren of slaves to compensation from the white grandchildren of slave owners, for the property and value created through this brutal human chattel system.

States Horowitz: "For all their country's faults, African-Americans have an enormous stake in America and above all in the heritage that men like Jefferson helped to shape. This heritage—enshrined in America's founding and the institutions and ideas to which it gave rise—is what is really under attack in the reparations movement." But this is a non sequitur of the highest order. Just because some advocates of reparations couple their demands with anti-Americanism does not at all mean that their goal is not justified; it does not mean that all arguments for reparations must be coupled with a denigration of this country. Certainly, that applies to the libertarian case.

Unfair?

The thought will perhaps occur to some that I have been unfair to Horowitz. After all, here he is criticizing the argument for reparations from all (non-black) citizens to all blacks, coupled with a healthy dose of socialism and anti-Americanism, and I am attacking him for overlooking the possibility that reparations from some whites to some blacks are justified. It might appear that I am guilty of launching a bit of an intellectual ambush upon this author.

I plead innocent of these charges. Horowitz is not merely rejecting one version of reparations; he is attacking the entire concept. I join with him for the most part, of course, in his dismissal of the case put forth by Randall Robinson, Jesse Jackson, John Conyers, Henry Louis Gates, Dorothy Lewis, Hannibal Afrik, Albert Thornton, and numerous professors of black "studies." But it is Horowitz's view that, having dealt with these straw men, he has demolished the entire argument for reparations. He has not, and this was the burden of my reply to him. Horowitz simply cannot be allowed to maintain, as he does, that his devastation of a weak and faulty case for reparations undermines all argument for this conclusion. And his unwarranted attack upon the rich, his mistaken embrace of what I have characterized as the Oprah Winfrey fallacy, must be addressed. This is no ambush, but rather a measured reply to an essay which in many ways is correct, but also contains numerous and grave flaws.

Objections

Let us consider a series of objections to the foregoing, some of which might be launched by Horowitz, others not.

1. "Most land in the south was stolen by carpetbaggers. Why wouldn't they owe compensation? Suppose the carpetbagger stole the land from the guilty slave owner, and then sold it to its present owner. Surely, the present owner would escape liability in this case."

If the carpetbagger (or his heirs, to whom he gave his ill-gotten gains) can be located, then the grandchildren of the slave have no case against the present occupier, but instead must obtain their compensation from the grandchildren of the carpetbagger. However, suppose, as is more likely, that the carpetbagger and his brood have vanished without a trace. Then we have only the grandchild of the slave, and the present (innocent) owner. The question is, which of them is the legitimate title holder? The libertarian answer is clear: the property must go to its rightful owner, the children of the slave.

According to Rothbard[28]: "suppose that a title to property is clearly identifiable as criminal, does this necessarily mean that the current possessor must give it up? No, not necessarily. For that depends upon two considerations: (a) whether the victim (the property owner originally aggressed against) or his heirs are clearly identifiable and can now be found; or (b) whether or not the current possessor is himself the criminal who stole the property. Suppose, for example, that Jones possesses a watch, and that we can clearly show that Jones's title is originally criminal, either because (1) his ancestor stole it, or (2) because he or his ancestor purchased it from a thief (whether wittingly or unwittingly is immaterial here). Now, if we can identify and find the victim or his heir, then it is clear that Jones's title to the watch is totally invalid, and that it must promptly revert to its true and legitimate owner. Thus, if Jones inherited or purchased the watch from a man who stole it from Smith,

---

[28] Rothbard, Murray N., The Ethics of Liberty, New York: New York University Press (1998 [1982], pp. 57–58); for more on the libertarian theory of private property rights, see Hoppe, Hans-Hermann, A Theory of Socialism and Capitalism: Economics, Politics and Ethics, Boston: Kluwer, 1989; Hoppe, Hans-Hermann, The Economics and Ethics of Private Property: Studies in Political Economy and Philosophy, Boston: Kluwer, 1993.

and if Smith or the heir to his estate can be found, then the title to the watch properly reverts back to Smith or his descendants, without compensation to the existing possessor of the criminally derived 'title.' "

In the context of our example, Jones is the present owner of the land, the carpetbagger is the thief, and Smith is the grandchild of the slave. To allow Jones to keep his land in the face of proof from Smith that he is the rightful owner is to not uphold legitimacy in private property rights; it is to denigrate it. If A is the rightful owner, B steals property from A, sells it to C, and then disappears, there is only one correct answer to the question of who should keep it, according to libertarianism: A. C is out of luck, unless he can somehow locate B.

2. "If a person is an unjust owner, can he legitimately bequeath his property? No. If not, then he cannot properly sell it either. Thus, the libertarian search for the successor of the original (and rightful) owner will also have to include those who purchased the land. Every land transaction after 1860 will have to be declared null and void. And why stop with 1860, since that date is arbitrarily based on the beginning of the war? In theory, there is nothing to preclude the requirement from going back in history until the beginning of time."

This sounds like a telling criticism of the libertarian theory of property rights, but it is not. Again we call upon Rothbard (1998, p. 57) to elucidate: "if we do not know if Jones's title to any given property is criminally derived, then we may assume that this property was, at least momentarily, in a state of non ownership … and therefore that the proper title of ownership reverted instantaneously to Jones as its 'first' (i.e., current) possessor and user. In short, where we are not sure about a title but it cannot be clearly identified as criminally derived, then the title properly and legitimately reverts to its current possessor."

The point is, the libertarian theory is actually a very conservative one, not at all calling for research in property titles back to the dawn of history. Unless proven otherwise, every extant property title is to be considered legitimate. The burden of proof, that is, rests squarely on the shoulders of those who wish to *overturn* duly registered property. If there is any historical research to be undertaken, it must be done by those who wish to refute already accepted claims, not those who wish to defend them.

In sum, this objection puts things in the exact opposite position from where they are, as far as practicality is concerned. It misconstrues the burden of proof.

3. "The white Southerners who permitted blacks to live on their land should not be held more responsible for reparations than Northerners who refused to even allow blacks to pass through their borders."

There are several problems here. First, it is not the case that before the Civil War slavery was confined to the South; yes, it predominated there, but this section of the country had no monopoly over the "curious institution." Second, compare all those who engaged in slavery vs. all those who did not, but would not allow blacks entry into their territory. Surely the former would be regarded by all, not just libertarians, as by far the more serious crime. That is, kidnapping is a major violation of human rights, while prohibiting immigration is at best only a minor one.[29] If so, then if heavy reparations are due to those who were enslaved, only light ones are due to those who were forcibly prevented from engaging in immigration.

4. "The slave owners fed and sheltered their property. These expenses should be offset against any debt owed by their progeny to the grandchildren of slaves. With any reasonable discount rate, since so many years have already passed, there will be little or nothing due to the children of slaves in reparations."

Suppose I kidnap you and keep you prisoner for a year. Whereupon I am caught by the forces of law and order, and argue, in my defense, mitigation in that I fed and sheltered you for this duration of time. This should be dismissed out of hand. For had I not fed and sheltered you in this context, I would have been guilty of the more serious crime of murder. That I am "only" charged with kidnapping results from the fact that at least I did keep you alive during your period of capture. In other words, feeding and housing you does indeed mitigate the charge of *murder*. But, as I am not being charged with that crime, only with kidnapping, this

[29] For a libertarian debate on whether immigration laws are per se criminal, see *Journal of Libertarian Studies: An Interdisciplinary Review*, Vol. 13, No. 2, summer 1998. If true, then all those who can prove that their grandparents would have immigrated to a given country have a reparations case under libertarian law not against all citizens of that nation, but only against the grandchildren of those few people specifically responsible for this law.

offset has already been made. To put this in the parlance of accounting, this objection incorporates the fallacy of double counting.

5. "White landowners paid freed blacks a form of private welfare after their emancipation. Many former masters allowed former slaves to stay on their land, and fed them too, as a matter of charity. These monies should be subtracted from any reparations owed."

The difficulty with this objection is that there were two separate acts—one of slaveholding, the other of charity—and it is not clear that the two are connected in any way. Let us return to the case where my grandfather stole a ring from your grandfather. In addition to this act of theft, this ancestor of mine also gave some charity to your grandfather. Does the second act mitigate the first? Not at all. Were my grandfather hauled into court on charges of stealing a ring from your grandfather, it would avail him nothing in defense, nor should it, that in a completely separate incident, he acted charitably toward your grandfather.

So, charity will not do. However, there is a kernel of truth in this objection, in that while mere charity will not suffice, reparations will. That is, had my grandfather given yours money not as an act of charity, but out of contrition and reparations, then and only then would this count in ameliorating the debt I now owe you.

Let us now return to the slave reparations case. Suppose that Oprah Winfrey can prove her great-grandfather was a slave on the XYZ plantation, and that the descendants of this owner owe her $x. Then from this, using the same rate of discount, should be subtracted whatever reparations—not charity—the master of XYZ gave to her ancestor. However, it should be noted that the burden of proof is now reversed. Oprah has, let us say, satisfied her burden of proof. But now the present holders of the XYZ lands, whoever they are, must prove that the original owner supported his ex-slaves not as a matter of charity, but out of a motive of repatriating money owed to them. If so, then the one can indeed be an offset against the other.

6. "The whites in the U.S. who bought the slaves purchased them not from freedom but from slavery, the state in which they were found in Africa. Shouldn't the original enslavers, then, bear a great deal of the burden? Perhaps there should be a search through the tribal history of Africa to discover the identities of all the descendants of enslavers dating back centuries?"

This is meant as a reductio ad absurdum of the libertarian position. The proper answer is to take the bull by the horns and accept the premise: yes, if the black slave catchers in Africa who first captured the slaves who were later to be sent to the United States can be identified, then the money they left to their grandchildren would become vulnerable to a lawsuit brought by the grandchildren of these US slaves. This is meant to sound preposterous, but instead it has all the earmarks of a just solution. Libertarian law cares not at all for the color of a person's skin. If he is a slave master, of whatever race, he is guilty of the crime of slave holding or slave capturing.

7. "Many blacks, after the war, were drafted into the army and sent west to slaughter Indians. Public slavery in effect replaced private slavery. Why focus on crimes further back in time rather than crimes more recent in time?"

There are several difficulties with this objection. For one thing, while a military draft and slavery are both crimes against humanity, there are surely relevant differences. For another, the answer to the question of which crimes to pursue, earlier or later ones, is "both." Just because the US government drafted newly freed blacks to kill Indians (for which compensation is due, from those responsible) does not for a minute allow a free ride to those guilty of earlier crimes. Libertarian punishment theory is a timeless concept. It matters not when or where or why a crime was committed. If it can be proven, there is a case for pursuing the victimizers, and for turning over the fruits of the crime to their rightful owners.

8. "The demand for slavery reparations is a diversion to put all Americans—black, white, brown—off their guard as tax slavery emerges on a global scale."

"It sounds farfetched, but hear my tale. Consider first how nonsensical is the reparations argument. Whites, none of whom are or were slave owners, would be making transfer payments to blacks, none of whom are or were slaves.

"Not even a 'sins of the fathers' rationale justifies race reparations. A majority of white Americans are descendants of people who immigrated to these shores after slavery had come to an end. Similarly, many blacks are descendants of people who arrived in the United States in the post-slavery era. Indeed, the millions of "preferred minorities" who have arrived in the last three decades are legally privileged compared to native born whites.

"To find descendants of slave owners and descendants of slaves would require more extensive racial genealogies than Nazi Germany and South Africa were able to assemble for their race-based policies. And how would we classify people with ancestors in both camps? Would they pay reparations to themselves? Would descendants of black slave owners pay reparations?"[30]

There is a difficulty with Roberts's characterization of taxes as akin to slavery, or, worse, an instance of it. A more accurate description of taxation is not slavery but theft. Both the tax gatherer and the holdup man demand money from you against your will. In contrast, the kidnapper and the enslaver, but neither the tax-man nor the robber, take over your physical body—if you give in to their demands. An objection might be that the tax collector comes to you at the behest of a majority vote, and offers services in return for the money he mulcts from you. Neither suffices. First, assume that not one but *two* highwaymen accost you, demanding your money. When you demur on grounds of democracy (they are philosophical thieves and are willing to discourse with you) they hold an election as to whether you should keep your money or give it to them, and they win by a majority two to one vote. The point is, you have not *agreed* to be part of this "election," no more than you have consented to be part of the "robber gang called the U.S. government."[31] Second, posit that these stickup men offer the "service" of giving you a paper clip in return for your money. Again, the point is not whether those who take your money by force give you something in return, but whether or not you have assent to the deal.

There are problems, too, with Roberts's dismissal of the arguments for reparations to today's blacks for the enslavement of their ancestors. First, I am not arguing this case on the basis of "sins of the fathers." Rather, reparations are justified because of "sins of the sons," namely, not giving up the property they never should have received from their sinning fathers

---

[30] Roberts, Paul Craig, "Taxing Away Freedoms," TownHall.Com Columnists, 7/21/01. See http://www.townhall.com/columnists/paulcraigroberts/pcr20010719.shtml, accessed on 7/21/01.

[31] See Spooner, Lysander, No Treason, Larkspur, Colorado, (1870) 1966).

in the first place, to the sons of those from whom it was stolen. This is a subtle difference, but an important one nonetheless.

Further, if indeed it is true that reparations would "require more extensive racial genealogies than Nazi Germany and South Africa were able to assemble for their race-based policies," so what. Perhaps we can do better than those two countries, genealogical-wise. And if we cannot, this is *still* not an argument against the *justice* of reparations, as maintained by Roberts, but only of the inability of the sons of slaves to prove their case. Based on the principle that "possession is nine tenths of the law," these disputed properties would stay in the hands of the white grandchildren of slave owners.

And last but not least, the phenomenon of mixed race children placed no insuperable barrier to our analysis. For it is unlikely in the extreme that any slave master would have given his *black* children any of his land or possessions. If so, then there will be no *black* descendants of slave owners who owe other children of slaves any reparations. But let us suppose that this is indeed the case. That is, Mr. X, the mixed race child of a white male slave owner and a black female slave,[32] is given some land by his father, which he duly hands down to his own descendants. These particular blacks would have no case for reparations in the present day since, by stipulation, they have *already* been given them. Roberts's problem is that he is analyzing the argument for reparations as if it is made on a racial basis. While this is indeed true for some proponents of this program,[33] this certainly does not apply to libertarianism.

[32] The opposite case is a possible, albeit less historically likely, occurrence.

[33] For example, see Robinson, op. cit.

11

Reparations, Once Again

I. Introduction

In this chapter we attempt to sketch out the libertarian view of reparations. Briefly, it is that reparations for slavery are indeed justified, but must be limited. The only justified recipients are the heirs of the slaves, not, for example, all black people now living in the United States. The only justified donors are the (mainly white) heirs of the slave masters, who never should have inherited wealth that did not properly belong to their parents; it would be improper to force, for example, all white people now living in the United States to pay reparations. This is at stark contrast to those on the right who oppose all reparations, and to those on the left who favor a far more unrestrained notion of reparations. In section "II. Philosophy" we give arguments in support of these contentions. Section "III. Objections" is devoted to responding to a series of objections to our thesis. We conclude in section "IV. Conclusion".

W. E. Block, *Property Rights*, Palgrave Studies in Classical Liberalism,
https://doi.org/10.1007/978-3-030-28353-7_11

II. Philosophy

In our view, which is based upon adherence to private property rights (Block, 1990; Hoppe, 1993; Locke, 1948; Paul, 1987; Rothbard, 1973, 32; Rozeff, 2005), reparations for past wrongs such as slavery and land theft are justified. States Block (2002, p. 54) in this regard: "Justified reparations are nothing more and nothing less than the forced return of stolen property—even after significant amount of time has passed. For example, if my grandfather stole a ring from your grandfather, and then bequeathed it to me through the intermediation of my father, then I am, presently, the illegitimate owner of that piece of jewelry. To take the position that reparations are always and forever unjustified is to give the imprimatur to theft, provided a sufficient time period has elapsed."

In 1865, at the close of the War to Prevent Southern Secession,[1] all slave masters should have been punished, retroactively, for the crime of slave holding.[2] They should have been enslaved, and their newly freed ex-slaves should have been set up as their new owners. Needless to say, the land and other property of the (mainly)[3] white ex–slave owners should have been given over to the new black slave owners, since a slave cannot own anything, but must give all his property to his master.

What, then, should be done at the present time in this regard? We are long past the time when full justice can be meted out to antebellum slave owners. But the land and other physical property that should have been turned over to the ex–black slaves went instead to the (mainly) white children of the slave holders. These people are totally and completely innocent of the crime of slave holding. It is impermissible to hold the

---

[1] There are some who call the "unpleasantness" of 1861 a "civil war." They are greatly mistaken. See on this Adams, 2000; Block, 2002a, 2002b, DiLorenzo, 2006; Gordon, 1998; Kreptul, 2003; McGee, 1994a, 1994b; Rothbard, 1967.

[2] Some might object that this constitutes ex post facto law. We support such law. We are not legal positivists (for a critique of this obnoxious doctrine, see Barnett, 1978; Groudine, 1980; Rothbard, 1998 [1982], 178; Simpson, 1987). Just because slavery was legal under the laws of the United States does not mean this conformed to a higher law, libertarian law, according to which it is impermissible for one person to forcibly enslave another. The case against ex post facto law is a weak one. Indeed, the Nuremberg Trials were based on a denial of the validity of this type of law.

[3] There were a few black slaveholders.

children responsible for the crimes of their parents. However, the land that was bequeathed to them from their slave holding parents was in effect stolen property, stolen from the slave who worked on the land. This, in justice, never should have been given to them in the first place.

Thus, any (black) grandchild of a slave should be free to demonstrate that his grandfather worked at thus and such a plantation, and thus is entitled to a pro rata share of those land holdings. This is the premise from which we begin our analysis.

Because of past wrongs—like slavery—does the government owe something to a certain group, such as black people? We answer in the negative. Certainly there is little doubt that the state directly facilitated slavery. But, were the government to discharge this obligation through taxation,[4] it would inevitably ensnare within its net all sorts of people who by no extent of the imagination were responsible for the forcible employment of human beings. For example, there are US citizens who only entered the country long after slavery ended. Were the government to give these reparations to all black people, again, injustice will be perpetrated, for many such recipients, also, are new entrants to the country.

How, then, should this repayment be funded? Reparations, at their root, should be based on property rights, that is, returning stolen property to its rightful owners, not retribution. Yet most debate seems to center on retribution, and why it is justified, or not.[5]

Before we attempt to place concepts like reparations into a consistent, logical, and moral context, let us examine the fact regarding the only method available to the state for securing money—theft. Frederic Bastiat (1962), in his pamphlet *The Law*, puts state-sponsored theft, which he refers to as "plunder," into scientific terms when he says:

> When a portion of wealth is transferred from the person who owns it, without his consent, and without compensation, whether by force or fraud,

[4] However, it would be entirely justified to seize the wealth improperly bequeathed to the heirs of the specific government officials responsible for slavery—the politicians and bureaucrats—and return these to the (black) heirs of the slaves.

[5] Earl Ofari Hutchinson has also answered (see: http://alternet.org/story/10680/) David Horowitz directly, although his analysis rests upon the type of statist premises that run counter to libertarian law.

to someone who does not own it, then I say that property is violated and an action of plunder is committed.

If someone stole something from you, having the state steal from someone altogether different does not really solve the problem, does it? And if the state robbed—or more accurately, allowed someone else to pilfer—something from your ancestors, does it make sense for them to now steal something from everyone else and give it to you? Not at all. All that said, and despite anything David Horowitz[6] (2000) might say, reparations are a legitimate issue.[7]

The question is not *if* the debt is owed. The questions are from whom it is owed, to whom it should be paid, and how best to fund that repayment. But in no case is it justified for the state to tax everyone so that some can get their property back, no matter how often this has been done in the past. That is so, unless we seek to place ourselves at the trough of stolen spoils the state necessarily creates. We have no desire to perpetuate theft, even for reasons as compelling as the debt based on slavery. Ironically, once one embraces the logic of property rights, the arguments against reparations cease to be reasonable from any reasonable perspective. It is a simple matter of proper assignment and recovery. But it does not involve the state—at least not in the form of taxation. The state cannot properly be used as tool of theft, even for ostensibly just reasons.

III. Objections

#1. Unique

Slavery was unique in American history. The limited reparations justified by libertarianism do not even begin to address the enormity of the problem.

---

[6] For criticisms of Horowitz (2000), although from very different perspectives, see Arceneaux (2005) and Block (2002).

[7] However, after reading *Twelve Years a Slave*, by Northup (1997), we were so incensed that we could easily empathize with those blacks who wanted to go out and extract a little personal repayment for themselves.

On the contrary, while the scope of chattel slavery was indeed large, the current population of people who have direct ancestry to either group, slave owners or slaves, represents a rather small proportion of the US population.[8] The argument for the enormity, then, is based upon the moral (and, frankly, libertarian) laws that slavery broke. Yet we herein are advocating a direct action that encompasses all the current descendants of slavery and the current value of that which was stolen from them. This action fully encompasses any "enormity" that can be reasonably expressed.

But further, this is not a contest we are now engaged in; however horrendous, slavery was not a unique event, calling for special laws. We are suggesting that we adopt a logical legal process and apply it to all issues consistently. Reparations based on slavery are to be sure a challenge for the law. But it is no more than part and parcel of the general law applying to the return of stolen property. Jurisprudence, here, it must be readily admitted, is complicated by the passage of much time since the original theft took place. But there is no doubt that just law will ignore this happenstance to the extent possible, and focus its attention on the issue just as it would in any other case of the return of stolen property.

Reparations for slavery are an excellent issue to examine because the amount of writing about it is plentiful[9] and the emotional baggage about it is rather full-figured. But, it is just an example of how the law of private property rights could be applied to a specific issue. We concede that under our plan there may be folks who will not get justice, whatever that may mean to them. But a simple application of first principles shows that consistent and universal justice will not be obtained from any state-sponsored approach either. The only result will be that injustice will be further exacerbated: other innocents, in addition to the great-grandchildren of slaves, will share in the unfairness.

[8] According to the 2000 US Census, the total number of African Americans is approximately 34,000,000 and the total population of the United States is approximately 281,000,000. This is 12.1%. Similarly, the total population of slaves in the United States in 1860 was approximately 4,000,000 and the total population of the United States was approximately 31,000,000, which is 12.7%. It seems clear that the 31,000,000 today are not all descended from the 4,000,000 from history. In other words, simply following the chain of familial connection, as the authors suggest, will account for all who are due payment.

[9] America, 1993; Arceneaux, 2005; Bittker, 1972; Horowitz, 2000, 2002; Robinson, 1998, 2000, 2002; Westley, 1998.

#2. An Apology Would Be Sufficient

Some may say, "if [pick your favorite mistreated racial group] could just get an honest apology from [pick your favorite mistreater of racial groups] that would mean *something*, would it not?" Not to put too fine a point on this, but the last time we participated in that pageant of American splendor known as commerce very little could be obtained in exchange for a heartfelt apology. (It could be that we shop in the wrong places, but we doubt it.) No, apologies avail nothing. Black people in 1865 should have obtained justice, restitution, 40 acres and a mule, and so on,[10] via conventional (and logical and moral) civil means. Their children are entitled to the present value of these benefits, to the extent they can demonstrate familial connection with slaves. And this wealth should come from those children and grandchildren of the slave owners, not from anyone else. Symbolic gestures such as apologies are for politicians, and at this point it should be pretty apparent what our views are in that regard.

#3. Why Does the Black Grandchild of the Slave Have to Prove Familial Connection?

This objection asks for the default position: from where do we start? This is very well established not only in libertarian law, but even in the mainstream: possession is nine-tenths of the law. The burden of proof is always and ever on he who would overturn extant property rights, even "when we know," or think we know, where justice lies in any one case. That is precisely for the courts to decide. Further, in stark contrast to all non-libertarian proposals for reparations, we seek to restrict both the payment and the receipt to only those who were directly involved. Proving familial connection therefore provides a ready barrier to any who might attempt

[10] The "40 acres and a mule" in our view was a rough approximation of what each slave would have been entitled to, on average, in 1865, under the libertarian legal code. Further, historical references speak directly to freed slaves being granted this sum as "payment" for their (immoral) incarceration. Ironically, although the US government of the time promised this sum to ex-slaves, it was never paid.

to feed themselves at any perceived trough of good fortune simply because they are of African descent.[11]

#4. Fair Race

In a fair race, all contestants line up at the same starting point, and since current descendants of slaves have endured not only the thievery, but also relatively poor economic position because of it, simply recovering property would be insufficient.

If we all *know* that the current societal set-up is a *direct result* of the thievery perpetrated on black people, how can we possibly start "fresh" now, even assuming we can assign proper ownership and transfer possession? This is a seminal question for black folk, because we all know that the scales were not initially balanced. In some sense, geographical, we were all at the same "starting" point, but some of us had whips in our hands, and others of us had our hands and feet in chains. If we start a new, fair race with such a historical deficit, how can anyone think this scenario is a fair one? In other words, is it really possible to simply transfer ownership now and call things "all square"? Our answer is that this is the only option available that is both just and conforming to libertarian law.

Even though mistakes were made and unfair advantages have been given to some, in a fair race, eventually, the better runner wins. Look at the example of American sports. For years, black folk were categorically and racially locked out of basketball, baseball, football, and so on. At present, however, black people are everywhere (on the field at least) and no one thinks it unusual. Certainly we cannot repay the debt to those who did not get their "shot" historically, but judging on the basis of how things are now, we have a good idea of what the situation would have been even then, a century and a half ago. Consider black quarterbacks in the NFL. Now they are so plentiful that almost no one can remember when it was commonly believed that black men didn't have the capacity to make the requisite split-second decisions. Can we go back in time and "make it right" for those men who *should have* gotten a fair shot but did

[11] Here, we explicitly adopt the default position that, unless matters can be shown otherwise, the natural progression is for parents to make their children their heirs.

not? No. But this is an argument, at least, for a more liberal interpretation of reparations than that offered by the libertarian.

There is a deeper insight in his question: "How can we just say, 'let's start now' when we *know* that the race would begin with some having an advantage based upon what their ancestors stole from them?" Consider the parable of a distance race being run on a track. One competitor is at the starting line for his race, ready to go. His opponent is at an entirely different starting line, some distance, maybe even over half the distance around the track behind that first runner. Looking at this scenario, there are several valid questions one could ask, which might include, although not be limited to:

1. Is this a fair race?
2. How can the competitor with the deficit be expected to compete?
3. Does not the fact of the race set-up virtually guarantee the outcome?

Here is our response to this very interesting objection: The analogy between life and a race can be pushed too far. Life is a positive-sum game; a track race is a zero-sum game. Everyone can "win" in the former case, each foot race has only one winner; the others are losers. Furthermore, the answer to questions 2 and 3 above would, maybe surprisingly, not be what might otherwise be obvious. For example, if either of the present authors was placed "ahead" of an Olympic marathoner in the second case, there is little doubt that no (reasonable) lead would likely be enough! Similarly, the same could be said for scenario three. Simply put, there are many, many set-ups that, while placing the present authors at an ostensible advantage, would most assuredly not guarantee them a win. In essence then, if the race is long enough, the better runner will almost always win.

However, we do not think that the libertarian goal is to start at the same starting point; this can never be achieved, in any case. Michael Jordan was born with springs in his legs; is this fair? Is he on the same starting line as the rest of us at least in terms of basketball? Of course not. So what? All this is irrelevant to justice. The libertarian goal is only to uphold private property rights, and, in this case, to return stolen property to its rightful owner. The aim here is not to start everyone on the same starting line, or to equalize opportunity, whatever that is. The aim here is the simple return of stolen property. We leave the race afterward up to those who wish to participate.

In any case, even assuming some sort of egalitarianism as the proper goal, land accounts for only some 10% of GDP (labor accounts for some 75%). So, what we are talking about here has to be kept in proportion. Far better for today's poor people to stop the theft against them that is still taking place, than to redress past injustices. But that is merely an economic argument, perhaps to be ignored. The justice of the matter is that past wrongs must be righted. But if so, the default position is present ownership, not starting lines in a supposed track race.

#5. Economic Disruption

Reparations of the sort advocated by libertarians would disrupt our economy. There would be vast transfers of property, if enacted. This would hurt the poor.

The libertarian position on reparations is very radical in theory, but rather conservative in practice, at least the further back one goes in history. For, if the presumption against present land ownership is to be overturned, evidence is required. And this is harder to come by the further back in history we must go, even apart from the fact that the more years ago, the less likely there is to be a written language in many cases. More importantly however, what we would establish, in the best-case scenario for the libertarian solution, is the current proper ownership of real property. No *a priori* assessment can therefore be made about either the socio-economic status of those from whom property is lawfully taken or those by whom property is lawfully acquired. We judge any ostensible danger to the poor as a red herring.

#6. Democratic Rejection

Reparations are unjustified, since our democracy has, at least so far, rejected them.

First, the previous actions of a state are irrelevant in regard to what may have happened that is in obvious conflict with libertarian law. Second, it is false to state that "our democracy has, at least so far, rejected them" unless one is speaking specifically about reparations to blacks for slavery. In the aftermath of World War II, Japan also had to pay reparations. The United States administered removal of capital goods from Japan, and the USSR seized Japanese assets in the former puppet state of Manchukuo. Further, again according to Hutchinson, "the U.S. government has shelled out billions since the 1960s to pay for resettlement, job training, education, and health programs for refugees fleeing Communist repression."[12]

More directly, though, democracy is hardly the be all and end all of justice. For example, if 51 men voted that rape is okay, and passed a law stating so, would that make the 49 men who thought it should be illegal somehow incorrect? Would that make the claims of the women who were molested after the law was passed less viable? Certainly not. Slavery, too, for that matter, persisted under democratic institutions. That hardly justifies the "curious institution." Thus, despite the absence of a plebiscite allowing it, the people who were wronged due to slavery, that is, the heirs of the slaves, have just cause to seek restitution. Period. The debate should be about *how* they should seek it, not *if* they may properly do so.

#7. Favor

Blacks do not deserve any reparations since whites did them a favor by kidnapping their ancestors, bringing them to the New World in chains, and then, subsequently, freeing them. The proof of this is that the black descendants of slaves are much better off, economically, socially, and in every other way, than the descendants of the African blacks who were not enslaved in the United States.

This is an oft-used argument that is, frankly, based upon a false premise. Simply put, it matters not one whit how the folks who were left in Africa fared since the time black people were kidnapped. How could it?

[12] "Ten Reasons for Reparations," Earl Ofari Hutchinson (2001), http://alternet.org/story/10680/.

Suppose A kidnaps B today, and feeds, clothes, and educates him, and so on. Subsequently, B's descendant grows up to be a world championship golfer. This happy occurrence does *nothing* to mitigate the original crime. Yes, it cannot be denied, this is a better result than what usually eventuates with kidnapping. But this objection is like trying to categorize a kidnapper as a Good Samaritan because it is later found out that had he not kidnapped his victim, a car would have hit her! This is highly problematic. The original crime is a free-standing event—against the most basic of libertarian laws: the sanctity of the human person. The subsequent history, full of twists and turns, is something else entirely.

#8. Black Slavemasters

Blacks do not deserve reparations for slavery since black Africans first enslaved other black Africans and sold them to the white slavers for the middle passage. As well, in the United States, some blacks owned other blacks as slaves.

Certainly, the issue is complex. One could argue that the tribal chiefs who took part in the original seizure of natives for sale to slave ships in Africa are culpable as well. Libertarian law is perfectly indifferent to skin color or epoch. It asks only if uninvited border crossings have taken place, and, if they have, it urges compensation. It may well be that the descendants of these African tribal chiefs, and of the black slave owners in the United States, owe a debt to the great-grandchildren of slaves. If this can be demonstrated, then reparations will be (partially) an intra-black matter. But, none of these considerations mitigates, even in the slightest, the claim that reparations are still owed by the descendants of white slave masters to their contemporaries who are the children of their black slaves. If a contemporary black person *knows and can demonstrate* the identity of the person who owned his great-great-grandfather, and, as well, the plantation on which he worked,[13] and wishes to sue for ownership of part of this land, and so on that he worked but that they inherited, libertarian law would support him.

[13] This applies to the senior author of this chapter.

Another version of this objection states that not only were slaves kidnapped by other blacks but also that since they did not actually own the land upon which they were held, and would not have, even had they been free, the return of the "stolen property" requires some type of complicated calculation. This objection represents at best a red herring for two main reasons. First of all, if libertarian law supports reparations, the complexity of the calculations is at best a secondary issue. Second, if libertarian law does not support reparations, the complexity of the calculations is irrelevant.

As an example, if one of the authors kidnaps someone, but eventually relinquishes "ownership" of that hostage via an exchange of money, is the recipient somehow exonerated of kidnapping as well? Of course not. And if that recipient takes that "living investment" and uses it in trade or direct business, was that money not still obtained unlawfully? Of course it was! Clearly, the secondary owner of the slave, the white plantation owner who made this purchase from the original African owner, is no less a law-breaker than the original seller of the slave.

The issue of multiple sales is thus another red herring. Simply stated, this is irrelevant. If the original kidnapper can be found or, more accurately, his descendants, he simply becomes an *additional* defendant, not a *replacement* defendant in either the civil suit or the dispute arbitration. The lawfulness of reparations under a libertarian paradigm is thus unaffected by this objection.

To the issue of value, positing arguendo that it is more than a secondary issue, standard financial calculations could be used to determine the value of the "property" involved. (As an aside, there was a time when conviction of kidnapping resulted in the death penalty, just like murder. It would therefore seem rather obvious that the taking of someone's freedom would be substantially more valuable than any "40 acres and a mule" that the slaves were supposedly promised after freedom was finally given.) It seems entirely that the value of the slaves relative to the value of the plantations where they worked must be proportional to one another otherwise selecting how many slaves to obtain for a plantation would have involved guessing versus economic considerations.[14]

[14] For the claim that, despicable though it was, slavery was run in a "business-like" manner, see Fogel and Engerman (1974).

Stated another way, if the land could have been successfully worked without the slaves, having them would have made little sense. Certainly every plantation did not have an identical number of slaves, ergo; there was a relatively simple and direct proportionality to the size of the plantation and the number of slaves needed and owned, abstracting from weather, terrain, and so on. If the size of the plantation required a certain number of slaves, then the amount due each slave would seem rather easy to compute. But these types of questions are for the courts to decide, and for the plaintiff to pursue. This chapter sets a libertarian framework for *why* the suit can be brought. It does not seek to determine, precisely, what the amount(s) of those damages should be.

#9. Non-constitutional

Blacks do not deserve reparations for slavery since neither the Constitution, nor our present laws, provide for any such legal remedy.

There are several problems here. First of all, the state's decision that something is illegal is entirely irrelevant to libertarian law. Governments have prohibited numerous personal and economic liberties since time immemorial. That does not make their acts licit.[15] Slavery (kidnapping followed by forced labor) is not wrong because of the constitution or the opinion of some human being with a black robe! With due respect to the judiciary law is above man, not man above law. Slavery is wrong, like stealing is wrong, like murder is wrong—regardless of what the folks with guns and power say. The rightness of what we can properly do to each other exists outside the parameters of what some document says, no matter how grandiose it might be. There is a higher law than the pretentious law of the constitution: libertarian law. Libertarianism bases law on the non-aggression axiom.

Suppose Congress, at the behest and advocacy of President Bush, now passes a law saying all left-handed red heads in the United States can be put to death. And, he proceeds to do just that. This is all entirely legal. It

[15] It is only a legal positivist who would equate government edicts with proper law. It is the task of the legislature to discern or discover just law. The obverse is simply not true, that whatever the legislators decree magically turns into proper law. See footnote 2, supra.

was passed by both houses of Congress. Only Ron Paul, we may suppose, voted against this new law. Still, this would be wrong. If Bush did this, he should be punished by law, even though what he did was legal. Ditto for slavery. Even though legal at the time, it still goes against libertarian law. The perpetrators of this should be punished. Property they illicitly passed on to their descendants should be taken away from them, if the rightful owners, the descendants of the slaves, can prove title. Reparations are based on this insight.

#10. Expansionist

Implementing any reparations solution via the laws of property in the courts would result a decidedly unlibertarian expansion of power by the courts.

This objection seems to assume that something as basic as dispute resolution must be eschewed by libertarians. This is highly problematic. In every manifestation of society envisioned, including the most anarchic possible, there will necessarily be disputes. As such, dispute resolution will be a necessity, unless men somehow turn into angels. This chapter simply explains why reparations could be pursued under a libertarian paradigm. It does not seek to *a priori* define every conceivable aspect of those proceedings. No analysis can possibly solve *every* possible problem, even related ones. There is such a thing as specialization and the division of labor in intellectual pursuits as there is in all others. The decision of whether those proceedings are civil, that is, handled in a court, or handled by an arbitrator, would occur in the aftermath of the adoption of the paradigm presented in this chapter.

We are confident, however, that these matters can be handled, since again, we place reparations in the arena of dispute resolution, where it rightfully belongs. The details thereafter are at worst irrelevant or at best secondary to the larger question this chapter seeks to answer. (It is comforting, however, for these types of objections to be raised, since they only exist in the case where reparations can actually be pursued, exactly as this chapter justifies!) As one additional point of justification, if the details of a dispute such as the return of stolen property, even property spanning several generations, cannot be handled via a libertarian dispute resolution paradigm, the type of anarchic society suggested by market anarchy cannot exist anyway.

#11. Details

"Assume that before the Civil War Tom owned Blackacre and used slaves to work his land. Further assume that descendants of slaves who worked Blackacre are identified. How should reparations proceed in the following circumstances?

1. The current owner of Blackacre is Tom's great grandson.
2. Blackacre was sold right after the civil war but the money was used to buy Blueacre. Blueacre is owned by Tom's great grandson.
3. Tom sold Blackacre and lost the money in the financial markets.
4. Blackacre is currently owned by Tom's great grandson. 99% of Blackacre's market value comes from improvements made to it since the civil war.
5. Tom's great grandson sold Blackacre in 1990. He used the money to finance consumption."[16]

First, we object to the characterization of what went on in the United States between 1861 and 1865 as a "Civil War." It was no such thing. A civil war occurs when there are two contending parties, each of whom wishes to rule the totality of which both are part. The Spanish Civil War of 1936 was indeed a civil war in that the Fascists and the Communists each wanted to govern all of Spain. So was this the case in the Russian Revolution of 1917. The Reds and the Whites both wished to serve as political masters over the entire country. But in 1861, while the North did indeed desire to control the South, this was *not* reciprocated. The South aimed to secede from the North, not command it.

We now turn to a reply to the specifics:

---

[16] An unusually active, able, and insightful referee of This Journal posed this challenge to us. We are delighted to respond to these eminently sensible calls for clarification. Indeed, we mentally kick ourselves for not having anticipated him in this regard. Well, better late than never.

1. The current owner of Blackacre is Tom's great-grandson.

Any great-grandchild of a slave of Blackacre who can prove this should be able to sue Tom's great-grandson, and collect an amount proportional to the number of slaves who worked there. For example, if there were 100 slaves on that plantation, this black grandchild should be able to receive damages. But the burden of proof rests with the latter.

2. Blackacre was sold right after the Civil War but the money was used to buy Blueacre. Blueacre is owned by Tom's great-grandson.

Tom's son (grandson, great-grandson) never should have received Blackacre in the first place. He owes all of it to all the (grand)children of the slaves, as the latter should have been given the entire plantation in 1865 to divide among themselves. Surely, Tom should not be allowed to escape this debt by converting Blackacre to Blueacre. So, the grandchildren of the slaves will have to content themselves with a share of Blueacre instead of Blackacre, assuming equal value of the two. But, suppose Blueacre is worth far less than Blackacre. Say, the former was 10,000 acres and the latter 10 acres of homogeneous land. Then, obviously, Tom is trying to escape his debt. The children of the slaves have a right to come after Tom's progeny for the difference in value between the two, as well as to attach Blueacre.

3. Tom sold Blackacre and lost the money in the financial markets.

Justice will not be done, unless we assume a God's eye view, and can trace exactly the path of the money. The blacks will be out of luck. Who can they sue?

But take another case; hopefully, this will be regarded as a friendly amendment to the referee's challenge. Suppose Tom lost Blackacre in a bet to Joe,[17] and Joe's, not Tom's great-grandchild now owns Blackacre. Then, Tom gambled with someone else's money (that, properly, of the slaves). He had no right to do so. That is, Joe would be out of luck if we,

[17] We assume this was a real bet, and not merely an attempt to hide resources. If the latter, see text, supra.

the forces of justice, could take a time machine and travel back to 1865. We would tell Joe to get his money out of Tom's carcass; for example, if Tom has no other resources, Joe is limited to a proverbial "pound of flesh out of Tom." But the lack of a time machine is irrelevant to the justice of the matter. The black grandchildren can sue Joe's grandchild, not Tom's. If Joe himself was not the proper, legitimate owner of Blackacre, then neither is his grandchild, the present owner.

4. Blackacre is currently owned by Tom's great-grandson. About 99% of Blackacre's market value comes from improvements made to it since the Civil War.

The black grandchildren are limited to the 1% of Blackacre that is attributable to the work of their grandfathers. Tom's great-grandson, after all, is an entirely innocent person. Yes, he received property that never should have been given to him, but he did homestead it ever since. That 1% would still be worth a lot; in any case, no less than if Tom's great-grandson had not been such a successful entrepreneur.

5. Tom's great-grandson sold Blackacre in 1990. He used the money for consumption.

This is variation on our "friendly amendment" scenario concocted and discussed under the heading of point 3, above. If Tom spent the proceeds of Blackacre's sale in 1990 on "wine, women and song," without a God's eye view, it is unclear as to whom the black grandchildren of slaves should direct their lawsuits. They are thus cheated of their patrimony.[18]

This case devolves into two others. First, suppose that after this 1990 sale, Tom's great-grandson has other (unrelated) wealth, or, second, is penniless. If the first assumption is true, then the black grandchildren can sue Tom's great-grandson for this other wealth. If the second, then the

[18] It may be worth noting here that we use as our "precedent" the normal proceedings of today's small claims court. It is quite possible to obtain a decision in favor of a plaintiff against a defendant who is unable to pay. In that case, the plaintiff is simply "out of luck," and the same would be true for our slave descendants above. In effect they can "win" and still not be paid if the defendant is insolvent.

black grandchildren are simply out of luck. True, Tom's great-grandson spent money not properly his on the "wine, women and song," from an overarching libertarian point of view. But, at the time, he was legally, and properly, the (innocent) owner of Blackacre. While we are perfectly willing to impose ex post facto law on malefactors, and we do regard Tom in this manner, hence the justification of reparations in the first place, we see Tom's great-grandson as an innocent.

IV. Conclusion

We conclude that slavery was wrong, despite the law of the land at the time, and the Constitution; that reparations are part and parcel of private property rights, not their abnegation; that reparations can be justified, but only in a *limited* way: they are to transfer property not from everyone, but only from those who inherited property that did not properly belong to their parents; and to only those who can demonstrate, beyond a reasonable doubt, that they are the descendants of slaves, and who, thus, in the ordinary course of events, would have inherited the wealth of their (great)-grandparents.

References

Adams, Charles. 2000. When in the Course of Human Events: Arguing the Case for Southern Secession. Lanham, MA: Rowman & Littlefield.

America, Richard. 1993. Paying the Social Debt: What White America Owes Black America. New York, NY: Praeger.

Arceneaux, Taniecea. 2005. "Reparations for Slavery: A Cause for Reparations, A Case Against David Horowitz," The Review of Black Political Economy, Vol. 32, No. 3–4, Winter–Spring, pp. 141–148.

Barnett, Randy E. 1978. "Toward a Theory of Legal Naturalism," The Journal of Libertarian Studies, Vol. 2, No. 2, Summer, pp. 97–108.

Bastiat, Frederic. 1962. The Law, New York: Foundation for Economic Education.

Bittker, Boris I. 1972. Reparations: The Case for Black Reparations. Boston: Beacon Press.

Block, Walter. 1990. "Earning Happiness Through Homesteading Unowned Land: A Comment on 'Buying Misery with Federal Land' by Richard Stroup," Journal of Social Political and Economic Studies, Vol. 15, No. 2, Summer, pp. 237–253.

Block, Walter. 6/10/2002a. "A Libertarian Theory of Secession and Slavery," http://www.lewrockwell.com/block/block15.html.

Block, Walter. 7/9/2002b. "Secession," http://www.lewrockwell.com/block/block18.html; reprinted: http://www.secessionist.us/secessionist_no8.htm; http://www.southernnationalist.org/secession_block.htm.

Block, Walter. 2002. "On Reparations to Blacks for Slavery," Human Rights Review, Vol. 3, No. 4, July–September, pp. 53–73.

DiLorenzo, Thomas. 2006. "Happy Secession Day." http://www.lewrockwell.com/dilorenzo/dilorenzo103.html.

Fogel, Robert W., and Engerman, Stanley L. 1974. Time on the Cross: The Economics of American Negro Slavery, Ann Arbor: University of Michigan Press.

Gordon, David, ed. 1998. Secession, State and Liberty. New Brunswick: Transaction Publishers.

Groudine, Candace J. 1980. "Authority: H.L.A. Hart and the Problem with Legal Positivism," The Journal of Libertarian Studies, Vol. IV, No. 3, Summer, pp. 273–288.

Hoppe, Hans-Hermann. 1993. The Economics and Ethics of Private Property: Studies in Political Economy and Philosophy, Boston: Kluwer.

Horowitz, David. 2000. "The latest civil rights disaster: Ten reasons why reparations for slavery are a bad idea for black people – and racist too." http://www.salon.com/news/col/horo/2000/05/30/reparations/index.html.

Horowitz, David. 2002. Uncivil Wars: The Controversy over Reparations for Slavery. San Francisco, CA: Encounter Books.

Hutchinson, Earl Ofari. 2001. "Ten Reasons Why Reparations," http://alternet.org/story/10680/.

Kreptul, Andrei. 2003. "The Constitutional Right of Secession in Political Theory and History." The Journal of Libertarian Studies, Vol. 17, No. 4, Fall, pp. 30–100; http://www.mises.org/journals/jls/17_4/17_4_3.pdf.

Locke, John. 1948. An Essay Concerning the True Origin, Extent and End of Civil Government, in E. Barker, ed., Social Contract, New York: Oxford University Press, pp. 17–18.

McGee, Robert W. 1994a. "Secession Reconsidered," The Journal of Libertarian Studies, Vol. 11, No. 1, Fall, pp. 11–33; http://www.mises.org/journals/jls/11_1/11_1_2.pdf.

McGee, Robert W. 1994b. "Secession as a Tool for Limiting the Growth of State and Municipal Government and Making it More Responsive: A Constitutional Proposal." Western State University Law Review, 21. Spring.
Northup, Solomon. 1997. Twelve Years a Slave, Academic Affairs Library, UNC-CH University of North Carolina, Chapel Hill, http://docsouth.unc.edu/northup/northup.html.
Paul, Ellen Frankel. 1987. Property Rights and Eminent Domain. Transaction Publisher.
Robinson, Randall. 1998. Defending the Spirit: A Black Life in America. Middlesex, England: Penguin.
Robinson, Randall. 2000. The Debt: What America Owes to Blacks. New York, NY: Dutton.
Robinson, Randall. 2002. The Reckoning. Middlesex, England: Penguin.
Rothbard, Murray N. 1967. "The Principle of Secession Defended." Colorado Springs Gazette Telegraph (Pine Tree Column), October 3.
Rothbard, Murray N. 1973. For a New Liberty. New York: Macmillan; http://www.mises.org/rothbard/newliberty.asp.
Rothbard, Murray N. 1998 [1982] The Ethics of Liberty. New York: New York University Press. http://www.mises.org/rothbard/ethics/ethics.asp.
Rozeff, Michael S. 2005. "Original Appropriation and Its Critics." September 1. http://www.lewrockwell.com/rozeff/rozeff18.html.
Simpson, A.W.B. 1987. "The Common Law & Legal Theory" & "The Survival of the Common Law System," Legal Theory & Legal History, Hambledon Press.
Westley, Robert. 1998. "Many Billions Gone: Is It Time to Reconsider the Case for Black Reparations?," 40 Boston College Law Review 429–476.

12

The Economics and Ethics of Land Reform

I. Introduction

Land reform can be defined as the forced transfer of the ownership of land from one person to another. This must be distinguished from the voluntary transfer of land from one person to another, such as ordinary buying and selling. In the latter case, there can be no true third party. All those involved in land purchases—agents, insurers, lawyers—are mere agents of one party or the other to the agreement. But in the former there must be a third actor, the one who forces one party to give up his land to a second party. This third party is typically the government. Were this third party not involved in the process, there could be no land reform.

In most land reform debates only two sides are represented. These two, together, dominate all such discussions. On the one hand there are those, usually called conservatives or right wing activists, who oppose land reform per se.[1] They maintain that such forced transfers are in total opposition to private property rights. From this perspective land reform must

[1] See LUDWING VON MISES, SOCIALISM 45 (J. Kahane trans., Yale University Press 1951); see also DAVID FRIEDMAN, THE FRASER INSTITUTE, MORALITY OF THE MARKET: RELIGIOUS AND ECONOMIC PERSPECTIVES 497–98, 506–07 (1985).

W. E. Block, *Property Rights*, Palgrave Studies in Classical Liberalism,
https://doi.org/10.1007/978-3-030-28353-7_12

be stopped, as private property rights are the very bedrock of civilization. Once these rights are breached all law, to say nothing of the economic well-being of the populace, is in grave danger.

On the other hand there are those, usually called socialists or left-wing activists, who maintain that land reform is justified *if and only if* the donors of the land are rich or powerful and the recipients are poor or powerless. Their argument is one of equity. Socialists maintain that the privileged of the world are few; they own vast tracts of land which are often not cultivated. In contrast, many people are poor and on the verge of starvation. They have the labor power necessary to feed themselves, but not the land upon which to do this.

One of the purposes of this chapter is to explore a third alternative in this debate, the libertarian or classical liberal position. This analysis is important for three reasons. First, the other two perspectives are at loggerheads. There is, seemingly, no possible reconciliation between them. It is possible that the introduction of a third philosophy of property rights and land reform may serve as an ameliorating device, allowing each of the other two parties to compromise with one another. Here, we speak not of compromise in the sense of adding up the differences and dividing by two, but rather of a principled compromise where each is able to retain the best part of its vision. Second, we shall maintain that while both the socialist and conservative views have aspects of justice on their side, neither has a monopoly in this regard. As presently constituted, both appear fatally flawed. Each philosophy, however, shares certain libertarian elements. If these can be brought out into the clear light of day, we can more closely approximate the truth of the matter. In this chapter, we shall attempt to offer the view that only the classical liberal vision is in accord with justice.

Finally, even if we cannot fully succeed in defending this rather ambitious claim, this exercise will still prove beneficial by providing a third alternative for society to consider. It may well be that this dialogue, now intellectually dead in its tracks, may take on some new light with the advent of a third viewpoint.

II. Libertarian Land Reform

A. The Libertarian Philosophy of Land Reform

What, then, is the libertarian philosophy of land reform? Such a theory maintains both that forced transfers of land from one person to another *are* justified, and that far from being incompatible with a strict regime of private property rights, land transfers are sometimes required by this doctrine. While these transfers are often from rich to poor, this is not required. It is even possible that justified land reform may enrich the wealthy and impoverish the poor. Conservatives may therefore find comfort in the fact that the libertarian position strongly upholds private property rights, while socialists may exult in the fact that land reform is not prohibited by the libertarian doctrine.

How can we reconcile these seemingly irreconcilable claims? It is simple. Valuable items are sometimes stolen. When these items are forcibly returned to their rightful owners, private property rights are protected. The following example supports this position:

> Suppose we are walking down the street and we see a man, A, seizing B by the wrist and grabbing B's wristwatch. There is no question that A is here violating both the person and property of B. Can we then simply infer from this scene that A is a criminal aggressor, and B his innocent victim?
>
> Certainly not—for we don't know simply from our observation whether A is indeed a thief, or whether A is merely repossessing his own watch from B who had previously stolen it from him. In short, while the watch had undoubtedly been B's property until the moment of A's attack, we don't know whether or not A had been the legitimate owner at some earlier time, and had been robbed by B. Therefore, we do not yet know which one of the two men is the legitimate or just property owner. We can only find the answer through investigating the concrete data of the particular case, i.e., through 'historical' inquiry.
>
> Thus, we *cannot* simply say that the great axiomatic moral rule of the libertarian society is the protection of property rights, *period*. For the criminal has no natural right whatever to the retention of property that he has stolen; the aggressor has no right to claim any property that he has acquired by aggression. Therefore, we must modify or rather clarify the basic rule of

> libertarian society to say that no one has the right to aggress against the *legitimate* or *just* property of another.
>
> In short, we cannot simply talk of defense of 'property rights' or of 'private property' *per se*. For if we do so, we are in grave danger of defending the 'property right' of a criminal aggressor—in fact, we logically must do so.[2]

The libertarian, then, must favor this "wristwatch" reform, as A is the proper owner of the stolen property, while B is merely its criminal possessor. Consider, however, the following situation: B, the thief, passed the watch down to B', his son, whereupon B", the grandson, inherited the watch and currently has possession. Presume also that had A not had the time piece stolen from him, it would have ended up the property of A", through a similar inheritance process. At this point A" goes to the police and demands the return of the watch from B". The latter objects that it is his *private property*, and to engage in the "wristwatch reform" described above constitutes socialism or communism. With our libertarian insights, however, it is easy to see the error of this response. Protecting B" under these conditions would not uphold private property rights, but rather would denigrate them. B" simply has no leg to stand upon. While he is not a thief, he is the possessor of what must be considered stolen property. To allow him to continue holding the watch would be to keep it from its rightful owner, A".

Of course, in this scenario the burden of proof rests squarely with A", the person attempting to alter and abolish present property titles. As the old legal adage goes, "Possession is nine tenths of the law," as it is the best evidence, in our uncertain world, of legitimate title. But this is only a presumption. With appropriate evidence, it can be defeated. If A" can prove he is the just owner, then the watch should be returned to him. If somehow the forces of law and order could travel back in time to capture B, the robber, they would be entitled to do more than merely relieve him of his ill-gotten gains.[3] While B" is entirely innocent of the original crime,

---

[2] MURRAY ROTHBARD, THE ETHICS OF LIBERTY 51–52 (1982).

[3] See generally RANDY BARNETT & JOHN HAGEL, ASSESSING THE CRIMINAL 309–21 (1977); Charles J. King, *A Rationale for Punishment*, 4 J. LIBERTARIAN STUDIES 151, 154 (1980); Stephan N. Kinsella, *A Libertarian Theory of Punishments and Rights*, 30 LOYOLA l. rev. 607, 613 (1997); Stephan N. Kinsella, *New Rationalist Directions in Libertarian Rights Theory*,

it would be a *denial* of private property rights to allow him to keep this stolen watch.

The problem with the conservative position is that it sometimes amounts to a defense of thieves. Since the conservative philosophy is linked with capitalism in the public mind, the free enterprise system is widely dismissed as merely upholding the "survival of the fittest," or of the claims of the rich against the poor. But nothing could be further from the truth. Free enterprise does not at all condone land, or any other kind, of theft; rather, this doctrine advocates the return of stolen property.

If the libertarian position deviates from the conservative philosophy, it also differs with the socialist view of redistribution from rich to poor. To put this another way, libertarians agree with the conservative advocacy of private property rights, but not with the claim that it constitutes a legitimate defense of all extant property titles. Rather, the libertarians agree with the socialists that forced transfer of property titles are sometimes justified when it is necessary to effectuate justice.

B. Property Redistribution

What is morally wrong with the socialist vision of coercively taking possessions from rich people and giving them to the poor? First, it is *theft*, and civilized societies have always looked askance upon such actions. To the extent that massive stealing becomes the order of the day, a social breakdown is the inevitable result. The Ten Commandments prohibit not only robbery, but even coveting the property of others.[4]

Additionally, egalitarians are unable to follow the Kantian imperative to make their principles the basis upon which all men act[5]; if we

12 J. LIBERTARIAN STUDIES 313, 321 (1996); Stephan N. Kinsella, *Punishment and Proportionality: The Estoppel Approach*, 12 J. LIBERTARIAN STUDIES 51, 57 (1996); Stephan N. Kinsella, *Estoppel: A New Justification for Individual Rights*, Reason Papers No. 17 (Fall 1992); Stephan Kinsella, *Inalienability and Punishment: A reply to George Smith*, 14 J. LIBERTARIAN STUDIES 79–93 (1998); MURRAY ROTHBARD, THE ETHICS OF LIBERTY 51–55 (1982).

[4] See *Exodus* 20: 1–17.

[5] See Immanuel Kant, Theory and Practice II, *Introduction to the Theory of Right*, in KANT'S POLITICAL WRITINGS (Hans Reiss ed. & H.B. Nisbet trans., Cambridge Univ. Press 1970).

may redistribute land and presumably money from rich to poor, then why may we not steal from the rich and give to the poor those characteristics which have allowed them to become wealthy in the first place? That is, assuming we had the ability to do so, we could take away the musical ability of Mozart, the athletic accomplishments of Michael Jordan, the entrepreneurial and innovational attainments of Bill Gates, the intelligence of Steven Hawking, and the sense of humor of Jay Leno. Were we to engage in such egalitarian redistribution, and continue the process until there were no difference between those rich and poor in talent and characteristics, we would have truly reduced the human race to the undifferentiated blob of a *Brave New World*.[6]

Third, there is simply no practical reason to engage in land reform from rich to poor if the goal is to help the poor attain a better standard of living. If there is one thing that most people have learned in the last few decades (or, in any case, *should* have learned) it is that the last best chance for lifting the poor out of poverty is not to give them the property of others, but rather grant them economic freedom.[7] In comparison to other factors, the redistribution of land does little to increase overall wealth.

Support for this position can be found in economist David Friedman's critique on the redistribution of Native American land in the United States, wherein he wrote,

> In the U.S. at the moment, if you gave the country back to the Indians, in some fair way where you didn't give them the buildings that are built on it, but just the land; and divided it fairly evenly among the Indians, it would not noticeably affect the distribution of income in the U.S. it wouldn't much affect how well off I am.[8]

---

[6] ALDOUS HUXLEY, BRAVE NEW WORLD (1946).

[7] See JAMES GWARTNEY ET AL., ECONOMIC FREEDOM OF THE WORLD 1975–1995 151–70 (1996); *see also* HERNANDO DE SOTO, THE OTHER PATH: THE INVISIBLE REVOLUTION IN THE THIRD WORLD 214–29 (1989); ANTHONY DE JASAY, THE STATE 208–32 (1985); HANS-HERMANN HOPE, A THEORY OF SOCIALISM AND CAPITALISM: ECONOMICS, POLITICS AND ETHICS 56 (1989).

[8] David Friedman, *Discussion*, in MORALITY OF THE MARKET: RELIGIOUS AND ECONOMIC PERSPECTIVES 505 (Walter Block et al. eds., 1985).

III. Homesteading

How, in the libertarian view, is an original claim to land justified? We begin our analysis with an excerpt of John Locke's homesteading theory, wherein he states:

> [E]very man has a *property* in his own person. Thus nobody has any right to but himself. The *labour* of his body and the *work* of his hands, we may say, are properly his. Whatsoever, then, he removes out of the state that nature hath provided and left it in, he hath mixed his labour with it, and joined it to something that is his own, and thereby makes it his property. It being by him removed from the common state nature placed it in, it hath by this labour something annexed to it that excludes the common right of other men. For this labour being the unquestionable property of the labourer, no man but he can have a right to what that is once joined.[9] [Emphasis added]

The above serves only as a starting point. Locke applies his theory only in cases where there is a superfluity of land. In other words, where there is enough virgin land so that no man can homestead it all, there is plenty left for the use of others. Libertarians, in contrast, believe the Lockean theory should be applied in all cases, whether or not there are sufficient land resources available for other people.[10]

What is the alternative to Locke in general or, more specifically, for the cases where excess land is not available? Several possibilities exist, the first of which is the claim theory. Under this approach, a man gets to own land or other natural resources merely by assertion. "I claim the sun, the moon, the stars, and the oceans," a man might say, and, if he is the first to do so, he thereby becomes the legitimate owner. The problems with this are legion. Who will know who has claimed what? There could be numerous people claiming the same thing at the same time; this theory offers no way to choose between them. According to folk wisdom, "talk

[9] JOHN LOCKE, *An Essay Concerning the True Original, Extant and End of Civil Government*, in TWO TREATISES OF GOVERNMENT. (P. Laslett, ed. 1960).

[10] *See* ROTHBARD, supra footnote 3, at 53.

is cheap." Anyone can say anything he wants, and as such, mere speech should not entitle anyone to own anything.

A second approach utilizes the apparatus of the state. With regard to unowned land, the government can give this property to its favorites, sell it to the highest bidder in an auction, or parcel it out on a first-come, first-served basis.[11] But why should politicians and bureaucrats own unused land? What did they do to deserve proprietary status? Even if the government sells the land instead of giving it away, the government already has far too many resources; why should they possess anymore?

Third, there is the doctrine of equal share for all individuals. To illustrate, if there are six billion of us, then we all own one-six-billionth of all virgin land. This is rather arbitrary, as we do not all own equal shares of anything else, up to and including human capital. The following example by Professor Rothbard illustrates the problem inherent in this theory: "it is difficult to see why a newborn Pakistani baby should have a moral claim to a quotal share of ownership of a piece of Iowa land that someone has just transformed into a wheatfield—and vice versa of course for an Iowan baby and a Pakistani farm."[12]

A fourth possibility is the theory of communal ownership with proportionate distribution of shares. In this view, we do not each own one-six-billionth of all virgin land on an *individual* basis; rather, we own it all, communally. In other words, before anything can be done with specific pieces of land, all of us, or at least a majority, must agree. This sounds like either a recipe for interminable committee meetings or, more likely, the concentration of power in a small set of the population.

A fatal flaw in all of these theories can be illustrated not with the ownership of land, but of something even more important, the human person. Civilized people agree to individual ownership of ourselves. This is consistent with homesteading. Initially, when we are born, we are unable to "homestead ourselves" or, rather, mix our labor with our own persons. Our parents perform tasks for us and thus, in a sense, "own" us throughout infancy.[13] Then, as we reach adulthood, we gradually take control over

[11] *See*, e.g., U.S. Homesteading Act, 12 U.S. Status at Large, 75 et seq. (1862).

[12] MURRAY N. ROTHBARD, FOR A NEW LIBERTY 35 (1973).

[13] More exactly, own the right to keep raising, or homesteading us. For the libertarian perspective on children, property and ownership. *See* id. at 97–112.

our bodies, or "homestead" them in effect, and thus come to own them fully. Perhaps an application of the abovementioned theories of property ownership to the ownership of people will prove insightful.

Under the *claim theory*, anyone could claim control over anyone else, provided only that he was the first to do so. This is a recipe for slavery on a grand scale, and must be rejected on that basis alone. Government ownership of people is similarly unacceptable. This merely shifts the slave master from the first claimant to the state. Or, to put this in another manner, it would hearken back to medieval days in Europe, or to oriental despotism, where the king was considered the literal owner, to do with as he wished, with all his subjects. Likewise, the theory of equal shares for all individuals is also unsatisfactory. Obviously, if we were to do things in this way, Michael Jordan and Bill Gates would have been given far more than an equal share. They would, at least partially, have to do the bidding of the rest of us. Who could argue in favor of ordering around some people merely because they were born with or developed extra talents and abilities? Finally, communal ownership also fails when it comes to control over human beings. If interpreted literally, no individual could so much as scratch his nose without the permission of at least a majority of six billion people. Under such a system, the human race would surely perish.

IV. The Pontifical Council's Document[14]

A. Concentration and Misappropriation of Land

The Pontifical Council ("hereinafter Council") often refers to the phrase "concentration and misappropriation of land" in a negative manner.[15]

---

[14] Roger Card et al., *Toward a Better Distribution of Land: The Challenge of Agrarian Reform*, NAT'L CATH. REP., Vol 34, No. 22 (April 3, 1998) [hereinafter *Presentation*]. Our commentary is based on the organization of the Presentation. We shall not discuss each and every section, as there is much repetition between them, and some are irrelevant to our concerns. Indeed, the organization of this document, or rather lack of it, makes a reply to it rather difficult. There are several recurrent themes of interest, and we will comment on all of them, but some are spread all throughout the document, stated in slightly different formats each time.

[15] *See* id. para. 1, 2, 4. Indeed, there are very few paragraphs in the entire document which do not criticize "land concentration."

But why must high concentration necessarily be equated with misappropriation? In the United States, there is high concentration in the computer, automobile, and movie industries, which are dominated by a handful of very large and prosperous entities. The same phenomenon occurs with regard to the ownership of agricultural land in the United States, where the farming sector is a significant contributor to overall economic wealth. There are sizable farms and ranches, such as in Texas and Montana, which are measured not so much in acres, nor even in hectares, but rather in square miles. Even so, apart from some Nader-ite attacks on "agribusiness," the large size of these farms has not led to, nor does it constitute, "misappropriation."

B. Developing Economies

The Council continually uses the term "developing economies" to refer to the poor nations of the third world. The use of this phrase is highly inaccurate. Characterizing an economically deteriorating nation as "developing" cannot possibly materially help any nation or its citizens. An acknowledgment of the truth is the first step in correcting the real problems these nations are facing. Denial is of little use in either economics or psychology. The point is that many of these countries are not developing at all; some are barely holding their own, while others are actually retrogressing from an economic development point of view. The Council's choice of words camouflages this reality.

1. Factors of Production

In the Council's economic analysis, "land … Given the predominantly agricultural nature of the economy … constitutes the fundamental production factor, *together with labor*, and the chief source of national wealth."[16] This is a curious conclusion. The document under consideration is concerned solely with land reform. This would imply, given the goal of economic development, that land is the key factor in production.

[16] Id. para. 1 (emphasis added).

Why, then, is the phrase "together with labor" added to the statement? Could it be that the writers of this document realize that land reform is not all that important, even to a predominantly agricultural nation? This realization comes from the fact that labor, on the margin, contributes far more to GDP than land.[17] Even in the undeveloped countries people own their own labor. Hence, this admission by the Council seriously undercuts their thesis.

This, however, is only the beginning of the problem. There are other factors of production beyond land and labor, most notably capital. But capital, based on savings and engendered by security of property rights, tends to avoid nations which engage in the socialist, egalitarian treat-ment' of land holdings, thus further leading to impoverishment. While no one can move land from one place to another, this immobility certainly does not apply to capital. The point is that the Council's thrust is in the direction of killing the goose which will, at least potentially, create the golden eggs.

2. Preferential Option for the Poor

The clergymen begin this section on a sound footing, with their embrace of the "preferential option for the poor."[18] It has been well said that a society may fairly be judged by how its poor are treated. If there is any obvious conclusion which must be drawn from an international economic comparison of countries, it is that the poor in rich nations are treated far more decently than those in the underdeveloped part of the world. If anything, the poor in places such as Switzerland, the United States, and Canada boast of more material possessions than even the middle class in many parts of the globe. Were Roger Cardinal Etchegaray, the author of the Council's land reformation document, serious about improving the lot of the poor in the third world, he would advocate economic development of the sort enjoyed in Europe, North America, Japan,

[17] In 1992, labor's distribution of the US income was 74.1%. In 1980 this figure was 75.9%, indicating only a slight variation. See Morgan Reynolds, ECONOMICS OF LABOR 55.

[18] *Presentation*, supra footnote 14, para.2.

and other such countries, that is, a great reliance on private property and free markets.

How did these wealthy nations achieve their present enviable economic status? Clearly, it was by embracing economic freedom, private property rights, and the rule of law.[19] Therefore, anything the clergy advocate in this direction will be helpful to the poor. But anything in the opposite direction will be harmful, and thus contrary to the preferential option for the poor, the presumed motivating axiom of the entire document. How well then does the cardinal's statement do when measured against these criteria? While there are some exceptions, the overall assessment, unfortunately, is negative. The analysis and evidence behind our assessment are explored below.

3. Latifundia

The Pontifical Council defines "latifundia" as "large land holdings, often belonging to absentee owners, where the land is worked on by hired labour, using out-dated farming techniques."[20] This would be unexceptionable but for the fact that the Council sees the latifundia as a basic cause of the problems of the third world.[21] What is the basis of this opinion? After all, as we have seen, "large land holdings" are characteristic of many countries with a vibrant agricultural sector, such as the United States and Canada.

Nor are "absentee owners" a barrier to economic development. Much real estate in advanced industrial nations is owned by people who do not

---

[19] *See generally* PETER T. BAUER, REALITY AND RHETORIC: STUDIES IN THE ECONOMICS OF DEVELOPMENT 38–52 (1984); see also PETER T. BAUER, EQUALITY, THE THIRD WORLD, AND ECONOMIC DELUSION 86–102 (1981); HERNANDO DE DOTO, THE OTHER PATH: THE INVISIBLE REVOLUTION IN THE THIRD WORLD 108–20 (1989; JAMES GWARTNEY ET AL., THE FRASER INSTITUTE, ECONOMIC FREEDOM OF THE WORLD 1975–1995 36–42 (1996); F.A. HAYEK, LAW, LEGISLATION AND LIBERTY (1973); HANS-HERMANN HOPE, A THEORY OF SOCIALISM AND CAPITALISM: ECONOMICS, POLITICS AND ETHICS 53–60 (1989); ADAM SMITH, AN INQUIRY TO THE NATURE AND CAUSES OF THE WEALTH OF NATIONS 52–63 (Edwin Cannon, ed. 1965) (1776).

[20] *Presentation*, supra footnote 14, para.2, n.2.

[21] *See* id.

live in their own high-rises. The corporation itself, emblem of economic success if ever there was one, is a paradigm case of "absentee ownership." Here, millions of people buy shares in companies which own land, mines, farms, resources all over a country, and, in the case of multinationals, all around the world. Surely stockholders are all "absentees." Are the clergy attacking the very idea of the corporation as economically unviable? One would have thought that with the toppling of the Soviet Union this sentiment would no longer be expressed quite so blatantly. It appears, however, that such thinking is wrong. Despite the Council's position, it is clear that an objective examination of economic reality shows that the criticism of the latifundia is misplaced.

4. Competence

The Council states that its land reformation document "is not a document of political intent, for that lies outside the Church's field of competence."[22] This issue would not have been brought up but for its entanglement with economics, since to do so would smack of *argumentum ad hominem*. It is not for us to state that only those with doctorates in economics are competent to analyze current economic issues, such as those involving the development of third world countries. However, since the Pontifical Council brought up this issue, perhaps it is appropriate to discuss it. In the Council's view, they are not competent to discuss political intent, but, presumably they are competent to discuss economic development. But why the difference? Are they not *theologians*, therefore, unqualified to also act as political scientists and economists? If so, what is the argument for competence in the latter but not the former?

5. Mortgage of the Past

The Council states that "[p]rivate appropriation of the land introduced serious distortions into the land market."[23] This sounds suspiciously like

[22] Id. para.2.

[23] Id. para.4.

an advocacy of Soviet- or Cuban-style collectivized farming, systems that have never been accused of being based upon "private appropriation." The Council proceeds to note five market distortions.[24] Before examining these in detail, it is necessary to set into context the bishops' charges. Clearly located in the socialist camp, they are stating that markets, capitalism, free enterprise, and so on are to blame for the plight of the poor, and that government action, such as taking land from the rich and giving it to the poor, is the solution.

The first market distortion is the government's forcing of indigenous populations into artificial groups and locating them on reservations. The reservations are often located in "infertile areas, far from [economic] markets or poor in infrastructures."[25] The problem is that the *government*, and *only* the government, has the legal power to force the geographic relocation of the populace. Additional examples of forced relocation include the creation and maintenance of a German ghetto for the Jews during World War II, zoning laws in general, and the "Jim Crow" legislation in the American South following the Civil War. The common denominator is that it is the *state* which imposes such mandates. How, then, can the blame rest with the *market*? Imprisoning specific portions of the population in infertile or otherwise inhospitable areas represents a "government failure," not a "market failure."

The second market distortion is "the imposition of discriminatory taxes on the produce of small indigenous farmers."[26] It can hardly be denied that this too is due to government action, not to market action. Ironically, this charge is most often raised by clergymen. The church itself advocates discriminatory taxes in the form of land redistribution. Although the church's redistribution plans generally favor the poor rather than the rich, who are traditionally the government's beneficiaries, *both* practices are discriminatory.

The third market distortion occurs when a pricing system is adopted that works in favor of large producers and to the disadvantage of small

[24] See id., para.4, n.5.

[25] Id. at 5(a).

[26] Id. at n.5(b).

farmers.[27] Price controls create this distortion and are clearly created by the government, not private citizens. Only the government has the legal power to impose price controls. A fourth distortion can be found in "the imposition of import barriers in order to protect the produce of large landowners from international competition."[28] Again, only the state has the capacity to set up barriers to international trade. Such barriers are indeed serious impediments to economic growth and are in need of control or elimination.

The final market distortion involves "the provision of public services and subsidies from which only large landholdings could, in actual practice, benefit."[29] At first glance, this seems consistent with *laissez-faire* capitalism. However, it is the government and not the market that is providing the services and subsidies. Taken on its face, it seems the argument should be to end business subsidies because they represent a market distortion. Then, the so-called "public services" would be provided privately. This comports with the libertarian philosophy.[30] However, the present authors believe that the Pontifical Council's document reflects the likelihood that the clergy may agree with this result more in principle than in practice.

C. Industrialization at the Expense of Agriculture

The Council's document is, for the most part, a socialist creed written in opposition to private property rights. Nevertheless, there are portions which support market theory and criticize government regulations. For example, the document attacks protectionism, exchange rate manipulation, and price controls.[31] Again, this comports with the classic liberal perspective. However, it is worth noting that the document appears to represent the product of a diverse committee composed of theologians

[27] Id. at n.5(e).

[28] Id. at n.5(d).

[29] Id. at n.5(e).

[30] *See* Rothbard, supra footnote 12, at 194–241.

[31] *See Presentation*, supra footnote 14, para.6.

with both pro- and anti-government sentiments.[32] It is apparent that there was little communication between the divergent groups.[33]

The Pontifical Council concludes that unwise government interventions in free enterprise have led to a "fail in farm income [which] has affected small producers so badly that many have been forced to give up farming."[34] The Council assumes that there are negative consequences when people are "forced to give up farming." However, this is not necessarily so. In the United States, the market has similarly "forced" people out of farming. The result has been an increase in productivity within both the agricultural sector and the industrial sector. This has led to enhanced income and wealth.

Strictly speaking, of course, the market can never "force" anyone to do anything. The market simply consists of no more and no less than the concentration of all voluntary economic interactions.[35] Perhaps a more accurate way of describing the process is that people are led by Adam Smith's "invisible hand"[36] to do that which is in the best interests of the economy. It is a result of the market that people have moved from the farm to the city where productivity is higher. The market may exert economic pressure on farmers to move to the city, but any given farmer in the United States is free to remain where he is. The result has been simply

[32] This has given rise to what can only be called the "Daddy likes me best" school of commentary. Since the PC has both pro- and anti-market elements, commentators from both sides have each stressed the parts of the document which favors their own position, and then claimed that the Church, or the Cardinal in this case, or the Pope in the case of several of the Papal Encyclicals, is "really on their own side." In sharp contrast, the present commentary has no ax to grind in this regard. If we say so ourselves, it is a straightforward political economic analysis of 'Toward a Better Distribution of Land" which notes that it contains support for, and criticism of, capitalism.

[33] Sometimes libertarians are accused of a similar sort of inconsistency, for we favor both economic (laissez-faire capitalism) and political liberty (civil liberties, free speech). In contrast, the overwhelming majority of commentators favor either economic but not civil liberty (conservatives) or civil, but not economic liberty (socialists). To champion both is thus to be held internally self-contradictory. However, in the libertarian philosophy, freedom is a seamless web, which must be pursued in any and all directions. The contradiction, then, takes place on both of these other places on the political economic spectrum, not on our own patch of it.

[34] *Presentation*, supra footnote 14, para.6.

[35] *Cf.* ROBERT NOZICK, ANARCHY, STATE, & UTOPIA 163 (1974) (stating the market consists of "capitalist acts between consenting adults").

[36] See SMITH, supra footnote 19.

that the farmer has had to accept a lower income because consumers place a higher value on goods made in the cities.

The Council, on the other hand, views the move toward industrialization as problematic per se. The church clearly favors reduced poverty. However, at the same time, the church seems to favor the maintenance of a farm-based economy. There appears to be a logical inconsistency here. The church wants to improve the conditions of the poor but not at the expense of farming.

D. Failure of Agrarian Reform

The Council discusses what it views as the reasons for the failure of past efforts in land reform.[37] In addition to the concentration problem, there is a failure of "preventing the expulsion of large masses of peasant farmers from the land that is still free, but which may be marginal."[38] However, this argument can be shown to be incorrect. Given that free enterprise is the key to economic development of third world countries and that private property rights are integral to free enterprise, then anything which promotes private property rights should in turn reduce poverty. The right to expel farm workers, if they are no longer needed, is a component of private property. Therefore, be it ever so counterintuitive, the right of expulsion is actually a means of *enhancing* overall wealth.

Additionally, the Pontifical Council's opposition to "migration to urban centers"[39] may be counterproductive. For example, the migration of black farm workers from rural states such as Mississippi and Alabama to urban areas such as Chicago, Detroit, and Philadelphia during the 1940s and 1950s resulted in economic growth. Surely the Council can recognize that it would have been economically disadvantageous for people to have stayed on the farms.

Economists place great value on the phenomenon of "voting with the feet" as an indicator of economic well-being. If there is a migration lasting several years in duration then the newcomers can tell those still on the

[37] See *Presentation*, supra footnote 14, para. 7.

[38] Id.

[39] Id.

farm of the benefits of city life. If those who had remained subsequently migrate to an urban center, then that migration provides strong evidence that life is better in the new venue. Historically this pattern has occurred under various circumstances. For example, there was traffic by Jews *out* of Nazi Germany, not into it. Similarly, the Industrial Revolution was beneficial for poor peasants who migrated to cities in spite of the factory hardships portrayed by socialists such as Dickens.[40] This pattern can also be found in pre-Mandela Apartheid South Africa. It can be deduced that South Africa was *better* for blacks than the alternatives available elsewhere because migration was *into* South Africa. The migration patterns criticized in the presentation demonstrate this pattern. When peasants continue to flock from farm to city, it is evidence that urbanization is an *improvement* in their lives. It is worth noting that churches are also clustered in cities and are less common in rural areas. The clergy too are "voting with their feet" by remaining largely urban.

E. Contradictions

The Pontifical Council seems to contradict itself when it calls for more government contributions to infrastructure as a necessary component of land reform and economic development. This is contrary to their notion that large landholders, not poor peasants, tend to benefit from these social services and subsidies.[41] Infrastructure generally includes items such as roads, harbors, lighthouses, electricity, other power sources, libraries, and public universities. Socialism is hardly the best way to provide such items. There is little doubt that private capital would be able and willing to invest in the infrastructure. However, the Council does not explain why it believes socialism will succeed and the market will fail in this regard.

The Pontifical Council also calls for "fixing prices" in order to enhance economic development.[42] This is in direct contradiction to its opposition

---

[40] See CHARLES DICKENS, OLIVER TWIST (Kathleen Tillotson ed., Oxford Press 1966) (1842).

[41] See *presentation*, supra footnote 14, para.7.

[42] Id. para. 8.

to "control of food prices."[43] It is clear that both cannot be correct. Either price controls are a force for economic development or they are not. Clearly, only the latter is correct. Prices have a role to play in economic growth. Prices coordinate the decentralized behavior of millions of consumers, sellers, entrepreneurs, workers, resource owners, and middlemen.[44] In this manner, uncontrolled prices based on private property coordinate the market. The only other alternative is central planning, which has always proven unsuccessful. The economic collapse of the Soviet Union is evidence of the negative effects of central planning.

The Council intends that "land reform" extend beyond taking the property of some and giving it to others. In addition to land redistribution, the Council calls for subsidies, subsidized credit, grants, government-funded improvements in infrastructure, "social services," and price fixing or price controls.[45] Clearly such programs require a great deal of money. The burden is likely to be borne by the taxpayers. Not only have taxpayers not been at all implicated in the (possible) latifundista land theft that contributed to land inequality, they are also less likely to benefit from the proposed improvements. Furthermore, the programs proposed are incompatible with free enterprise. Finally, the Council recognizes that past attempts at land reform have been accompanied by massive corruption; yet, the Council favors this course of action without providing any means to prevent corruption from again occurring.

F. The Management of Agricultural Exports

1. Debt Repudiation

As in the case of land reform, the libertarian can agree with the socialist as to the propriety of debt repudiation, at least in principle, while disagreeing as to the specific justification. In contrast, the conservative, with an imprecise understanding of private property, rejects this course of

---

[43] Id. para. 6.

[44] See MISES, supra footnote 1, at 53; see also F.A.HAYEK, THE CONSTITUTION OF LIBERTY 112 (1960).

[45] See *presentation*, supra footnote 14, para. 8.

action outright. The left-wing individual defends both land reform and debt repudiation on egalitarian grounds believing that as long as the poor gain, the case is made.

Consider, for example, an illegitimate government, such as in Cuba. Suppose that a new libertarian regime somehow takes over this troubled island nation. Does this new government have the responsibility to pay off the creditors of Fidel Castro and his fellow criminals? People who have purchased Cuban bonds fall into two classes: those who did so under duress, and those who made willing contributions, either out of ideological support for Cuban-style communism, and/or because the interest rates were attractive to them. The determination of whether to pay the latter is quite simple. Those willing lenders were cooperators, or perhaps even conspirators, with a government that is composed of criminals. Therefore, no repayment is necessary; indeed, it would be highly improper. The payment obligation is not as easy to determine in the situation where innocent people were forced to buy Castro's bonds. Yes, they should be able to sue Fidel and his minions in order to collect their debt. Their lien against these people should be a high one. In that sense, there is no debt repudiation. On the other hand, it would be totally impermissible for the new regime to tax innocent Cubans to repay these debts. To do so creates a new set of innocent victims to compensate the first set of victims.

Of course, a practical question to consider along with repudiation is the future impact on borrowing. Repudiation makes it is less likely that new borrowing will occur. Further, a substantial difference exists between socialists repudiating debt because the lenders are rich and the borrowers poor, and the libertarians doing so because the lenders have cooperated with thieves. In the former case, the bond market may close off entirely or charge such high rates of interest as to impede future borrowing. With the latter case there is not enough historical evidence to render an opinion about this essentially empirical issue.

2. Agrarian Dualism

It is almost an article of faith among clerical commentators on business subjects that selling goods for the export market is uneconomic. According to the Council, "[i]f the market prompts small farmers to grow export crops, this often takes place at the expense of production intended mainly for their own consumption, thus putting farming families at considerable risk."[46] This view amounts to economic illiteracy. The only way the market can "prompt" anyone to do anything, farmers or industrialists, large or small, is by holding out the prospect of greater profits. Should American wheat farmers stop their production for export, and instead produce something consumed in the United States, such as apple pie? Should German exporters of Volkswagens cease and desist, and instead manufacture wiener-schnitzel, something beloved of local consumers? Should a small family firm in the tulip bulb industry of Holland cancel production for the world market because "unfavorable climatic or market conditions can lead to a vicious circle of hunger, so that such families contract debts that then force them to give up ownership of their land"?[47] To ask these questions is to answer them.

The business world is unpredictable. Indeed, it is the essence of the entrepreneurial function to bear risk. There are no guaranteed safe havens—any businessman, no matter how powerful, must risk financial loss. This applies to exporters and importers, as well as those who produce for the local market. Self-sufficient family farms, beloved of the clergy, like small family groceries, can also prove to be uneconomic.

It is one thing to use the cloak of theology to give good business consulting advice; even this is problematic, as it exceeds the competence of the authors. It is quite another to give erroneous opinions, cloaked under the authority of the church, which might well be believed by unsophisticated people in the third world. This is no way to promote the "preferential option for the poor."[48]

G. Expropriation of the Land of Indigenous Populations

According to the Council, "the rights of the indigenous inhabitants have been ignored when the expansion of large scale agricultural concerns …

[46] Id. para.10.

[47] Id.

[48] Id. para.2.

(and industry) … have been decided."[49] The clergy are absolutely correct in claiming that Indian lands have been stolen throughout history. They are on morally firm ground in implying that these wrongs should be righted, despite claims to the contrary from conservatives who favor the status quo in terms of land ownership, believing that any forced changes would be a violation of private property rights.

However, the clergy here tread on thin ice in several regards. First of all, "large-scale" agriculture, hydroelectric, mineral, oil, and timber interests are not the only ones to have ridden rough shod over native property rights. Small concerns have also done so. Second, these thefts, or takings, are by no means as extensive as thought of in some quarters, at least on Lockean grounds. The fact of the matter is that we are talking about people with essentially stone-age technology who were for the most part incapable of homesteading property. Much, but not all, tribal behavior consisted of hunting and gathering, not in mixing their labor with the land as in farming. To be sure, then, such people would be the legitimate owners of all the berries they had gathered and animals they had killed, and so on, as well as of their northern and southern camping grounds, and the right of access from one to the other. But a mere handful of natives could not have homesteaded anything approaching the entire territory of the continental United States before the arrival of the Europeans. The point is, Lockean-Libertarian homesteading theory requires that the Indians mix their labor with the land; that they transform it in some way. This, for the most part, they failed to do, and therefore cannot be considered its legitimate owners. While they would be considered proper owners of the relatively small areas where they pitched their tents and farmed, they would not be the owners of the vast areas in which they traveled and hunted.

Finally, "the burden of proof' rests with those who wish to alter property titles. Otherwise, we are reduced to claim theory for all property. An individual can claim he is the rightful owner of another's land or wristwatch, but unless he can offer proof of his contention there is no warrant for transferring these items from the one to the other. Yet, the Council goes so far as to admit that "the origins of' Indian ownership claims to

[49] Id. para.11.

land "are lost in memory."[50] If so, how can any rational court grant these claims? They state further that" [i]ndigenous populations can also run the absurd but very real risk of being seen as 'invaders' of their own land."[51] But where is it engraved in stone that this is "their own land"? If they never in justice owned the land in the first place, and then others arrived who did homestead it, then it is not at all incorrect to characterize the natives as "invaders," not of their own land, but of the land of these later arrivals.

The libertarian theory is not merely an excuse for the status quo, as is that of the right wing. It is not merely the dressing up in more sophisticated clothing of the conservative head in the sand attitude toward land reform. Yet it may well *appear* this way when we consider very ancient wrongs, or those done to people with stone-age technology who thus have no written records to support their claims. However, with regard to more recent events where there is physical evidence of robbery (e.g., the Nazis and the Jews, the Americans and the Japanese in the early 1940s, and even black pre–Civil War slavery in the United States) the libertarian and conservative conclusions as well as underlying analyses are very different.

H. Violence and Complicity

The clerics quite properly oppose "terror." But one man's terror may be another man's self-defense. Property rights are the only way to tell if A's fist is imposing on B's face, or if B's face is attacking A's fist. Consider again Professor Rothbard's analysis of "A, seizing B by the wrist and grabbing B's wristwatch."[52] Who is aggressing against whom in this action? It all depends upon who is the rightful owner of the timepiece. If the property belongs to B, then A is indeed the terrorist.

The same thing appears to have occurred between the latifundistas and the landless peasants. The clergy see the former as using violence on the latter, and too quickly assume they are guilty of terror. But if the land

[50] Id.

[51] Id.

[52] See supra text, pp. 3–8.

properly belongs to the large latifundistas, then all those who squat on their property, or trespass upon it, or attempt to take it over, are the real criminals. Property rights determine terror; without this understanding, we cannot possibly distinguish an invasion from self-defense.

Suppose that landless peasants "sat in" on church property, attempting to turn these edifices devoted to worship to housing for themselves. Would not the reaction of the priest be to call in the police for eviction, thus resorting to what these trespassers would see as "terror"? And what of the defense of "protests of workers who are forced to work at an inhuman pace for wages that often do not cover their travel and living expenses"?[53] This Council charge is economically incomprehensible. The wage depicted by the clergy would have to be below that of subsistence level. Even slaves were paid a wage greater than "living expenses" in terms of food and shelter; otherwise they would have perished. Wages are determined in markets based on productivity. This must of necessity be higher for free men than slaves, if only because there are no costs of guarding the former from escape which must be deducted from the former's productivity. Thus, *ceteris paribus*, free labor must always be paid more than slaves. And if slaves are paid enough to keep them alive, free persons must be paid even more. Thus, this charge is an untenable one.

I. Legal Recognition of Ownership Rights

The Council complains of the fact that it is difficult "for small farmers to obtain legal recognition of ownership rights over land that they have been farming for a long time and of which they are the de facto owners." The problem with this is that there can be no such thing as de facto ownership where a different person has actual title to the land, and is thus the de jure owner.

How could such a situation arise? One possibility would be for a tenant to farm land for many years for an absentee owner, and then, suddenly, to declare that he, the farmer, was the real owner, and that the landlord to whom he had been paying rent for decades was not. Another

[53] *Presentation*, supra footnote 14, para.12.

would be the case of an owner of land who allowed a passerby to take a shortcut through his property, so much so that over the years a path was worn by his footsteps; whereupon the traveler, instead of being grateful to the owner, asserts his access rights.

Were this sort of thing countenanced by the courts, it would place into disrepute private property, and with it, capitalism, the system which has brought about modem civilized standards of living. Alternatively, no one would ever allow passerby access to one's land; and tenancy would become a thing of the past. This would run counter to the preferential option for the poor, as they are people of limited means, who cannot afford to buy homes, cars, farms, and so on, and are thus the main beneficiaries of tenancy.

J. Environmental Concerns

The authors of this report worry that without seizing the land of the latifundistas, there will be an "over-exploitation of natural resources without concern for environmental sustainability or without considering the intergenerational continuity of family property."[54] Environmental degradation, running out of resources, extinction of species, and other legitimate environmental concerns simply have nothing to do with who owns the land, provided only that it is held in private, not public, hands. The reason for this is rather straightforward. When an individual or family farmer or large firm in the agriculture business industry owns land, or a cow, or a tractor, they tend to take care of them. They do not overuse these resources, or dissipate them. If they fail to act in this manner, they suffer the full attendant losses.

In very sharp contrast, when items such as these are owned in common through coercion, when no one really owns them but all may partake in their use, they are in great danger. Under such circumstances, the user is

---

[54] Id. para.14. In another section, the clerics express the view that "inequalities in the distribution of land ownership set in motion a process of environmental degradation that is hard to reverse." Id. para. 21. For a critique of this sentiment, see *Pollution Trading Permits as a Form of Market Socialism, and the Search for a Real Market Solution to Environmental Pollution*, 1 FORDHAM ENVTL. L.J. 46, 51–57 (1994).

not confronted with the full costs of his actions. For example, a farmer would be foolish to allow his sheep to graze too long on his own land, since if he does, the grass will be eaten down to its roots, and will not regrow easily. He has every incentive to preserve this land for another day, for if he does, he is assured that his sheep will be the ones who benefit. On the other hand, if the pasture is compulsorily held in common by all shepherds, then none of them has an economic incentive to act in this environmentally and economically sound way. Here, if he moves his sheep up the mountain to another less accessible pasture, he has no guarantee at all that when he returns to the more convenient one, the grass will be held for his animals. On the contrary, it is almost certain that someone else will come along and allow their sheep to overgraze.

K. The Credit Market

The Council takes the position that "[i]n rural areas, there is often no legal credit market, so that small farmers have to turn to money lenders if they need loans, thus exposing themselves to risks that can lead to the partial or even total loss of their land—for property speculation is usually the real focus of such moneylenders' operations."[55] There are numerous economic fallacies espoused here. First, a confusion exists in the passage between the geographical and the legal spheres. Lack of a legal credit market results from jurisprudence and not location. When an enactment forbids credit, or sets interest rate maximums, it can apply to *either* rural or urban areas. No presumption exists, as the clergymen contend, that this law applies with greater feverishness to the rural milieu rather than the urban.

Second, money lenders *are* part of the credit market. While the clergy thinks all money lenders loan at very high rates, this is not always the case. Basically, what determines the rate of interest in a given society is time preference: the impatience of the populace to consume now, as opposed to deferring gratification for the future. If the former, then a high interest rate ensues; if the latter, a low one. Imagine a society com-

---

[55] *Presentation*, supra footnote 14, para.15.

posed primarily of seven-year-old school children, each of whom would gladly give up five candy bars tomorrow to have one today. Very few of them would be willing to lend at almost any interest rate, and most would be willing to borrow at virtually any cost. Interest rates will thus be very high, regardless of other occurrences. At the opposite end of the spectrum are people who "save for a rainy day." They are willing to lend money even at low rates of interest, and rarely borrow, even when it is cheap to do so. A low interest rate will prevail in such a society. In other words money lenders, and the interest rates they charge, are merely the messengers for the underlying economic realities.[56]

Finally, the real cause of artificially high interest rates stems from laws prohibiting usury. Imposing ceilings upon interest payments creates a situation where only individuals with good collateral obtain loans, which tend to be large enterprises. Small businesses and other risky borrowers with little collateral and poor repayment records have to deal in the black market, at much higher interest rates because of the laws against usury; the lender, as a law breaker, cannot rely upon the courts to help collect bad debts. Only exorbitant interest rates compensate a lender enough to risk loans to such enterprises. This means that the "risks" are borne not by the small borrowers whose interests the counsel think they are defending, but by the usurious money lenders. The small and/or risky borrower does not face risk, but rather faces either astronomical interest to attract the loan or the inability to obtain financing at all.

Property speculation, or any other kind, does not represent the evil that the Council believes. Instead, the market process of speculation places goods and services into the hands of those who value them greatest, as demonstrated by willingness to pay. The speculator helps stabilize price differentials so that the same price for the same commodity, apart from transportation and other such costs, prevails everywhere. For example, if oranges are selling for one dollar in Miami and two dollars in Boston, the speculator will take advantage of this difference by purchasing cheap southern oranges and transporting them north. The first part

---

[56] For more on this subject, see MURRAY ROTHBARD, MAN, ECONOMY AND STATE 74–120 (1993); EUGEN BOHM-BAWERK, CAPITAL ANFL INTEREST 35 (George Hunke & Hans Sennholz trans., Libertarian Press 1959) (1884); Walter Block, *The Negative Rate of Interest: Toward a Taxonomic Critique*, 2 J. LIBERTARIAN STUD. 121, 124 (1978).

of this operation raises the prices of oranges in Miami, and the second part lowers them in Boston.

While money lenders may sometimes speculate in land, and land speculators may sometimes lend money, the two professions are not at all economically connected, as the clergymen espouse. The only common bond between lenders and speculators mirrors the bond between middlemen and landlords: all four are cordially hated by socialists as emblematic of capitalism.

L. Idle Land

The counsel states, with regard to the case for breaking up the latifundias, and redistributing them to the handless poor, that "[s]uch large landholdings are often poorly cultivated, or simply left uncultivated for speculation."[57] If these holdings represent stolen property then a strong moral case exists for redistributing them not to the poor, but to the children of the victims. However, to offer "poor cultivation" as a reason for hand reform implicitly acknowledges the legitimacy of these property titles; in effect, the clergy argue that, even if the latifundistas had clear and legitimate title to their hands, they should still lose their land on grounds of poor cultivation.

If true, more land would exist to redistribute than to merely the latifundias in the third world. Anything left idle would be fair game. For example, Mr. A goes on a year-long holiday for a trip around the world. He leaves his home vacant and loses ownership in it. Mr. B doesn't use his 15 speed bicycle, tennis racket, or fishing rod for five years; long before that time, his property rights in these items lapse. Miss C doesn't wear her blue dress for a few years, with the same result. Farmer D utilizes his land only eight months of the year, allowing it to lie fallow for the remaining four months. A teenager leaves his childish toys in the attic; when he tries to recover them, he is told he no longer owns them. An old man sticks his money in his mattress for years, "for a rainy day," and thereby loses it.

---

[57] *Presentation*, supra footnote 14, para.32.

The problem of this philosophy, apart from the blatant unfairness of seizing idle property, is that it disregards Keynes's "precautionary motive."[58] People value their possessions whether they "use" them or not. Alternatively, and perhaps preferably, people do not always use them in normally accepted standards. The point is, Mr. A's home, Mr. B's sports equipment, miss C's dress, farmer D's land, the teenager's toys, and the old man's money are not really "idle." They only appear so to outsiders. One man's lack of cultivation or idleness is another man's valuable contemplation or financial support against the unknown future. If the goods did not provide services, if they were truly idle, they would be sold. Thus, people occasionally sell their homes, dresses, toys, and so on. Are there no church-owned bibles, organs, churches, surplices, wine, automobiles, or wafers that go unused for any appreciable amount of time? If so, these would be forfeited under the philosophy adumbrated by the Council.

M. The Lack of Infrastructures and Social Services

In the view of the Pontifical Council, "small farmers are forced to depend on local markets to sell their produce ... They are also dominated by traders whose monopolistic position means that farmers are forced to accept the price offered if they want to sell their produce."[59] The clergymen illuminate an important issue, but their lack of economic sophistication distorts its perception. The clergy raise the issue of marketing boards, which are government entities that prohibit farmers from selling to anyone but themselves. Also, the boards typically purchase at prices far below levels farmers could otherwise attain, whether on local or world markets.[60] These monopsonists[61] exploit farmers, particularly small ones who cannot bribe their way out of these regulations or otherwise avoid them.

---

[58] JOHN MAYNARD KEYNES, GENERAL THEORY OF MONEY, INTEREST AND MONEY 215–225 (1936).

[59] *See Presentation*, supra footnote 14, para.17.

[60] *See generally* supra footnote 19 and accompanying text.

[61] A monopsonist is the opposite of a monopolist. The monopolist is the only legal seller (e.g., the post office, a medallioned taxi cab) in a given market, while a monopsonist is the only legal buyer (a marketing board to which all farmers are forced to sell). Under this system, it is illegal to sell agricultural products to anyone else other than the official marketing board.

The flaw with the cardinal's analysis is that the boards are government entities, not a part of the market. To label them "traders" confuses markets with central planning and economic freedom with economic coercion. Nor could it be otherwise. If these underdeveloped countries were dedicated to capitalism, then any local private person would be a monopsonist, who served as the sole purchasing agent for small farmers and bought at below–world market prices would earn vast profits. However, this would attract other competitors into the industry, both local and multinational, which would compete with the original monopsonistic one to buy farm produce. With greater demand, prices paid to farmers, even *small* ones, would increase until the profits earned in the industry reached market standards, abstracting from risk.

Why, then, do the clergy, being aware of monopsonistic exploitation of small farmers, not call for an end to governmental marketing boards? Presumably, the answer is that they have cast their lot, and their moral authority, with socialist central planners, not free enterprise, and marketing boards play an integral role in this philosophy. To frontally attack statist marketing boards would undermine their moral and intellectual underpinnings.

N. Economic Consequences

The Council complains of "the pegging of farm wages at low levels."[62] "Pegging" refers to governmental setting of wage rates. Pegging at levels below equilibrium would be equivalent to setting wage maximums. This can cause labor shortages. The clergy, perhaps unfamiliar with technical economic usage, do not refer to this situation. Instead, somewhat confusingly, they mention ordinary functioning of the labor markets and not governmental interference. To wit "this pegging is a result of the simultaneous rise in supply and fall in demand or farm labour."[63]

If true, it causes both happiness and regret. Farm workers will receive less compensation, which means they are not needed in agriculture, but,

---

[62] *Presentation*, supra footnote 14, para.18.

[63] Id.

rather, they are in relatively greater demand elsewhere, presumably in industry. If so, this would roughly follow the US pattern, where virtually the entire populace engaged in farm labor in the eighteenth century and virtually no one farms at the close of the twentieth century.[64]

IV. Conclusion

There is massive suffering on the part of the poor in the underdeveloped countries of the world. However, this is due to central planning, socialism, and a public ethic which views with great suspicion profits, free markets, individual initiative, and entrepreneurship—it is not at all the fault of free enterprise and private property rights.

This story exists the world over. Well-meaning critics, ignorant of the niceties of economic science, see abject poverty and misinterpret its causes. They have still to learn Adam Smith's lesson that the wealth of nations stems from economic freedom, not its absence. The theological critics fail to see the deleterious effects of government control and, instead, espouse the same policies that created the plight of the poor in the first place.

It cannot be denied that there has been land theft, occurring in both the economically underdeveloped part of the globe and the developed nations. Land reform, based on returning stolen property from the children of the thieves to the children of the victims, is justified. But the burden of proof must reside on those who would overturn extant property titles. This requirement vitiates against the undoing of robbery buried in the sands of time, against the very poor who do not have access to records which can prove their claims, and against native peoples lacking written records. Thus, while the libertarian message on land reform is a very radical one in theory, it is rather conservative in application. It is radical in theory because it is open to the possibility, which is rather unexpected given its almost total unanimous rejection on the part of those who ostensibly favor private property rights.[65] On the other hand,

[64] See THE STATISTICAL ABSTRACT OF THE UNITED STATES (1998).

[65] See TOM BETHELL, THE NOBLEST TRIUMPH: PROPERTY AND PROSPERITY THROUGH THE AGES 35 (1998). For a response, see Walter Block, *Review Essay of Tom Bethell*, 3 Q.J. AUSTRIAN ECON. 65 (1999).

as a practical matter, the libertarian perspective on land reform cannot be expected to support changes in extant land titles between Jews, Arabs, Palestinians, and so on, since their disputes go back for thousands of years; nor for Indians vis-à-vis white settlers in the United States for lack of written records. This view may, however, buttress claims from Japanese Americans stemming from World War II expropriation.

If the church wishes to promote the interests of the poor, if it desires to take to heart "the preferential option for the poor," instead of continually urging socialistic welfare schemes that only impoverish them, it must make itself more knowledgeable about economics. Then, as easy as falling off a log, the clergy will realize that the last best hope for the poor are the institutions of free enterprise, precisely the ones responsible for the relatively vast wealth enjoyed in the western industrialized nations.

Part IV

Other Property Rights Issues

13

Eminent Domain: A Legal and Economic Analysis

I. Introduction

The primary concept underlying the US Constitution is that of a limited government whose powers are both checked and balanced. A case in point is the Fifth Amendment, which limits the exercise of eminent domain in two ways: a taking must be for "public use," and "just compensation" must be paid to the owner. However, the long line of Supreme Court cases culminating in *Kelo v. City of New London*[1] has successfully obliterated both of those limitations. Citizens whose private property is taken by the government are not justly compensated, nor are those takings limited by "public use."

After this introduction, we critically discuss takings for the purpose of economic development. Section "III. [Un]Just Compensation and Serbonian Bogs" is given over to difficulties with just compensation. The burden of section "IV. Urban Planning and the Real Estate Holdout" is to analyze, from an economic point of view, urban planning and the real estate holdout. In section "V. Assembling Roads Without Eminent Domain" we take on a radical objection to our thesis: how can land be

[1] 125 S Ct. 2655 (2005).

W. E. Block, *Property Rights*, Palgrave Studies in Classical Liberalism,
https://doi.org/10.1007/978-3-030-28353-7_13

assembled for roads and highways without the utilization of eminent domain? The purpose of section "VI. Maybe Private Use Is Better than Public Use" is to challenge the usual presumption that land subject to eminent domain be limited to public use: we ask, given that the government has already seized private property, whether it is a foregone conclusion that public use is to be preferred to private use.

II. Economic Takings

Kelo is consistent with a Supreme Court precedent; its only distinction is that the Court now fully and overtly accepts "economic development" as an appropriate "public use." In retrospect, the decision that was most destructive of any rational definition of the term was undoubtedly *Berman v. Parker*.[2] In *Berman*, the Court defined public use as anything a legislature wants it to be: "When the legislature has spoken, the public interest has been declared in terms well-nigh conclusive." Furthermore, the term represents values "spiritual as well as physical, aesthetic as well as monetary."[3] *Berman* and *Kelo* both approved takings for purposes of economic development and therein lies the problem.

The *Kelo* majority claims that promoting economic development is a traditional, long accepted function of government. Perhaps that is true, but taking from one private party to give to another is a violation of the fundamental social compact, and "against all reason and justice."[4] Furthermore, the practical problem with using eminent domain to foster economic development is that it often fails. The redevelopment project at issue in *Berman* ultimately failed, as have several others, including the Poletown GM project in Michigan, and Cincinnati's downtown: Poletown's busy commercial strip was replaced with vacant and burned-out buildings when GM did not expand as planned, and instead of a Nordstrom store, downtown Cincinnati now has a municipal parking lot. Even where an economic development taking does not result in

[2] 348 U.S. 26 (1954).

[3] Id. at 33.

[4] Kelo, 125 SCT at 2671 (O'Connor, J. dissenting).

further depression, it is likely that the area at issue would have improved without the use of eminent domain.

A second practical problem with the Supreme Court's interpretation of "public use" is that it gives too much power to local, state, and national legislatures. As a result, legislatures have both the power and the incentive to use eminent domain irresponsibly and unjustifiably, at the expense of working-class neighborhoods. Such was the case with Sunset Manor subdivision in Missouri, where a city council, in an effort to increase its tax base with a new shopping mall, apparently manipulated studies so that it could declare the subdivision blighted.

A third very serious problem with economic takings—indeed any takings—is that they undermine private property rights, the bedrock of a well-functioning economy. If property rights are jeopardized, homeowners and small businesses lose the incentive to invest in property. Economic incentives, based upon individual property rights, are essential for economic growth, as shown by the work of economist Hernando de Soto,[5] as well as demonstrated by the fall of the Soviet Union.

III. [Un]Just Compensation and Serbonian Bogs

Just as the Supreme Court has destroyed any rational meaning of the term "public use," so has it wrecked the meaning of "just compensation." The compensation granted under current Supreme Court authority is unjust, even though the underlying theory seems plausible. The Court defines "just compensation" as requiring that the owner of condemned property be put in as good a financial position as if his property had not been taken, meaning that the owner should be paid the "fair market value:" "the price a willing buyer would pay a willing seller in the open market."[6]

---

[5] Hernando de Soto, The Other Path: The Economic Answer to Terrorism (Basic Books 2000).

[6] *See* United States v. 564.54 Acres of Land, 441 U.S. 506, 510 (1979); United States v. Miller, 317 U.S. 369, 373 (1943); Olson v. United States, 292 U.S. 246, 255 (1934) (all holding that just compensation requires that the owner be put in substantially the same position pecuniarily as if he would have been if his property had not been taken.).

The "fair market value" method as used by courts is a fiction that makes sense only to attorneys who enjoy cavorting in Serbonian bogs, from which extrication is impossible.[7] It certainly does not make sense under either economics or traditional common law. To begin with, there is no willing seller in this equation, and the only willing buyer is the government. Market value, as ascertained by realtors, refers to the price an interested buyer would pay and assumes that the seller will accept a reasonable price given local market conditions. In contrast, the judicial definition of "fair market value" is circular because it uses one unknown variable (fair market value) to define a second unknown variable (willing seller).[8]

Regardless of semantics, the "fair market value" scheme is legally insufficient because it excludes all consequential damages, thus failing to fairly compensate owners for losses that would be otherwise included in tort damages. Thus, business owners lose business profits and goodwill, removal costs, relocation costs, litigation costs, and demoralization costs.[9] Homeowners lose any value that could be attributed to emotional or historical attachment to the property.[10] This exclusion of consequential damages from the plaintiff's losses in eminent domain cases is unjust: the clause was not designed to protect the thing owned, rather it was designed to protect the owner of the thing.[11]

The Radical (but Effective) Solution: Repeal the "Takings" Clause

While excluding economic takings might temporarily rejuvenate "public use," it does nothing to remedy the interpretation of "just compensation." Courts and takings-minded legislatures could still torture language to find that a proposed economic development project has a "public use."

[7] Parker B. Potter Jr., *Surveying the Serbonian Bog: A Brief History of a Judicial Metaphor*, 28 Tul. Mar. L. J. 519, 521 (2004) (tracing the origin of the term to Milton's Paradise Lost).

[8] Id.

[9] Id.; *see also* Michael DeBow, *Unjust Compensation: The Continuing Need for Reform*, 46 S.C. L. Rev. 579 (1995).

[10] *See* id. at 87–88.

[11] Richard A. Epstein, Takings: Private Property and the Power of Eminent Domain 52–53 (1985).

The best solution is to return to common law by repealing the takings clause and forcing governments to justify their actions as if they were any other private party.

Governments would be forced to develop plans that would avoid taking property from one private person and giving it to another. Where they insisted on doing so, they would be forced to give compensation according to traditional tort law on conversion, and thus forced to give just compensation. "The measure of damages recoverable in an action for the wrongful taking of property is ordinarily the market value of the thing converted, fixed as of the time and place of the conversion, with interest from the date to the time of trial."[12] Normal compensatory damages would be available for loss of goodwill and other "subjective" damages. Punitive damages might also be available for a particularly recalcitrant governmental entity whose taking the jury found particularly offensive—subject, possibly, to the reasonable, proportionate limitation the Supreme Court recently placed on punitive damage awards.

IV. Urban Planning and the Real Estate Holdout

One of the most interesting of all architectural developments is the phenomenon of pie-with-a-missing-slice-shaped buildings. We have all seen these. Typically there will be a gigantic high rise edifice, but not shaped at its base as we might expect, as an unbroken square, rectangle, or circle, or some such other regular geometrical figure. Instead, there will be a missing piece, on which is often perched an older home. The architect might bemoan the lack of artistic or intellectual integrity of such a development, but those who favor markets and private property will see a certain beauty in them, an economic aesthetic, as it were.

What is the source of such constructions? In most cases, a private developer was able to buy up all the lots on an entire city block except for one tiny parcel. When all purchase offers failed to convince the "holdout"[13]

[12] Morris v. Pearl Street Auction Co., 22 N.E.2d 740, 741 (Ohio Ct. App. 1939).

[13] Walter Block, *Herbie the Holdout*, Frasier Forum, Oct 1989, at 28–30.

to sell, the entrepreneur decided to go ahead with construction in any case but was limited to an irregular plot of land. Hence, the structurally misshapen building.

This is the sort of thing that cannot be witnessed in any communist or dictatorship-run country. The central planners would simply not tolerate such uncooperativeness on the part of the holdout. Instead, it is a badge of honor for a capitalist nation, predicated upon the sanctity of private property rights.

On a moral level, it is easy to see that the misshapen edifice is preferable to the unblemished geometrically correct one. The former is predicated on voluntariness; no one is coerced into doing something against his will. The latter in sharp contrast is the result of violence or the threat of violence.[14] This is ethically problematic, in that it cannot in principle be distinguished from armed robbery.[15]

But even on the more mundane economic level, there is something to be said on behalf of misshapen constructions that may emanate from holdout or opportunistic behavior. First of all, there is simply no way to distinguish such commercial interaction from any other normal business interaction. There are no objective criteria on the basis of which we may say that one man is an obstreperous holdout, while another refuses to sell to the developer for other reasons. All we can know if we take on the role of the disinterested economist is that A offers to purchase something from B, and the latter declines.

Second, let us posit, arguendo, that there is indeed a discernible difference in the motivation underlying these supposedly two different behaviors (holdout and ordinary refusal to sell). Then, still, albeit paradoxically, it makes more economic sense to rely on a private property rights regime which sometimes but not always eventuates in misshapen

[14] If there is any doubt about this, let someone attempt to "hold out" against a governmental condemnatory order and see what happens to him.

[15] But is not a duly processed taking compatible with, and even based on, the constitution? Well, yes, at least as interpreted by the Supreme Court. However, as Spooner has shown, this is not a binding document, since no one signed it, and it would be improper to interpret voting, or taxpaying, as implicit consent to the constitution. *See* Lysander Spooner, *No Treason: The Constitution of No Authority and A Letter to Thomas F. Bayard* (1870) (Larkspur, Colorado: Rampart College 1966), http://www.lysanderspooner.org/notreason.htm.

structures than one which allows some to ride roughshod over others with the goal of avoiding such architecture. Why? Because there are two and only two economic systems possible; all others are merely theme and variation on one of these two. They are, first, *laissez-faire* capitalism, where each owner decides for himself how his property is to be used, and second, central planning, where the authority makes such determinations. But if we have learned anything whatsoever from the fall of the U.S.S.R. and the crumbling of the Berlin Wall, it is that central economic direction is a snare and a delusion. This applies to the Soviet style of planning as well as urban planning on the basis of which *Kelo* uncomfortably perches.

V. Assembling Roads Without Eminent Domain

The opponent of eminent domain must squarely face the issue that without this type of legal recourse, we would have no roads or highways, or, at the very least, far fewer than the optimal mileage in this regard. This seems like a bigger challenge. For buildings can be constructed without expropriation; the result is likely to be only an aesthetically challenged edifice. But with thoroughfares, the result would appear to be nothing at all, in the face of the holdout.

How, then, would road assembly work in the absence of eminent domain? There are several ways. First of all, just as there is more than one way to skin a cat, there is more than one path that can be taken between any two points: for example, between Baton Rouge, Louisiana, and British Columbia, Canada, to mention places where the present authors sometimes reside. One possibility is a direct route, taking in effect the hypotenuse, something that does not exist at present, not at least in the form of major highways. A second alternative is to go west from Baton Rouge on Interstate 10, and then north on Interstate 5 when we reach California. A third option is to start out in a northerly direction, along what is now Interstate 55 and then turn west, tracing out roughly along the space now occupied by Interstate 90. Both these second plans call for going along the sides of a right triangle, the apex of which would be where, respectively, Los Angeles and Chicago are located.

There are almost an infinite number of other paths lying between the second and third tracings out of the two right triangles,[16] with the hypotenuse or direct route being only one of these. The point is that the firm that wishes to build a road between Louisiana and British Columbia need not, at least initially, *purchase* any land at all. Rather, they can, at the merest fraction of the cost, buy *options* to assemble land. Say, there are 100 feasible routes between the start and end points of our prospective road. Agents can be sent out in secret to purchase these options along all of them. As soon as, or, rather, when and if a holdout appears, who demands appreciably more for his parcel than would be justified by what farms or forest land normally commands in the given neighborhood, all efforts along that particular route can cease.

That alone ought to suffice. After all, while there are no private highways that have ever been put together, there are other long thin things that have: railroads. P.J. Hill built them without any eminent domain powers, whatsoever. But suppose, just suppose, that each and every one of these 100 routes runs into a holdout. Or, take the case where one single individual owns a long thin strip of land stretching all the way from Chicago to Los Angeles, this blocking our putative road at all points. The answer to this challenge[17] is to tunnel under, or build a bridge over, this man's landholdings.[18] Yes, this might be a bit more expensive, but, if it is far less than what the "blockader" is demanding, a reasonable presumption, it will be the most feasible option to take.

The obvious objection to this "modest proposal" is the *ad coelum* doctrine. According to this perspective, it would be illicit for our road company to tunnel under, or bridge over the holdout's land, since he owns whatever lies below him, all the way down, in a decreasing cone-shaped

---

[16] This is only approximately true, given that the contours of the Rocky Mountains sharply reduce the pathways that can be taken. Some would say that the possible paths would be radically decreased due to this consideration, but they have not reckoned with the tunneling option, to be discussed below.

[17] Gordon Tullock, *Comment on 'Roads, Bridges, Sunlight and Private Property', by Walter Block and Matthew Block,* Journal des Economistes et des Etudes Humaines, Vol. 7, No. 4, December, pp. 589–592 (1996); Block vs. Epstein, op. cit.

[18] Walter Block and Matthew Block, *Roads, Bridges, Sunlight and Private Property Rights,* Journal Des Economistes Et Des Etudes Humaines, Vol. VII, No. 2/3, June-September 1996, at 351–362; http://141.164.133.3/faculty/Block/Blockarticles/roads1_vol7.htm.

mass, to the core of the earth, and, also, in an increasingly sized cone-shaped area as we move in an upward direction, all the way to the heavens.

But the *ad coelum* doctrine is itself open to a whole host of criticisms.[19] One would be a pragmatic one: it would make air flight impossible, as *every* landowner over which an airplane appears could charge the latter whatever price he wished. This would not constitute a mere single hold-out which might or might not be able to be overcome. This doctrine would be the death knell of air carriers, period.

Another objection is more philosophical: why should someone who owns a square mile of the surface of the planet be entitled to control land hundreds or even thousands of miles below his acreage? He never homesteaded[20] so much as a square inch of any of it. To be sure, the tunnel built below him may not be so close to his holdings that it causes cave-ins of his buildings. Similarly, why should he be justified in determining what takes place 30,000 feet above his property? And, just how far above him do his supposed property rights extend? Certainly, airplanes should not be allowed to "buzz" him by flying only a foot above his head. But can he literally own the air space all the way to Mars? To the next solar system? The courts have quite rightly refused to accommodate so outlandish a doctrine.

VI. Maybe Private Use Is Better than Public Use

One last final but very, very radical point. Given that for better or worse, and we have argued the latter in this paper, there are to be takings. Should they be limited to the purpose of promoting public uses,[21] as

[19] Walter Block, *Roads, Bridges, Sunlight and Private Property: Reply to Gordon Tullock*, Journal des Economistes et des Etudes Humaines, Vol. 8, No. 2/3, June-September 1998, at 315–326; http://141.164.133.3/faculty/Block/Blockarticles/roads2_vol8.htm.

[20] Hans-Hermann Hoppe, Hans-Hermann, The Economics and Ethics of Private Property: Studies in Political Economy and Philosophy (Boston: Kluwer 1993); John Locke, *An Essay Concerning the True Origin, Extent and End of Civil Government*, in E. Barker, ed., Social Contract 17–18, (New York: Oxford University Press 1948; Ellen Frankel Paul, Property Rights and Eminent Domain. (Transaction 1987); Michael S. Rozeff, *Original Appropriation and Its Critics*, September 1, 2005, http://www.lewrockwell.com/rozeff/rozeff18.html; Murray N. Rothbard, *For a New Liberty*, (Macmillan, New York 1973); http://www.mises.org/rothbard/newliberty.asp.

[21] Such as national defense, roads, lighthouses, and courts. For the argument that there is no such thing as a public good, for example, that the doctrine of public goods is entirely fallacious, *see*

most critics argue, or should they be for the private use of other people? In other words, given that the courts condemn the land of private party A, should only the government be able to use this property, or, can the state properly turn around and give or sell A's property to private party B. At first blush, this is preposterous. After all, given that we do not want to forcibly take A's property away from him, limiting the use to which it may be put to "public" uses at least decreases the incidence of such goings-on. However, *given* that this unjustified act has already taken place, and has, heroic assumption coming up here, no implications for future such practices, are there any cogent reasons for wishing to allow B to enjoy the fruits of A's labors? Yes, there are. It all depends upon the stance one takes toward the government. If one sees it as an unmitigated robber gang,[22] then there is at least a case for preferring that A's property ends up in B's hands,[23] for the latter is at least relatively innocent.

VII. Conclusion

It is time to end this legal, economic, and philosophical discussion of eminent domain. On the legal front, we conclude that this initiative is incompatible with Constitutional emphasis on takings for public use and the requirement of just compensation. In our economic analysis, we cast doubt on the notion that takings actually promote economic welfare.

Walter Block, *Public Goods and Externalities: The Case of Roads*, The Journal of Libertarian Studies: An Interdisciplinary Review, Vol. VII, No. 1, Spring 1983, at 1–34; Walter Block, *National Defense and the Theory of Externalities, Public Goods and Clubs*, The Myth of National Defense: Essays on the Theory and History of Security Production, in (Hans-Hermann Hoppe, ed., Auburn: Mises Institute 2003), at 301–334; Anthony De Jasay, Social Contract, Free Ride: A Study of the Public Goods Problem (Oxford University Press 1989); Hans-Hermann Hoppe, *Fallacies of the Public Goods Theory and the Production of Security*, The Journal of Libertarian Studies, Vol. IX, No. 1, Winter 1989, at 27–46; Jeffery Hummel, *National Goods vs. Public Goods: Defense, Disarmament and Free Riders*, The Review of Austrian Economics, Vol. IV 1990, at. 88–122; http://www.mises.org/journals/rae/pdf/rae4_1_4.pdf.

[22] *Spooner*, supra footnote 15; Murray N. Rothbard, The Ethics of Liberty, (Humanities Press, Atlantic Highlands, N.J. 1982).

[23] We make another heroic assumption here that B is an innocent party and not part and parcel of an illegitimate governmental undertaking.

Philosophically, we reject the doctrine of *ad coelum* and ask, in this era of Big Government, if, given a taking has already occurred, it will really promote the public weal to add more property to the public sector and would not be better to simply focus on providing compensation that really is just.

14

Eminent Domain: A Legal and Economic Critique

Introduction

This article offers a legal and economic analysis and critique of the eminent domain doctrine. The first section gives an overview of the historical development of the concept. Section "II. Eminent Domain as Interpreted by US Courts" continues on to discuss major cases and problems with jurisprudential trends in US Supreme Court interpretation of the Takings Clause, and section "III. An Economic Analysis of Eminent Domain" provides an economic analysis of the concept from a libertarian perspective. In section "IV. Conclusion", the article concludes quite radically that granting a limited government the power of eminent domain (or expropriation, as the concept is known in Canada), is unnecessary, ill-conceived, and should be eliminated.

W. E. Block, *Property Rights*, Palgrave Studies in Classical Liberalism,
https://doi.org/10.1007/978-3-030-28353-7_14

I. Historical Background

Plato and other ancient Greek philosophers saw no limits on governmental powers: all ownership interests derived from the ruler's good favor, which could be revoked at will.[1] The concept that governmental powers should be limited, including that of taking private property, developed out of Western Christian legal tradition, beginning with the concept that church and state should be separate.[2] Grotius, the seventeenth-century jurist, originated the term "eminent domain."[3] Grotius held that the state possessed the power to take or destroy property for the public's benefit, but he further believed that when the state so acted, it was obligated to compensate the injured property owner for his losses.[4] Blackstone, too, believed that society had no general power to take a landowner's private property, except on payment of a reasonable price.

"So great ... is the regard of the law for private property, that it will not authorize the least violation of it; no, not even for the general good of the whole community. If a new road ... were to be made through the grounds of a private person, it might perhaps be extensively beneficial to the public; but the law permits no man, or set of men, to do this without the consent of the owner of the land."[5]

In practice, however, eighteenth-century colonial legislatures regularly took private property with little or no compensation, sometimes when the owner had failed to develop his property but more often when the legislature wanted to build a public road.[6] The first state constitutions lacked just compensation clauses, partly because of republican conceptions of property and of rights, but also because the drafters originally had faith in legislatures.[7] Over time, however, the colonials justifiably lost

---

[1] *See generally* Plato, The Republic.

[2] *See*, for example, The Bible Mt 22:17 When asked whether it was lawful to pay taxes, Jesus replied, "Render unto Caesar the things which are Caesar's, and unto God the things that are God's."

[3] John E. Nowak & Ronald D. Rotunda, Constitutional Law § 11.11, at 424–25 (4th ed. 1991).

[4] Id.

[5] 1 Blackstone 135.

[6] William Michael Treanor, Note, *The Origins and Original Significance of the Just Compensation Clause of the Fifth Amendment*, 94 Yale L. J. 694, 695 (1985).

[7] Id. at 700.

this faith and gained a new concern for the protection of individual property rights.[8] The Vermont Constitution of 1777, the Massachusetts Constitution of 1780, and the Northwest Ordinance of 1787 all required just compensation for the governmental taking of private property.[9]

Madison's takings and just compensation clause, as incorporated in the US Constitution's Fifth Amendment, was built upon Grotius's concept that a government is morally obligated to pay for its interference with private property: "private property [shall not] be taken for public use, without just compensation." Thus, the Fifth Amendment imposes two distinct conditions—two checks—on the exercise of eminent domain: "the taking must be for a 'public use,' and 'just compensation must be paid to the owner.'"[10] Originally, this power applied only to the federal government, but the passage of the Fourteenth Amendment expanded its scope to include state and local governments as well.

As drafted that hot summer in Philadelphia, the US Constitution did not include any reference to eminent domain. Nor was there a lack of any such mention of concern to those who objected to the document. James Madison drafted the Bill of Rights, including the Fifth Amendment, in an effort to increase the chances of Constitutional ratification. The primary concern at the time was that the new federal government would be too strong, and the Bill of Rights was desired as a further check on it. Madison added the Takings Clause because he was keenly concerned with protecting private property rights,[11] and it was adopted in a slightly modified form with little or no debate in Congress.[12]

Apparently the clause was not considered particularly significant because most members of the Constitutional Convention simply doubted that the federal government would exercise its power of eminent domain and that, therefore, consuming time with a discussion of this trivial

---

[8] Id.

[9] Id.

[10] Brown v. Legal Foundation of Wash., 538 U.S. 216 231–232, 123 S. Ct. 1406, 155 L. Ed. 2d 376 (2003).

[11] *See* Jack N. Rackove, Original Meanings 330–31 (1996).

[12] William Michael Treanor, Note, *The Origins and Original Significance of the Just Compensation Clause of the Fifth Amendment*, 94 Yale L.J. 694, 708–09.

concern would make little sense.[13] Rather, the debate centered around whether or not the Constitution should include a Bill of Rights. Those concerned with the protection of property from the Federal Government may have found convincing the argument that Madison advanced in Federalist Ten. Thus, they may have believed that the Bill of Rights, and the Takings Clause it contained, was "superfluous and absurd" because the structure of the national government as established by the Constitution adequately protected property interests and other rights.[14] A Bill of Rights was superfluous because it would merely state that "we should enjoy those privileges of which we are not divested."[15] Those in support of a Bill of Rights, however, had fears (now justified under *Kelo v. City of New London*[16]) that without a Bill of Rights, and even with one, the powers granted to the federal government under the Constitution were such that the inevitable result was tyranny.[17] Nevertheless, at the time of the ratification, neither side was particularly concerned with the language of the Takings Clause included in the Fifth Amendment.

II. Eminent Domain as Interpreted by US Courts

The Supreme Court has had three main difficulties in interpreting the Eminent Domain clause, as can be seen by examining jurisprudential trends. The three problems include deciding when a governmental action constitutes a taking,[18] what is meant by public use, and what is just

---

[13] Id.

[14] William Michael Treanor, *The Original Understanding of the Takings Clause and the Political Process*, 95 Colum. L. Rev. 782, 835 (1995) (Hereinafter "*Original Understanding*").

[15] James Wilson, Speech Oct. 6, 1787, *reprinted* in Ralph Ketcham, ed., The Anti-Federalist Papers and the Constitutional Convention Debates 184 (Signet Classic 2003).

[16] 545 U.S. 469, 125 S. Ct. 2655 (2005).

[17] *See The Address and Reasons of Dissent of the Minority of the Convention of Pennsylvania to their Constituents* (December 18, 1787), *reprinted* in Ketcham, supra footnote 15, at 237–256.

[18] *See generally* Richard A. Epstein, Takings: Private Property and the Power of Eminent Domain (Harvard University Press 1985). Roy Whitehead & Walter Block, *Environmental Takings of Private Water Rights: the Case for Full Water Privatization*, Environmental Law Reporter 11162–11176 (2002).

compensation. In other words, the Court has had problems with all three components of the clause. In all three instances, Supreme Court jurisprudence has succeeded in enlarging the government's powers at the expense of private owners. Each will be examined in turn.

A. Takings

Originally, the understanding of the Takings Clause was that compensation was required when the federal government physically took private property but not when government regulations limited the ways in which property could be used.[19] In 1922, however, the Court held that compensation must be provided when a government regulation "goes too far" in diminishing the value of private property.[20] Determining what is "too far" has created a body of law that recent commentators have described as "a mess."[21] The problem is finding a sensible and stable balance between the individual's right to enjoy and use his property against the government's interest in protecting and promoting the health, safety, and welfare of the community.

Generally, the Court has upheld land-use regulations as valid exercises of a government's police power. For example, the government may always impose taxes and can impose serious burdens without compensation—such as zoning decisions that cause properties to precipitously lose value, or which create noisy highways nearby, or which stop an owner from a "noxious" use. It was against this background that the Court considered the case of David Lucas and his South Carolina property.[22] Mr. Lucas bought two very expensive beachfront residential lots, intending to build single-family homes on them. However, two years later, the South Carolina Legislature passed a law barring him from erecting any permanent habitable structures on his land, thus instantly rendering his property virtually valueless.[23]

---

[19] Treanor, *Original Understanding* supra footnote 14, at 782.

[20] Pennsylvania Coal v. Mahon, 260 U.S. 393, 415 (1922).

[21] Treanor, Original Understanding supra footnote 14, at 782; Daniel A. Farber, *Public Choice and Just Compensation*, 9 Const Commentary 279, 279 (1992); Saul Levmore, *Just Compensation and Just Politics*, 22 Conn. L. Rev. 285, 287 (1990).

[22] Lucas v. South Carolina Coastal Council, 505 U.S. 1003, 1006–7 (1992).

[23] Id. at 1007.

Reasoning that a regulation becomes a taking if it compels the property owner to suffer a permanent physical "invasion" of his property, or "denies an owner economically viable use of his land," or fails to "substantially advance a legitimate state interest,"[24] the Supreme Court held that as the law left Lucas's lots without economic value, it was a taking. In *Dolan v. City of Tigard*, the Court similarly found a taking where a municipal development plan conditioned a building and expansion permit on an existing business owner's, dedicating a portion of her property for storm drainage and for a bicycle/pedestrian pathway.[25] In reaching these decisions, the Court developed a new two-part test: in order *not* to be termed a taking, a permit condition imposed by government: (1) must have an "essential nexus" to a legitimate state interest; and (2) must be "roughly proportionate" to the projected impacts of the proposed development.[26]

Unfortunately, this rule of rough proportionality has led to a new morass of cases in the lower courts. In one such case, the Maryland Supreme court held that a city's conditioning approval of a subdivision on its sacrificing an entire residential lot as a recreational space was *not* a taking,[27] a result apparently inconsistent with *Lucas* and *Dolan*. Thus, the new test has led to inconsistent, irreconcilable holdings just as had the old one. There is still no consensus on what constitutes a taking.

B. Public Use

Historically, the courts have employed two interpretations of the "public use" exception to the bar against governmental takings: a narrow view and a broad one. The narrow view was that property could be taken only if it was to be used by the public in general: this led to the "public purpose" line of cases. So, for example, in the colonial era, one constructing

---

[24] Nicole M. Lugo, Case Note, *Dolan v. City of Tigard: Paving New Bicycle Paths Through the Thickets of the Fifth Amendment's Takings Clause*, 48 Ark. L. Rev. 823, 829 (1995).

[25] Dolan v. City of Tigard, 512 U.S. 374, 396, 114 S. Ct. 2309, 2322 (1994).

[26] Dwight H. Merriam, *What is the Relevant Parcel in Takings Litigation?*, in 1999 Zoning and Planning Law Handbook 353, 370 (Deborah A. Mans ed. 1999).

[27] City of Annapolis v. Waterman, 745 A.2d 1000, 1012 (MD 2000).

a mill (the equivalent of a public utility) under the Mill Acts was liable only for limited damages if his mill caused flooding to up-stream neighbors[28]: "[a]pparently, the contribution of water power to the general well-being and advancement of the public trumped the rights of the private landowner."[29]

In the nineteenth century, many early decisions held that governments lacked the power to permit the non-consensual taking of private property for private use, based on natural law theories or on state constitutional language. They held that actual use by members of the public was essential to justifying a taking.[30] Thus, an incidental, amorphous benefit accruing to the public after taking land and transferring it to a private party was insufficient to satisfy the "public use" limitation on eminent domain: "public use" meant that the government controlled the use of the property or that the entire public had a right to utilize the property in a physical sense.[31]

However, this "use by the public" standard, which was adopted by the majority of the states, became difficult to apply. This was because of the loopholes, limitations, and evasions which courts giving lip services to the majority view utilized to allow expanding industrialization and the quick exploitation of natural resources felt to be necessary at the time.[32] For example, one court found that the construction of a railroad satisfied the public use definition, but another reached the opposite conclusion.[33] The US Supreme Court was of little help in defining public use. Even

---

[28] Charles E. Cohen, *Eminent Domain After Kelo v. City of New London: An Argument for Banning Economic Development Takings*, 29 Harv. J.L. & Pub. Pol'y 491, 501 (2006).

[29] Alberto B. Lopez, *Weighing and Reweighing Eminent Domain's Political Philosophies Post-Kelo*, 41 Wake Forest L. Rev. 237, 256 (2006).

[30] Id. at 505–06.

[31] John Lewis, A Treatise on the Law of Eminent Domain in the United States §164 (Chicago, Callaghan & Co. 1888).

[32] Philip Nichols, Jr., *The Meaning of Public Use in the Law of Eminent Domain*, 20 B.U.L. Rev. 615, 624 (1940). *See* id. at 618–24 (giving details of evasions). *See also* Errol E. Meidinger, *The "Public Uses" of Eminent Domain: History and Policy*, 11 Envt'l L. 1, 24(1980).

[33] *Compare*, for example, Aldridge v. Tuscumbia, Courtland, & Decatur RR., 2 Stew. & P. 199, 203 (Ala. 1832) (upholding the exercise of eminent domain for purposes of constructing a railroad), *to* Pittsburg, Wheeling & Ky. R.R. v. Benwood Iron-Works, 8 S.E. 453, 467 (W. Va. 1888)(reversing a lower court decision to allow a railroad company to condemn land pursuant state statute) (cited in *Lopez*, supra footnote 29, at n.132.

when the Court recognized that state court decisions were a quagmire, the Court itself used circular reasoning rather than a definition: it stated that an irrigation plan which took land from some farmers to benefit other landowners was consistent with the narrow "public use" definition because "the irrigation of really arid lands is a public purpose, and the water thus used is put to a public use."[34] Consequently, critics not unreasonably concluded that the expansive nature of what counted as a "public use" posed a substantial threat to the right of private property.[35]

Another line of cases involved a broader conception of "public use" by deferring to legislatures' definitions of the term.[36] "[W]hen the legislature has declared the use or purpose to be a public one, its judgment will be respected by the courts, unless the use be palpably without reasonable foundation."[37] In other words, the public use is what the legislature said it was (so much for checks, balances, and an independent judiciary).

Finally, in its 1954 seminal decision *Berman v. Parker*, the Supreme Court abandoned the "narrow" definition of public use entirely, and defined *public use* as a generalized benefit to the "public welfare": "[t]he concept of the public welfare is broad and inclusive. The values it represents are spiritual as well as physical, aesthetic as well as monetary."[38] This decision meant that Berman lost his non-blighted commercial property, which was to be transferred to another private party simply because it was in an area designated by Congress for redevelopment[39]: a public agency created by Congress's District of Columbia Redevelopment Act had been granted eminent domain powers to acquire blighted areas in DC and then transfer the condemned properties to private parties who agreed to initiate projects that conformed to their overall redevelopment plan. Berman's business happened to be in that area, though the premises themselves were not blighted.

[34] Fallbrook Irrigation District v. Bradley, 164 U.S. 112, 164 (1896) (cited and quoted in *Lopez*, supra footnote 19 at 263.

[35] *Lopez*, supra footnote 29, at 260 (and citations therein).

[36] United States v. Gettysburg Electric R. Co., 160 U.S. 668 (1896).

[37] Id. at 680.

[38] Berman v. Parker, 348 U.S. 26, 33 (1954).

[39] Id. at.

The next important Supreme Court case, *Hawaii Housing Authority v. Midkiff*, similarly allowed the government to acquire land by eminent domain and then transfer it to private parties it deemed qualified, though the circumstances were unusual: rather than a blighted area determination, Hawaii had determined that a "feudal land tenure system," created by Hawaii's traditional aristocracy, had distorted the residential property market, and thus governmental seizure and resale to private parties was justified.[40] In reaching its decision, the Court further entrenched *Berman*'s broad basis for testing the constitutionality of a taking: [we] "long ago rejected any literal requirement that condemned property be put into use for the general public," and the beneficiaries of an eminent domain action need not constitute "any considerable portion" of the community.[41]

The most recent Supreme Court decision in this line, *Kelo v. City of New London*, is fully in keeping with the policies developed under *Berman*. Like many other New England cities, New London was experiencing economic difficulties in the 1990s: one of its primary employers, the Naval Undersea Warfare Center, closed, and the city's population had diminished.[42] A Connecticut state agency identified New London as a "distressed municipality," enabling the New London Development Corporation ("NLDC") to use its power of eminent domain to acquire property for development purposes.[43] The NLDC decided that, once acquired, the property would be transferred to Pfizer, Inc., in the hope that it would be "a catalyst to the area's rejuvenation."[44] Susette Kelo, Wilhelmina Dery, and several other homeowners challenged the exercise of eminent domain as a violation of the Fifth Amendment's "public use" stricture.

---

[40] Hawaii Housing Authority v. Midkiff, 467 U.S. 229, 232 (1984). Traditionally, an island high chief controlled the land, assigning it for development to subchiefs, who would then reassign the land to lower-ranking chiefs, who would administer the land and govern farmers and other tenants. As a result, 49% of Hawaii's land was owned by State and Federal Governments while another 47% was controlled by the feudal system, causing a severe shortage of land available for housing.

[41] Id. at 243–44.

[42] Kelo v. City of New London, 125 S. Ct. 2655, 2658 (2005).

[43] Id. at 2660.

[44] Id. at 2659. Pfizer had plans for a $300 million research facility, and the development was to include a hotel with restaurants and shopping, marinas, a pedestrian "riverwalk," 80 new residences, a new US Coast Guard Museum, and other office and retail venues. Id.

In a controversial and fragmented decision, the Court's holding was in line with *Berman*, postulating that it had "repeatedly and consistently rejected" the narrow test since the end of the nineteenth century. The majority stated that the narrow interpretation had fallen out of favor over the course of time due to the difficulty of its application and the changing needs of society: the narrow test required answers to questions such as "what proportion of the public need have access to the property?" and "at what price?"[45] The fact that the City's "carefully formulated" plan was designed to create jobs and increase the community's tax base, as well as provide residential and recreational use, so that it "unquestionably serve[d] a public purpose" was enough of a "public use" to justify the exercise of eminent domain powers.[46]

In dissent, Justice O'Connor, joined by Justices Rehnquist, Scalia, and Thomas, argued that the majority deleted "the words 'for public use' from the Takings Clause of the Fifth Amendment."[47] She also asserted that the plurality had veered from *Berman* and *Midkiff* by upholding an exercise of eminent domain with only remote public benefits.[48] While *Berman* and *Midkiff* involved taking land from private parties and subsequently redistributing it to other private parties, the acquisition of the land led directly to a public benefit, regardless of the subsequent transfer: a harmful use was eliminated by the taking to remove blight in *Berman* and to break the land oligopoly in *Midkiff*,[49] but there was no such purpose in *Kelo*.

In his separate dissent, Justice Thomas agreed that *Kelo* erases the "public use" stricture from the Constitution but condemned the majority opinion even more vehemently than had Justice O'Connor: "Defying [the] original understanding that only public necessity could justify violating the 'sacred and inviolable rights of private property,' the Court replaces the Public Use Clause with a '[P]ublic [P]urpose' Clause, … or perhaps the 'diverse and Always Evolving Needs of Society' Clause, a

[45] Id. at 196.
[46] Id. at 2659, 2665.
[47] Id. at 2671 (O. Connor. J., dissenting).
[48] Id. at 2675.
[49] Id. at 2674–75.

restriction that is satisfied, the Court instructs, so long as the purpose is 'legitimate' and the means 'not irrational.'"[50] Justice Thomas then described the public use basis of the majority reasoning as being against all common sense: a costly urban-renewal project whose stated public use was only a vague promise of new jobs and increased tax revenue, suspiciously agreeable to Pfizer Inc.[51] Instead, Justice Thomas argued, in keeping with the Constitution's common law background, the clause was intended to be a most-needed limit on the government and should be interpreted in context with other carefully chosen Constitutional language. The government is allowed to take private property only if it provides "just compensation" and only if the taking is for the government's or the public's own use.[52] Thus, the Takings Clause allows the government to take property only if the government owns, or the public has a legal right to use, the property.[53] Neither the narrow nor the broad line of cases correctly followed the original, natural reading of the clause.[54]

Kelo has resulted in a widespread debate on the fiscal and ethical consequences of using economic development to justify the exercise of eminent domain. The fiscal concern is that such government-sponsored redevelopment projects are both costly and unsuccessful. In other words, the use of eminent domain to take property from one private entity and give it to another with the aim of promoting economic development is counterproductive as well as unconstitutional.[55] For example, the Washington DC redevelopment project at issue in *Berman* ultimately failed and the legislation creating it was repealed.[56] A similar project in the Poletown area of Detroit, Michigan, involving General Motors also

---

[50] Id. at 2677 (Thomas, J. Dissenting).

[51] Id.

[52] Id. at 2680.

[53] Id. at 2679.

[54] Id. at 2682.

[55] Art Rolnick & Phil Davies, *The Cost of Kelo*, 20 Fed. Reserve Bank Region 12 at *8 2006 WLNR 11063440 (June 1, 2006).

[56] Housing and Community Development Act of 1974, Pub. L. No. 93–383, § 116, 88 Stat. 652 (codified at 42 U.S.C. § 5316 (2000); see 42 U.S.C. §§ 1450–1451 (sections omitted pursuant to § 5316); *see also* Jane Jacobs, The Death and Life of Great American Cities 311–14 (Vintage Books 1992) (criticizing urban renewal and public housing programs as "inherently wasteful ways of rebuilding cities."

flopped, leaving a strip of abandoned and burned-out properties instead of the pre-taking busy commercial area. And, Cincinnati's downtown area gained only a municipal parking lot when Nordstrom ultimately backed out of a redevelopment plan.[57] The mere declaration of an eminent-domain-backed redevelopment plan can itself lead to anticipatory "condemnation blight" where properties lose value precipitously in advance of the actual exercise of eminent domain power.[58] Even where an economic development taking has resulted in an economically improved area, the area at issue would likely have improved on its own through the operation of the market without the use of eminent domain.

The ethical concern is that promiscuous redevelopment takings lead to nefarious overreaching by legislators in concert with large business entities, victimizing private parties and small firms. Specifically, business interests who want to purchase property for redevelopment at low cost will be motivated to persuade legislative bodies to grant them eminent domain support and then use this power to bully smaller businesses. In one such case, when a landlord refused to allow an expansion, a Target store secured eminent domain power from the local government and forced its landlord to allow the expansion.[59]

The reverse is also possible: legislative bodies, greedy for additional tax dollars, will use indefensible methods to either cause areas to be blighted or declare them blighted and then grant eminent domain taking powers simply to raise their tax base.[60] One recent case illustrates exactly this sort of nefarious overreaching, as well as the potential for fiscal irresponsibility: a city council allegedly hired first one appraiser and then another in an effort to have an aging, working-class subdivision in St. Louis declared "blighted," so that it could be slated for redevelopment.[61] The council wanted to replace the subdivision with a shopping mall in an effort to

[57] Id. at *7.

[58] Dale A. Whitman, *Eminent Domain Reform in Missouri: A Legislative Memoire*, 71 Mo. L. Rev. 721, 757 (2006).

[59] Dale A. Whitman, *Eminent Domain Reform in Missouri: A Legislative Memoire*, 71 Mo. L. Rev. 721, 736 (2006).

[60] Richard A. Epstein, *Kelo: An American Original*, 8 Green Bag 2d 355, 360 (2005).

[61] Peter W. Salsich, Jr., *Privatization and Democratization – Reflections on the Power of Eminent Domain*, 50 St. Louis U. L.J. 751, 755 (2006), discussing controversy surrounding the exercise of eminent domain with regard to a development project in the St. Louis suburb of Sunset Hills.

increase the city's tax income, and so the World War II era subdivision was termed "blighted" despite the fact that the only problems the appraiser could find were bedrooms in some basements, front porches which had settled, and some windows were too small to allow escape in an emergency.[62] Despite the fact that the City Council granted it eminent domain authority, the developer hired to redevelop the area could not secure financing, and so the project eventually failed, leaving a number of homeowners caught between a contract to purchase a new home but no purchaser for the old one.

In response to *Kelo* and perceived problems posed by the exercise of eminent domain for economic redevelopment purposes, 32 states passed or were in the process of enacting legislation banning economic development as a "public use" within a year of the *Kelo* decision.[63] Even the US Congress passed a bill preventing the use of federal money in connection with a federal, state, or local economic redevelopment taking where private entities would be the primary beneficiaries.[64]

C. Just Compensation

Theoretically, the Supreme Court has interpreted "just compensation" as requiring that the owner of condemned property be put in as good a position pecuniarily as if his property had not been taken[65]; however, the

---

[62] Id.

[63] *See* Castle Coalition, Enacted Legislation, available at www.castlecoalition.org/legislation/passed/index.html, *listing* post-*Kelo* eminent domain legislation.

[64] Transportation, Treasury, Housing and Urban Development, the Judiciary, the District of Columbia, and Independent Agencies Appropriations Act for FY 2006, Pub. L. 109–115, Title VII, § 726 (Nov. 30, 2005): "No funds in this Act may be used to support any Federal, State, or local projects that seek to use the power of eminent domain, unless eminent domain is employed only for a public use: *Provided*, That for purposes of this section, public use shall not be construed to include economic development that primarily benefits private entities…."

[65] *See* United States v. 564.54 Acres of Land, 441 U.S. 506, 510 (1979); United States v. Miller, 317 U.S. 369, 373 (1943); Olson v. United States, 292 U.S. 246, 255 (1934); Campbell v. United States, 266 U.S. 368 (1924); Seaboard Airline R. Col. V. United States, 261 U.S. 299, 304 (1923) (all holding that just compensation requires that the owner be put in substantially the same position pecuniarily as if he would have been if his property had not been taken).

compensation granted is widely recognized as consistently under-compensatory.[66]

Under eminent domain practice, the expropriating agency must first attempt to purchase the property through free negotiation on the open market before resorting to condemnation.[67] Nevertheless, the owner of the property at issue will usually understand that an eminent domain action is threatened if he refuses to sell on the government's terms, and therefore as a practical matter, even this "free negotiation" has a coercive nature. Once the owner has refused and the agency brings the threatened action, although the condemned owner is theoretically due a full and perfect equivalent to the property taken, practical difficulties have made it necessary for the courts to develop and follow working rules to enable determination of that value.[68] This particularly concerns holdout landowners whose actions purportedly could drive up the price of the property until the government offers compensation higher than the market price[69] and equal to or greater than the value of the property to the government. The primary "working rule" is that of the "fair market value."

Unfortunately, it has been widely recognized that the "fair market value" scheme fails all three of the basic criteria courts use to judge whether a compensation scheme is effective: it fails to ensure that landowners are fairly compensated for their loss, fails to promote efficient use of the Takings Clause, and does not prevent opportunism.[70] Landowners are systematically under-compensated for the loss of their property. Business owners lose business profits and goodwill, removal costs, litigation costs, appraisal fees, and demoralization costs.[71] Homeowners and

---

[66] Michael DeBow, *Unjust Compensation: The Continuing Need for Reform*, 46 S.C. L. Rev. 579, 580 (1995).

[67] Patricia Munch, *An Economic Analysis of Eminent Domain*, 84 J. Pol. Econ. 473, 473 (1976).

[68] *See* 564.54 Acres of Land, at 511; United States v. Cors, 337 U.S. 325, 332 (1949); United States v. Fuller, 409 U.S. 488, 490 (1973); United States ex rel. Tenn. Valley Auth. v. Powelson, 319 U.S. 266, 280 (1943); Miller, 317 U.S. at 375.

[69] *But see* Bruce Benson, *The Mythology of Holdout as a Justification for Eminent Domain and Public Provision of Roads*, 10 Independent Review 165–194 (Fall 2005), arguing that whatever the "holdout" demands *is* the market price.

[70] Nathan Burdsal, Note, *Just Compensation and the Seller's Paradox*, 20 Brigham Young U. J. Pub. L. 79, 82 (2005), and sources cited nn.14–19.

[71] Id.

neighborhoods are uncompensated for any value that could be attributed to emotional or historical attachment to the property, in addition to litigation costs, appraisal fees, and any other indirect costs.[72]

Additionally, the market value method is inefficient because the government cannot incorporate all of the costs associated with the takings and thus fails to consider opportunity costs. It presumes that the only costs it will pay are the "fair market value" costs and fails to take into account administrative and litigation costs. The former are astronomical: obtaining legislative authorization of eminent domain power, drafting and filing the complaint, serving process, securing a formal appraisal, and so on.[73] Similarly, the latter can also be extremely high. In one California case, a jury awarded a family who paid $878,000 for their property $1,070,000, plus $620,000 in attorney fees.[74] Third, even assuming that opportunism—rent seeking (as it is sometimes termed)[75]—is something to be discouraged, the fair market calculus is ineffective: generally the fair market value system rules prevent landowners from receiving more compensation than the appraised market value of their property but encourages opportunistic behavior by administrators, attorneys, and litigants.[76]

Moreover, the market value method is a poorly defined fiction. Fair market value is properly defined as the price that a willing buyer would pay a willing seller in the open market.[77] The reality in an eminent domain/taking context is that the willing buyer is the government, but there is no willing seller.[78]

---

[72] *See* id. at 87–88. *See also* United States v. Bodcaw Co., 440 U.S. 202, 204, 99 S. Ct. 1066, 1067 (1979) (holding that appraisal expenses and expert witness expenses are not part of the "just compensation" required by the Fifth Amendment).

[73] *See* Burdsal, supra footnote 70, at 85, 90; Thomas Merrill, *The Economics of Public Use*, 72 Cornell L. Rev. 61, 77–78 (1986).

[74] *Property Rights Victories*, The Orange County Register, Nov. 26, 2000, cited in Burdsal, supra footnote 46, at 90.

[75] *See* Walter Block, *Watch your Language* (Feb. 21, 2000), critiquing this terminology, available at; http://www.mises.org/fullarticle.asp?control=385&month=17&title=Watch+Your+Language&id=19

[76] Id. at 89.

[77] Kirby Forest Indus. v. United States, 467 U.S. 1, 10 (1984); United States v. 564.54 Acres of Land, 441 U.S. 506, 511 (1979); Almota Farmers Elevator & Warehouse Co. v. United States, 409 U.S. 470, 474 (1973); United States v. Virginia Elec. & Power Co., 365 U.S. 624, 633 (1961); United States v. Miller, 317 U.S. 369, 374 (1943).

[78] *Burdsal*, supra footnote 70, at 91–92.

"Oftentimes, the state claims it is offering a "fair market value" for the property it seeks to seize, but this is a sham. The market price for something is, by definition, the price that both parties consent to. In a fair market exchange, each party gives up something he values less for something he values more, or else he wouldn't agree to it. It is only through such a voluntary transaction that we can determine what something's market value is in the first place. Market value is not universal, but particular to the assets exchanged in a specific transaction. For any given piece of property, there can be no market value without market exchange."[79]

Thus, the judicial definition of fair market value for purposes of an eminent domain taking is confusing, circular, and a complete fiction in the eyes of economists.

Consequently, as interpreted by the Supreme Court, the takings clause has been gutted: neither *taking*, nor *public use* nor *just compensation* has any consistent, sensible meaning. At this point, under the US Constitution, as interpreted by the Supreme Court, federal, state, and local governments are effectively free to take or legislate-away any property, pay the owner some paltry sum, and then resell the property to another private entity.[80]

In part, the antifederalists' fear that we were creating far too powerful a government has come to pass.[81] Contrary to Madison's original intent, due to inconsistent and politically driven Supreme Court interpretation, adding the Eminent Domain clause to the Bill of Rights has resulted not in protecting individuals' rights but in circumscribing them instead. Furthermore, giving the government a vague, theoretical power to take property from individuals implies that it is capable of determining the

---

[79] Anthony Gregory, *The Trouble with "Just Compensation,"* (Dec. 5, 2006), available at http://mises.org/story/2379.

[80] Happily, state and local governments are free to provide protection higher than that provided in the US Constitution as interpreted by the Supreme Court. *See* supra text at footnote 63–64 discussing post-Kelo legislation; *Whitman*, supra footnote 58 at 744, discussing "heritage value" measure of compensation as provided by Missouri statutes. *But see* id. at 758 pointing out that the post-Sunset Hills, Missouri legislation would not have benefited owners who had sold their homes under the mere threat of eminent domain.

[81] *See* supra text accompanying footnotes 15–17.

public good, thus implying that a country is an enterprise association with a collective goal.[82] This is contrary to Madison's vision of the United States as a commercial republic grounded in a multiplicity of individuals' interests.[83]

III. An Economic Analysis of Eminent Domain

According to conventional wisdom, some things will simply be unavailable to us as a society without the governmental employment of eminent domain. Preeminent examples include highways, pipelines, railroads, sewer lines, water pipes, long tunnels, indeed, anything long and thin that requires miles and miles of extended narrow space. Why? Well, in all likelihood, the territory required to build these amenities will be in the hands of hundreds, and maybe thousands of different property owners.[84] The odds are that at least one of them will hold out for vast amounts of money if his land is to be used for this purpose, thus threatening the entire enterprise. Even those who cordially dislike the coercion necessary to expropriate[85] private property rights are thus likely to acquiesce in such seizures of private property, since for them a world without such long thin things (LTTs) would be scarcely tolerable.

In contrast to conventional wisdom, in our judgment, a system based strictly on private property rights where all actions are strictly limited to voluntary ones and thus no land seizure is legal is far preferable to one where coercion is legal, even if the result is that LTTs cannot be built. In other words, for us, the motto "justice though the heavens fall" is relevant to real-world public policy analysis; it should not be something that merely garners lip service and is not incorporated into actual decision-making.

[82] Michael Oakshott, On Human Conduct 119, 139, 181, 153–58, 234–5, 286, 315 (Oxford University 2003); *see also* Hayak, supra footnote 83, at 94–98.

[83] James Madison, Federalist 10.

[84] This is true in the modern day. This sort of "conventional wisdom" will readily concede that in a bygone era, it was possible to construct LTTs without the benefit of eminent domain. For example, J.J. Hill was able to build railways with no government help (DiLorenzo, 2004).

[85] In Canada, eminent domain is called expropriation.

Happily, however, it is our claim that this stark choice is not one that actually confronts us. We do not have to choose between economic freedom and no LTTs on the one hand, and, on the other, LTTs but a curtailment of private property rights and liberty. We can, proverbially, have our cake and eat it too. We can retain our western civilization-based appreciation of private property rights, and, also, have long thin things.

The argument for the necessity of eminent domain goes as follows: any time anyone starts building one of these LTTs, the holdout problem will arise. Even though there is an obvious benefit to all, say, 5000 individual property owners from agreeing to take part as a part owner if need be in the LTT creation, each one has an even greater incentive to be a holdout because then he can reap even greater benefits.

Having stated the economic case for eminent domain, we now move to a refutation of it, beginning by showing that potential holdouts are not likely to hold out for any length of time. They themselves are likely to recognize that (1) the gain to be realized by holding out is minimal, (2) holding out will place them in an awkward position vis-à-vis their neighbors, and (3) even if they persist in holding out, the likely result is a crooked LTT, not no LTT, because (4) there is likely to be little additional expense to the developer in choosing a less direct route.

A. Holdout Profits

The holdout can reap these even greater benefits *only* if the enterprise goes through to completion. Assume the following values per acre of farmland, of the 5000 owners stretching, say, between Louisiana and California,[86] where we are thinking of building our new road.

If LTT is not built	$10	If LTT is built	$10,000
Successful holdout	$1 trillion	Unsuccessful holdout	$10

The point here is that the $1 trillion windfall is a will-o-the-wisp. It is theoretical. It does not exist. It will never take place. If a holdout insists upon this ridiculous amount, or anything like it, that will be the end of the project. It simply will not be built.

[86] The authors of the present paper make their homes in these two states.

Therefore, and to the extent to which these 5000 property owners (and by extension, all such people) are motivated by greed or profit seeking, and not by a desire merely to balk the travel plans of everyone else, this holdout threat is not a serious one. Some evidence for this: only a small percentage of people are anti-social in this way. Similarly, only a small percentage of the citizenry engage in serious crimes such as murder and rape.[87] Most people are decent and motivated not only by self-interest in terms of maximizing their own profits or revenues but even by the good of others or society in general (how else can we account for the widespread practice of charitable giving in the United States).[88] This is perhaps the most important of the points made here. For, if it is stipulated that most people have an overwhelming desire to become richer, not a desire to stubbornly reduce everyone else's welfare, then human nature is in *favor* of LTTs being built under a regime of economic freedom (and eminent domain authority is unnecessary).

It cannot be denied that bargaining power will play a role here.[89] The only point being made at present is that the holdout, if he is motivated by greed rather than sheer bloody-mindedness, will realize that if he insists upon the proverbial $1 trillion, he will get nothing from the LTT since it will not be built. Thus, he will have to settle for a more "reasonable" amount for his land. We move, then, from the horror story of the holdout who prevents the road or pipeline from being built to one who is merely trying to maximize the value of his landholdings. If the developer offers a flat $10,000 per acre for land that previously was worth $10 per acre and states that if a single owner demands more he will build elsewhere, it is entirely possible that even the limited bargaining power help by each land holder will greatly decrease.

---

[87] The United States has the highest incarceration rate in the world, see study available at http://www.google.ca/search?hl=en&q=The+U.S.+has+the+highest+incarceration+rate+in+the+world+&btnG=Search&meta= and it is only 500 per 100,000, statistics at http://www.ojp.usdoj.gov/bjs/glance/incrt.htm.

[88] *See* Giving Statistics, available at http://www.charitynavigator.org/index.cfm/bay/content.view/cpid/42; http://nccsdataweb.urban.org/FAQ/index.php?category=31, presenting statistics analyzing the sources of widespread charitable giving in the United States.

[89] *See generally* Adam Clanton, *Enforcing Individual Rights in an Industrial World: Legal Rules and Economic Consequences*, 4 Georgetown J. L. & Pub. Pol. 165 (Winter 2006).

B. Peer Pressure and the Holdout's Plight

Consider the plight of the holdout. All the neighbors are positively *hungering* for the LTT to come through, so that their land can increase in value from $10 per acre to $10,000, in the example given above. There is this one holdout in town demanding the never-to-be attained $1 trillion. None of the townsfolk will have anything to do with the holdout or his family. Yet, still, provided these other people don't use violence against him, there may well still be some few holdouts, out of our assumed sample size of 5000. But this phenomenon, alone, ought to reduce the number of such holdouts to a more manageable size.

C. Non-straight or Crooked LTTs

An alternative way of dealing with holdouts is simply to work around them, and this is where crooked or non-perfectly straight LTTs come in. Given that only a *very* small percentage of the population will be motivated to hold out through pure malevolence,[90] if, by odd chance, one of them pops up on what would have been a straight LTT route, the developing company[91] can always choose a more circuitous path. That is, they can build around the holdout's property. This option, in itself, is likely to discourage holdouts.

There is such a phenomenon as potential competition. The last thing that the extant railroad wants is a competitor to be built parallel to his own operation, a few miles distant from his own. Once this occurs, the capital value of his own holdings will plummet. Therefore, *competition* is in operation even if no such alternative route yet exists. The present railroad will not likely price too high for its services,[92] lest the profits earned thereby tempt a competitor to actually enter the field.

---

[90] Or terminal stupidity. It is possible that some may yet hope for that bonanza of $1 trillion, but in any free enterprise society worthy of the name, it is likely people of this ilk will not end up owning any large tracts of land.

[91] For the argument that private interests will likely be able to build LTTs, and the government is therefore not needed at least in the case of roads, see Block, Walter. 2007, forthcoming. *Privatize The Highways*. Auburn, AL: The Mises Institute.

[92] We are now assuming a free market environment, where giving bribes to the legislature to prevent the entry of alternative firms is not an option.

In like manner, the same considerations apply to the would-be holdout, standing in the way of the LTT development. The last thing such a property owner would want would be for the road or pipeline to be sited elsewhere, in a place such that the demand for his own land would not increase at all. In other words, the holdout faces potential competition from every other landowner whose property could be used by the LTT developer as an alternative to his own. This phenomenon, alone, ought to put something of a spike into the wheels of the holdout.

D. Developer's Expenses in the Absence of Eminent Domain Authority

No great or inordinate expenses would likely have to be undertaken by the firm attempting to build the LTT. It could purchase options[93] to buy land along any given route, at a relatively modest price. Then, if a holdout refused to cooperate, this company could turn to an alternative route.

Consider the attached diagram 1. There are six "curved" paths between the starting and ending points of our road, in, say, New Orleans and San Francisco, in addition to the straight one, A. These six are, respectively, B, C, D, E, F, and G. The entrepreneur who wants to build a highway or pipeline between these two cities can purchase options to buy land at a relatively modest price. If and when he runs into a holdout demanding an inordinate price, he merely refrains from exercising his options along that one route and simply reroutes.

Diagram 2 furnishes a variation on this theme. Here, instead of "curved" alternative routes, there are jagged or crooked alternative routes as mentioned in the previous section. When a holdout appears, an end run may in this way be made around him and his property. Admittedly, this will be more expensive. Assuming the LTT is a pipeline, additional pumps may have to be placed at the corners in order to keep the oil moving. Or, if the LTT is a road, traffic will have to slow down to accommodate the extra curvature to a greater degree than otherwise on the private

[93] Walter Block & Richard A. Epstein, *Walter Block v. Richard Epstein, Debate on Eminent Domain*, 1 NYU J. L. & Lib. 1144–1169 (2005).

road.[94] Nevertheless, as long as the present discounted capital value of these losses is lower than the amount the holdout is demanding for his land, the LTT project will be undertaken. The additional costs provide an upper limit on what might have to be paid to the holdout.[95]

E. Extreme Holdouts: The Worst-Case Scenario in the Absence of Eminent Domain

The worst-case scenario for advocates of our position that LTTs can be built by private enterprise without resort to eminent domain is the sort of holdout situation depicted in diagram 3. Here, the proposed road is to be laid out in an east-west direction, and the land owned by the holdout runs north-south, overlapping each and every one of the alternative east-west routes that might otherwise be followed by the developer. That is, holding X overlaps routes A, B, C, D, E, F, and G.

The first thing to be said about this scenario is that it is an extremely unlikely one. Any firm economically strong enough to own such a large parcel of land is unlikely in the extreme to take on the role of holdout.

---

[94] An example of this is the kind of rerouting that occurred in Worcester, Massachusetts, with the building of US Interstate 290, near exit 11. The road curves around the College of the Holy Cross, which was politically strong enough to "hold out" against the straight-line development of this thoroughfare, which might well otherwise have occurred. See map available at http://www.mapquest.com/maps/map.adp?formtype=address&country=US&popflag=0&latitude=&longitude=&name=&phone=&level=&addtohistory=&cat=&address=1+College+St&city=Worcester&state=MA&zipcode=01610-2322.

[95] It might be thought that the authors of the present paper look upon the holdout as some sort of "enemy." After all, but for him, our case would be easy to make that eminent domain laws are unnecessary in a free society. Nothing could be further from the truth. As it happens, we look upon the holdout with a certain wry approval. Yes, he can be a pest, but his presence is emblematic of the essence of private property rights in a free society. For example, you will never see an edifice constructed under the control of the USSR with a "piece" cut out of it. All such buildings are squares or regular rectangles. It is evidence of the relative freedom prevailing in the United States that every once in a while there will be a high rise edifice with an irregular base. Sometimes, there is (or was) a little house belonging to a holdout in this space. Sometimes, an empty lot. In one case on Canal Street in New Orleans, a Sheraton hotel was built over and around an old drugstore whose owner held out—thus the high-rise was built lacking a pyramidal section in its base, in which nestled the drugstore. Apparently, when the owner died, the heirs sold the property to Sheraton, which promptly tore down the drugstore and filled in the missing piece. Such anomalies bear testimony to the protection of property rights and freedom from contract, two concepts which are bulwarks of commercial success in the United States.

Much more plausible would be that such an enterprise would want to become partners with the developer, contributing its land in return for an ownership share in the LTT. Nor is it reasonable to assume, at last, that the landowner in this case could "hold up" the developer for the theoretical \$1 trillion. True, the LTT, subject to what follows below, cannot be built without the cooperation of the owner of this strategic parcel, but it is equally true that the development will not take place if the landowner attempts to obtain the entire profits therefrom. No, here there will be a bargaining situation, with economic theory unable to determine each parties' shares of the ensuing revenues.

But, even if such a situation were to ensue, the developer is not without a strategy that will likely overcome the holdout's roadblock. Assuming the geographical situation makes it impossible for the LTT to be sited around the holdout's parcel, the developer can still tunnel under his land or bridge over it.[96] While this would be more expensive than building a road on the surface it, like the crooked LTT, places an upper limit on what the holdout can ask as payment for his property: he cannot expect any more than the cost of this bridge or tunnel.[97]

---

[96] Walter Block & Mathew Block, *Roads, Bridges, Sunlight and Private Property Rights*, VII *Journal Des Economistes Et Des Études Humaines* 351–362 (June-September 1996).

[97] According to the *ad coelum* doctrine, the owner of surface land also owns territory stretching below it, in a decreasing cone shape, all the way down to the center of the earth, and up into the heavens, in an increasing cone shape. But this doctrine is incompatible with the libertarian principle of homesteading. Walter Block, *Homesteading City Streets; An Exercise* in Managerial Theory, 5 Planning and Markets 18–33 (September 2002), available at http://www-pam.usc.edu/volume5/v5i1a2s1.html; http://www-pam.usc.edu/; Walter Block, *On Reparations to Blacks for Slavery*, 3 Human Rights Review 53–73 (September 2002); Walter Block & Guillermo Yeatts, *The Economics and Ethics of Land Reform: A Critique of the Pontifical Council for Justice and Peace's "Toward a Better Distribution of Land: The Challenge of Agrarian Reform*, 15 Journal of Natural Resources and Environmental Law 37–69 (1999–2000); Block v. Epstein, supra footnote 95; Block, Walter. 1990. "Earning Happiness Through Homesteading Unowned Land: a comment on 'Buying Misery with Federal Land' by Richard Stroup," *Journal of Social Political and Economic Studies*, Vol. 15, No. 2, Summer, pp. 237–253; Hans-Hermann Hoppe, The Economics and Ethics of Private Property: Studies in Political Economy and Philosophy, (Kluwer Academic Publishers 1993); John Locke, *An Essay Concerning the True Origin, Extent, and End of Civil Government*, in E. Barker, ed., Social Contract 17–18 (Oxford University Press 1948); Ellen Frankel Paul, Property Rights and Eminent Domain (1987); Murray N. Rothbard, *For a New Liberty* (Macmillan, New York 1973), available at http://www.mises.org/rothbard/newliberty.asp; Michael Rozeff, *Original Appropriation and its Critics* (September 1, 2005), available at http://www.lewrockwell.com/rozeff/rozeff18.html and thus must be rejected in the free society of which we are speaking. After all, the owner of surface land never came within 500 miles of "mixing his labor" with territory 500 miles below it. For

F. Precluding: Feasibility of the Holdout's Last Defense

Even in the face of a bridge or tunnel, the potential holdout is not without a possible response of his own. He could try to homestead the land above his property, *all* of it, in an attempt to preclude the LTT firm from bridging over his property, or below, *all* of it, in an attempt to preclude the LTT firm from tunneling[98] under his property. This anticipatory homesteading, however, would be very expensive. For, by definition, the LTT is *thin*, while the property in question is anything but. The holdout, moreover, would be like the first speaker in a debate: however high he built, or however deep he tunneled, the LTT developer would have the option of besting him in either direction. The developer only has to homestead land sufficient for his tunnel or pipeline; the holdout must do so for his *entire* subterranean property. Assume that the holdout wishes to forestall the developer, and he needs a cubic mile to do so. In very sharp contrast indeed, the landmass needed for the Chunnel was far less per mile of length. Thus, the developer has a gigantic advantage over the holdout.

Building an underground blocking wall would of course be cheaper than building an underground cubic edifice, but it would not suffice. For the developer can work around it. Suppose the wall is oriented north-south. Then, all the builder of the road or pipeline need do, apart from going under it, is to travel to the end of it, onto someone else's property with their permission, of course, thus obviating the entire purpose of the plane. Think of the Maginot Line.

Consider the situation in the opposite direction: above, not below. The impeder would have to build a wall, say, 30,000 feet high into the air the entire width of his property to stop airplane travel. But if so, then the planes could travel at 35,000 feet.

---

criticisms of ad coelum, see Rothbard (1982). One practical difficulty with ad coelum is that air flight would be rendered just about impossible.

[98] Block & Block, supra footnote 93; Block, Walter. 1998. "Roads, Bridges, Sunlight and Private Property: Reply to Gordon Tullock," *Journal des Economistes et des Etudes Humaines*, Vol. 8, No. 2/3, June-September, pp. 315–326, available at http://141.164.133.3/faculty/Block/Blockarticles/roads2_vol8.htm; Compare to Gordon Tullock, Comment on "Roads, Bridges, Sunlight and Private Property," by Walter Block and Matthew Block, 7 Journal des Economistes et des Etudes Humaines, 589–592 (December 1996).

G. The Advantage of Surprise

The LTT company has another advantage over the potential holdout: surprise. Only the developer knows where it intends to build. There is only so much the holdout can do to preclude *all* LTT options. And each of these can be *highly* expensive. For example, it is no accident that airplanes reached flying altitudes long before anyone thought to build walls high into the air in order to be bought off by them. To be fair, however, this argument is specious because such activities would not have been accepted by government courts even assuming such constructions were feasible.

Consider the same argument with regard to downward constructions rather than upward. Assume the owner of a roadway of some 3000 miles, stretching, say, from Baltimore to Seattle wishes to adopt the role of holdout against any north-south LTT development that wishes to pass under its holdings. It will have to begin by building something or other, down, down, down. How far down? This is unclear and highly problematic since no matter how deeply it claims land below its surface holdings by such "homesteading," all the builder of the north-south amenity has to do is undercut him by a few feet.[99] Moreover, and this is the crucial point, the "defense" will have to protect a perimeter stretching for the entire 3000-mile length of the extant road.[100] In very sharp contrast, all the "offense" needs to do is to find one weak spot: a place along this gigantic distance where either the holdout road owner has not built in a downward direction at all or has done so only to a shallow depth. Then, it is

[99] By how many feet below person A's land must person B build? The libertarian criterion is that B not interfere with the peaceful legitimate use of A of his property. So, again, we ask, how many feet below must B build below A's holdings? It depends upon how solid is the land involved, and what exists on the surface. If we are talking of the island of Manhattan, which is virtually solid rock, where there are buildings on the surface extending no more, typically, than 100 feet underneath, then not too far below at all: the rock is strong enough that the buildings above will not cave in. If territory near New Orleans is under discussion, then very deep indeed, as well as the extra cost required to prevent water seepage. For this land is swampy (query: where have all the swamps gone? Answer: they have been replaced by wetlands.) If A has an apple orchard, then B cannot get too close to the trees' roots lest he interferes with their growth. If there are only corn plants there, whose roots do not extend down as far, then B can build much closer to the surface.

[100] We abstract from the possibilities of making end runs up and down either the Atlantic or the Pacific Ocean.

game over. Imagine one football team which has to defend a line 3000 miles wide and another that merely has to break through at any one point,[101] to get an even clearer idea of the enormous difficulties placed upon the holdout.

H. Specialization and the Division of Labor

Specialization and the division of labor will also give an advantage to the developer *vis-à-vis* the holdout. The onus and expense of developing new techniques of digging tunnels, and expertise in using old ones, will rest on the side of the developer, not the holdout. Although this seems at first glance to be an advantage for the holdout, this is not the case because the LTT developer will likely specialize in only this type of enterprise, whereas the holdout will be involved, entirely, in a completely different industry; perhaps farming or ranching. Thus, any technological breakthroughs in tunneling will be in all likelihood first and to a greater degree mastered by the former than the latter.

Remember, the ethos of homesteading incorporates, at least potentially, a race between the developer and the holdout to see which of them can first build real or preventative tunnels or bridges. Given differential specialization in this sort of thing, the advantage once again lies in the direction of society being able to have LTTs without requiring eminent domain laws.

I. Feint

But this does not even begin to exhaust all the advantages enjoyed by the LTT developer in his "war" with the holdout. All the developer has to do is make a foray, a feint. He can bruit it about that he is intending to build a road or pipeline, where he has no intention of locating. Immediately, under a fully free enterprise system with no eminent domain and fully

[101] Well, ok, not a single geometrical point. Rather, a distance necessary to accommodate the north-south LTT. For a pipeline, what is this, ten feet? For a four-lane highway, perhaps 100 feet, including shoulders.

wedded to homesteading, all would-be holdouts will be sent a-quivering. They must rush to homestead land below their surface holdings, and *deeply* too, the better to make it impossible for the builder to move in that direction without making payments. This, to say the very least, will occasion vast expenses on the holdouts' part. Let a few instances of this boy falsely "crying wolf" type activity occur, and be publicized, where the holdout went to great expense all for naught, and when the real plan becomes actualized, such people will think twice before acting in this manner.

Indeed, "holdout" is a misnomer. It implies that the property owner who wishes to make a "killing" by either altogether preventing[102] or charging a very high price for his land needs merely "holdout." That is, sit tight, do nothing, wait for the LTT-er to come begging, hat in hand. Nothing could be further from the truth. Very much to the contrary, "holding out" is by far a more activist event. The holdout must initiate a very expensive homesteading effort in order to preclude the possibility of someone going under, above, or around his surface landholdings. Better nomenclature, instead of holdout, so as to emphasize this activist or initiatory element, might be "precluder," or "forestaller," or "preventer," or "prohibiter," or "rejecter," or "stopper."[103]

There is a strong analogy between these sorts of "games" and the predatory price-cutting Rockefeller was accused of in the 1911 antitrust suit against him.[104] According to the conventional wisdom, all the advantages

[102] A thousand pardons. If the holdout totally prevents the LTT, he garners nothing from his preventative efforts.

[103] Getting a "stop" in basketball takes great initiative, talent, and athleticism. It is by no means a passive accomplishment.

[104] Standard Oil began as an Ohio partnership formed by industrialist John D. Rockefeller, his brother William, Henry Flagler, chemist Samuel Andrews, and silent partner Stephen V. Harkness. *Standard Oil Co. of New Jersey v. United States*, available at http://www.answers.com/topic/standard-oil-co-of-new-jersey-v-united-states (hereinafter "*Answers*". The period following the war of 1861–1865 was a time of unparalleled growth for the American economy, attributable to several factors: the emergence of national markets for manufactured products, the innovation of new technologies capable of manufacturing goods in larger quantities, and the generation of vast amounts of capital necessary for financing this growth. Eleanor M. Fox & Lawrence A. Sullivan, *Antitrust – Retrospective and Prospective: Where Are We Coming From? Where Are We Going?*, 62 N.Y.U. L. Rev. 936, 937–38 (1987). By the late 1870s and early 1880s, companies were seeking ways to obtain relief from unrelenting competition as well as innovating ways to organize and manage increasingly giant enterprises. *See* id. at 939, *Answers*; *also* Kolko, Gabriel. 1963. *Triumph of*

lay with Rockefeller. He could cut prices in one area, make up the shortfalls from the other divisions of his gigantic corporation. When the local was driven to the wall, Standard Oil would jack up prices there, and use the proceeds to launch yet another price war elsewhere. But as has been eloquently shown, all the target had to do was temporarily shut down. In this way the local price cutter would suffer tremendous losses, and the entire process could not even get underway.[105] In a similar manner, the advantage here, at least initially, appears all on the side of the holdout. All

---

Conservatism, Chicago: Quadrangle Books. According to most historians, one such enterprise was Standard Oil, which absorbed or obtained control over most of its competition in Cleveland Ohio, and then throughout the northeastern U.S., putting numerous small companies out of business (for an alternative view, see John McGee, *Predatory Price Cutting: The Standard Oil (New Jersey) Case*, The Journal of Law and Economics 137–169 (October 1958)). Rockefeller pioneered the trust as a legally enforceable way to unify control over a large number of corporations: trust certificates for common stock in the different corporations were exchanged among industry leaders, and by virtue of holding this common stock, the trust gained legal control over member corporations. Often a trust resembled a cartel because it concerned itself primarily with price and output decisions, not with the firms' actual operations. *Fox* at 940.

Negative reaction to the business trusts led to the Sherman Antitrust Act in 1890. 15 U.S.C. §§ 1–7 (1988). Although Ohio successfully sued Standard Oil and compelled the dissolution of its trust in 1892, the company separated off only Standard Oil of Ohio, without relinquishing control. *Answers*. When in 1899 New Jersey changed its incorporation laws to allow a single company to hold shares in other companies in any state, the Standard Oil Trust was legally reborn as a holding company. Eventually, the US Justice Department sued Standard Oil of New Jersey under the Sherman Act, and Standard Oil was forced to separate into 34 companies, each with its own distinct board of directors. Id. These companies formed the core of today's US oil industry, including ExxonMobil, ConocoPhillips, Chevron, Amoco and Sohio (now BP of North America), Atlantic Richfield, Marathon, and many other smaller companies.

For a critique of all anti-trust legislation as incompatible with free enterprise and private property rights, see Anderson, William, Walter Block, Thomas J. DiLorenzo, Ilana Mercer, Leon Snyman, and Christopher Westley. 2001. "The Microsoft Corporation in Collision with Antitrust Law," *The Journal of Social, Political and Economic Studies*, Vol. 26, No. 1, Winter, pp. 287–302; Armentano, Dominick T. 1999. *Antitrust: The Case for Repeal*. Revised 2nd ed., Auburn AL: Mises Institute; Block, Walter. 1994. "Total Repeal of Anti-trust Legislation: A Critique of Bork, Brozen and Posner, *Review of Austrian Economics*, Vol. 8, No. 1, pp. 35–70; Boudreaux, Donald J., and DiLorenzo, Thomas J. 1992. "The Protectionist Roots of Antitrust," *Review of Austrian Economics*, Vol. 6, No. 2, pp. 81–96; DiLorenzo, Thomas J. 1996. "The Myth of Natural Monopoly," *Review of Austrian Economics*, Vol. 9, No. 2, pp. 43–58; http://www.mises.org/journals/rae/pdf/rae9_2_3.pdf; DiLorenzo, Tom and Jack High. 1988. "Antitrust and Competition, Historically Considered," *Economic Inquiry*, July; McChesney, Fred. 1991. "Antitrust and Regulation: Chicago's Contradictory Views," *Cato Journal*, Vol. 10; Murray N. Rothbard. 1970. *Man, Economy and State*, Los Angeles, Nash; Shugart II, William F. 1987. "Don't Revise the Clayton Act, Scrap It!," 6 *Cato Journal*, 925; Smith, Jr., Fred L. 1983. "Why Not Abolish Antitrust?" *Regulation*, Jan-Feb, 23.

[105] See generally John McGee, supra footnote 104.

the latter has to do, supposedly, is to costlessly hunker down, and wait to "pounce" on the LTT developer. Not so, not so. Thanks to the phenomenon of libertarian homesteading, he must take a far more active and expensive role. He must preclude the LTT developer from making an end run (around), an under run (tunnel), and an over run (bridge) around him. There are not one, nor two, but *three* margins on the basis of which the developer can operate. The holdout must defend himself in all these dimensions, and perhaps for naught.

J. Homesteading

What is the precluding holdout going to *do* with the land lying significantly below his surface holdings in order to demonstrate homesteading? If he merely empties it, for example, "builds" a big underground hole, the LTT may be placed therein, without any harm to the precluder. That may well be his cheapest course of action, but it will avail him nothing in terms of accomplishing the task he sets for himself. The tunnel will in no way interfere with the big hole in the ground.[106] If he places land mines throughout, making it impossible for anything, ever, to be built there, he is no longer a holdout, even an active one. Now, he is taking himself out of the realm of a person who wants to cash in big by threatening to prevent someone else from building an LTT. He is violating the libertarian law prohibiting aggression against non-aggressors. Unless, that is, he posts information attesting to their exact location, so that the rights of other homesteaders (LTT) are not violated. But, then, it is always possible for the LTT to dig deeper. Knowing that, the holdout will be tempted to dig very deep indeed, sowing landmines as he goes. It goes without saying that this would be a very expensive proposition, and perhaps unnecessary if the LTT is engaging in a feint. It is also a hypothetical so unlikely that it reaches the absurd and laughable.

[106] Can the forestaller object that he wants to "contemplate" the big hole, for example, use it for aesthetic purposes? He cannot. *See* Walter Block, "Homesteading, *Ad Coelum*, Owning Views and Forestalling." (unpublished)

K. Optimal Number of LTTs?

It is entirely possible, and even likely, that there will be fewer miles' worth of LTTs under a regime of full economic freedom than with rampant statism. It is difficult to see how this can be denied. The government can, if it wishes, subject an inordinately large amount of land to expropriation. Its only limit in this regard is that it dare not do so much of it that it risks its own continued power. Reactions to *Kelo* showed that there are limits of tolerance, at least when the land is turned over to private people pursuing private interests, instead of used for "public" purposes.[107]

But rational public policy lies not in the direction of maximizing LTTs. Rather, it is predicated on attaining the *optimal* amount of them. The government is likely to overbuild. For example, consider the case of the "bridge to nowhere" where a few dozen Alaskans were to have an entire such edifice built for their own personal use.[108] Compared to that, in the absence of eminent domain powers, the market will certainly underbuild. But what is the *optimal amount* of LTTs? As with any such question, the proper answer can only emanate from the workings of the *market*.[109] But the free market is defined as the concatenation of commercial events based on *private property* and economic freedom. How

[107] *See* supra text accompanying footnotes 47–64, discussing reactions to *Kelo*. Of course, for the radical libertarian, it might be preferable to use land seizure in this way. At least the land stays in the private sector, always a desideratum. Stephan N. Kinsella, A Libertarian Defense of Kelo and Limited Federal Power (August 28, 2005), available at http://www.lewrockwell.com/kinsella/kinsella17.html; *see also* Block, Walter. 2006. "Coase and *Kelo*: Ominous Parallels and Reply to Lott on Rothbard on Coase," *Whittier Law Review*, Vol. 27, No. 4, pp. 997–1022; Epstein, Richard. 2005. "Blind Justices: The scandal of *Kelo* v. New London." *Wall Street Journal*, July 3. http://www.opinionjournal.com/extra/?id=110006904.

[108] http://www.google.com/search?hl=en&q=bridge+to+nowhere&btnG=Google+Search.

[109] See the socialist calculation literature on this vital point: Boettke, Peter J. 2001. *Calculation and Coordination: Essays on Socialism and Transitional Political Economy*. London: Routledge, 2001. http://www.mises.org/etexts/cc.pdf; Ebeling, Richard M. 1993. "Economic Calculation Under Socialism: Ludwig von Mises and His Predecessors," in Jeffrey Herbener, ed., The Meaning of Ludwig von Mises, Norwell, MA: Kluwer Academic Press, pp. 56–101; Hayek, F.A. 1948. "Socialist Calculation I, II, & III," *Individualism and Economic Order*, Chicago: University of Chicago Press; Herbener, Jeffrey M. 1996. "Calculation and the Question of Mathematics," Review of Austrian Economics, 9(1), pp. 151–162; Hoff, Trygve J.B. 1981. Economic Calculation in a Socialist Society, Indianapolis: Liberty Press.

these institutions can be logically reconciled with the expropriation of private property, for *any* purpose, is difficult to say.

There are other problems with eminent domain.[110] These have to be set against, on utilitarian grounds, the diminution of land devoted to LTTs, compared to what would eventuate on the free market. This holds true even if we take as optimal the mileage devoted to them under eminent domain (a heroic assumption). In other words, let us say, *arguendo*, that the ideal percentage of land allocated to LTTs is 5%. Stipulate that under a regime of full free enterprise with no exceptions for expropriation, only 3% of land will be so used. And, crucial point here, that with legal land seizure, this figure goes up to 10%.

The problem is, this 5% figure has no basis in fact; it is entirely made up for purposes of illustration. In the real world, only the market offers a non-ambiguous optimal allocation of resources. If, hypothetically speaking, with no government intervention whatsoever, the market allocates 70% of the money spent on chalk and cheese to the latter, and 30% to the former, well, then so be it; we are justified in claiming that this is the *optimal* allocation of resources. There is simply no other ratio, such as 60-40 or 80-20 that has any basis in fact, and on the basis of which we can criticize the market's 70-30 decision. Presumably, if either of these two other allocations were more in keeping with the preferences of the market actors, there would be forces brought to bear moving society in whatever direction is called for. For example, if 80-20 cheese to chalk were the extant allocation, and 70-30 the ideal one, there would be profits earned in cheese, and losses in the chalk industry, until we approached the optimum.[111] And the same applies to the "proper" allocation of land to LTTs and for other purposes.

[110] *Kelo* (2005) is only the last in a long line of such cases. See on this Block, 2006; Epstein, 2005; *Kelo*, 2005; Kinsella, 2005.

[111] It is an Austrian economic insight that the market rarely if ever, and if so, only temporarily so, settles at any such optimal point. Rather, tastes and the supply and demand for substitutes and complements of these two goods are always changing. The market, then, is a process, which at all times "aims" at congruency between tastes and supply and demand for items, on the one hand, and allocations of them on the other. Richard M. Ebeling, Richard M., ed., Money, Method, and the Market Process, (Kluwer Academic Publishers 1990): David Gordon, *What Should Anti-Economists Do?* Review of The market process: essays in contemporary Austrian economics (Peter J. Boettke and David L. Prychitko; Edward Elgar, 1994. XV + 304 pgs. (Mises Review, Spring 1995), available at http://www.mises.org/misesreview_detail.asp?control=81&sortorder=issue.

L. Cartels

The argument that LTTs can be built only under a regime of eminent domain is similar to the analysis of cartel breakup. Yes, each cartel member has an incentive to join the cartel. Given proper inelasticity in the relevant range, he can do better by cutting back on production a bit. However, once in the cartel, he has a strong incentive to "cheat"; to get everyone else to cut back, except himself. While encouraging others to do so, and acting as if he is going along, but all the while refusing to engage in any cutbacks on his own, he can garner even greater profits than by actually fully cooperating in this venture. In that way he can benefit in two different directions, not just one. He gains as a cartel member from the fact that every other member reduces productivity, thus raising the price by a greater percentage amount than the loss in quantity. He improves his lot, further, as a cartel "cheater," since he suffers no loss in product brought to market; indeed, he can even increase his output to some degree, as long as he is not so greedy as to completely counteract the cutbacks of his partners.

However, successful cartels *do* exist: They are called (large) business firms.[112] Any theory, such as the one that says cartel-like behavior cannot survive, is thus rendered invalid.

"A common argument holds that cartel action involves *collusion*. For one firm may achieve a 'monopoly price' as a result of its natural abilities or consumer enthusiasm for its particular product, whereas a cartel of many firms allegedly involves 'collusion' and 'conspiracy.' These expressions, however, are simply emotive terms designed to induce an unfavorable response. What is actually involved here is *co-operation* to increase the incomes of the producers. For what is the essence of a cartel action? Individual producers agree to pool their assets into a common lot, this single central organization to make the decisions on production and price policies for all the owners and then to allocate the monetary gain among them. *But is this process not the same as any sort of joint partnership or the formation of a single corporation?*"

[112] Rothbard, Murray N. (1993 [1962]). *Man, Economy, and State*, 2 vols., Auburn, AL: Ludwig von Mises Institute, p. 572; http://www.mises.org/rothbard/mespm.pdf.

Let it not be argued that the analogy between the cartel cheater and the holdout is not an apt one. The situations are congruent. The "cheater" and the holdout each attempt to gain ground at the expense of those with whom, if they cooperate with them, will earn them extra revenue. The cheater cooperates with the other cartel members, and then turns around and supposedly stabs them in the back. Precisely the same is true of the holdout. The only way his land can increase in value is if the LTT gets constructed. This requires the cooperation of numerous economic actors. And, yet, the holdout slips the knife into all those others, without whose cooperation the money-making LTT cannot be constructed.

The traditional argument is that a cartel is subject to break up from two sources. First, the internal cheating previously discussed: each member has an incentive to look as if he is cutting back on production but not actually doing so. Second, there is outside entry. If the cartel is successful, profits in the industry will rise. This will attract newcomers who are anxious to benefit from this success. But as new entry occurs, supply will increase and profits decrease until the cartel is no more. However, as Rothbard has shown, given that large firms are but agglomerations of smaller business entities, it cannot be said that all cartels fail.[113]

M. Summary of the Economic Analysis

Let our enthusiasm for the LTT developer *vis-à-vis* the holdout not be misinterpreted as our favoring of the former in contrast to the latter. Did you ever see, gentle reader, a high rise building that was not regularized from a geometrical point of view? Looked at from above, it appeared to be a circle or a rectangle with a little part cut out of it? This is an indication that a real estate developer was unable to convince a recalcitrant holdout to sell his property, and went ahead with construction despite that fact. But a building with a sliver sliced out of it is a testimony to economic freedom. You will not find anything of the kind in areas controlled by our good friends, the Communists. No, irregular building patterns are a monument to free enterprise. It is imperative for the survival

[113] Id.

of civilization that private property rights be upheld, and allowing hold-outs to, well, hold out, is a necessary part and parcel of that system. Our only point is that it is unlikely in the extreme that protecting the private property rights of the holdout will cost us LTTs.

IV. Conclusion

The strength of common law is its flexibility and the judiciary's ability to craft different resolutions for different fact patterns, in contrast to traditional civilian jurisdictions where the only sources of law are statutes and regulations. However, this very strength can also be a weakness when case law leads to inconsistencies and incoherence. Such has been the case with eminent domain. Such inconsistencies and incoherence tend to bring into disrespect all of law. And yet law and the rule of law are what hold us together as a society. It is what distinguishes us from the barbarians. If our civilization is to be protected, at least insofar as jurisprudence is concerned, we must strive mightily to eliminate, or at least radically reduce, aspects of the law that are given to such capriciousness. Expropriation certainly fits this bill. Nor, the point we have attempted to make in our economic analysis is eminent domain necessary if we as a society are to be able to enjoy the "long thin things" that, presumably, "justify" governmental takings in the first place. In the absence of eminent domain, governments and private entities will still be able to build long thing things because holding out is simply not in any individual's long-term interest. And even were an individual to hold out due to pure meanness, the developer is likely to build over, under, or around his property.

While ancient governments may have been perceived of as all-powerful, since the Enlightenment, the understanding has been that it is the people who ultimately hold power, and it is the people whose rights must be protected. Some of the most important of these rights include the free market, the right to own property, and freedom of contract. Eminent domain has simply proven to be economically unsound as well as incompatible with these rights and should, therefore, be eliminated.

15

Canadian Aboriginals: A Debate

This is a debate between Walter Block and Lorne Gunter on public policy with regard to Canadian Aboriginals and human rights legislation.

The exchange of opinion between Block and Gunter began with the latter's publication in the *Edmonton Journal*. Block responded, Gunter replied, and several rejoinders followed, a baker's dozen in all. (The times of day of the messages may not perfectly match the order as correctly depicted below, because the two correspondents were located in different time zones).

I. Gunter

Aboriginal stalling on rights must end; 30-year 'temporary' exemption to human rights law has benefited some band leaders.

Canadian aboriginal leaders have for decades flown all over the globe eagerly denouncing this country's human rights record against them.

What none has ever mentioned (at least none that I know of) is that aboriginal governments are themselves exempt from Canada's most fundamental human rights laws.

W. E. Block, *Property Rights*, Palgrave Studies in Classical Liberalism,
https://doi.org/10.1007/978-3-030-28353-7_15

The very rights violations they accuse non-native governments of, their own governments are unaccountable for.

Thanks to a "temporary" clause in the 1977 Canada Human Rights Act (CHRA), charges of bigotry, discrimination and harassment of the kind frequently levelled against non-aboriginal society cannot be brought against native councils and organizations.

After three decades of being shielded against the provisions of the CHRA, it is past time aboriginal governments were brought under the act's mandate.

Equality cuts both ways.

Abe Lincoln once said that "he who would be no slave must consent to have no slave." It works the same for aboriginals and human rights. The very rights aboriginals insist they be granted they must themselves be prepared to grant their own people—and be held accountable when they do not.

The CHRA was initially suspended on reserves and among native bureaucrats so they could ready themselves to abide by it. Federally regulated businesses were given very little time to adjust, even though the act eventually imposed on them billions of dollars of costs in making their services accessible to the disabled and equalizing their pay scales between predominately male and female jobs.

In pushing forward their bill to bring natives under the CHRA, the Tories have offered aboriginal leaders 18 months to get ready to comply. The leaders in turn have demanded three years, pointing out that is how much time the provinces were initially given.

But it should be remembered, aboriginal governments have already had 30 years to get ready. Giving them 33 is not likely to improve their implementation.

Also, at the same time as native organizations are complaining that Ottawa refuses to ratify the United Nations declaration on the rights of indigenous peoples, they themselves are working with the three federal opposition parties to block the Tory human rights bill.

Why the duality?

I can only guess it is because the UN declaration is a one-way street that works in their favour, whereas bringing them under the provisions of the CHRA would place obligations on those same leaders that they vehemently do not want.

They are all in favour of rights agitation when they stand to benefit from it, such as when it is their demands for equality, land claims and funding.

But they want nothing to do with having to protect women's rights on reserves or individual property rights.

Leaders and the non-aboriginal politicians who are supporting them have offered three arguments against passing the Tory bill at this time—all of them specious: The legislation threatens native notions of "collective" rights because the CHRA is too focused on individual rights, it was drafted without sufficient consultation of aboriginal people and most native governments have too little money to cope with the complaints that could be brought against them.

To the extent that natives practice "collective" rights, those rights are protected by the Charter.

Since the Charter supersedes the CHRA, there can be little fear the Supreme Court will adjudicate in favour of the individualistic CHRA if called to decide between it and the aboriginal-rights clause of Charter.

The charge that the bill was drafted without sufficient consultation with those who will be affected by it is similarly facile.

The government has heard scores of native objections, it merely disagrees with most of them and has decided to press on regardless.

People frequently do that. They confuse being heeded with being consulted.

Unless the consulter ends up adopting their recommendations, they convince themselves they have not been consulted. Or that the consultation process was flawed. Or that there were poor communications.

Not necessarily. The government knows native leaders' objections, it just believes those objections are stall tactics designed to maintain leaders' power over native populations.

Finally, there is the claim that aboriginal governments are too poor to implement the CHRA without a lot more money from Ottawa.

First and foremost, this claim is getting tiresome. It is native leaders' response to every problem: Give us more money.

At present, Ottawa spends about $5800 for every non-native man, woman and child, and nearly $20,000 for every native one.

Sure, people with greater needs are going to warrant greater spending. But if $20,000 per capita is not enough, how much will be? $40,000? $50,000?

Because of aboriginals' so-called collectivist approach to governance, individuals are forbidden from owning property on reserves, most federal monies are paid to the band rather than to individuals (so the chief and council get to decide who gets paid and how much), too many women who have married non-natives are denied their rights by their own bands and there is little accountability among far too many leaders.

Maybe the collectivist approach then—and not non-native culture—is responsible for aboriginal plight.

And any change to federal law that weakens the collectivist mindset is helpful.

II. Block

Dear Lorne:

Instead of bringing the Indians under the evil human rights law, wouldn't it be more libertarian to advocate that the rest of us get out from under this pernicious legislation?

Best regards,

Walter

III. Gunter

But so long as we postpone the inevitable clash between equally politically correct groups (such as Aboriginals and women), then there will be no political will to change such laws.

Only once more voters have come to realize that modern human rights theory is nothing more than a hodge-podge of group-power adjudication—the state choosing winners and losers from among competing groups based on the political value of each group—will things change.

Until then, making such laws apply to all is not only fair but also a good way to irritate more people faster.

– Lorne

IV. Block

Slavery is wrong. Suppose I could free only 10% of the slaves. Your argument implies that until ALL the slaves are freed, none should be freed. I find that highly problematic.

V. Gunter

No, Walter. You've got it backwards.

Ten percent of Canadians are now slaves because of their leaders' exemption from the human rights law. The other 90% of us aren't as well served by the law as we would be by its repeal. But the 10% who are slaves would be better off under the imperfect law than they are now without it.

Native leaders don't want to be exempt from human rights law so they can make their people freer than the rest of us. They demand exemption so they can keep them down without interference from the rest of society, which (to the extent we support the exemption) makes us complicit in the subjugation.

We would be making Aboriginal individuals freer than they are now by including them in the law. Then we can work on making us all free—native and non-native—by eliminating the law. But the latter is going to take years of voter education.

– Lorne

VI. Block

The numbers don't matter. Suppose I could free only 90% of the slaves. By your logic, I should not do so, since I can't free them all.

I agree with you about the motives of the native leaders, but I don't think that is germane to our discussion.

You are calling for the expansion of an unjust law, when, I think, as a libertarian, you should be calling for an end to it.

(You could also call for dividing up all the Indian lands among all the Indians so that they own it individually; that would stop the unjust power of the Indian leaders, but this is an entirely separate issue)

VII. Gunter

No.

If there are two classes of slaves—one (10%) really fettered and the others (90%) less so—and I can get the 10% brought up to the 90%'s level, I should. Even if the 90%'s level is unjust, it is less unjust than the 10%'s. Even if I can't free the 90%, I've still done something useful for freedom by elevating the 10%.

VIII. Block

Why is it "elevating" the majority of natives by imposing an unjust law on them? They could as easily have been elevated WITHOUT violating their rights (you do agree with me that "human rights" laws against discrimination are really a violation of real rights, do you not?) by privatizing all their land, no?

Let me put this in other words.

The majority of natives are suffering under unscrupulous leaders. I'm sure we agree on this. There are two ways to help them

1. Privatize all their lands. This eliminates, in one fell swoop, the power of the leaders. It is entirely just
2. Impose "human rights" on all Indians. This, too, will cut the power of the leaders. But it is unjust.

You chose option 2. That is not the libertarian option

IX. Gunter

Sure. But that isn't happening anytime soon. So in the meantime, they're better off under the law than not.

Earlier in this chain you said I had suggested that it was better to wait to free all slaves than to free just a few. I think that is now what you are suggesting with Aboriginals—that we should do nothing to make them even slightly freer, but instead wait for the day when their land can be privatized, etc.

That's the ideal. You'll get no argument from me there. But it is a long way off. In the interim, their circumstances can be made slightly better by bringing them under the current human rights law, so I think we should.

– Lorne

X. Block

Just because something is good for natives or can make "their circumstances … better" does not mean it is compatible with libertarianism.

It would be undoubtedly beneficial for Indians if all whites would transfer 50 IQ points to them, at the point of a gun (assuming we had the technology to do this). But this would not be compatible with libertarianism.

XI. Gunter

True. But how can making them live less free than they could be while they wait to be truly free be consistent with libertarianism?

Sometimes victory can only be won incrementally. Give them a small taste of individual liberty and perhaps Aboriginals will become allies in the fight for a full helping.

Right now, because Aboriginal governments are exempt from the Canadian Human Rights Act, individual natives cannot bring suits against their chiefs for discriminatory practices—such as hiring or dismissal from on-reserve jobs based on one's last name. They cannot sue band governments in most circumstances for negligent treatment. Reserve women who marry non-natives can be stripped of their status and booted from their band-owned homes. Residents on few reserves can own their own plot of land and the house on it. They cannot borrow capital to start a business because they have no equity.

Instead, all federal monies are paid to the band council who then decides which of their friends and supporters get band jobs, houses and development grants.

Would it be better for all to level the CHRA and the commission that enforces? Undoubtedly. But the practical truth is that that is not going to happen soon. It will take years of re-education of public thinking and several small baby steps before citizens are willing to take such bold action.

So what are natives supposed to do in the meantime? Continue to live like serfs to their own Aboriginal barons?

For them, CHRA protection would be an improvement, a step closer to freedom. So I don't understand your objection to granting them that admittedly imperfect improvement during the 20 to 30 years, or more, it is going to take to get to the ideal.

—Lorne

XII. Block

Look at who you are "in bed" with: every lefty, pinko, "human rights" group in the country. Doesn't that give you pause for thought?

What any individual, such as you are I, advocates, will have but a marginal effect on actual events. It is up to us, I think, to advocate things compatible with libertarianism.

Would it be ok with you if I sought publication for this correspondence?

XIII. Gunter

I'm always uncomfortable when I am on the same side of an issue with the left. It does make me pause. But I suppose the law of probability dictates their going to be partly right by accident on one issue every few years.

So long as I get to see (and have some say over) the final version of anything you can get published, I'm OK with it.

XIV. Block

Well, then, thanks. Since you got the first word on this, with your initial essay, I'll take the last word. And here it is: it has been a pleasure debating this issue with you. And I don't think our cordiality with each other stems, only, from the fact that we agree on the overwhelming majority of issues. It goes deeper than that.

16

Space Environmentalism, Property Rights, and the Law

I. Introduction

A considerable body of academic literature exists on the subject of space law, despite the fact that very few human beings have ever been to outer space, and substantial presence beyond the earth's orbit still seems to be in the rather distant future.[1] Among those proposing detailed, centralized regulatory regimes for a realm that so far has little, if any, need for them are anti-market[2] environmentalists who, not content to attend merely to

[1] Others have been more optimistic about the rate of growth in outer-space activities. *See*, for example, Amanda L. Moore & Jerry V. Leaphart, *Manipulation and Modification of the Outer Space Environment: International Legal Considerations*, in Proceedings of the Twenty-Fifth Colloquium on the Law of Outer Space 15, 17 (1982) ("Experts assure that lunar surface mining can be accomplished in the near term future defined as no later than 2000 A.D. and perhaps as soon as 1990.").

[2] We include this modifier on the ground that some environmentalists favor private property rights and free enterprise. In our view, "free market environmentalism" is not a contradiction in terms. *See* Terry L. Anderson & Donald R. Leal, Free Market Environmentalism (1991); Walter Block, *Environmentalism and Economic Freedom: The Case for Private Property Rights*, 17 J. Bus. Ethics 1887 (1998); Walter Block, *Environmental Problems, Private Property Rights Solutions*, in Economics and the Environment: A Reconciliation 281(Walter Block ed., 1990); Walter Block & Roy Whitehead, *The Unintended Consequences of Environmental Justice*, 100 Forensic Sci. Int'l 57 (1999); Thomas DiLorenzo, *Does Capitalism Cause Pollution?*, 38 Washington University Center for the Study of American Business Contemporary Issues Series (1990); Murray N. Rothbard, *Law, Property Rights, and Air Pollution*, 2 Cato J. 55 (1982); Richard L. Stroup et al., *Progressive*

W. E. Block, *Property Rights*, Palgrave Studies in Classical Liberalism,
https://doi.org/10.1007/978-3-030-28353-7_16

the earth's pollution problems, are concerned about the possible future pollution of the moon and other celestial bodies such as Mars. This article considers the ideas of these individuals—whom we will call socialist space environmentalists[3]—and rejects them.

We find proposed environmental programs for outer space not only philosophically ill-founded but also economically and pragmatically unjustified. In their place, we propose an alternative: a regime of pure private property and strict liability. Though our approach might be considered radical if proposed for the earth,[4] we maintain that it is an entirely appropriate policy for outer space and celestial bodies.

A. Types of Environmentalism

Few, if any, human beings would self-identify as enemies of "the environment." After all, everyone wants clean air to breathe and clean water to drink and does not want anyone to invade his person or property with harmful substances without permission. People who go this far—and only this far—with their environmentalism probably comprise the majority of humanity. They can be said to be adherents of *anthropocentric* environmentalism.[5] Anthropocentric environmentalists can be found across the political spectrum. For example, voices ranging from the right[6] to the extreme Marxist left[7] have called for unprecedented global government intervention to combat perceived environmental threats to human

Environmentalism: A Pro-Human, Pro-Science, Pro-Free Enterprise Agenda for Change (Nat'l Ctr. for Pol'y Analysis, Dallas, Tex.), 1991; Roy Whitehead & Walter Block, *Environmental Takings of Private Water Rights: the Case for Full Water Privatization*, 32 Envtl. L. Rep., 11162 (2002); Roy Whitehead & Walter Block, *Environmental Justice Risks in the Petroleum Industry*, 24 Wm. & Mary Envtl. L. & Pol'y Rev. 67 (2000).

[3] In contrast, the present authors characterize themselves as free market private property space environmentalists.

[4] Nonetheless, a substantially similar scheme *has* been proposed for the earth. *See*, for example, Rothbard, supra footnote 2.

[5] Alyson C. Flournoy, *In Search of an Environmental Ethic*, 28 Colum. J. Envtl. L. 63, 80 (2003).

[6] *See*, for example, Richard A. Posner, Catastrophe: Risk and Response (2004).

[7] *See*, for example, Barry Commoner, Making Peace with the Planet (1990); Paul Ehrlich, The Population Bomb (1968); Paul Ehrlich & Anne Ehrlich, Extinction: The Causes and Consequences of the Disappearance of Species (1981); Al Gore, Earth in the Balance: Ecology and the Human Spirit (1992).

well-being. Others, however, have advocated *laissez-faire* capitalism as the appropriate means to protect the environment to maximize human well-being on Earth.[8] For the anthropocentric environmentalist, non-human creatures and objects are valuable to the extent that humans value them—they have no "intrinsic" value apart from this.[9]

In the second half of the twentieth century, another type of environmentalism came to the fore: *ecocentric* environmentalism. (Ecocentric environmentalism is also sometimes referred to as "deep ecology," to contrast it with the "shallowness" of anthropocentric concern for the environment.)[10] Originated by Aldo Leopold, who conceived the idea of the "land ethic," ecocentric environmentalism holds that the environment itself is intrinsically valuable and that human beings themselves have value only to the extent that they play a role in, and support, this environmental whole.[11] According to radical ecocentrism, only "ecological wholes (such as species, ecosystems, the land or the biotic community) … have a value in themselves … and … the value of the ecological parts … is determined by how far they contribute to the survival and well-being of the ecological whole."[12] The ecocentric view is not limited to concern for animals or even plants but to the entire Earth, dirt and

---

[8] *See* supra footnote 2; *see also* Louis De Alessi, *Private Property Rights as the Basis for Free Market Environmentalism*, in Who Owns the Environment? (Peter J. Hill & Roger E. Meiners eds., 1998); Tibor R. Machan, *Pollution and Political Theory*, in Earthbound: New Introductory Essays in Environmental Ethics (Tom Regan ed., 1984).

[9] For an economic critique of the notion of intrinsic value, see James M. Buchanan, Cost and Choice: An Inquiry in Economic Theory (1969). *See also*, generally, L.S.E. Essays on Cost (James M. Buchanan & George F. Trilby, eds., New York Univ. Press 1981) (1973); William Barnett, II, *Subjective Cost Revisited*, 3 Rev. Austrian Econ. 137, 137–38 (1989); Roy E. Cordato, *Subjective Value, Time Passage, and the Economics of Harmful Effects*, 12 Hamline L. Rev. 229 (1989); Thomas J. DiLorenzo, *The Subjectivist Roots of James Buchanan's Economics*, 4 Rev. Austrian Econ. 180 (1990); Jacob Halbrooks, *Value and the Environment*, Mises.org, Mar. 27, 2002, http://www.mises.org/story/922.

[10] *See* Tal Scriven, Wrongness, Wisdom, and Wilderness: Toward a Libertarian Theory of Ethics and the Environment 147 (1997).

[11] *See* Flournoy, supra footnote 5, at 81–82; John Grim, *Indigenous Traditions and Deep Ecology*, in Deep Ecology and World Religions: New Essays on Sacred Ground 35, 40–41 (David Landis Barnhill ed., 2001).

[12] Mikael Stenmark, Environmental Ethics and Policy Making 85 (2002); *see also* Holmes Rolston, III, *Ethics on the Home Planet*, in An Invitation to Environmental Philosophy 107, 133 (Anthony Weston ed., 1999) ("Earth does not belong to us; rather we belong to it…. Earth is really the relevant survival unit.").

rocks included.[13] Everything on Earth, except for humans, is seen as possessing "intrinsic value" (i.e., value somehow derived from itself, not from man), which is destroyed or threatened by any human tampering at all.[14]

The real-world implications of this philosophy can be seen, for example, in the activities of the Earth First! organization, which is known for, among other things, putting spikes in trees so lumberjacks or mill workers who cut them may be injured or killed.[15] Earth First! leader Richard Foreman states the ends of ecocentric environmentalism bluntly: "We advocate bio-diversity for bio-diversity's sake. That says man is no more important than any other species.... It may well take our extinction to set things straight."[16]

To be fair, not all ecocentric environmentalists go this far. Advocates of what could be called "strong" (but not "radical") ecocentric environmentalism value both the environmental whole (independently of its value to humans) and human beings as individuals.[17] "Weak" ecocentric environmentalists similarly value both but ultimately are willing to put humans first.[18]

Ecocentric environmentalists typically speak in terms of the Earth, "bio-diversity," and the "biosphere."[19] Indeed, radical environmentalists who subscribe to the "GAIA hypothesis" consider the Earth itself to be a "superorganism" and see the Earth goddess Gaia (or "Mother Earth") as

---

[13] The land ethic "enlarges the boundaries of the community to include soils, waters, plants, and animals, or collectively: the land." Gary D. Meryers, *Old-Growth Forests, the Owl, and Yew: Environmental Ethics Versus Traditional Dispute Resolution Under the Endangered Species Act and Other Public Lands and Resources Laws*, 18 B.C. Envtl. Aff. L. Rev. 623, 657 (quoting Aldo Leopold, A Sand County Almanac 202–03 (1949)).

[14] *See* George Reisman, *Environmentalism in the Light of Mises and Menger*, 5 Q. J. Austrian Econ. 3, 11 (Summer 2002).

[15] Block, *Environmentalism and Economic Freedom: The Case for Private Property Rights*, supra footnote 2, at 1896 n.5.

[16] Robert James Bidinotto, *Environmentalism: Freedom's Foe for the 90s*, The Freeman, November 1990 (quoting M. John Fayhee, *Earth First! and Foremost*, Backpacker, September 1988, at 21).

[17] Stenmark, supra footnote 12, at 85.

[18] Id. at 89.

[19] *See*, for example, Mary Anne Warren, *The Rights of the Nonhuman World*, in Environmental Philosophy: A Collection of Readings 109 (Robert Elliot & Arran Gare eds., 1983) (stating that environmentalists show concern for the "planetary biosystem" and the "biotic community" as a whole).

"an embodiment and distinctly a personification of the intrinsic value of the Earth."[20]

Considering this strong focus on the Earth, one might expect that we would be spared the down-with-humans-up-with-dirt-and-rocks rhetoric with respect to man's activity beyond the earth. Many ecocentrists, however, appear ready to expand their area of concern to any place man might travel. Thus, as we are arguably poised to move significantly into outer space and other celestial bodies in the next few decades, we already have calls for "cosmo-centric" environmentalism[21] or "astroenvironmentalism."[22] Howard A. Baker writes approvingly, "With an environmental approach, protection of the outer space environment and its sub-systems is the priority," not "ensuring that outer space can be used for [human] space activities."[23] "Outer space, a source of wonder and inspiration for centuries, deserves to be preserved *in its original pristine state, for its own sake* and for future generations to enjoy," writes Bernard K. Schafer.[24] Another writer states, "[W]e must ensure that our presence [in space] does not defile what remains one of the few accessible pristine areas."[25]

---

[20] Erazim Kohák, The Green Halo: A Bird's-Eye View of Ecological Ethics 129 (2000).

[21] Ulrike M. Bohlmann, *Planetary Protection in Public International Law*, in Proceedings of the Forty-Sixth Colloquium on the Law of Outer Space 18, 27 (2003).

[22] *See* Ryder W. Miller, *Astroenvironmentalism: The Case for Space Exploration as an Environmental Issue*, 15 Electronic Green J. (2001), available at http://egj.lib.uidaho.edu/egj15/miller1.html.

[23] Howard A. Baker, *Protection of the Outer Space Environment: History and Analysis of Article IX of the Outer Space Treaty*, in 12 Annals of Air & Space L. 143,166 (Nicolas Mateesco Matte, ed., 1987).

[24] Bernard K. Schafer, *Solid, Hazardous, and Radioactive Wastes in Outer Space: Present Controls and Suggested Changes*, in Law, Values, and the Environment: A Reader and Selective Bibliography 395, 399 (Robert N. Wells, Jr. ed., 1996) (emphasis added). One wonders whether the "future generations" of which he speaks are intended to be human beings. If so, this represents an inconsistency in his world view, which, presumably, denigrates human beings of whatever generation, now *or* in the future. This author seems to think humans (now and in the future) can "enjoy" outer space—apparently by looking at it and knowing it is there—as long as they leave it in its pristine state. But, people cannot own views. If they did, there would be an over-determination of property rights: millions of people would own Disney World and the Grand Canyon, and it would no longer be clear as to who had rights to alter these amenities. *See* Walter Block, "Homesteading, ad coelum, owning views and forestalling," (Unpublished).

[25] April Greene Apking, Note & Comment, *The Rush to Develop Space: The Role of Spacefaring Nations in Forging Environmental Standards for the Use of Celestial Bodies for Governmental and Private Interests*, 16 Colo. J. Int'l Envtl. L. & Pol'y 429, 433 (2005).

Ryder W. Miller lists among space environmentalism's goals the declaration of "celestial bodies [as] pristine wildernesses that need to be protected rather than frontiers to conquer;" prohibition of "terraforming" of celestial bodies (e.g., attempting to transform Mars into an earthlike planet where humans could live); "safeguarding against the introduction of non-terrestrial life to and from celestial bodies"; and prohibiting all property ownership by both governments and private parties[26] in space.[27]

Space environmentalists Paul F. Uhlir and William P. Bishop, quoting Harry H. Almond, Jr., suggest five principles to guide space environmental policy: (1) "environmental balance" (with "substantial weight given to intrinsic environmental values"); (2) conservation of resources ("The natural resources of outer space must not be exploited in a wasteful or environmentally damaging way."); (3) "*Absolute liability for wrongful or negligent acts to the space wilderness and the duty to restore conditions to the status quo ante*"[28]; (4) demilitarization; and (5) permission for "states" to use and explore space, provided they abide by the first principle of "environmental balance."[29] They also call for zoning laws for celestial bodies to restrict the uses to which land can be put.[30]

[26] Even NASA is calling for more private initiatives in space travel and exploration. *See* Lucy Sherriff, *Private Enterprise Needed in Space: NASA*, The Register, Nov. 17, 2005, available at http://www.theregister.co.uk/2005/11/17/nasa_private_investment/; *see also* George Knapp, *The Ultimate Public-Private Partnership*, Las Vegas Mercury, July 8, 2004, available at http://www.lasvegasmercury.com/2004/MERC-Jul-08-Thu-2004/24250261.html. On the other hand, nothing in this paper should be interpreted as our support for any such initiative. In our view, the market should be left alone to determine just how much investment should go to this area. Certainly, no government subsidies would be justified. For a general critique of NASA as a socialist enterprise and support of private entrepreneurial decision making in this arena, *see*, for example, William L. Anderson, *The Trouble with NASA*, The Free Market, Apr. 2003, available at http://www.mises.org/freemarket_detail.asp?control=434. *See also* Robert Murphy, *A Free Market in Space*, The Free Market, Jan. 2005, available at http://www.mises.org/freemarket_detail.asp?control=525.

[27] Miller, supra footnote 22.

[28] This suggests a legal system in which rocks, dirt, and other inanimate objects somehow have standing to sue those who have disrupted them. Presumably environmentalists would bring these claims on the rocks' behalf, as they did for trees in *Sierra Club v. Morton*, 405 U.S. 727 (1972). On that case, and some economic problems of standing to sue for "existence value," *see* Donald J. Boudreaux & Roger E. Meiners, *Existence Value and Other of Life's Ills*, in Who Owns the Environment? 153, 177–79 (Peter J. Hill & Roger E. Meiners eds., 1998).

[29] Paul F. Uhlir & William P. Bishop, *Wilderness and Space*, in Beyond Spaceship Earth: Environmental Ethics and the Solar System 183, 203–04 (Eugene C. Hargrove ed., 1986) (citing Harry H. Almond, Jr., *A Draft Convention for Protecting the Environment of Outer Space*, in Proceedings of the Twenty-Third Colloquium on the Law of Outer Space 101–02 (1980)) (emphasis added).

[30] Id. at 205.

Even relatively moderate, generally anthropocentric observers appear to have been influenced by the ecocentrists' views and have called for the preservation of pristine "wilderness" areas on celestial bodies. Glenn H. Reynolds and Robert P. Merges, for example, generally favor private property rights but make an exception for "environmental research and conservation preserves," which would place "10 to 15 percent of the area capable of being developed" off-limits.[31] They offer no argument to support this notion but instead state, "It should not be necessary at this point to defend such an idea."[32] Similarly, Lawrence D. Roberts calls for "[r]estrictions on development which gradually open the high frontier over time" on inhospitable bodies and a "precautionary principle" restricting development where life might have once existed, presently exists, or could potentially exist.[33] Others with no otherwise-apparent hatred for the human race make passing reference to the necessity of some degree of space environmentalism.[34]

We do not intend to attack the radical ecocentric environmentalists directly in this paper. The absurdity of "intrinsic" value or value independent of the existence of human beings has been well-refuted elsewhere,[35] so we need not rehash those arguments here. Besides, we assume rather reasonably that the majority of our readers are anthropocentrists or at least moderate ecocentrists who do not favor the human race's demise over and above any disturbance of the rocks of the solar system. And, of course, there is little use in trying to rationally persuade

---

[31] Glenn H. Reynolds & Robert P. Merges, Outer Space: Problems of Law and Policy 176 (1997).

[32] Id.

[33] Lawrence D. Roberts, *Ensuring the Best of All Possible Worlds: Environmental Regulation of the Solar System*, 6 N.Y.U. Envtl. L.J. 126, 153, 158–59 (1997).

[34] *See*, for example, Steven Freeland, *Up, Up and … Back: The Emergence of Space Tourism and its Impact on the International Law of Outer Space*, 6 Chi. J. Int'l L. 1, 20 (2005) (declaring laws against "littering" by space tourists "imperative" to avoid "additional disruption to the space environment"); Kelly M. Zullo, Note, *The Need to Clarify the Status of Property Rights in International Space Law*, 90 Geo. L.J. 2413, 2442 (2002) ("Renewable licenses [for space ventures] should be granted liberally unless … the proposed activity would cause an unacceptable degree of harm to the Earth or outer space environment. An unacceptable degree of harm may include ventures that would leave excessive debris, produce harmful radioactive waste, or some other demonstrable damage."). For an alternative view on littering, see Walter Block, Defending the Undefendable, 210–16 (Fox & Wilkes 1991) (1976).

[35] *See* supra footnote 9.

adherents of a religion, including nature worshipers, with rational arguments—they will believe what they will believe regardless of what we may write here. Further, their position amounts to a logical or internal contradiction. They wax eloquently about overpopulation.[36] Yet they all, each and every one of them, have the power to reduce the number of the earth's inhabitants by precisely one. The fact that they are still here, complaining bitterly of too many people utilizing too few resources, shows that they do not take their own views seriously. If they do not, why should we? These people might likely argue (not totally unreasonably, given their premises) that they reduce the population more by sticking around and persuading others not to have children, and so on. However, if this were true, then, when they were no longer able to convince people of the merits of their position (say, due to old age or infirmity), they would commit suicide. They might well do so publicly, in order to better promote the overpopulationist movement. To the knowledge of the authors of the present paper, this has *never* been done. Actions speak louder than words.

Instead, we intend to argue to our fellow anthropocentrists and even moderate ecocentrists that one would have to be a *radical* ecocentrist to seriously embrace any sort of space environmentalism that goes beyond a regime of full private property rights and strict liability for harms to private property. There is simply no legitimate philosophical or pragmatic argument to the contrary. Nor, we will show, does international law demand anything more than this.

B. What Is the Space Environment?

To speak of a "pristine" environment outside of the planet Earth is a rather strange thing to do, given how utterly unpleasant the rest of the solar system (and, as far as anyone knows, the universe) is. The planet Mercury, for example, has no atmosphere, and portions of its surface become hot enough to melt tin. Other parts, however, remain cold enough to keep ice from crashed comets perpetually frozen—and there is nothing remotely pleasant in between. Mercury is, in one writer's words,

[36] *See* Ehrlich, supra footnote 7; Ehrlich & Ehrlich, supra footnote 7.

"geologically dead. It has not changed significantly in several *billion* years."[37]

Venus is even worse—"a good substitute for Hell."[38] Its atmosphere is a "choking shroud of almost pure carbon dioxide" (a gas much hated by environmentalists on earth) complemented by "thick clouds of battery acid."[39] Its atmospheric pressure is 92 times that which exists on the earth's surface, so any visiting astronaut in a spacesuit would be "crushed instantly."[40] And the mean surface temperature is 480°C—even hotter than Mercury, and hot enough "to melt tin, zinc, and lead."[41]

Earth's moon is relatively less hateful, but it has no atmosphere, of course, and "has never supported liquid water," let alone life.[42]

"Mars is not alive. It is dead, and looks as if it has been that way for a long time. No conclusive evidence for life there, either now or in the past, has ever been found."[43] Its atmosphere consists mostly of deadly carbon dioxide,[44] and its mean surface temperature is −23°C.[45]

The planets further out are even worse, so bad that it is difficult to imagine that they could be of any use at all to humans, except perhaps as something for tourists to fly past and admire. Jupiter, Saturn, Uranus, and Neptune are covered in extremely cold, giant, stormy mixes of toxic liquids and gasses.[46] Tiny Pluto apparently no longer counts as a planet[47] and has a surface temperature of −230°C and an atmosphere of nitrogen (good) and methane (poison).[48] There is talk of a tenth planet, but we are

[37] Mark A. Garlick, The Story of the Solar System 52 (2002) (emphasis added).

[38] Id. at 58.

[39] Id.

[40] Id. at 58, 60.

[41] Id. at 60. It may seem strange that Venus is further from the sun than Mercury, and, yet, hotter. This is due to its thick atmosphere of carbon dioxide, which creates a "greenhouse effect."

[42] *See* id. at 66.

[43] Id. at 72.

[44] Id. at 74.

[45] Id. at 72.

[46] *See* id. at 86–106.

[47] Dennis Overbye, *Vote Makes It Official: Pluto Isn't What It Used to Be*, N.Y. Times, Aug. 25, 2006, at A13.

[48] Garlick, supra footnote 37, at 112.

not competent to pronounce on its status.[49] Some of these distant planets' moons might be of some use to humans but are nonetheless wholly inhospitable. For example, one of Jupiter's moons, Europa, is covered in water ice and may have liquid water and possibly some sort of microscopic life beneath its frozen surface. And Saturn's moon Titan has, like Earth, a mostly nitrogen atmosphere—at negative 180 degrees.[50]

Where there is no atmosphere, as on the moon, the environment is far from healthy. Spaceships and spacesuits must be well shielded to protect against the sun's radiation. "A hypothetically unprotected astronaut would receive (in the absence of solar flares) about 10 rems of radiation per year. In comparison, the average person on the face of the earth receives only about .1 rems of radiation per year from background sources (e.g., from the earth and from space)."[51] The presence of solar flares makes matters much worse—their high-energy protons "can cause the release of lethal doses of secondary radiation, such as gamma rays, when they collide with spacecraft."[52]

All of that may sound bad, but in fact the space environment is only going to become worse, much worse, even if we humans never reach other celestial bodies. That is because, as the eons pass, our sun will eventually change to a "subgiant" star, then a Red Giant, then a nebula, then a White Dwarf, then a Black Dwarf. In the end, all of the planets, including Earth, will lose their atmospheres and exist at a temperature just a few degrees above absolute zero, the coldest temperature possible.[53]

Thus, in sum, the space environment is so bad right now that, from anything other than a rock-and-dirt-worshiping perspective, it could not

---

[49] *See* Kenneth Chang & Dennis Overbye, *Planet or Not, Pluto Now Has Far-Out Rival*, N.Y. Times, Jul. 30, 2005, at A1.

[50] Garlick, supra footnote 37, at 97.

[51] Schafer, supra footnote 24, at 427 n.19 (citing Michael Freeman, Space Traveller's Handbook: Every Man's Comprehensive Manual to Space Flight 154 (1979)).

[52] Reynolds & Merges, supra footnote 31, at 13.

[53] Garlick, supra footnote 37, at 127–42. Lest we depress our readers too severely, we note that author Robert Ringer suggests using this "ice ball" scenario as an opportunity to recognize that one's day-to-day problems are relatively insignificant. *See* Robert J. Ringer, Winning Through Intimidation 40–43 (1974).

get much worse—except that billions of years from now, it will get worse, and there is nothing anyone can do about that.[54]

II. Property Rights and Problems of Space Pollution

A. Is Space Pollution Even Possible?

Considering the solar system's present and future environmental state, the idea of space pollution becomes absurd to anyone apart from those who believe that whatever is "natural" is best, including even the eventual frozen desolation of our solar system. The reality is, virtually nothing human beings could do to the solar system could likely make it less livable or less useful than it is now.

Air pollution? As we have seen, there is no air on the moon—and to the extent that our neighboring planets have an atmosphere at all, it is almost entirely carbon dioxide, which is toxic and the bane of environmentalists here on Earth when it is produced by our automobiles.[55] Thus, nothing we could do to other celestial bodies could make the "air" more toxic than it already is. Water pollution? There is no surface liquid water, anywhere but Earth. Radiological pollution? As we have seen, there already is dangerous radiation in space against which humans must shield themselves. The Mars atmosphere may limit the amount of radiation on its surface—but if one cannot live there anyway without special protection (given the poison-gas environment), just how much worse would some radiation here and there make the planet? Also, Martian soil is believed to be highly toxic, to the extent that it could even threaten completion of any manned mission there.[56] Any human vehicles or structures

---

[54] Another antidote to depression: if we do not blow each other up before that, it is at least possible that long before this time, man will have learned the techniques necessary to bring us to not only other planets but other solar systems, more welcoming ones.

[55] On the enmity between environmentalists and carbon dioxide on Earth, *see*, for example, Gore, supra footnote 7, at 22.

[56] Nat'l Research Council, Safe on Mars: Precursor Measurements Necessary to Support Human Operations on the Martian Surface 28 (2002), available at http://newton.nap.edu/books/0309084261/html/28.html.

there would have to be specially protected by something like "mega-Rust-Oleum" to avoid destruction from this planet's violent sandstorms.[57]

Thus, to speak of pollution or contamination of space in the abstract—apart from human beings' property rights—makes no sense.

B. Air and Water Pollution in Space

Lawrence D. Roberts suggests that "[u]biquitous commons resources on Earth such as air and water will likely pose the same kinds of environmental challenges for space developers as they do for Earth developers," adding, "The need to recycle such valuable commodities will require stringent regulation of the discharge of hazardous byproducts into the waste stream."[58] We find this implausible. To the extent that there would be any air or water on the moon or elsewhere in space, how would it get there? It could only be from humans who brought or created it there. Where would it be found? Inside the space vehicles or other structures individuals brought to or built on the lunar (or Martian) surface. And here we get to the key of space environmental policy: to protect humans' environment in space, we need only protect their private property rights in whatever settlement they establish there.[59]

On Earth, such a policy, though philosophically sound, has historically presented some technical difficulties. For example, on our planet, it may be difficult to determine which factories contributed to victims' air or water pollution and in what amounts, as contaminants may travel imperceptibly over long distances.[60] Pollution victims may also suffer very small harms individually such that a lawsuit would cost them more than it was worth.[61] Those problems are far from insurmountable in the earthbound

---

[57] Benjamin Wallace-Wells, *Mars or Bust*, Rolling Stone, Feb. 23, 2006, at 45, 50.

[58] Roberts, supra footnote 33, at 154.

[59] In fairness to Roberts, he recognizes this point at least to a limited extent. *See* id. at 149 ("With regard to the inhospitable resources of the solar system, any environmental regime should begin with the management of property rights."); Id. at 151 ("Enforcement, in most cases, is a matter of individual property owners upholding their personal interests.").

[60] *See* Rothbard, supra footnote 2, at 88.

[61] Richard A. Posner, Economic Analysis of Law § 13.5 (5th ed. 1998).

context[62]—indeed, technological advances and the availability of class-action lawsuits should make them decreasingly problematic—but they do exist.

In space, however, apart perhaps from radiological poisoning, some sort of unmistakable physical invasion would be necessary for anyone to pollute anyone else's air or water. Thus, enforcement of a strict-liability regime for pollution should be simple and effective.

C. Other Pollution on the Moon and Celestial Bodies

Roberts also sees a need for environmental regulation on the moon to prevent pollution from lunar dust.[63] The extent to which this would be a problem requiring regulation is, however, unclear, given the moon's lack of an atmosphere. Further, given the moon's size and its likely sparse population even once humans begin exploiting it, it seems those using the moon for mining and those using it for recreational purposes or for a good view of the Earth would rationally spread themselves apart. With relatively few parties and a strong incentive to spread out, we can imagine that parties might bargain in advance to avoid conflicts or later to eliminate them.[64]

Of course, to the extent that polluters (whether by dust, chemicals, radiation, or anything else) arrive at the moon first, they may establish property rights there, *including the right to "pollute."* Where no one has already homesteaded lunar or planetary land, a mine or factory owner may homestead an easement to emit dust, and other potential pollutants, over the surrounding area that his operation affects.[65] Then new arrivals

[62] For example, if courts had continued to allow individuals to bring lawsuits for air pollution from the nineteenth century through the present, an environmental forensics industry would almost certainly be capable of determining sources of harm from air pollution. *See* Morton Horwitz, The Transformation of American Law: 1780–1860 (1977); Walter Block, *Private Property Rights, Economic Freedom, and Professor Coase: A Critique of Friedman, McCloskey, Medema, and Zorn*, 26 Harv. J.L. & Pub. Pol'y 923, 929–30 (2003).

[63] Roberts, supra footnote 33, at 154.

[64] A relatively low number of parties makes bargaining more likely (though perhaps not certain if transactions costs are high). *See* Posner, supra footnote 61, at § 3.8; Ronald H. Coase, *The Problem of Social Cost*, 3 J.L. & Econ. 1 (1960).

[65] *See* Rothbard, supra footnote 2, at 77.

will know that they should not locate in the area the established industrial operation affects unless they are willing to subject themselves to the industry's by-products. Not only is this philosophically sound from a property-rights perspective,[66] but it also should present little burden in practice because of the moon's likely sparseness for a very long time.

On the other hand, where the owners of hotels, golf courses, "wilderness" preserves, and the like arrive first, they will homestead their land, including the right not to be disturbed by pollution. Should someone trespass upon their property with any form of pollution, they will be entitled to both damages and injunctive relief, just as pollution victims were in Great Britain and the United States through the 1830s.[67]

D. Space: The Ultimate Waste Dump

One of the most promising uses for space is, of course, as a waste dump. This should be cause for environmentalist celebration, not alarm.

For example, rational observers recognize that nuclear electric power is far better for the environment than fossil fuels, which pollute the air and cause countless health problems for those of us who breathe in the pollution.[68] An important problem, of course, comes in the form of the radioactive waste produced, which, though small in quantity, remains hazardous for a very long time.[69] Once space flight becomes sufficiently affordable, the answer of what to do with this waste becomes simple: send it on a long, long trip.[70] Who but the most fanatical "cosmo-centrist" could be disturbed by sending all of our toxic waste to, for example, Venus, an already hellish place where no human being or other living

[66] Such an act would be characterized as "coming to the nuisance."

[67] *See* Block, *Environmentalism and Economic Freedom: The Case for Private Property Rights*, supra footnote 2, at 1890; *see also* Horwitz, supra footnote 62.

[68] *See*, for example, Petr Beckmann, The Health Hazards of NOT Going Nuclear 122 (1977) ("Every 1,000 MW of nuclear power that replaces coal-fired power saves between 20 and 100 lives a year.").

[69] *See* id. at 102 (noting also that while it is correct to say that nuclear waste remains hazardous for thousands of years, the problem is not as threatening as it might seem, nor as threatening to human health in the short or long term as the burning of fossil fuels).

[70] *See* Ty S. Twibell, Note, *Space Law: Legal Restraints on Commercialization and Development of Outer Space*, 65 UMKC L. Rev. 589, 631 (1997).

creature will likely ever go? Even if we were to take the nuclear waste to someplace humans might want to go, such as the moon or Mars, the physical quantities of such waste are small enough that it would require only minimal space.[71] The only colorable objection to this is that the waste might pose a risk to people on Earth as it leaves the atmosphere (e.g., if the ship carrying it explodes or crashes, as NASA vehicles are wont to do[72]). But presumably that risk would ever decrease as the private sector moves further into the space transportation field and space technology advances. For example, a space elevator would not entail the high risks or costs of ordinary space flight.[73] And, of course, carriers of hazardous waste would be strictly liable for any harm—which, along with their financial investment, would encourage them to take extreme care.

Another potential benefit would be to move polluting industrial operations off-planet.[74] Again, environmentalists who really care about the well-being of humans or life generally (as opposed to rocks and dirt per se) should delight in this prospect.

E. "Wilderness" Preserves

As noted above, Reynolds and Merges call for 10–15% of the moon (and presumably any other celestial body at which humans may someday arrive) as a "preserve."[75] They make no argument to support this view,

---

[71] *See* Beckmann, supra footnote 68, at 99–111 ("If all of the US power capacity were nuclear, the total amount of wastes per person per year would amount to one aspirin tablet.... If the entire US electrical capacity were nuclear and ran at the present [1977] rate for 350 years, the volume of wastes would amount to a cube 200 feet on a side.").

[72] For example, NASA lost two space shuttles and 14 astronauts in just 114 flights. Tariq Malik, *NASA's New Moon Plans: 'Apollo on Steroids'*, Space.com, Sept. 19, 2005, http://www.space.com/news/050919_nasa_moon.html. In 1999 alone, it also lost two Mars spacecraft and a $246 million infrared telescope which failed shortly after launching. *Nasa's Disastrous Year*, BBC News, Mar. 22, 2000, http://news.bbc.co.uk/1/hi/sci/tech/686674.stm.

[73] *See* Kenneth Chang, *Not Science Fiction: An Elevator to Space*, N.Y. Times, Sept. 23, 2003, at F1.

[74] *See* Roberts, supra footnote 33, at 148.

[75] Reynolds & Merges, supra footnote 31, at 176. *See also* Robert P. Merges & Glenn H. Reynolds, *Space Resources, Common Property, and the Collective Action Problem*, 6 N.Y.U. Envtl. L. J. 107, 124–25 (1997). Incidentally, Reynolds and Merges also call for "development preserves"—territory set aside to give to poor non-spacefaring nations later. Reynolds & Merges, supra footnote 31, at 176.

however, and even explicitly state that they believe no such argument is necessary.[76] The radical environmentalists go further, of course, and want earthly governments to declare all of outer space an untouchable "wilderness."[77] We find the alleged need for official wilderness preserves less obvious.

Indeed, this seems rather a strange preoccupation. As we have noted already, there seems to be plenty of room up there for everyone and every purpose imaginable. Right now space is de facto 100% wilderness preserve, and it is difficult to imagine humanity making a significant dent in that number anytime soon. After all, even vast amounts of the relatively hospitable continents of North America and Australia have minimal population density, even excluding national parks and other areas governments have so far placed off-limits. Environmentalists have also purchased land for the purpose of keeping it vacant and preserved on Earth[78]; there is no reason they could not do so in space—or rather than purchase simply homestead because it is there for the taking.

Governments have little incentive or ability to determine which parts of any celestial body are best used as wilderness preserves or which are best put to other purposes.[79] One can imagine that such determinations may be corrupted by the inevitable influence of special interests, just as special interests have influenced terrestrial environmental laws to the benefit of polluters.[80] Indeed, the US government's management of its national parks has been dismal, as have the environmental records of governments, especially socialist governments, generally.[81] Thus, if optimal preservation of that which is valuable to scientists and other admirers

---

[76] Reynolds & Merges, supra footnote 31, at 176.

[77] *See*, for example, Miller, supra footnote 22; Schafer, supra footnote 24.

[78] These groups include, for example, the Nature Conservancy and the Audubon Society. *See* John Brätland, *Externalities, Conflict, and Offshore Lands*, 8 Indep. R. 527, 540 (2004).

[79] *See* id.

[80] On the ability of polluters to "capture" centralized agencies ostensibly intended to regulate them, *see*, for example, Andrew P. Morriss, Bruce Yandle & Roger E. Meiners, *The Failure of EPA's Water Quality Reforms: From Environment-Enhancing Competition to Uniformity and Polluter Profits*, 20 UCLA J. Envtl. L. & Pol'y 25, 26 (2001–2002).

[81] *See*, for example, Block, *Environmentalism and Economic Freedom: The Case for Private Property Rights*, supra footnote 2, at 1889; Fred L. Smith, Jr., *Sustainable Development–A Free-Market Perspective*, 21 B.C. Envtl. Aff. L. Rev. 297, 305–06 (1994).

of pristine lunar wilderness is the goal, the answer again is strictly enforced private property rights.

It is entirely unjust for "wilderness" advocates to use government to prevent others from developing their property in space. As Glenn Reynolds has noted, theirs is essentially an "aesthetic view masquerading as a religious one."[82] They may speak in terms of intrinsic value, but they really seek to use the law to forcibly place their personal aesthetic preferences—their own human desires—above those of others, and above the welfare of the human race. By and large, they have been allowed to do this on earth, albeit only partially. Unfortunately, there is no reason why space should be any different. As we have seen, however, in space there is even less cause to cater to their desires. Perhaps, then, they will not succeed as well in the heavens as they have on earth.

F. Terraforming

"Terraforming" would involve transforming an alien environment (Mars being the obvious candidate) to give it a climate more like Earth's.[83] Fantastic though it sounds, this is likely to be technologically feasible on the fourth planet.[84] Essentially, it would involve initiating "global warming" through the release of Carbon tetrafluoride (CF4) into the now very sparse Martian atmosphere, raising the temperature by ten degrees Celsius within several decades, which would cause an increase of water vapor in the atmosphere, further warming the planet.[85] With that accomplished, humans could release "methanogenic and ammonia-creating bacteria into the now-livable environment,"[86] creating even more greenhouse gases. "The net result of such a program could be the creation of a Mars with acceptable atmospheric pressure and temperature, and liquid water

[82] Glenn Harlan Reynolds, *Space Law in the 21st Century: Some Thoughts in Response to the Bush Administration's Space Initiative*, 69 J. Air L. & Com. 413, 422 (2004).

[83] Id. at 419.

[84] Id. at 420 (citing Martyn J. Fogg, Terraforming: Engineering Planetary Environments (1995)).

[85] Id. at 420.

[86] Id. (quoting Robert Zubrin, Entering Space: Creating a Spacefaring Civilization 37 (1999)).

on its surface within fifty years of the start of the program."[87] Mars would not then have a breathable atmosphere "but would support crops and allow people to move around without spacesuits."[88]

Of course, those who want to preserve the outer space environment in its "pristine" form can be expected to oppose this.[89] Some already have.[90] From an anthropocentric environmentalist perspective, however, we find no problem with terraforming.

If no one owned property on Mars before terraforming apart from the terraformers, property rights certainly would not be an issue—the terraformers would have a right to do as they please with presumably large parts of the planet.

That is, terraformers could make whatever use they see fit or as much of Mars as they could homestead before other homesteaders arrived, apart from the land already taken over to use as a base for their operations. Strictly speaking, they could not claim even one square inch of the rest of the surface, as, by assumption, they would not have directly "mixed their labor with"[91] any of it. In the scenario we are positing, their actions were limited to setting off gases. Of course they would have a tremendous advantage in terms of homesteading over any other later arrivals.[92]

If other property owners did exist, they would of course likely welcome the change because it would make their own property more useful to

[87] Id. (quoting Robert Zubrin, Entering Space: Creating a Spacefaring Civilization 37 (1999)).

[88] Id.

[89] A battle between "reds" who want to preserve a pristine Mars and "blues" who want to terraform occurs in an acclaimed series of science-fiction novels. *See* Kim Stanley Robinson, Red Mars (1992); Kim Stanley Robinson, Blue Mars (1993); Kim Stanley Robinson, Green Mars (1996).

[90] *See* Reynolds, supra footnote 82, at 421 ("The character of these objections is likely to reveal much about the environmental movement, or at least about those making them."); *see also*, for example, Ryder W. Miller, *The Case Against Terraforming Mars*, Space Pol'y Dig., May 22, 2003, available at http://www.gyre.org/news/article/3273.

[91] *See* John Locke, *An Essay Concerning the True Origin, Extent and End of Civil Government*, in Social Contract 17–18 (E. Barker, ed., 1948); *see also* Hans-Hermann Hoppe, The Economics and Ethics of Private Property: Studies in Political Economy and Philosophy (1993); Murray N. Rothbard, The Ethics of Liberty 32 (New York University Press 1998) (1982); Murray N. Rothbard, For a New Liberty 34–35 (Ludwig von Mises Institute 2002) (1973); Walter Block, *Earning Happiness Through Homesteading Unowned Land: A Comment on 'Buying Misery with Federal Land' by Richard Stroup*, 15 J. Soc. Pol. & Econ. Stud., 237 (1990).

[92] For an analogous case regarding intellectual property, see N. Stephan Kinsella, *Against Intellectual Property*, 15 J. Libertarian Stud. 1 (2001) (explaining that the first creator of an idea has an advantage in reaping the economic benefits from the idea even if he cannot own it).

them. (In economic terms, they would enjoy *positive* externalities of the terraformers' activity. Instead of "coming to the nuisance," they would be coming to its very opposite.) But some Mars property owners—especially scientists trying to research the planet's history—might not welcome the radical changes to the planet. Still, the right to be protected against weather one finds undesirable has never been recognized, to our knowledge.[93]

On the other hand, the very notion of externalities, whether positive or negative, is highly problematic. This concept is very subjective[94]: "one man's meat is another man's poison." A home painted with psychedelic colors will be off-putting to most people but attractive to some. To take a case from our present concern, the search for extraterrestrial intelligence (SETI) is seen by many as a progressive step[95]; an attempt to uncover other species in the galaxy with whom we humans can interact. However, an entirely different interpretation of this initiative could be that it is very dangerous, in that it might only call attention to ourselves with regard to a superior but evil species, who will either enslave or eat us.

Of course, non-property-owning environmental activists on Earth—those most likely to challenge terraforming—would have no standing to challenge this process of development. Again, their aesthetic tastes should not be given priority over those with an actual stake in the matter (i.e., property owners) and over the good of the human race generally.

G. What If There's Life?

Some observers, such as Roberts, believe that bodies "with the potential for harboring biotic or prebiotic activity" present a special case for which different rules must apply. Roberts states that where life exists or even potentially exists, we must apply the "precautionary principle," which would place the burden of proof on those engaged in a "challenged activ-

---

[93] For a rejection of the notion of a right to weather of a particular type in the context of global warming on Earth, see Reisman, supra footnote 14, at 14.

[94] *See* supra footnote 9.

[95] *See* Dennis Overbye, *When It's Not Enough to Say 'Take Me to Your Leader,'* N.Y. Times, Mar. 5, 2002, at F1.

ity" and prohibit development that threatens evidence of past life or the existence of present or "potential" life.[96] We disagree.

First, we note that there is no evidence that life exists or has ever existed anywhere in the solar system except Earth.[97] Further, there is a strong consensus that to the extent that life might exist or have ever existed elsewhere, such as on Mars or Europa, it is limited to extremely simple microscopic organisms.[98] The likelihood of sentient or even plant life existing elsewhere in the solar system appears to be zero, and the question of life on planets outside the solar system is very hypothetical, even for an article on space law.[99] Therefore a presumption against the existence of *actual* life where no evidence to the contrary exists seems proper.

Further, space environmentalists have failed to make the case that environmental regulations are necessary to protect whatever extraterrestrial life (or evidence thereof) may exist. Humans are fascinated by the prospect of the existence of any kind of extraterrestrial life. Anyone who bothers to go to space for any purpose is likely to be interested in checking for signs of past or present life on his property (or prospective property) before acting in a way that might destroy it. For the intellectually uncurious, there would still be financial incentives. For example, scientific or environmental organizations could offer prize money for the discovery of evidence of extraterrestrial life; a property owner who discovers evidence of life could sell scientists, journalists, and others rights to access, study, and publicize information about the discovery. Only governmental intervention (e.g., stripping individuals of property rights when something of scientific interest is found on their property) is likely to cause incentives to run in any other direction.[100]

---

[96] Roberts, supra footnote 33, at 157–60. For more on the precautionary principle, see Steven A. Mirmina & David J. Den Herder, *Nuclear Power Sources and Future Space Exploration*, 6 Chi. J. Int'l L. 149, 164 (2005).

[97] *See* Bruce Jakosky, The Search for Life on Other Planets 2 (1998).

[98] Id. at 4.

[99] The most earthlike planet known is 21,000 light-years away and has a surface temperature of −370°F. Dennis Overbye, *Search Finds Far-Off Planet Akin to Earth*, N.Y. Times, Jan. 26, 2006, at A21.

[100] This has happened on Earth. For example, the Endangered Species Act encourages people to kill and hide any endangered species on their property (in the vernacular, "shoot, shovel, and shut up") so they do not lose their property rights. *See* Andrew P. Morriss & Richard Stroup, *Quartering*

Suppose there were the proverbial "little green creatures" discovered on Mars or on any other planet humans colonized. What rights would they have? What obligations would we have to respect these rights? (If they were smarter/stronger than we, the shoe of course would be on the other foot.) There are several options. If they had the intelligence/ability of dogs or cats, then we would treat them as we now do those animals. But suppose they were intermediate between us and the smartest of earth animals (chimps, porpoises), or had human qualities but looked like a cross between an octopus and a giraffe. According to Rothbard,[101] if they could communicate with us, promise to respect our personal and property rights, and adhere to such undertakings, then and only then would we be obligated to treat them as we do each other (well, better, hopefully).

III. International Law and the Space Environment

Despite a relatively large amount of academic writing *about* space law, relatively little space law actually exists for the obvious reason that there has so far been minimal need for it. Still, several international agreements comprise that space law which does exist—and space environmentalists may attempt to use it as a weapon against development. We argue, however, that the international agreements to which the United States is a party do not demand a restrictive environmental regime for outer space and celestial bodies.

A. The Test Ban Treaty

The Limited Test Ban Treaty of 1963 ("Test Ban Treaty"), signed by the United States, the Soviet Union, and Great Britain, forbids any "nuclear explosion … in the atmosphere; beyond its limits, including outer space;

Species: The 'Living Constitution,' the Third Amendment, and the Endangered Species Act, 30 Envtl. L. 769, 795 (2000).

[101] Rothbard, For a New Liberty, supra footnote 91, at 156; *see also* Tibor Machan, Putting Humans First: Why We Are Nature's Favorite (2004).

or underwater, including territorial waters or high seas," as well as in "any other environment if such explosion causes radioactive debris to be present outside the territorial limits of the State under whose jurisdiction or control such explosion is conducted."[102] Reynolds and Merges describe the treaty as primarily environmental in intent, seeking to prevent "global nuclear contamination," though it had military effects.[103]

We see nothing objectionable in this treaty's ban on the use of nuclear weapons.[104] If states or anyone else want to bind themselves not to conduct certain activities, that seems appropriate. Certainly an inability to detonate nuclear weapons in space will not hamper development there and should even encourage it to the extent that it reduces the threat of nuclear annihilation those of us on earth face and eliminates the threat of an electromagnetic pulse that could affect electronic equipment[105] and thereby violate property rights.[106]

The Test Ban Treaty also implicitly prohibits nuclear fission as a means of space propulsion.[107] Again, to the extent that states wish to bind themselves not to do certain things in space, that seems appropriate, just as any private party can agree to refrain from particular actions. The terms of the Test Ban Treaty require the signatories to "prohibit" nuclear explosions "at any place under [their] jurisdiction or control"[108]; this would not seem to bind private parties beyond the confines of the Earth. Reynolds and Merges also suggest that if non-signatory nations allow nuclear propulsion, the signatories are likely to follow suit in the interest of competition.[109] To the extent that repudiation of this aspect of the Test Ban

---

[102] Treaty Banning Nuclear Weapon Tests in the Atmosphere, in Outer Space and Under Water, U.S.-U.K.-U.S.S.R., art. I, Aug. 5, 1963, 14 U.S.T. 1313 [hereinafter Test Ban Treaty].

[103] Reynolds & Merges, supra footnote 31, at 54.

[104] For a libertarian analysis of weapons in space and on the heavenly bodies in a different than earthly context, *see* Walter Block & Matthew Block, *Toward a Universal Libertarian Theory of Gun (Weapon) Control*, 3 Ethics, Place & Env't 289 (2000).

[105] *See* Reynolds & Merges, supra footnote 31, at 59.

[106] Former US Secretary of State Dean Rusk noted, "I can think of no other way to more massively increase the pollution of outer space than to allow the arms race to move out there." Dean Rusk, *Star Wars: The Nuclear/Military Uses of Space*, in Beyond Spaceship Earth: Environmental Ethics and the Solar System 315, 318 (Eugene C. Hargrove ed., 1986).

[107] Reynolds & Merges, supra footnote 31, at 61.

[108] Test Ban Treaty, supra footnote 102, art. I.

[109] Reynolds & Merges, supra footnote 31, at 61.

Treaty would encourage private parties to use nuclear propulsion, and thereby facilitate space activities, we see it as a laudable step.

B. The Outer Space Treaty

The Multilateral Treaty on Principles Governing the Activities of States in the Exploration and Use of Outer Space, Including the Moon and Other Celestial Bodies ("Outer Space Treaty")[110] is the foremost document in international space law.[111] The United States and other spacefaring countries have signed it. Primarily, the Outer Space Treaty limits the activities of governments in space. Most significantly, it prohibits them from claiming sovereignty over outer space "including the moon and other celestial bodies,"[112] prohibits "nuclear weapons or any other kinds of weapons of mass destruction" in space,[113] and allows the moon and other celestial bodies to be used "exclusively for peaceful purposes."[114] As with the Test Ban Treaty, we find nothing objectionable here. Governments have been responsible for massive pollution, millions of human deaths,[115] and countless invasions of property rights on Earth; to the extent that they agree to keep their hands off and weapons out of space, that appears favorable from both environmental and property-rights perspectives.[116]

---

[110] Treaty on Principles Governing the Activities of States in the Exploration and Use of Outer Space, Including the Moon and Other Celestial Bodies, U.S.-U.K.-U.S.S.R., Jan. 27, 1967, 18 U.S.T. 2410 [hereinafter Outer Space Treaty].

[111] *See* Steven A. Mirmina & David J. Den Herder, *Nuclear Power Sources and Future Space Exploration*, 6 Chi. J. Int'l L. 149, 158 (2005) (calling the Outer Space Treaty "the cornerstone of international space law"); Reynolds & Merges, supra footnote 31, at 62.

[112] Outer Space Treaty, supra footnote 110, art. II.

[113] Id. art. IV.

[114] Id.

[115] *See* R.J. Rummel, Death by Government (1994).

[116] Some have argued that the Outer Space Treaty effectively abolishes both government and private property in space. Reynolds, however, argues that a consensus exists to the contrary—that is, property rights are allowed. Glenn H. Reynolds, *International Space Law: Into the Twenty-first Century*, 25 V and. J. Transnat'l L. 225, 230 (1992). But the idea that the Outer Space Treaty proscribes private property persists among some commentators, and the status of private property rights in space therefore remains uncertain. See, for example, Heidi Keefe, Essay, *Making the Final Frontier Feasible: A Critical Look at the Current Body of Outer Space Law*, 11 Santa Clara Computer & High Tech. L.J. 345, 350–60 (1995); Leo B. Malagar & Marlo Apalisok Magdoza-Malagar, *International Law of Outer Space and the Protection of Intellectual Property Rights*, 17 B.U. Int'l L.J. 311, 345

Some argue that Article IX of the Outer Space Treaty calls for environmental restrictions.[117] It provides, *inter alia*, that exploration of celestial bodies must be conducted "so as to avoid their harmful contamination and also adverse changes in the environment of the Earth resulting from the introduction of extraterrestrial matter."[118]

Baker concedes that this rule is essentially anthropocentric—that is, "harmful contamination" simply means contamination that hurts other humans.[119] Nothing in Baker's idea necessarily conflicts with the private property, strict-liability regime we propose; to the contrary, it is fully consonant with it. And to us, it appears to be the most logical reading of the treaty—that is, if contamination of the space environment is, as we have argued, inconceivable except from the perspective of property-rights violations, then the Outer Space Treaty creates no protection for the space environment per se.

Schafer argues that Article VIII of the Outer Space Treaty prohibits the contamination of the space environment.[120] Article VIII provides: "Ownership of objects launched into outer space, ... and of their component parts, is not affected by their presence in outer space...."[121] Schafer reads this provision as establishing "a responsibility to deal with all of the incidence of ownership of such an item, including the contamination it

(1999); Uhlir & Bishop, supra footnote 29, at 196 (noting that this prohibition will preserve space "wilderness"). This debate is beyond the scope of this article, but we note that a considerable consensus does exist that, even if the Outer Space Treaty does not allow for private property rights, it *should* allow for them so entrepreneurs will have an incentive to go there. See, for example, Kurt Anderson Baca, *Property Rights in Outer Space*, 58 J. Air L. & Com. 1041, 1083–85 (1993); Julie A. Jiru, Comment, *Star Wars and Space Malls: When the Paint Chips Off a Treaty's Golden Handcuffs*, 42 S. Tex. L. Rev. 155, 169–73 (2000); Twibell, supra footnote 70, at 613–19; Keefe, at 350–60; Wayne N. White, Jr., *Real Property Rights in Outer Space*, in Proceedings of the Fortieth Colloquium on the Law of Outer Space 370 (1998); Zullo, supra footnote 34, at 2438–44.

[117] *See*, for example, Molly K. Macauley, *Flying in the Face of Uncertainty: Human Risk in Space Activities*, 6 Chi. J. Int'l L. 131, 144 (2005); Uhlir & Bishop, supra footnote 29, at 196–97.

[118] Outer Space Treaty, *supra* footnote 110, art. IX.

[119] *See* Baker, supra footnote 23, at 163 ("[I]t was never intended that the protection offered by the avoidance of harmful contamination principle would extend to the environments of the Moon and other celestial bodies *per se*.").

[120] Schafer, supra footnote 24, at 404.

[121] Outer Space Treaty, supra footnote 110, art. VIII.

may cause the space environment."[122] Although Schafer is concerned with preserving the environment per se, his argument only supports the notion of respect for property rights in space. Therefore, Article VIII of the Outer Space Treaty is congruent with, not contrary to, our proposed property-rights regime and does not establish any environmental protection beyond it.

C. The Liability Convention

Another major agreement is the 1972 Convention on International Liability for Damage Caused by Space Objects ("Liability Convention").[123] It holds nations strictly liable for damage caused by their (or their citizens') space objects to aircraft in flight or objects on Earth, and applies a "fault" standard for damage to other space objects. The Liability Convention, however, does not address protection of the space environment apart from human-made "space objects" and therefore does not call for any sort of space environmentalism.[124]

D. The Moon Treaty

A treaty that *does* seem to call for space environmentalism is the 1979 Agreement Governing the Activities of States on the Moon and other Celestial Bodies ("Moon Treaty").[125] It requires signatories to "take measures to prevent the disruption of the existing balance of [the moon's] environment, whether by introducing adverse changes in that environ-

---

[122] Schafer, supra footnote 24, at 404.

[123] Convention on International Liability for Damage Caused by Space Objects, U.S.-U.K.-U.S.S.R., Mar. 29, 1972, 24 U.S.T. 2389 [hereinafter Liability Convention].

[124] This is in sharp contrast to the Convention on International Trade in Endangered Species of Wild Fauna and Flora ("CITES"), Mar. 3, 1973, 27 U.S.T. 1087, the aqueous analog to the Liability Convention. CITES specifically rules out and condemns private property rights as a means of protecting endangered species. *See* Jonathan Adler, *Do Conservation Conventions Conserve?*, in Sustainable Development: Promoting Progress or Perpetuating Poverty? (Julian Morris ed., 2002).

[125] Agreement Governing the Activities of States on the Moon and Other Celestial Bodies, G.A. Res. 34/68, U.N. Doc. A/RES/34/68 (Dec. 5, 1979) [hereinafter Moon Treaty].

ment, by its harmful contamination through the introduction of extra-environmental matter or otherwise."[126] It also proclaims the moon and its resources "the common heritage of mankind."[127] Its terms also apply to other celestial bodies.[128]

What precisely the Treaty means by "the existing balance" of celestial body's environment is unclear. As for "harmful contamination," the Moon Treaty does not define the term, but again, in light of our discussion above, this phrase could possibly be interpreted to mean that property rights must be respected.

In any event, the Moon Treaty is of virtually no practical consequence, because "no major space power has signed it."[129] Further, observers agree that it is unlikely that the United States will ever join, because it not only would impose environmental restrictions but also would prohibit property rights[130] and essentially impose a space welfare or global wealth redistribution program, under which profits from wealthy nations' space ventures would have to be shared with the governments of poor non-spacefaring countries.[131] Not even the Soviet Union, despite its communist ideology, was willing to agree to that.[132] Therefore, though it receives attention in academic literature, the Moon Treaty will not directly affect space environmental law in the United States.

---

[126] Id. art. 7.

[127] Id. art. 11. For an analysis of this concept, see Kemal Baslar, The Concept of the Common Heritage of Mankind in International Law (1998); for applications of this concept to the earth's oceans, see Jan van Ettinger et al., *Ocean Governance and the Global Picture*, in Ocean Governance: Sustainable Development of the Seas (Peter Bautista Payoyo ed., 1994); for a critique on the ground that it interferes with private property rights, and opens the door to the tragedy of the commons, *see* Roy Whitehead, Jr., Catherine Gould & Walter Block, *The Value of Private Water Rights: From a Legal and Economic Perspective*, 9 Alb. L. Envtl. Outlook J. 313 (2004).

[128] Moon Treaty, supra footnote 125, art. 1.

[129] Rosanna Sattler, *Transporting a Legal System for Property Rights: From the Earth to the Stars*, 6 Chi. J. Int'l L. 23, 30 (2005); *see also* Reynolds & Merges, supra footnote 31, at 116 ("Absent adoption by the major space powers, the Moon Treaty is unlikely to play a major role in the future.").

[130] *See* Sattler, supra footnote 129, at 30; Twibell, supra footnote 70, at 598.

[131] *See* Kevin V. Cook, Note, *The Discovery of Lunar Water: An Opportunity to Develop a Workable Moon Treaty*, 11 Geo. Int'l Envtl. L. Rev. 647, 664–70 (1999).

[132] Reynolds and Merges, supra footnote 31, at 116.

IV. Conclusion

As we have shown, space environmentalism lacks a legal or economic justification, and its only philosophical foundation is a most extreme form of environmentalism to which very few people seriously subscribe. For the good of the human race, and because it is just, the law should continue to allow private parties to use space for whatever human purposes they see fit within the limits of private property rights.

17

Coase and *Kelo*: Ominous Parallels and Lott on Rothbard on Coase

In its *Kelo* decision, the Supreme Court upheld Connecticut's decision to use its eminent domain powers to take property from one set of private owners and give it to another set of private owners.[1] The state defended this plan on the grounds that the former group of owners was using their property in a less efficient manner than would the latter.[2] There are ominous parallels between this decision, which amounts to no more than thinly veiled theft, and the works of Ronald Coase and the "Law and Economics" movement spawned by his 1960 publication.[3] To wit, this philosophy can be used to buttress *Kelo*. Indeed, we need look no further than this literature for a spirited albeit entirely wrong-headed notion that courts are justified in ruling, in property rights disputes, not in favor of the historical owners, but rather on the side of those they think can make the "best use" of the property; for example, so as to maximize economic welfare, or economic efficiency, or the gross domestic product (GDP), or

[1] *Kelo v. City of New London*, 125 S. Ct. 2655, 2669 (2005).

[2] *See* id. at 2658.

[3] R. H. Coase, *The Problem of Social Cost*, 3 J. L. & Econ. 1 (Oct. 1960).

W. E. Block, *Property Rights*, Palgrave Studies in Classical Liberalism,
https://doi.org/10.1007/978-3-030-28353-7_17

as in *Kelo*, all of them plus the tax base.[4] This topic is addressed in part I of the present chapter.

In part II we turn to a defense of Coase by Lott.[5] Coase argued that in the zero transactions costs world, it did not matter, at least as far as resource allocation was concerned, which of two parties to a dispute over property rights was the winner.[6] And that in the positive transactions costs world, the proper role of the judge was to maximize wealth, and that this could be done by finding in favor of the most efficient user of the property under dispute, the one who would have ended up with it in the zero transactions cost scenario.[7] Rothbard disputed Coase on both of these points.[8] Lott disagreed with the Rothbardian position.[9] This part of the present chapter defends Rothbard against the criticisms of Lott.

I. Coase and *Kelo*: Ominous Parallels[10]

A. Introduction

Part I of the present chapter is devoted to the thesis that there is an ominous parallel between Coase and *Kelo*.[11] There is a strong similarity because both this economic-philosophical treatise and the Supreme Court decision of 2005 support the proposition that when there is a dispute over property rights, it should be settled on the basis of societal wealth maximization, or gross domestic product (GDP) enhancement, or economic efficiency, or so as to expand the tax bases as much as possible,

---

[4] 125 S. Ct. at 2658.

[5] *See* John R. Lott, *A Note on Law, Property Rights, and Air Pollution*, 3 Cato J. 875 (Winter 1983–1984) (available at http://www. cato.org/pubs/journal/cj3n3/w3n3-15.pdf).

[6] *See* Coase, supra footnote 3.

[7] Id. at 16.

[8] *See* Murray N. Rothbard, *Law, Property Rights, and Air Pollution*, 2 Cato J. 55 (Spring 1982), reprinted in *The Logic of Action Two* 121–70 (Walter Block ed., The Fraser Institute 1990) (available at http://www.mises.org/rothbard/ lawproperty.pdf).

[9] Lott, supra footnote 5, at 875.

[10] Peikoff used the phrase "ominous parallels" in the title of his book of that same name. Leonard Peikoff, *The Ominous Parallels* (Stein and Day Pub. 1982).

[11] *See* Coase, supra footnote 3; *Kelo v. City of New London*, 125 S. Ct. 2655 (2005).

rather than in favor of whoever holds title to the property in question and thus is the rightful owner.[12] This is ominous in that it is only the historical-based genesis of property that deserves to be considered a property rights system at all. A legal regime that will alter property titles willy-nilly in favor of those who the Court in its far less than infinite wisdom decides is the most efficient user of the property in question does not even deserve the honorific, private property rights system. Rather, it is the absolute, total, and complete abnegation of any such institution.

In section B we review Coase. Section C is devoted to an examination of *Kelo*, to determine if it is indeed based on the work of Coase, the Nobel Prize winner in Economics in 1991.[13] I make the case in section D that what these two bodies of thought have in common, their "ominous parallels," spell the death knell for civilization as we have known it. In section E we discuss how the Coaseans, the followers of the master, fare in this regard. We conclude part I of the chapter in section F.[14]

B. *Coase*[15]

According to Coase, there are two basic possible states of the world.[16] In the first, transactions costs, defined as the cost of finding people to bargain with, setting up a contract, monitoring it, adjudicating it, and so on, are zero or at the very least substantially below the possible benefits of the

[12] *See* id.

[13] The Nobel Foundation, http://nobelprize.org/economics/laureates/ (last updated Oct. 10, 2005).

[14] There is an interesting debate concerning the implications of *Kelo* for federalism and decentralization. As this discussion is peripheral to our present interests, we content ourselves with merely noting it. *See generally* Stephan Kinsella, *Woops, They Did It Again (Bad Supreme Court! Bad! Bad!)*, http://blog.mises.org/blog/archives/003745.asp (June 23, 2005); N. Stephan Kinsella, *A Libertarian Defense of 'Kelo' and Limited Federal Power*, http://www.lewrockwell.com/kinsella/kinsella17.html (June 28, 2005); Roderick T. Long, *Federalism and the Bill of Rights: The Pros and Cons of Kelo*, http://www.lewrockwell.com/long/long14.html (July 8, 2005); Tibor R. Machan, *Kelo v. New London City, CT, versus the Free Society*, http://groups.msn.com/TiborsPlaceontheWeb/general.msnw ?action=get_message&mview=1&ID_Message=1311 (July 6, 2005); Ron Paul, *Lessons From the Kelo Decision*, http://www.lewrockwell.com/paul/paul259.html (July 5, 2005).

[15] For another attempt to link Coase and *Kelo*, *see* Frank Speiser, *Imminent Eminent Domain: Paying Tribute in Collectivist Society*, http://www.strike-the-root.com/51/speiser/speiser1.html (June 28, 2005).

[16] *See generally* Coase, supra footnote 3.

commercial endeavor.[17] Here, it does not matter how the judge rules between two contending parties in terms of resource allocation.

Suppose there is a dispute between a railroad emitting dust, sparks, and smoke particles, for example, and a farmer whose nearby haystacks are being ruined. Assume that a smoke prevention device costing $75 would completely ameliorate the problem and that the damage to the agriculturalist is $100 if not addressed in this manner.

There are only four possibilities. First, if the court rules in favor of the railroad, the farmer will pay the polluter, say, $90 to install the device, even though the law (the judicial finding) does not compel him to do so. The farmer will garner ten dollars ($100 he saves in straw, minus the $90 bribe) while the railroad will gain $15 (the $90 bribe minus the installation cost of $75). Total wealth will register at $25.

Second, if the court comes down on the side of the farmer, he will save $100, at the cost of $75 to the railroad, with society (the two of them) again $25 to the good. So, the judicial decision *does not matter* in terms of whether the smoke prevention device will be installed or not.[18] However, Coase's analysis is open to criticism because it fatally assumes that the farmer, in this case, has the wherewithal to make the $90 bribe. If he does not, that is, if the hay is only of psychic, not market value, he cannot make this payment, and, thus, even in the zero transactions costs world, the judge's opinion will determine resource allocation.[19] According to Coase:

> I now turn to the case in which, although the pricing system is assumed to work smoothly (that is, costlessly), the damaging business is not liable for any of the damage which it causes. This business does not have to make a payment to those damaged by its actions. I propose to show that the allocation of resources will be the same in this case as it was when the damaging business was liable for damage caused.[20]

[17] Id. at 15–16.

[18] Or, more generally, how resources will be allocated.

[19] Walter Block, *Coase and Demsetz on Private Property Rights*, 1 J. Libertarian Stud. 111, 112 (Spring 1977) (available at http://www.mises. org/journals/jls/1_2/1_2_4.pdf).

[20] Coase, supra footnote 3, at 6.

Matters are very different, for Coase, in the high transactions cost (or real) world. Here, the judicial finding very much matters for resource allocation, for there can be no post-judgment reallocation of resources; whatever emanates from the court will not be able to be undone by the marketplace.[21] For example, to continue using the numerical illustration above, the third alternative, if the court rules in favor of the farmer, he will insist upon the installation of the smoke prevention device; and this is "good" for society, as $75 will have been spent in order to garner a savings of $100, for a pure gain of $25.

However, in the fourth and last case, suppose the bench decides in favor of the railroad. It will refuse to install this machine. Will the farmer be able to bribe the railroad into doing so as he did before in the previous example? After all, the gain to agriculture will be $100, the loss to the transportation industry only $75. Surely the two sides can come together? They *cannot*, since we are now assuming either an infinitely high transactions cost world, or, at least, one in which the expenses of transacting such arrangements are much higher than any gains that could be made (think hundreds of railroads and thousands of farmers and the practical impossibility of bringing them all into an agreement).

In such a situation it is imperative for Coase that the judge makes the "correct" decision, in favor of the farmer, given our numerical example.[22] His advice to the bench is that it rules in such a manner that resources are allocated "rationally," the GDP is maximized, and, in our example, as we have seen, in favor of the farmer.[23]

For Coase, it is simply not true that the railroad is the instigator of a trespass, or a property rights violation, and that the farmer is the innocent victim.[24] Rather, it is a reciprocal problem. Yes, if the trains were not running, there would be no problem with the haystacks. But also, and equally true for Coase, were the haystacks not located where they are, then the engines would not be problematic.[25] In his words:

---

[21] Id. at 15–16.

[22] Id. at 19.

[23] Id.

[24] Id.

[25] Id. at 2.

> The traditional approach has tended to obscure the nature of the choice that has to be made. The question is commonly thought of as one in which A inflicts harm on B and what has to be decided is: how should we restrain A? But this is wrong. We are dealing with a problem of a reciprocal nature. To avoid the harm to B would inflict harm on A. The real question that has to be decided is: should A be allowed to harm B or should B be allowed to harm A? The problem is to avoid the more serious harm. I instanced in my previous article the case of a confectioner the noise and vibrations from whose machinery disturbed a doctor in his work. To avoid harming the doctor would inflict harm on the confectioner. The problem posed by this case was essentially whether it was worth while, as a result of restricting the methods of production which could be used by the confectioner, to secure more doctoring at the cost of a reduced supply of confectionery products. Another example is afforded by the problem of straying cattle which destroy crops on neighbouring land. If it is inevitable that some cattle will stray, an increase in the supply of meat can only be obtained at the expense of a decrease in the supply of crops. The nature of the choice is clear: meat or crops. What answer should be given is, of course, not clear unless we know the value of what is obtained as well as the value of what is sacrificed to obtain it. To give another example, Professor George J. Stigler instances the contamination of a stream. If we assume that the harmful effect of the pollution is that it kills the fish, the question to be decided is: is the value of the fish lost greater or less than the value of the product which the contamination of the stream makes possible.[26]

Note that Coase's views on reciprocality can be given both a positive *and* a normative interpretation. That is, my claim is that this author means his thesis to be taken in both ways.

In the former case Coase is in effect predicting that judges *will and have* decided cases as if reciprocality is the proper relation.[27] That is, in his terminology, the results of these lawsuits can be interpreted as the court seeing not that A is criminally violating the rights of B, and penalizing the former, but rather as if plaintiff and defendant on are the same legal plane.[28] Thus, the legal remedy is not to punish the evildoer, for there is

[26] Id. (citations omitted).

[27] Id.

[28] Id.

no such thing in these cases. Rather, given that both parties are innocent, the desiderata is to decide the case in favor of the person who *would have* (contrary to fact conditional) enjoyed the resource in the zero (or low) transactions costs' world. Namely, award the property right to the most "efficient" user of it and ignore the property rights in question.

But it is also possible to interpret Coase in a normative manner. To wit, that the judge, if he is to be rational, *should* look at these cases in such a way. That is, the jurist *should* realize that there is no right and wrong, no good and bad in any of these cases. Rather, Coase is calling upon him to decide these cases such that wealth is maximized, rather than justice be done.[29] In effect, whoever wins the case no injustice can be perpetrated, since justice is not an issue here.

C. *Kelo*

The *Kelo* decision does not mention Coase.[30] Nevertheless, it is informed by that article to its very roots. Do I go so far as to say that the judicial authors of *Kelo*, in failing to cite Coase, were guilty of at least failure to acknowledge a source, and, at worst, of plagiarism? I do not. My thought is that Coase has so completely permeated the legal profession—this article is the most cited in all of the economic literature—that no such citation was needed.[31]

In this case, a private organization, the New London Development Corporation (NLDC), expropriated land from several homeowners in order to upgrade their property into a shopping mall, office center, and other amenities.[32] It cannot be denied that this was done with the permission and encouragement of the city government of New London, Connecticut; they thought it would bring more taxes to their coffers.[33]

---

[29] Id.

[30] *See generally Kelo v. City of New London*, 125 S. Ct. 2655 (2005).

[31] Fred R. Shapiro, *The Most-Cited Law Review Articles Revisited*, 71 Chi.-Kent L. Rev. 751 (1996) (reporting that Coase, with 1741 citations, is far ahead of the next most cited article, which only has 359 citations).

[32] *Kelo*, 125 S. Ct. at 2658–60.

[33] Id. at 2658–59.

Nevertheless, it was a *private* non-profit group that was the actual land thief.[34] This is hardly the first case on record of the U.S. judiciary riding roughshod over private property rights, for purposes not even alleged to be on behalf of public use (such as roads, tunnels, bridges).[35] Yet it is perhaps the most blatant, in that there was much less of a fig leaf of public use involved than ordinarily.[36] "Justice Thomas distinguishes "public use" from "public purpose."[37] He states: "This deferential shift in phraseology enables the Court to hold, against all common sense, that a costly urban-renewal project whose stated purpose is a vague promise of new jobs and increased tax revenue, but which is also suspiciously agreeable to the Pfizer Corporation, is for a 'public use.'"[38]

It seems particularly egregious to many commentators that it was a private concern, not a governmental one, which was responsible for the land theft of eminent domain in this case. Kinsella provides an alternative to this viewpoint:

> For the libertarian, the main concern is to reduce the number or likelihood of such acts of theft; and to minimize the harm done when it does occur. But once a person's land is taken, it is hard to see how he suffers extra harm due to the way the state uses the property—whether they use it to build a road, or military base, or sell it to Costco. In fact, some libertarians might prefer that their land be transferred to private hands for peaceful purposes such as a mall or strip center or condo instead of being used by the inefficient state.[39]

---

[34] Id. at 2659; *See also* Stephen Bainbridge, *They Can't Take That Away From Me... Unless They Can*, http://remotefarm.techcentralstation.com/062305C.html (June 24, 2005).

[35] *See Haw. Hous. Auth. v. Midkiff*, 467 U.S. 229, 233, 235 n. 3 (1984) (forcing a landlord to give property titles to tenants to promote an egalitarian scheme of redistribution); *Berman v. Parker*, 348 U.S. 26, 28–34 (1954) (the taking of an apartment house for urban renewal to combat slums, even though it was conceded that this specific dwelling was sound).

[36] *See generally* Walter Block, *Road Socialism*, 9 Int. J. Value-Based Mgt. 195 (1996), http://walterblock.com/publications/road_ socialism.pdf (For a critique of eminent domain even in the case of highways and streets); Richard A. Epstein & Walter Block, Debate, *Epstein vs. Block: Do We Really Need Eminent Domain?* (U. Chi. Sch. L., May 13, 2004), in ___ N.Y.U. J. L. & Liberty ___ (audio version available at http://www.mises.org/media.aspx?action=showname& ID=443).

[37] *Kelo*, 125 S. Ct. at 2677 (Thomas, J., dissenting).

[38] Id. at 2677–78.

[39] Stephen Kinsella, *A Libertarian Defense of 'Kelo' and Limited Federal Power*, ¶ 6, http://www.lewrockwell.com/kinsella/kinsella17.html (June 28, 2005).

Consider this statement by Justice O'Connor: "The specter of condemnation hangs over all property. Nothing is to prevent the State from replacing any Motel 6 with a Ritz-Carlton, any home with a shopping mall, or any farm with a factory."[40]

Think in terms of the railroad and the farmer in Coase and any two claimants for land in any of these cases decided by the Supreme Court. Cannot we just "hear" Coase in the background opining that it is not a matter of right and wrong, not an issue of property rights, that *all* of these contending parties are in a relationship of "reciprocality" with one another and that the justice *should* rule in favor of that party such that the GDP, or the tax base, or some other desiderata be maximized?[41]

This insight of O'Connor's is couched in terms of *Kelo*, but with a little poetic license, we can also read it as an utter rejection of the Coasean philosophy:

> Any property may now be taken for the benefit of another private party, but the fallout from this decision will not be random. The beneficiaries are likely to be those citizens with disproportionate influence and power in the political process, including large corporations and development firms. As for the victims,[42] the government now has license to transfer property from those with fewer resources to those with more. The Founders cannot have intended this perverse result.[43]

Justice O'Connor is precisely correct in her anticipation that *Kelo* would likely have negative repercussions on the poor. There is a large body of literature attesting to the fact that "urban renewal" made possible only by eminent domain, actually amounts to "Negro removal."[44]

---

[40] *Kelo*, 125 S. Ct. at 2676 (O'Connor, J., dissenting) (citations omitted).

[41] *See* Coase, supra footnote 3.

[42] *See* John Fund, *Property Rights Are Civil Rights: Opposition to the Kelo Decision Crosses Racial and Party Lines*, ¶¶ 2,3,7, http://www.opinionjournal.com/diary/?id=110006941 (accessed Mar. 22, 2006) (making the point that the victims will tend to be poor and black).

[43] *Kelo*, 125 S. Ct. at 2677 (O'Connor, J. dissenting).

[44] *See Kelo*, 125 S. Ct. at 2687 (Thomas, J., dissenting); Martin Anderson, *The Federal Bulldozer: A Critical Analysis of Urban Renewal, 1949–1962*, 7–8 (Cambridge, MIT Press 1964). *See also* http://www. google.ca/search?hl=en&q=negro+removal&btnG=Google+ Search&meta= (accessed Mar. 22, 2006); *Kennedy's Vast Dominion: The Supreme Court's Reverse Robin Hoods*, ¶8, http://www. opinionjournal. com/editorial/feature.html?id=110006862 (accessed Mar. 22, 2006).

However, there are exceptions to this general rule. In a delicious bit of irony, or perhaps poetic justice, there is a movement afoot to do unto the majority Judges of the Supreme Court in *Kelo* what they have done to the losing plaintiffs in this case; they are trying to use eminent domain to expropriate the homes of all those responsible, starting with Justice Souter.[45]

Here is Justice O'Connor's minority report again:

> Under the banner of economic development, all private property is now vulnerable to being taken and transferred to another private owner, so long as it might be upgraded—*i.e.*, given to an owner who will use it in a way that the legislature deems more beneficial to the public—in the process.[46]

No truer words have ever been said. There has been such a sense of outrage at the injustice of the majority opinion in *Kelo* that the Pfizer Company, which had been thought to have been involved in the Connecticut eminent domain controversy, took pains to distance itself from it.[47]

D. *The Ominous Parallels*

Having set out Coase in section B and *Kelo* in section C, we are now ready to consider their similarities.

Here is an insight from the *Economist* that puts the similarity in context:

> Put simply, cities cannot take someone's house just because they think they can make better use of it.
>
> Otherwise, argues Scott Bullock, Mrs. Kelo's lawyer, you end up destroying private property rights altogether. For if the sole yardstick is economic benefit, any house can be replaced at any time by a business or shop (because they usually produce more tax revenues). Moreover, if city

[45] Ron Strom, *This land was your land: Supreme Court justice faces boot from home? Developer wants 'Lost Liberty Hotel' built upon property of David Souter*, http://worldnetdaily.com/news/printer-friendly.asp? ARTICLE_ID=45029 (June 28, 2005).

[46] *Kelo*, 125 S. Ct. at 2671 (O'Connor, J., dissenting).

[47] Pfizer Inc., *Pfizer Statement on Eminent Domain*, http://www. pfizer.com/pfizer/are/news_releases/2005pr/mn_2005_0627.jsp (accessed Mar. 22, 2006).

> governments can seize private property by claiming a public benefit which they themselves determine, where do they stop? If they decide it is in the public interest to encourage locally-owned shops, what would prevent them compulsorily closing megastores, or vice versa? This is central planning.[48]

Precisely. Suppose this quote from the *Economist* did not mention *Kelo* but rather Coase. Would that have made any difference to the truth of the contention? Not at all. This sentiment applies to both, equally.

There is in effect a "reciprocal" relationship between Kelo and her embattled fellow property owners, on the one hand, and on the other hand, those who would pillage them and steal their land under cover of legal authority. If Coase were sitting on the Supreme Court, it is difficult to avoid the conclusion that he would have voted, enthusiastically, for the majority. Why? Not so much that he is concerned with enhancing the "tax base." Rather, that he would take this as a proxy variable with maximizing GDP, or wealth, or "efficiency" in his terms.[49] Just as he rules in favor of the hypothetical railroad, or farmer, depending upon his assumption as to which is the more efficient user of the rights to pollute or to prevent pollution, so too would he come down on the side of whichever of the contending parties for any real estate would more greatly enhance its value.[50]

E. *The Coaseans*

The number of Coaseans is not quite as large as the number of grains of sand on all the beaches of the world, but in the fields of law and economics, they have cut quite a swath. It is fair to say that this school of thought is totally dominant in these two academic disciplines and particularly in the sub-field that combines them both. It will be impossible to measure all of the practitioners in this regard against the *Kelo* litmus test, but let us consider the views of at least a few of the more prominent members.

---

[48] Economist.com, *Eminent Domain: Despotism by Stealth*, ¶¶ 17–18, http://www.economist.com/World/na/displayStory.cfm?story_id= 3672769 (Feb. 17, 2005).

[49] *See* Coase, supra footnote 3, at 3–8, 29–34.

[50] Id.

1. Richard Posner[51]

According to this author:

> The only justification for eminent domain is that sometimes a landowner may be in a position to exercise holdout power, enabling him to obtain a monopoly rent in the absence of an eminent domain right. The clearest example is that of a right of way company, such as a railroad or a pipeline, which to provide service between two points needs an easement from every single one of the intervening landowners. Knowing this, each landowner has an incentive to hang back, refusing to sell to the right of way company except for an exorbitant price. Each hopes to be the last holdout after the company has purchased an easement from every other landowner—easements that will be worthless if it doesn't obtain an easement from that last holdout…
>
> Right of way companies are not the only private enterprises that can make an argument for the use of the eminent domain power. The argument is available in other cases in which a large number of separately owned contiguous parcels have to be acquired for a project that will create greater value than the parcels generate in their present use. It is impossible to tell from the opinions in the Kelo case whether that was such a case. Pfizer had decided to build a large research facility adjacent to a 90-acre stretch of downtown and waterfront property in New London and the City hoped that Pfizer's presence would attract other businesses to the neighborhood. The plaintiffs' residential properties were on portions of the 90-acre tract earmarked for office space and parking, and it might have been impossible to develop these areas for those uses if the areas were spotted with houses (the plaintiffs owned 15 houses in all in the two areas).[52]

There are difficulties with this position. First of all, Posner has an incorrect view of monopoly.[53] The only way anyone can attain a monopoly position, profit or rent it matters not, is through a government grant

---

[51] Posner and Coase, of course, have their differences. However, for present purposes, there are no distinctions to be drawn between these two University of Chicago professors.

[52] Richard Posner, *The Becker-Posner Blog: The Kelo Case, Public Use, and Eminent Domain*, ¶¶ 5,7, http://www.becker-posner-blog.com/archives/2005/06/the_kelo_case_p.html (June 26, 2005).

[53] Walter Block, *Total Repeal of Anti-trust Legislation: A Critique of Bork, Brozen and Posner*, 8 Rev. Austrian Econ. 35, 55–68 (1994).

of privilege; for example, if the state prohibits competition. How does Posner know when a "holdout" problem occurs? He offers us no criteria on the basis of which this can be determined. Every purchaser, of anything, at any time, would like to buy on better terms than those for which he finally settles. Similarly, this author's use of "exorbitant price" is unscientific. "Exorbitant" compared to *what*? Again, we are vouchsafed no objective criterion that will determine whether a price is "exorbitant."[54] Then there is the fact that only a moron would "[purchase] an easement from every other landowner."[55] Any sensible entrepreneur, in contrast, would first buy *options*, and then exercise them if and only if *all* of his targets had agreed in advance to sell.[56]

Posner announces it is "impossible to tell" whether *Kelo* describes a situation in which one single large development would be worth more than the present "large number of separately owned contiguous parcels."[57] But the implication is clear: *if* this were the case, then Posner in his role as judge, and Coasean, would indeed rule with the majority in *Kelo*. That is to say, Posner, like Coase, has no more respect for a system of private property rights, at least theoretically, than any cut-purse thief.

Let us consider one more statement by this author:

> The Court was mindful of the possibility of abuse of the eminent domain power; it made clear that there would not be a public use if all a municipality did was take property from one person and give it to another, with no showing of an increase in overall value.[58]

---

[54] The clear implication for a statist such as Posner is that if a price is "exorbitant" then the government must step in and force it to be lowered. In the aftermath of Hurricane Katrina, there is a movement afoot to stop price "gouging." Posner, presumably, would favor this bit of economic illiteracy. For an antidote to it, see http://www.google.com/u/Mises?hl= en&submit.x=0&submit.y=0&&q=price%20gouge.

[55] Posner, supra footnote 54, at ¶ 5.

[56] Or, he would build a bridge over, or a tunnel under, any such "holdout." *See* Walter Block, *Roads, Bridges, Sunlight and Private Property: Reply to Tullock*, 8 J. Economistes Etudes Humaines 315 (June/Sept. 1998); Walter Block & Matthew Block, *Roads, Bridges, Sunlight and Private Property Rights*, 7 J. Economistes Etudes Humaines 315 (June/Sept. 1996); Epstein & Block, supra footnote 38; Gordon Tullock, *Comment on "Roads, Bridges, Sunlight and Private Property," by Walter Block & Matthew Block*, 7 J. Economistes Etudes Humaines 589 (Dec. 1996).

[57] Posner, supra footnote 54, at ¶ 7.

[58] Id. at ¶ 5.

But, suppose "a municipality … [took] property from one person and [gave] it to another, with … [a *guaranteed*] showing of an increase in overall value."[59] Then, would this be justified in Posner's view? It is difficult to resist the notion that it would; that Posner would support such a forced transfer of property, under these stipulated conditions. But if so, then his view is open to any number of reductios ad absurdum. For example, that rape would be justified if the rapist valued this act more than the victim disvalued it.[60] That O.J. Simpson was justified in murdering his wife, since, if we but posit that he derived greater pleasure from this act than she lost therefrom.[61] Of course, all this verges way past being silly, since there is simply no way to make any such determinations. Interpersonal comparisons of utility constitute no less than a basic economic fallacy.[62]

2. Steven Medema and Richard Zerbe

According to these authors, "the goal of the legal system should be to establish a pattern of rights such that economic efficiency is attained."[63]

And again: "[T]he goal of such a system is to minimize harm or costs."[64]

It is only in the "real" or high transactions costs scenario that these claims even come into play. For, as we have seen, in Coase's view, on the zero transactions costs assumption, these goals are *always* attained.[65] If the court awards the property rights under contention to the "wrong" man, no problem arises; the "right" one will buy him out.[66] Matters are entirely different in the real world of high transactions costs. Here, no

---

[59] Id. (emphasis added).

[60] Walter Block, *O.J.'s Defense: A Reductio Ad Absurdum of the Economics of Coase and Posner*, 3 Euro. J.L. & Econ. 265, 275 (1996).

[61] Id.

[62] *See* Murray N. Rothbard, *Toward a Reconstruction of Utility and Welfare Economics*, in *The Logic of Action One* 211, 225–27 (Edward Elgar Publg. 1997).

[63] Steven G. Medema & Richard O. Zerbe, Jr., *The Coase Theorem*, in *The Encyclopedia of Law and Economics* vol. 1 836 (Bougdewin Bouckaert & Gerrit De Geest eds., Edward Elgar Publg. 1999).

[64] Id. at 837.

[65] *See* Coase, supra footnote 3.

[66] Id. at 6–8.

post-judicial finding transfers of rights can easily or possibly at all effected. Thus, for "efficiency" to be attained, the *court* will have to get it right in the first place. And, what, in turn, does this imply? Of course, for the Coaseans, this means that when there are two parties contending over a given piece of real estate, it must be awarded to the one who can make better or more efficient use of it. Thus, if there is a dispute between a small homeowner and a large Donald Trump casino, or in Justice O'Connor's words, between a "Motel 6 [and] a Ritz-Carlton,"[67] it is the latter who should and must prevail, property rights be damned.

3. David Friedman

This author faithfully reflects Coase's emphasis on the supposed reciprocal nature of property:

> [A]n external cost is not simply a cost produced by the pollutor (sic) and born (sic) by the victim. In almost all cases, the cost is a result of decisions by both parties. I would not be coughing if your steel mill were not pouring out Sulfur Dioxide. But your steel mill would do no damage if I (and other people) did not happen to live down wind from it. It is the joint decision—yours to pollute and mine to live where you are polluting—that produces the cost.[68]

He then answers our question of the farmer vs. the railroad or the land developers vis-à-vis Susette Kelo and her neighbors:

> [T]he law should define property in such a way as to minimize the costs associated with the sorts of incompatible uses we have been discussing—factories and recording studios, or steel mills and resorts.[69]

[67] *Kelo v. City of New London*, 125 S. Ct. 2655, 2676 (2005) (O'Connor, J., dissenting) ("The specter of condemnation hangs over all property. Nothing is to prevent the State from replacing any Motel 6 with a Ritz-Carlton, any home with a shopping mall, or any farm with a factory.").

[68] David Friedman, *The Swedes Get it Right* ¶ 14, http://www.daviddfriedman.com/Libertarian/The_Swedes.html (accessed Mar. 7, 2006) (reprinted from Liberty Magazine).

[69] Id.

Although he does not address himself, specifically, to the *Kelo* question, there is little doubt that were he to do so, he would vote with the majority if he thought that this was the best way to "minimize the costs,"[70] and with the minority if he thought that GDP could be maximized by allowing the homeowners to keep their property. But either way, he would *ignore* private property rights.

I have a challenge for this author, and, indeed, for all other Coaseans. Suppose one man had normal eyesight, and another was completely blind. Would it not be justified for the state to inaugurate a program of forced eye transfer from the normal two-eyed person to the one who is completely blind? Surely, it would reduce costs, or increase total or social wealth, if both of them had one eye. For the second eye, while beneficial to depth perception, is almost, economically speaking, a mere decoration. It seems clear that the blind man will gain far more from having one eye (sight) than the normal man will lose (better depth perception) from having his number of eyes reduced from two to one.

Suppose a Coasean were on a court charged with deciding the proper ownership of this second eye, which is now located in the head of the normal man. It is difficult to see how he could get out of supporting such a forced transfer. But this is a powerful reductio ad absurdum of this entire system.

4. Richard Epstein

I readily concede that this author disagrees with the *Kelo* decision. He starts off on a very strong note: "Last week's regrettable 5-4 decision in *Kelo v. City of New London* marks a new low point in the Supreme Court's takings jurisprudence."[71]

Or at least he thinks he does. But matters are not so clear when Epstein declares of Justice Stevens the view that:

[70] Id.

[71] Richard A. Epstein, *Blind Justices: The Scandal of Kelo v. New London* ¶ 1, http://www.opinionjournal.com/extra/?id=110006904 (July 3, 2005).

> New London had made its case when it asserted, without evidence, that the new projects would both increase tax revenues and create new jobs. It hardly mattered that its projections had been pulled out of thin air and were already hopelessly out of date when the case reached the Supreme Court.[72]

Suppose, however, that there *was* "evidence," strong evidence, to the effect that "the new projects would both increase tax revenues and create new jobs"[73] and enhance wealth as well. Suppose the "projections" were not "pulled out of thin air" and were very much up to "date." Then what?

While Epstein is a strong advocate of compensation for takings, he has no principled argument against eminent domain.[74] Indeed, he explicitly supports it, and agrees with Posner's view on the supposed "hold-out" problem:

> [A]ssume that the owner of a mine (who has no choice on where to dig) can get his ore to market only by ferrying it over scrub lands owned by another individual. That second landowner can demand a huge chunk of the mining profits for his trivial contribution to the overall venture. For over 100 years, the Supreme Court has allowed the state to condemn the obstructing property for the mine owner upon payment of just compensation, here measured by the trivial losses sustained by the obstructing landowner. The net gains from blocking the holdout are huge.[75]

There are several difficulties with this position. First, the owner of the mine does indeed have a choice: he can open a mine anywhere in the world, or not at all. He is no helpless victim. Second, on what basis does Epstein denigrate the contribution of the second landowner as "trivial?" In doing so this University of Chicago professor is taking on the unwarranted role of economic central planner, surely not a comfortable role for him, given his otherwise proclivities toward free enterprise. Third, Epstein

[72] Id. at ¶ 4.

[73] Id.

[74] *See generally* Richard A. Epstein, *Takings: Private Property and the Power of Eminent Domain* (Harvard U. Press 1985).

[75] Epstein, supra footnote 71, at ¶ 6.

supports the Supreme Court's century-long practice of land theft, on these spurious grounds, albeit limited to "public purposes," such as lighthouses, military installations, and roads.[76] But in doing so he is helping to set up a slippery slope, down which the Supreme Court just slid in *Kelo*.

F. Conclusion

The Coasean chickens have come home to roost. This applies, as we have seen, to both Coase and the Coaseans. If the public is outraged at *Kelo*, they need look no further than the University of Chicago-based "Law and Economics" movement, shaped pretty much entirely by this group of intellectuals and their followers in academia. The populace would be entirely justified in taking such a stance, as these professors provide the scholarly justification for judges running amuck with our sacred and precious private property rights. Coase has provided a "hostile environment" for our traditional values that reject and oppose land theft.

II. Reply to Lott on Rothbard on Coase

Coase started off the ball rolling in this regard with his claim that there were two possible states of affairs: a world with zero transactions costs,[77] and one with positive (or, indeed, very high) transactions costs.[78] In the former case, he maintained, it would not matter one whit for resource allocation how a judge ruled between contending parties over private property rights; the most efficient user of the property would keep them.[79] Either he would be awarded them by the court, in which case his opponent would not be able to bribe them out of his possession, or the court would award them to the least efficient user, in which case, the most efficient user would bribe his legal opponent into allowing him to keep

[76] *See* Epstein, supra footnote 71.

[77] Coase, supra footnote 3, at 2.

[78] Id. at 6.

[79] *See* id. at 2–6.

these rights.[80] In the latter case, high transactions costs made it impossible for there to be any post-decision reallocation of rights.[81] Then, Coase's advice to the judge was to make the award to the most efficient user of the resource.[82] This was the one who, in the zero transactions cost world, would have ended up possessing the resource under contention. In this way, Coase argued, wealth, or gross domestic product (GDP), would be maximized, which he saw as the proper goal at which judges should aim.[83]

Rothbard and several of his followers took Coase to task on both these claims.[84] Regarding the zero transactions costs scenario, Rothbard argued that the more efficient user who lost the lawsuit would only be able to bribe the less efficient user who won it if he had the wherewithal with which to finance it.[85] He need not be assumed to have it, particularly if his more efficient use is in the form of personal psychic benefits,[86] which cannot be converted into cash. Coase had specifically anticipated an objection to his thesis based on wealth effects, but that was entirely another matter.[87] All this meant was that Coase acknowledged that the court's decisions would necessarily effect the division of wealth between the two contending parties but had nothing to do with whether or not the loser could bribe the winner into allocating resources in his preferred manner.

As for the high transactions costs world, Rothbard and several of his supporters held up to scorn and derision the notion that the most efficient user of the resource should be given them.[88] First of all, this would

---

[80] Id. at 6.

[81] Id. at 15–16.

[82] *See* id.

[83] *See* id. at 1.

[84] *See* Murray N. Rothbard, *Law, Property Rights, and Air Pollution*, 2 Cato J. 55 (Spring 1982) (reprinted in *Economics and the Environment: A Reconciliation* 233 (Walter Block ed., The Fraser Inst. 1990)).

[85] Id. at 58.

[86] *See* Walter Block, *Ethics, Efficiency, Coasean Property Rights and Psychic Income: A Reply to Demsetz*, 8 Rev. Austrian Econ. 61, 64 (1995); Walter Block, *Coase and Demsetz on Private Property Rights*, 1 J. Libertarian Stud. 111, 112 (1977).

[87] Coase, supra footnote 3, at 43.

[88] For critiques of Coase on Rothbardian lines, *see* Block, supra footnote 86; Block, *Road Socialism*, supra footnote 36; Cordato, North, Rothbard, & Stringham, supra footnote 19; and Timothy

thrust the judge into the role of central planner, one for which he was particularly ill-suited.[89] Second, there was no way the court could know who was the "better" user of any given resource.[90] Third, every time relative prices changed, there would be a presumption that so would property rights. For example, if the point at issue was between the owner of wandering cows and a neighboring cornfield farmer, then when the meat-to-vegetable price ratio is high, the court will likely find for the cowboy, and when low, for the grower. But this is not so much a property rights system as the *absence* of one. And fourth, by refusing to look at the *past* in order to solve this dispute, the Coasean judge opened himself up to all sorts of dilemmas, for example, that O.J. Simpson was justified in murdering his wife, and that enslavement and rape are sometimes wealth maximizing and thus ought to be legalized.[91]

D. Terrell, *Property Rights and Externality: The Ethics of the Austrian School*, 2 J. Mkts. & Morality page# (Fall 1999).

[89] The Austrian side of the socialist calculation debate maintained that *no one* could accomplish any such task in any case. *See* Peter J. Boettke, *Why Perestroika Failed: The Politics and Economics of Socialist Transformation* (Routledge 1993); James Dorn, *Markets True and False in Yugoslavia*, 2 J. Libertarian Stud. 243 (Fall 1978); Richard M. Ebeling, *Economic Calculation Under Socialism: Ludwig von Mises and His Predecessors*, in *The Meaning of Ludwig von Mises* 56 (Jeffrey Herbener ed., Kluwer Academic Press 1993); Nicolai Juul Foss, *Information and the Market Economy: A Note on a Common Marxist Fallacy*, 8 Rev. Austrian Econ. 127 (1995); David Gordon, *Resurrecting Marx: The Analytical Marxists on Freedom, Exploitation, and Justice* (Transaction 1990); Hans-Hermann Hoppe, *A Theory of Socialism and Capitalism* (Kluwer Academic Pub. 1989); Ludwig von Mises, *Socialism* (LibertyPress/LibertyClassics 1981); Morgan O. Reynolds, *The Impossibility of Socialist Economy*, 1.2 Q. J. Austrian Econ. 29 (Summer 1998); Murray N. Rothbard, *The End of Socialism and the Calculation Debate Revisited*, 5 Rev. Austrian Econ. 51 (1991); Joseph T. Salerno, *Postscript: Why a Socialist Economy is 'Impossible'*, in *Ludwig von Mises, Economic Calculation in the Socialist Commonwealth* 51 (Ludwig von Mises Institute 1990), David Ramsey Steele, *Posing the Problem: The Impossibility of Economic Calculation Under Socialism*, 5 J. Libertarian Stud. 99 (Special issue, Winter 1981).

[90] It is a basic element of Austrian economics that costs are alternatives foregone, and hence *subjective. See* William Barnett II, *Subjective Cost Revisited*, 3 Rev. Austrian Econ. 137 (1989); James M. Buchanan, *Cost and Choice: An Inquiry into Economic Theory* (Markham 1969); Roy E. Cordato, *Subjective Value, Time Passage, and the Economics of Harmful Effects*, 12 Hamline L. Rev. 229 (Spring 1989); Thomas J. DiLorenzo, *The Subjectivist Roots of James Buchanan's Economics*, 4 Rev. Austrian Econ. 180 (1990); Roger Garrison, *A Subjectivist Theory of a Capital Using Economy*, in Gerald P. O'Driscoll & Mario Rizzo, *The Economics of Time and Ignorance* (Basil Blackwell 1985); Ludwig von Mises, *Human Action* (Regnery 1949); Mario J. Rizzo, *The Mirage of Efficiency*, 8 Hofstra L. Rev. 641 (1980); Murray N. Rothbard, *Toward a Reconstruction of Utility and Welfare Economics*, reprinted in *The Logic of Action* vol. 1, 225 (Edward Elgar 1997).

[91] Block, supra footnote 62, at 272.

Lott disagreed with the Rothbardian position.[92] It shall be the task of this part of the present chapter to subject that article to criticism.

Lott starts off on a strong note: "In fact, the Coase theorem is true by definition. If transaction costs are lower than the grains from agreement and there are no wealth effects, then resource allocation will not be altered by the redistribution of property rights."[93]

Let us start off with a minor criticism first.[94] Claims being true "by definition" are, for the Chicago school-oriented empirical scientists, highly problematic. For the Chicago tradition is one of logical positivism.[95] While there are to be sure some methodological differences between Coase and his fellow Chicagoans, one does not go far out on the limb to claim he is surely more of an empiricist than a praxeological Austrian, as implied by Lott.[96]

Now for a major criticism, or, at least, one more relevant to the issue at hand. The phrase "and there are no wealth effects" opens up a can of worms, but it is one, happily, that this author addresses.[97] Lott quite properly notes Rothbard's objection on the ground of "psychological factors" and offers two possible interpretations of this phenomenon.[98] The first of these, that psychological considerations are merely a different kind of opportunities foregone[99] does not at all apply to Rothbard,[100] whereas the second, the one offered by Block[101] and cited by Rothbard,[102] certainly does.

[92] *See* John R. Lott, *A Note on Law, Property Rights, and Air Pollution*, 3 Cato J. 875 (Winter 1983–1984).

[93] Id. at 875.

[94] This is minor only in the present law and economics context. Actually, it is of the first importance in determining whether economics is an empirical or deductive science.

[95] Milton Friedman, *The Methodology of Positive Economics*, in *Essays in Positive Economics* 7 (U. Chi. Press 1953).

[96] *See* Lott, supra footnote 92.

[97] Id. at 875.

[98] Id. at 876.

[99] Id.

[100] *See* Rothbard, supra footnote 84.

[101] *See* Block, *Coase and Demsetz on Private Property Rights*, supra footnote 86.

[102] Rothbard, supra footnote 84, at 57–58.

Let us quote Lott in full on this point, to reduce the possibility of miscommunication:

> This brings us to a second possible interpretation of Rothbard's objection to the Coase theorem. This second argument is advanced by Walter Block (1977) in a paper Rothbard cites.[103] The analogous argument to the railroad and farmer is that while the farmer places this additional $900,000 value on the orchard, he neither 'has the money' to pay the railroad up to $1 million (if the railroad's foregone profits were that high) nor would he want to pay that much money, for if he did he would no longer want to own the orchard. If Rothbard meant either one of these points, then the response is simply that he has violated the zero wealth effects assumption of the theorem. That is, the level of his wealth does determine whether the farmer will purchase the nonpecuniary benefits he receives from running the orchard. Wealth effects do not exist in the case of a strictly profit- maximizing firm, but only where individual consumption is occurring as in the case Rothbard mentions.[104]

My problem with Lott's treatment is that he is widening "the zero wealth effects assumption of the theorem" far beyond what Coase himself stipulated; he is in effect making it up as he goes along, in order to protect Coase from legitimate criticism. Coase stated in this regard:

> But as the payment would not be so high as to cause the cattle-raiser to abandon this location and as it would not vary with the size of the herd, such an agreement would not affect the allocation of resources but would merely alter the distribution of income and wealth as between the cattle-raiser and the farmer.[105]

What Coase is saying is that while the judge's decision would indeed alter the relative wealth of the two disputants, resource allocation would be invariant with regard to the judge's decision in the zero transactions

[103] Lott, supra footnote 92, at 876 n. 2 ("Rothbard's statement (p. 59, n. 6) that 'there may well be farmers so attached to their orchards that *no price* would compensate them,' leads one to believe that, like Block, he is forgetting Coase's assumption of zero wealth effects.").

[104] Id. at 876.

[105] Coase, supra footnote 3, at 5.

costs world or, as Lott would have it, with "[t]ransactions costs … smaller than the gains that can be realized by agreement between the parties."[106] The "wealth effect" Coase is talking about is the relative "distribution of income and wealth" between the winner and loser of the court finding.[107]

Lott is attempting to stretch this to cover something never even mentioned by Coase—the issue of whether or not the loser of the court decision would have enough income or wealth with which to finance the bribe to the winner, in case he lost the decision.[108] This is a *very* separate topic from the one concerning the fact that the wealth of the winner will increase while the wealth of the loser will decrease.

Perhaps a numerical example will clarify this crucially important distinction.

Suppose, then, that a poor man and a rich man are contending over the ownership of a flowerpot. The former places a value on it of $1000, while the latter $100. If the judge awards the flowerpot to the poor man, that is the end of the story; the rich man will not attempt to purchase it from him. But suppose that the court finds in favor of the rich man. Now, according to the Coase theory, the poor man, valuing it at $1000, is supposed to be able to buy it from the rich man for some price lying in between these two levels. For example, if the poor man offers the rich man $400 for the flowerpot, both of them will gain. The poor man will profit from the deal to the extent of $600 ($1000–$400) while the rich man will earn $300 on the deal ($400–$100).

But where, pray tell, will the poor man get the $400 with which to purchase this item? We may suppose he is *very* poor and simply does not have this amount of money at his disposal. Ah, but what about that $1000? He values the flowerpot at this amount, does he not? Yes, he does. Well, if so, cannot he go to the bank and borrow the $400 necessary to finance the purchase of it from the rich man? Out of his $600 profit, he can certainly pay off his debt, with a significant amount of money to spare. Yes, indeed, he could do so, if this flowerpot *had any value to anyone else; that is, if it had market value*. But suppose that it does *not*. That

---

[106] Lott, supra footnote 92, at 875.

[107] Coase, supra footnote 3, at 5.

[108] Lott, supra footnote 92, at 876.

is to say, the poor man values the flowerpot *not* because of its market value but simply on the basis of psychic evaluation. This amount of money, $1000, is what he would accept for its *sale*, but he *has* no money of his own. He cannot make the purchase with his own funds. It will *not* serve as collateral the bank will recognize since no one but the poor man values it at all. Sorry, the rich man values it at $100. But this is entirely irrelevant. The poor man has *no* money at all; nada, zip, bupkes, nothing. For him, the $100 he must pay the rich man for it is an astronomical sum.

There are two ways to reply to Lott on this matter. One, this is simply *not* a "wealth effect" as contemplated by Coase.[109] What that author meant by this phrase was something very different: that he was entirely cognizant that the court's decision would determine the relative wealth of plaintiff and defendant.[110] Two, I concede that this flowerpot—psychic wealth example *is* a "wealth effect." But, then, there are *two different* wealth effects: the one mentioned by Coase, and this *very* distinct psychic income one. There is no way around the conclusion, however; Rothbard and Block discerned a real error in Coase.[111] Lott, in supporting Coase vis-à-vis Rothbard and Block, is also mistaken.[112]

It is more than passing curious that Lott focused mainly on the zero transactions cost world or where the benefits of reallocating resources were greater than such costs.[113] For Coase, this model was the relatively uninteresting one.[114] This Nobel prize-winning economist has long held that the positive transactions cost world, where the benefits of reallocating resources were less than such costs, was by far the more interesting

[109] *See* Coase, supra footnote 3.

[110] Id. at 19 (Coase maintained, only, that the allocation of resources, e.g., who would end up with the flowerpot, would be independent of the judicial finding. But this, we can now clearly see, was a mistake. The flowerpot will be retained by the poor man if he is judicially awarded it; if not, he will not have the means to bribe the rich man into giving it to him).

[111] *See* Rothbard, supra footnote 84; Block, supra footnote 86.

[112] *See* Lott, supra footnote 92 (This error committed by Lott is similar to that made by Demsetz, *Ethics and Efficiency in Property Rights Systems* & *Block's Erroneous Interpretations*, supra footnote 19. The latter author also criticized Block, *Coase and Demsetz on Private Property Rights*, supra footnote 86, but was responded to in Block, *Ethics, Efficiency, Coasean Property Rights and Psychic Income: A Reply to Demsetz* & *Private Property Rights, Erroneous Interpretations, Morality and Economics: Reply to Demsetz, see* supra footnote 19).

[113] Id. at 875.

[114] Coase, supra footnote 3, at 15.

one.[115] Here, since transactions costs are so high, the judicial decision is definitive not only for Coasean wealth effects but for allocational decisions as well. And it is precisely in this model that Coase and the Coaseans have taken their most severe criticisms.[116]

One last point. In the conclusion of his work, Lott states as follows: "In summary, Rothbard's piece is disappointing in that he misunderstands the opposing arguments. The whole debate is especially unfortunate since it is between natural allies (for instance, both stress the subjective nature of cost and that all costs are opportunity costs)."[117]

In my view, nothing could be further from the truth. Of course, it cannot be denied that on *some* issues, Coase and Rothbard come out on the same side. Both, for example, favor privatization of the airwaves. But as far as the subjective nature of costs and the doctrine of opportunity costs, the two might as well come from different planets. All throughout Coase, there are numerical examples of costs.[118] Rothbard would reject these out of hand as essentially unknowable to third parties such as courts, the very institutions relied upon by Coase to make judgments on the basis of them.[119] It is the same with opportunity costs. These are the next best alternatives foregone whenever one chooses. As such, they are necessarily private and subjective. No judge can know of anyone's opportunity costs. Yet, it is on the basis of these that the Coase-inspired judge must render his decisions, in the real world of high transactions costs.

---

[115] *See* id.

[116] *See* supra footnote 88.

[117] Lott, supra footnote 94, at 878.

[118] *See* Coase, supra footnote 3.

[119] Rothbard, supra footnote 84, at 126.

18

Landsburg on Crime

Steven E. Landsburg, political economic maverick extraordinaire, and supposed advocate of free enterprise, has written a paper on theft and externalities entitled "Property Is Theft: When protecting your own property is stealing from others." In it, he calls for greater government intervention into the economy, more taxing, regulating, and subsidizing; and he does so on the ground that only in this way may we become more economically efficient. Where was he when the Politburo needed commissars?

In his view, there are several ways to protect your home or car from theft. One is to do so in an ostentatious way. For example, a burglar alarm with a sign posted on your front door, advertising its presence; or the "Club," which is fastened to the steering wheel, making it impossible for the robber to turn the vehicle. While this might turn some criminals onto the paths of righteousness, the dedicated member of this "profession" is more likely to seek easier, softer targets, that is, houses and autos without such visible protection.

States Landsburg, "When your neighbor installs a burglar alarm, thoughtful burglars are encouraged to choose a different target—like *your*

W. E. Block, *Property Rights*, Palgrave Studies in Classical Liberalism,
https://doi.org/10.1007/978-3-030-28353-7_18

house, for example. It's rather as if your neighbor had hired an exterminator to drive all the vermin next door."

In contrast, there are hidden protections against break-ins and theft. If the robber does not know which cars or houses are defended against his depredations but knows for sure that a significant number of them are, then he is more inclined to leave this field entirely. Here, each potential victim who protects himself protects his neighbors and indeed all others, as well.

Landsburg explains:

> The 'Lojack' is a hidden radio transmitter that can be activated after your car is stolen, to lead police to the thief (or, better yet, to the chop shop that employs the thief). The transmitter is hidden randomly within the car, so thieves cannot easily find it and deactivate it. The Lojack is completely hidden. There's no way to look at a car and know whether it has a Lojack installed. So unlike, say, the Club, a Lojack will never prevent any particular car from being stolen; it will only increase the chance of its being recovered. But from a social point of view, the Lojack has the huge advantage of *helping* your neighbors rather than hurting them. The Club convinces thieves to steal someone else's car instead; the Lojack convinces thieves not to steal.

From this, our author concludes that unseen safety devices are not only a vast improvement over flamboyant ones, but that the former are to be supported by law, the latter condemned and legally penalized. He not only says, in effect, "Lojack, good, the Club, bad;" he also maintains that we should subsidize the Lojack, and tax the Club.

But this, splutter, splutter, amounts to socialism, okay, okay, to fascism (socialism is outright government ownership; fascism, stylistically different only, favors heavy government regulation, as does Landsburg). He does so for the oft-used reason on the part of neoclassical economists, "market failure." It is only a slight exaggeration to define successful mainstream economists as those who have, more cleverly than their peers, discerned more and more "market failures" in more and more obscure places. If Landsburg were just an ordinary economist, this would not really bother me too much. But, as he is widely seen as a free enterpriser, I find this perturbing in the extreme.

What are the specifics? Let us allow Landsburg to tell the grisly tale himself:

> By the criteria that economists usually employ, this suggests that Lojacks should be heavily subsidized, just as visible security systems—like my neighbor's home burglar alarm or the Club—should be taxed. When you're doing something that makes strangers better off, you should be encouraged to do more of it.
>
> If we all used the same insurance company, you might expect that company to supply the appropriate subsidy. As long as your Lojack reduces the number of insurance claims, the company should be willing to pay you to install it. But with multiple insurance companies, that doesn't work so well: A company that insures only 10 percent of the populace will reap only 10 percent of the Lojack's benefits, and so will undersubsidize them. Worse yet, large insurance discounts are illegal in many states.
>
> The media have recently paid a lot of attention to research on other kinds of self-protection, most notably the work of John Lott and David Mustard on concealed handguns. But the Lojack research is in many ways more informative, because the authors were able to do a thorough job of distinguishing between benefits to the *purchaser* of a Lojack and benefits to the community at large. That discrepancy is the sort of thing that leads markets to fail—in this case by providing too many Clubs and not enough Lojacks.

Now for the (long overdue) criticisms of Landsburg.

First, minor point, he ought to change the title of his paper. As he has it: "Property Is Theft: When protecting your own property is stealing from others." In saying that "property is theft," Landsburg is provocatively putting himself on the side of the avowed enemies of civilization.

For example, according to Proudhon (Proudhon, Pierre-Joseph. 1966 [1840]. *What Is Property?* New York: Howard Fertig. p. 131. Quoted from Stewart Edwards (ed.) 1969. *Selected Writings of Pierre-Joseph Proudhon*. New York: Anchor Books. p. 124.):

> If I had to answer the question 'What is slavery?' and if I were to answer in one word, 'Murder,' I would immediately be understood. I would not need to use a lengthy argument to demonstrate that the power to deprive a man of his thoughts, his will and his personality is a power of life and death, and

> that to enslave a man is to murder him. Why, then, to the question 'What is property?' may I not likewise reply 'theft,' without knowing that I am certain to be misunderstood, even though the second proposition is simply a transformation of the first?

Second, there is that bit about "When protecting your own property is stealing from others." Surely, when Jones installs a Club, he is not exactly *stealing* from his neighbors. Rather, at worst, he is *deflecting* the attention of car thieves from himself to others. But the same can be said about anyone who locks his bicycle or the front door of his house when his neighbors do not.

Third, his attack on the Club is totally unwarranted. With it, one piece of property that might have been looted is saved. It is hardly the Club owner's fault that the monster then turns around and rips off somebody else's car. Further, the example set by the Club is socially useful; more people will protect themselves. A more reasonable way to look at the Club is as a totally innocent attempt to safeguard private property.

Fourth, the analogy with "vermin" is highly problematic. The neighbor is just as free to employ the services of an exterminator. A better way to look at the matter is this: suppose *everyone* utilized the Club. Then, there would be no shifting about of criminal attentions from one victim to another. Cars, all cars, would be better protected. The problem, here, lies not with those who utilize exterminators and the Club; rather, it lies with those who do not.

But what of this charge of "market failure?" This false indictment of free enterprise stems from the fact that Landsburg has not read and digested Hazlitt's most famous book, where he admonishes us to trace the effects of a given policy or phenomenon as far as possible; not only in the short run, but also in the long run; not as it affects only some people, but all. Why, then, can the market not ensure that people use the Lojack instead of the Club (assuming roughly equal costs between them; if these are radically different, then all bets are off)? It is because the relevant market has been already preempted by the government. It has not been allowed to operate. It has been nationalized (or statized or municipalized). It has disappeared. There can be no "market failure" here because this simply is no "market."

I refer, of course, to roads, streets, highways, avenues, lanes, and all other vehicular thoroughfares where automobiles are to be found. Not one of them is a part of the market. Suppose streets were all privately owned. Let us posit, arguendo, that Landsburg is totally correct in his comparative analysis of the Lojack and the Club, and that these two protective devices are equally costly. Is there any doubt that the road owner would either compel the former and forbid the latter, or, at the very least, charge people in such a way for street use to bring about the same state of affairs? That is, do exactly what Landsburg is calling upon the government to do: subsidize the Lojack and penalize the Club. Nor is there any doubt that if the road owner did not pursue precisely this policy, he would lose out in the competition between different firms in his industry.

So, of course, the market can internalize the externality about which Landsburg is (properly) concerned. That is, *if* a market is allowed in the first place. If not, it is a bit much on Landsburg's part to blame the market ("market failure") for something the government has forbidden to it. For more on this, see my article Block, Walter. 1983. "Public Goods and Externalities: The Case of Roads," *The Journal of Libertarian Studies: An Interdisciplinary Review*, Vol. VII, No. 1, Spring, pp. 1–34.

19

Debate on Eminent Domain

On May 10, 2004, a debate took place between Walter E. Block, Harold E. Wirth Eminent Scholar Endowed Chair and Professor of Economics at Loyola University New Orleans, and Richard A. Epstein, James Parker Hall Distinguished Service Professor of Law and Director, Law and Economics Program at the University of Chicago, and the Peter and Kirsten Senior Fellow of the Hoover Institution. The debate took place at the University of Chicago and was organized and moderated by J.H. Huebert, who was at that time a law student at the University of Chicago and is now a clerk at the US Court of Appeals. What follows is a very lightly edited transcript of the proceedings of that debate. All participants wish to acknowledge a debt of gratitude to Lew Rockwell, president of the Mises Institute, for financially supporting this event.

J.H. Huebert: Our debaters today are Professors Richard Epstein and Walter Block. Both men have long lists of achievements, but I will only introduce them briefly in the interests of time. Prof. Richard Epstein, as most of you know, is a Professor of Law here at the University of Chicago and one of the world's foremost classical liberal scholars. He is the author of numerous books, including a highly influential one addressed to the topic we are discussing here today, called *Takings: Private Property in the*

W. E. Block, *Property Rights*, Palgrave Studies in Classical Liberalism,
https://doi.org/10.1007/978-3-030-28353-7_19

Power of Eminent Domain. Professor Walter Block is a member of the economics department at Loyola University, New Orleans, and a leader of the Austrian School of Economics. He is an outspoken critic of the Chicago School of Economics and is also the author of the provocative book *Defending the Undefendable: The Pimp, Prostitute, Scab, Slumlord, Libeler, Moneylender, and Other Scapegoats in the Rogues Gallery of American Society*.

The topic of our debate today is "Do we really need eminent domain?" Professor Epstein will argue that we do, and Professor Block will argue that we do not. Here is the format: Block will begin with a 15-minute opening statement, followed by Epstein. Then, each will respond to the other with an eight-minute rebuttal. After that, we will go to a question and answer format, with debaters alternating in the order of their responses. Dr. Block, you may begin.

Walter Block: Usually, a debate is the sort of a thing where there is blood on the floor afterward, which students always like to see. I hate to disappoint you, but I think that there will be less blood on the floor than otherwise expected, because I do agree with Richard that under certain circumstances eminent domain is justified. But there will be some blood flowing later on because we do have some substantive disagreements.

Do you know the difference between a living room and a bathroom? The joke is, if you say "no," I say, "Don't come to my house." Well, the analog joke is: do you know the difference between coercion and voluntary agreement? Between using, initiating force against innocent people, on the one hand, and consent, on the other hand? If you don't know the difference between those two things, I say, "Don't get into political economy."

This debate is about political economy. Now, I admit that Richard does know this difference; further, that he is an impassioned defender of liberty and non-coercion in, maybe, 99% of all cases. However, he does have some reservations. He says that there are certain things that can trump the requirement not to initiate force. Namely, he denies that non-coercion is always a legal good, coercion always a legal bad. Examples for him include necessity, public goods, the holdout, the free-rider. Whereas, in my case, nothing trumps this principle. I am rabid on this issue. The non-aggression axiom is the essence of libertarianism, and I brook no disagreement with it in my philosophy.

Eminent domain is okay within a condominium development or restrictive covenant or based on some sort of prior consent. But what about outside of a condominium development? Suppose we are now talking about "out there" as in the case if somebody wants to widen a highway or build a new road and there is a holdout. To me, the issue comes down to the question of whether the US government is an agreed upon institution. Is it a club? Are we all part of this club called USA? If so, then we have already agreed to be bound by whatever the majority wants, and presumably, eminent domain could be one such policy. And that would be fine.

For my claim is that consent can turn what would otherwise be a legal bad into a legal good. For example, assault can turn into non-assault. Consent can turn what is a mugging into boxing. We don't put boxers in jail, even though what they do is punch each other, and in other contexts, we would do just that to them for such behavior. But since they both consented to punch and be punched above the belt, it turns from a legal bad into a legal good.

This occurs, similarly, with sex. Consent turns rape into seduction. Now, rape and seduction might look exactly alike to an outside observer. The woman who is being raped might not protest, for example, if there is a threat that the rapist will kill her baby in the next room if she doesn't cooperate. A third party might not be able to tell whether it is rape or seduction, but surely, her consent is crucial. With it, it is seduction. Without it, it is rape.

What about eminent domain? Well, if there is prior consent, then eminent domain is justified. Here is where I agree with Richard. For example, in a condominium development. I used to live in one. Every house there had to be painted the same color; you couldn't have a picket fence, because all of them were required to be in the same style.

Such institutions featured an agreement to be bound by majority rule, within certain limits. Suppose they wanted to widen an internal road and this necessitated eliminating, or reducing, the size of several members' front lawns. Then, since everyone had previously consented to the condominium contract, all those negatively affected were required to go along with this decision. I think that eminent domain of this sort is justified.

Now for the blood on the floor. I believe that the US government is not a voluntary organization. Thus, its eminent domain is not consistent with libertarianism. In contrast Richard argues that it is. To buttress my case I first turn to arguments from authority. Here is a quote: "The theory which construes taxes on the analogy of club dues or of the purchase of the services of, say, a doctor only proves how far removed this part of the social science is from scientific habits of mind" (Schumpeter, Joseph A. 1942. *Capitalism, Socialism and Democracy*, New York: Harper, p. 198).

Here is another quote from Franz Oppenheimer (Oppenheimer, Franz. 1926. *The State*. New York: Vanguard Press, pp. 24–27): "There are two fundamentally opposed means, whereby man, requiring sustenance, is impelled to obtain the necessary means for satisfying his desires. These are work and robbery, one's own labor and the forcible appropriation of the labor of others. I call one's own labor and the exchange of one's own labor for the labor of others the economic means. While the unrequited appropriation, where I would add requited appropriation too, of the labor of others will be called the political means. The state is the organization of the political means."

In my view, the state is based on theft. To see this, let us go back to the day of creation of this group called the United States of America. Suppose we are in the wilds of western Pennsylvania somewhere in 1776, and a tax collector comes to Mr. Jones and says, "Hey, Mr. Jones, guess what? We just started this new group called the United States of America." And Jones says, "Oh, that's nice. I wish you the best of luck. We'll be good neighbors. I always get along with my neighbors, and I'll get along with you all." The tax collector replies: "You don't understand. You have got to be part of this group." And Jones says, "Why do I have to be part of the group? I'm not a joiner. I don't like joining groups. I don't want to join this particular group. I'll be peaceable, I won't attack you if you don't attack me." Whereupon states the tax collector: "You don't understand. You've got to be a member. This is not a voluntary matter. This is coercive." I put it to you that this is a moral outrage. It is disgusting. It is despicable to go to an innocent person and threaten to use force against him when he has not done anything of the sort to you.

Here is a quote from my colleague, friend, and debating partner, Richard, who says, in his *Reason Magazine* interview (http://www.reason.org/aofr.html): "No government at all? A large society with no central authority offers an open invitation to some sleazy individual to consolidate power in his own name. The constitutional government uses deliberation. Anarchist's void at the center promotes the totalitarian rule, not individual liberty."

I think this is wrong on many different levels. First, if we are worrying about totalitarians and sleazy individuals, we have to realize that monopoly usually creates the worst product possible; competition is a superior process. The reason we have reasonably good ties and wristwatches and shirts and stuff like that and pretzels too is because we have competition in these arenas. If somebody makes a lousy pretzel, Richard won't eat that pretzel, and that pretzel place goes broke. Whereas, if they make a good pretzel like Ryder's pretzels (Epstein has this product in front of him on the desk and is snacking on it while Block is speaking—ed.), which I'm sure is a good pretzel, he'll go back and buy more pretzels from them.

But the same result obtains in guarding against bad guys, capturing, trying, and imprisoning them. Why should it be different? Why should competition be good for pretzels and shirts and ties and wristwatches, and not for protection against criminals? Competition brings about a better product, in general, because it weeds out inefficient providers of the good or service. I am sure that Richard would agree. Why should this not be true in all industries, including those devoted to dealing with bad guys?

Here is one indication of this. Consider what the Federales are doing. They are creating more problems than they are solving. A very high proportion of the people now in jail are there for drug crimes. But this is a victimless crime, and in a libertarian society, these prisoners would all be free.

What Richard is saying is, if I understand him correctly, is that if there are just a bunch of us individuals, we need a national government to rule over us because we are more than likely to run amuck and rape and murder each other. The market can't be relied upon to stop this, so we need a government. I argue against this, now, by analogy: national government is to individuals as world government is to national governments. Notice that the countries of the world are in a state of anarchy with regard to each other. There is not now a world government; there is no UN with any such powers. So the country of Canada and the country of Venezuela are now in a state of anarchy with regard to each other, just as I would be with regard to any individual residing here, if we didn't have a national government. Richard's argument logically implies advocacy of world government. If national government is justified because there is no single entity ruling over the locals, well then, so is world government, for precisely the same reason: because there is no single entity ruling over the various nations.

There are problems with any such scheme. If we had a world government, India and China between them would rule the entire planet. There would be no other place to run to, if you did not like the way they ran things. But this is mere consequentialism, unworthy almost of even mentioning, because we are interested in principle and justice. And the principle is that it is just plain wrong to initiate violence against people. It is wrong to force them to join a club. If you force them to join a club, it is no longer a voluntary club.

Another point is that Richard's position implies no right of secession. This, in turn, implies slavery. Look, the only thing wrong with slavery was that you could not quit. If you could quit, it would be no problem. It's a pretty good deal: You get fed three meals a day, you pick cotton and sing a song—and then the guy pulls out the whip, and you would say, "Wait, I quit." And he says, "No, you can't quit." You can't secede from slavery. We southerners still resent the War of Northern Aggression. People in Chechnya have every right to leave Russia. People in Taiwan have a right to be free of their Chinese masters. The two-country solution in Israel and Palestine is legitimate. But if it is justified to leave or quit en masse, it's also justified to secede a state at a time or a county at a time or a city at a time or a family at a time or even an individual at a time.

Consider the situation if an individual can secede and keep his property, not just emigrate and be forced to sell his land but depart from the political union and keep his property intact for himself. This is all that the guy in western Pennsylvania wanted to do: keep his property. When the tax collector told him he was free to leave but could not stay and keep his property, the only proper response is, "But that is land theft." If you can secede, and stay on your own land, that is equivalent to anarchism, or free market anarchism.

Let us now consider government defense. Is government necessary for defense? It seems to me that it is more like a protection racket. The Mafioso comes and says, "Look, I'll protect you. Pay me money." And the guy says, "Oh, that's okay. I don't need protection." Replies the gangster: "You don't understand. You pay me and then I'll protect you. Mainly from me." And the government adds: "I'll make you pay even if I don't protect you."

The point is that there's no unanimity in the government. What about the poor pacifist? Why should he be forced to contribute for defense? I defy anyone to tell me the difference, apart from great P.R., between the United States government and a Mafioso hooligan gang. It is the same thing. There is no difference.

Here is a paradox. Inside the condominium, eminent domain, takings, and expropriations are justified, since they were agreed upon, beforehand. Outside the condominium, in the real world out there, eminent domain, takings, and expropriations are not needed. Take the holdout problem. You are thinking of building a road from New Orleans to Chicago, and all of a sudden, some guy, Huebert over here (Block is now referring to the moderator of the debate—ed.), who owns property right in the middle of your prospective highway says, "Ha, ha. I'm not selling my land for any amount of money" so you can't build the road. That's the argument of the road statists.

There are various ways to deal with that challenge. First, there is not one but several possible routes that can be taken between New Orleans and Chicago. One, of course, is an exact straight line between them. But it is also possible to take several slightly circuitous routes, each of them extending out, a mile or two east or west, from the most direct. If there is a holdout on any one of these paths, the builder can utilize another.

Another response is to tunnel under Huebert the holdout's land or build a bridge over it. Libertarians do not believe in ad coelum. In that doctrine the owner of a square mile of the earth's surface also owns a cone of territory down to the center of the earth and also the air up towards the heavens, and, presumably, any heavenly bodies that wander into this area. Under this rule, no one could build over, or tunnel under, anyone else's land without the surface owner's permission. This would effectively require eminent domain if things like roads, pipelines, water and sewer lines, etc., were to be constructed.

Libertarians reject ad coelum and instead adopt homesteading, or "mixing your labor with the land," as a way of establishing ownership. Since nobody homesteaded a hundred yards underneath or above his farm or house, assuming a hundred yards is sufficient to tunnel under, the developer could overcome the holdout challenge by building a tunnel right under, or a bridge right over it.

Did you ever see a city block entirely taken up by a high rise except for a little sliver of land on which appears a little cottage? Did you ever see that? This is evidence that the land assembly negotiations didn't succeed. You won't find that in the Soviet Union. This phenomenon is a testimony to the virtues and the freedom of capitalism and free enterprise. Namely, that sometimes people don't make deals even though those who believe in making interpersonal comparisons of utility think that the cottage should have been taken down and the entire block given over to the large building. I say that this is a magnificent example of the operation of the free enterprise system.

A third response to the holdout problem is not to purchase land outright, but, rather, options. You buy options to buy land. The land in question might be worth, say $10,000. You pay a landowner on each of the prospective paths of the highway $100 and say to him, "Look, I'll give you $100. You keep it. And if I want, I could exercise the option to buy the land within a certain time period at the agreed upon price of $10,000." You buy options all over the place, relatively cheaply, and then if you get one holdout, you just go to another route.

Here is a quote from Richard, "Low level frauds used to mislead sellers about buyer's intentions." If I understand him correctly, by low-level frauds, he means that if you buy an option, you don't tell people what you're trying to do. You are guilty of fraud. But I think this is mistaken. I don't think it is fraudulent.

Another point, roads were originally privately owned. So much for the need for eminent domain. By the way, now that they are run by the government, they kill 40,000 people a year.

Now consider the concept of fair compensation in eminent domain. Huebert steals $100 from me. He is a philosophical robber so he is willing to engage me in dialogue about this and I say to him, "This is unfair. You stole $100 from me." He says, "Tut-tut. Here is a piece of chalk in compensation." How could it be fair compensation unless I agree? Remember, the key is consent, not giving compensation. Thanks for your attention. (Applause.)

Richard Epstein: Walter, talking with you always makes for an interesting conversation. Let me respond.

First of all, the question here is not whether we think that the distinction between coercion and consent has no traction. Clearly, if you are trying to figure out how to organize any kind of society, just or otherwise, a system, which entirely rests on coercive arrangements will in fact be the Gulag and we all ought to deplore it. The issue, rather, is whether or not the distinction between consent and coercion is so absolute that one would say that whenever there is consent, the transaction ought to be blessed, and that whenever there is coercion, the transaction ought to be damned.

What is the difference between the strong or radical libertarian such as Walter, and the more moderate or restrained classical liberal such as myself? It is that we classical liberals believe that there is a very strong presumption in favor of consent over coercion, but we do not believe that this is an absolute. The question is, what counts as a reason for the exceptions, and how is it that we can implement them and put them into practice?

If you start looking at the consent side of the situation, there are ways in which it can be undermined. Here is one of the examples that Walter gave, which I don't think came out quite right. He said that if you use force against a woman, it is coercion and rape, but if you don't use force, it is seduction. I was waiting to hear a word like "love" or a phrase like "genuine passion" because "seduction" itself has strong negative connotations. The reason is that there are transactions that are induced by various forms of fraud, and the question under these circumstances is whether or not the fraud will negate the voluntariness of any particular arrangement, whether for business or pleasure. Within the standard framework of a libertarian analysis, the answer, I think, should be "yes" at least if the cardinal sin in law is force and fraud.

My problem with Walter, here, is that he did not actually condemn fraud. He said that the fundamental principle was that of non-aggression, which seems to speak only to the use of physical violence and does not deal with such things as nondisclosure, concealment, or outright lying. So, one of the problems that you should immediately be aware of is that within the libertarian framework, there is a debate as to whether or not fraud should be covered under the prohibition, or if it is only naked force that is a legal wrong.

In dealing with this consent situation, at least within the context of government, there is also another very large body of law which is extremely important. It addresses the situation when you hold a resource for which the consents you obtained are not going to be valid. For example, suppose the government announced that the only time they are going to allow you to use the roads is if you agreed to waive all your rights for the compensation of property taken from you in an independent action. Most of us would say, and I think intuitively we would be correct, that the ability to contest to exaction of individual consent does not succeed within the standard libertarian framework. If you have the power to withhold something absolutely, or the power to grant it absolutely, you have the power to grant it subject to a condition or not. Ergo, the government wins.

The reason the conventional analysis is so dubious about that syllogism is that it is deeply worried, in all of these cases, about the problem of monopoly and coordination. The reason why most classical liberals are not libertarians is that they think the nature of the social problem is not just to minimize the danger of fraud, or rather force and fraud, but, also, to minimize the dangers associated with fairly serious coordination problems. Walter, I think, makes too light of these. They also stand in the way of human happiness and success. Consider the case that we are talking about, here. I think the usual rule is that no matter how much any individual wants to consent to the waiver of these particular constitutional rights, in virtue of the fact that the conditions involved have nothing to do with the safe operation of the roads, but, rather, constitute a design to extend government power, we would not accept the waiver. Interestingly enough, even if you were dealing with private roads, whose owners enjoyed monopoly positions, there would be a limit of the conditions that their owners could impose for access. The desire to find some way to discipline certain monopolies long antedates Roosevelt's New Deal. The general common law that allowed for the regulation of rates also allowed for judicial scrutiny of any conditions that might be imposed on the use of these private roads.

In other words, the doctrine of unconstitutional conditions often applies to government actions because they rely on state monopoly power. But to the extent that there are any forms of private monopolies, the same sorts of worries continued to apply.

So, if you are going to look at the issue of consent, you ought not to treat it as non-problematic and, self-evidently understood, as I think Walter does. There are certain very important limitations that have to be accepted with respect to the operation of that particular doctrine.

Regarding the use of force and coercion, or the threat thereof, similar kinds of ambiguity also arise. There is no doubt that ordinary aggression by individuals against other individuals counts as a legal wrong. There is also no doubt that there are immense problems in trying to figure out when there is an altercation between two or more individuals, who is the initial aggressor and who used force in self-defense. The uncertainty with respect to the application of the principle in the individual case is what led every serious political thinker, from Hobbes to Locke, and beyond, to the conclusion that self-help and self-judgment was not a reliable way in which to organize a political society. A rational legal system requires a neutral third party to sit in judgment so as to be able to introduce some degree of impartiality for the resolution of these kinds of disputes.

One could hope, in many cases, that you would be able to set up these tribunals by some kind of consensual arrangement. But, generally speaking, as the population size rises, the likelihood that there will be consent within the group is in fact much lower. If you start looking at this fellow in western Pennsylvania mentioned by Walter, it may well be that he says, "Well, you know, I'm a perfectly peaceable guy, and if you are a good neighbor to me, oh United States, I'll be a good neighbor to you." But suppose it turns out that he is lying. Now the whole question of anticipatory self-defense arises. Do you attack him before he attacks you, or do you have to wait? Generally speaking, when you are trying to work out these kinds of political arrangements where there are huge numbers of individuals, you cannot handle the coordination problem with a geographical hodge-podge, where the effective scope of sovereignty turns out to be the boundary lines of the western Pennsylvania's farmer Jones' world.

Walter is quite right to say that competition in marketplaces clearly dominates government coercion and monopoly. But there is no way that these wonderful pretzels (Epstein at this point grabs and waves around some snack food on the table in front of him –ed.) would have been able to reach our vending machines unless there were a system of public roads over which they could travel. There is no way that the seller would have been able to get them here to the University of Chicago unless there had been at least a modicum of social order which, generally speaking, only a well-organized state can provide. So if you are trying to understand what eminent domain's power is all about, what it says in effect is that the coordination problems we face in upholding society, in assembling pipelines and highways for pretzel delivery, etc., are very serious, and there is no way we can attain our desired individual goals without a limited government, armed with, among other things, eminent domain powers.

Now, Walter tries to do this by giving you a series of arguments, both of which, I think, are wrong. One concerns a practical matter, and the other a doctrinal issue. Consider the question of what else you own when you own some part of the surface of the earth. Here, Walter argues against the entire history of both Roman and common law by assuming that ownership applies only to surface rights. (An additional error of his is that he speaks of the ad coelum doctrine, which applies to ownership rights above the surface, when he meant to refer to the ad inferos doctrine, which pertains to ownership rights below the surface). Both of his contentions are wrong. Walter's view that ownership is confined to surface rights has been uniformly rejected for all sorts of very clever and sensible reasons.

Does a person who is only four foot tall own only up to six foot high into the air with respect to his land, whereas somebody who is six feet tall gets eight feet? Can you in fact claim additional airspace above your land by building upward? Can somebody who occupies the land next to you cantilever over your property, so as to prevent the building from taking place? Every serious property lawyer who has thought about this has said that the trick in the system of possession is to make sure that you require as little as possible, not as much as possible, to generate a stable system of ownership rights. This will allow people to manage, to generate ownership claims over particular physical objects.

Ownership of land on the surface of the earth runs in both directions precisely because it eliminates incredible problems that would arise if subsequent strategic actions would allow you to build on top of or below the land of your neighbor. One of the most famous cases in the takings law, called *Pennsylvania Coal Co. v. Mahon*, 260 US 393 (1922) against the coal company had to do with the problem when you start digging out coal underneath the surface and the ground starts falling in. The question is whether or not the owner of the coal was under a duty to support the land and improvements of the surface owner during the course of his mining operations. In principle the question could go either way. In most cases the surface and the subsurface mineral rights are owned by the same person in virtue of the *ad inferos* rule. When they are divided, if in fact the parties want to create easements by contract, which allow the owner of the mineral rights to dig without worrying about support, that is just fine: allocate that risk by the deed, and register it to bind all third parties. But to argue that when you own the surface, you do not also legally possess the subsurface, means that anyone could burrow under you, and your land will be at risk from cave-ins, etc. You now have to contract to get protection from him.

What this maneuver does in effect is save the libertarian theory from the holdout problem by creating an impossible original delineation of rights, which makes it impossible for anybody to get productive value out of his own land. It is not a trade, I think, that any rational legal theorist or private entrepreneur would want to make in these sorts of cases.

Now let us consider Walter's second problem. He has a rather odd definition of property rights. The libertarian definition, as he puts it, is much more narrow and much weaker than the traditional definition of property rights. Walter shows us this "wonderful" illustration to the effect that there are lots of different ways to get from New Orleans to Chicago and back. Of course, when you are trying to build a highway, you are not just trying to build a one-way road between two cities. You might also like to stop in Memphis along the way, or maybe Springfield or St. Louis. Look at the routes taken by all the interstate highways built in the United States as a case in point. Once you start adding in those constraints, it seems pretty clear that this particular scenario of private voluntary transactions, with or without options, is going to be a dismal failure.

There are probably, at a guess, a hundred thousand or more landowners from whom you would have to assemble rights of way in order to build any one of these routes between Chicago and New Orleans. If you announce that there are only six or eight alternative routes that you could have, each one of which could be blocked by one landowner under the circumstances, that would be a recipe for disaster. You just need to have a rate of noncompliance under these circumstances of well under one tenth of one percent in order to throw the entire system of interstate highways into a shambles. It simply cannot be denied that the holdout problem is very, very devastating.

We know this empirically. Just consider the holdout problems associated with small surface plots of land, which are located above large pools of oil, where, in fact, cooperation amongst the surface holders would allow you, relative to non-cooperation, to increase the yields from these pools by five- or ten-fold. The empirical evidence that has been gathered shows that once you get more than four or five people on the surface who have to coordinate their activities with respect to the pools below, you never come up with any form of agreement. Instead you get these incredible, wasteful "picket fences" where everybody starts to drill down at their boundary line in order to commandeer as much of the pool under the surface of their own land. The net effect is that everybody is left worse off than if there were cooperation.

These examples show us what is profoundly wrong with Walter's version of the libertarian state. You don't want to treat this wealth of empirical evidence attesting to the importance of the holdout problem with the sort of easy dismissive attitude that he did. If you are looking at the nature of various kinds of human actions, which involve the use of coercion, we know enough about human motivation that nobody, even a pervert, will engage in coercive actions against some other individual unless he thinks there is some kind of return or net benefit for himself. The core of good sense, with respect to the libertarian position, is that, generally speaking, if we are involved in ordinary individual actions of aggression, we know that there is going to be a fundamental imbalance between the benefits and the harms of coercive behavior. If I start hauling off at Huebért, he is going to be a systematic loser, I may turn out to be a winner. But we also know: (a) I am not going to compensate him so as to let us know whether or not my gains are greater than his loss, and (b) We know empirically even when compensation is not possible, if I kill him in order to make my life a little bit more pleasant for a day, we are willing to do what Walter says we can't do: make interpersonal comparisons of utility, and stop me.

I dare say there are none of us who would think, for example, in the rape case, that a happy ten minutes for a guy is sufficient utility to justify a life of shame, degradation, physical humiliation and abuse, psychosis that can be induced in a woman, not to mention her possible death. We make interpersonal comparisons of utility in those cases all the time. With regard to that kind of extreme case, I don't think there is anybody who thinks about this with the slightest bit of detachment, who would say that global judgment turns out to be wrong.

So, what is it about the eminent domain case, or the taxation case, that distinguishes this from the straight coercion case that Walter talks about? The answer is that the distribution of benefits you get from the proper use of government powers, relative to the distribution of benefits from private uses of coercion and murder and rape cases, is so fundamentally different. In that little exchange in *Reason Magazine* to which Walter referred, I said that the reason the hard libertarian principle is wrong is because it systematically and absolutely and in all cases precludes the use of centralized force by a government. It does so under those kinds of circumstances in which there is a net benefit for the individuals who, in fact, are subject to the coercion in question.

Go back to the oil and gas pool that I referred to a moment ago; that is exactly the way in which the system starts to work. What happens is, by telling each of these characters that you may put, for example, one and only one well on your property, each of them is being coerced—in the sense that they are being limited as to what they can do. But each of them benefits from the parallel coercion imposed upon the other persons who own land above the pool. So the person who is coerced now finds that his production goes down by 10% because he can't have those other 40 wells on his land. But then, to counterbalance that, he finds out that it rises by a far greater percentage by virtue of the like restrictions that are imposed upon the property of all these other individuals.

To the radical or extreme libertarian the only question you ask is whether or not there is or is not coercion involved in the transaction. To the classical liberal, my own tradition, you ask another question. Do we or do we not move from a regime of non-coercion to one of coercion? Or, can we say that we have created a situation in which the welfare of all the individuals has been improved, to some extent, as a result of the state action? It was exactly that kind of a logic which led people, looking at the inconveniences associated with the state of nature, to introduce a form of "social contract" theory to explain how it was that you justify the state. And, it seems to me, that this move contains really a very important insight.

Let me conclude by mentioning two other points.

One of them concerns that the eminent domain principles I have criticized. In my book *Takings*, I talk about how it is that the use of state force is justified against sovereign individuals only to the extent that it provides them with a net benefit greater than the coercion involved. This is in fact a position which has been systematically repudiated everywhere in the United States and elsewhere in the free world. Most scholars favor a much larger role for state power. After I wrote my *Takings* book, I was not, for the most part, attacked as a sell-out by people who stood on the right, and insisted that I had made too many concessions to state power. In addition, I was attacked as a zealot and worse from the left because, in effect I said that if you follow the principles I supported, you could get pretty strong evidence that virtually every major social welfare reform introduced under the New Deal was flatly unconstitutional. That is to say, this is not a position which is toothless against the arguments associated with government taxes.

How does this work? What happens is that the argument relies on a lot of private analogies and tries to push them a little bit further. For example, if you go back and you read opponents of large government such as Adam Smith, they use the partnership example in trying to explain why a flat tax ought to be preferred over a progressive tax. The argument was in a partnership all individuals have to contribute in proportion to their shares or their gains, their fraction of the cost, and that principle of proportionality becomes a useful rule of thumb to figure out how you would organize taxation in a public state. If you realize that once you eliminate one major source of redistribution and coercion by flattening the tax and eliminating various exercises of government power, what remains is an eminent domain power. This doesn't easily lend itself to massive forms of abuse; in fact this could be quite closely tracked, if only you had a government that cared to do it.

The last point I want to mention is that you have to be very much aware of questions of scale. I am very much worried about the problems associated with world government precisely because I think the monopolistic tendencies of these states, if they follow the pattern of the European Union, for example, will be disastrous. But, there is a big difference between governments and individuals. It is very difficult to imagine any kind of stable situation if you have hundreds of thousands of people in very close proximity to one another without a common authority. Whereas if you have a much smaller number of government players under their separate controls, you can get that form of stability because of a mutual acknowledgment of the gains from trade associated with it. Sometimes defensive positions require less to maintain themselves than offensive positions require to overrun them.

The argument here is not that classical liberals such as myself favor the current system of separate nation-states because it is perfect. Any system, whether it be monopoly or private, is going to have to figure out how you minimize cost under different types of uncertainty. What we can say with some degree of confidence, and I will end on this note, is that within the domestic political realm, a limited government will do better than no government at all. This holds true even if we are confident that, when we're worried about the potential source of abuses in the international realm, that a comprehensive world government is likely to do more abuse than a system of well-run national governments. Thank you. (Applause)

Huebert: Professor Epstein gave both an opening statement of 15 minutes and also a rejoinder of 8 minutes. I now call upon Professor Block for an eight-minute response; then we will go to the question period.

Block: I don't think there's anything wrong with seduction. Part of seduction is taking a shower or wearing a nice suit of clothes. I don't think it is fraudulent to try to seduce someone. I don't think that full disclosure is necessary. If you have to disclose, that is a positive obligation, anathema to libertarians.

With regard to monopoly, there is no such thing as a private monopoly. There can only be publicly aided monopoly. Monopoly is a grant of state privilege based on coercion. There is no such thing as a private monopoly.

In my publications on private roads, I made the point that right now when you buy a house, you get title insurance to make sure that you are the real owner of it. Under a regime of private roads, you would have to get access insurance, namely, assurance that you could get in and out of your house and onto the road and not have to become a world-class pole-vaulter or get a helicopter. The road owner would contractually obligate himself not to pull that sort of stuff on you because he wants you to buy the house contiguous to his road in the first place.

I don't think public roads are necessary for pretzel delivery. We have had private highways long before we had public ones. The initial thoroughfares were private turnpikes, and I don't see why you couldn't have them today.

I think Richard misunderstands the ad coelum doctrine. If the tunnel builder causes a cave-in for the owner of the surface land, obviously he is building too close to the surface. That would be a violation of the surface owner's property rights. But if you, left him, say, 50 feet, and there was firm terrain between the top of your tunnel and the bottom of his basement so that there would never be a cave-in, then and only then would you be justified in burrowing under his land holdings. Why does he own the area way below his surface property? He didn't homestead it. And if you believe in first possession, prohibiting the tunnel or the bridge is incompatible with that doctrine as well.

This solution eliminates all the oil well problems. The surface owner didn't do anything with the oil that would entitle him to own it. The first guy who discovered, developed, and tapped into that oil lake is the only rightful owner. Anyone else putting a pipe down to this lake is stealing his oil. There is only one just owner. You don't need any "coordination."

Consider the system of statism we now have. Rudy J. Rummel calculates the total number of noncombatants killed by their own governments during the twentieth century as 169,198,000 (Rummel, R. J. 1994. *Death By Government*, New Brunswick, NJ: Transaction Table 1.2, http://www.hawaii.edu/powerkills/20TH.HTM). That is not due to war. This figure is apart from wars. This is just due to states killing their own residents. A hundred and seventy million of them and many, many more millions died due to wars between governments. Surely, anarchy could do no worse.

Richard in his *Takings* book tells a story of two pies. He says there is a small pie without the government and a much bigger pie with this institution in charge. I would reverse it and say that when the government comes on stage, the pie shrinks because of its inherent coercion. There is a lack of a sense of a proportion here. The state has been one of the institutions that killed more people than anyone else; robber gangs don't come close, rapists don't come close. Richard is embracing this evil institution in order to make it easier to get roadways built. I don't think that that's justified at all.

In his response to me, he ignored my challenge about telling me the difference between a government and a mafia or protection racket and a government. Maybe he will answer that later, during the question and answer section of this debate.

I don't like this idea of anticipatory self-defense. It seems like that is what the US is doing now. We have several hundred military bases in every country known to man and some unknown to man. We have soldiers posted in some countries that have not yet even been discovered. I'm just kidding here. We have got military bases there too. There is an awful lot of anticipatory self-defense. How about waiting until we see the "whites of their eyes?"

Richard also favors the doctrine of necessity that justifies all sorts of violations of private property. Well, I put it to him right here and now that there is a necessity. There are people presently starving in Africa, and he has a nice suit of clothes, a wristwatch, pretzels, a nice house. I say that he is acting incompatibly with his own doctrine. What he should do is sell his house, sell his car, sell all the possessions that he has over and above what is needed just for some sort of hand-to-mouth existence. Take that money and, because of necessity, give it to all the starving people. If he doesn't do it, and so far he has not, then he is acting incompatibly with his own view. He is guilty of a performative contradiction.

Huebert: We now enter the third phase of the debate, questions from the audience and responses from the debaters. No matter to whom a question is addressed, the debaters will alternate as to their order of response.

Question 1: Professor Block, how can you mount an attack on eminent domain, even while accepting the social contract? I mean, to take a common example, suppose you're in a condo complex. There are still some things that a condo cannot do to you. There is such a thing as a social contract, but eminent domain is not one of the things that the government can or should do.

Block: I would say that it depends upon the specific condominium contract. If you believe the government is a legitimate institution, it depends upon what powers we ceded to them in order to get this much-vaunted protection out of them. Yes, there are certain things that the condominium association can't do. They can't shoot you, but they can widen the internal road, or narrow it, or take away one of your rooms if permission for so doing is stated in the contract. And if not, they shouldn't be able to do it.

Epstein: There's no question that with condos it is easy, because it all starts with a single owner who can supply a blueprint for dividing up the land. The point is that after you divide it up in an effort to sell shares to people, what kind of protections you give them. They are remarkably similar to those that we find in the United States' constitution. There is no condominium association which it allows you to take this or that private room and turn it into a common recreation room, but there are rules that allow assessments to be laid usually proportionally to various benefits that are received. This becomes very tricky because some of these benefits benefit only some members of the unit and some benefit others. So you have all these battles. But that is the easy case. The turnpike case is not one like that because all these private turnpikes are only assembled in the first place with the use of eminent domain powers and then handed off to private parties. So there is always a situation of state franchises and private development, which in fact is perfectly consistent with the basic situation but is not consistent with Walter's theory.

Question 2: It seems like, Professor Epstein, that you are arguing, that rape is wrong only because of costs and benefits considerations. I certainly don't form such decisions in that way. And I don't think that very many other people do either. Instead, we make decisions based on what is right and wrong. It isn't that we ignore the consequences, but, we have a certain system of moral rules that we follow. It would not even be possible to do it your way because we cannot make such interpersonal comparisons of utility. I am a philosophy student at Washington University and one of the things you learn is that utility is subjective. It is inside your head, and you can't take it out and look at somebody else's and put them on a scale. So, even if you wanted to make moral decisions this way, you couldn't.

Epstein: That is an interesting question, but I think you are confusing two things. One is the question of where and how do you make these decisions. It would be utterly ruinous as a moral and a practical matter to use a form of act utilitarianism for rape. If we did this with respect to each particular instance of rape, we would have to determine whether or not the satisfaction on one side was sufficiently greater than the harm on the other side to warrant imprisonment. The reason we have categorical rules is because if you look around and see what is generally happening, you can't imagine many situations, which would go the other way; that is, where the benefits of a rape would exceed its costs. The last thing you want to do is to give accused rapists in individual cases the opportunity to plead a utilitarian defense, because you know that there is a great danger that phony special pleading will override your basic judgment. In other words, your background norm says that the gain from rape is 10, while the loss is 100,000. Then the defendant's lawyer says, "That's just a general average. In my client's case, the gain was enormous and the prostitute didn't much care anyhow, so the cost was trivial."

So that what happens is we do make, and we have to make, utilitarian judgments all the time with respect to aggregate norms. This is one of the things we are worried about in the problem of administration. If you allow judicial decisions to be made particularistically in individual cases, the entire system will suffer a rapid degeneration.

Now, there are a couple of things about this problem which show how tricky and treacherous some of these judgments turn out to be. Consider the domain of charitable work, which even in a libertarian world is perfectly fine. The only way we decide to whom we are going to extend contributions, on the grounds that they are needy, is to be able to make utilitarian judgments about comparative need. For example, that somebody who is desperately hungry and hasn't had anything to eat for 4 days can use a bowl of soup more than I can use my 19th bowl of soup after having just slurped down 18 bowls.

I submit to you if the radical subjectivity you think appropriate for moral philosophy was correct, then not only would you misunderstand the arguments that I made with respect to rape, but you would render the entire area of imperfect obligations for charitable work completely unintelligible. Completely unintelligible. You simply could not explain the common patterns of behavior. If you cannot explain what utility differences are, why it is that you would make a voluntary contribution for no consideration in exchange to some people and not to others? And even with respect to categorical judgments, for example, we have a categorical judgment based "on moral grounds against murder," right? And this holds true even with consent. Then you would have to figure out if Walter is correct, why we retain that prohibition. It is only because of the general abuse in practice.

When you think of people who are desperately ill, racked with pain, suffer from euthanasia-type circumstances, the categorical judgments on the authenticity of consent do not seem to fit the particular cases. You get the enormous moral question as to whether or not you now have a subrule of cases to deal with euthanasia as opposed to the general prohibition.

Let me ask Walter a question. Your version of libertarianism has nothing to do with any system property rights ever known to mankind. On the area of oil rights, ad coelum, anything you care to mention, it is just completely at variance. So just answer a simple question: would you or would you not accept consent as a defense to murder?

Block: Yes, I would certainly accept consent as a defense to murder because I believe in the right of assisted suicide.

Epstein: No, no. I said general defense to murder in all cases, obviously in cases of rape. That is, alleged rape. Everyone says consent; otherwise, you don't have marriage. But the question is whether or not you think it operates the same way. The point I am making is that there are institutional judgments which you are blind to. Would you accept consent to a standard case of murder brought by this mythical public prosecutor who, in your world, doesn't exist? And then you say, "Yeah, I killed Huebert, but he wanted me to do it. He asked for it."

Block: I would accept this as a defense if I killed Huebert and he said it was okay if there was some sort of evidence for that claim. If he had written a letter or taped a video stating that he wanted me to kill him. That would prove that it was assisted suicide as opposed to murder, and I would accept it as evidence.

I want to talk about this rape business and interpersonal comparisons of utility. Here is a quote from another of Richard's books (Epstein, Richard A. 1995. *Simple Rules for a Complex World*, Boston: Harvard University Press; p. tba) "A unit of wealth is worth more to a poor person than a rich one." In my view, you are giving away the store when you say anything like that. You can justify all sorts of non-libertarian and even non-classical liberal welfare schemes. If you are justified in taking money from a John D. Rockefeller or a Bill Gates because they have 19 bowls of soup and give it to some poor guy without any, then you have justified every leftists' vision of the welfare state.

There are cases where we can say that a rape victim loses less than a rapist gains if you use interpersonal comparisons of utility in a loose sense. I really have no objection to doing so. But the existence of charity does not prove an interpersonal comparison of utility in the strict technical sense. Charity can be justified without resorting to that concept in a non-technical sense. People do look around them and see others in worse shape and they want to help them.

What about the case of a prostitute who is used to having sexual intercourse all the time, and the rapist who, say, was in jail for 20 years and was really desperate for sexual services. One could then, using this loose sense of interpersonal comparisons of utility, say that utility will increase if we allowed that rape to occur. I still say, along with the questioner, that this is a moral obscenity. And yet, this is the objection that the Coase, Posner, Epstein, and the University of Chicago Law and Economics tradition is wide open to. They maintain that maximizing wealth is the be-all and end-all of legal theory. If that's your criteria, then you get these anomalous cases where utility clearly runs the other way.

In Africa, nowadays, they have this view that if you have sex with a virgin, you get cured of AIDS. This isn't true of course, but suppose it were. Suppose that if you have sex with a virgin—non-consensual sex, therefore, rape—you will no longer have this dread disease; you will save your own life. Maybe we should legalize or even favor rape in these cases? Only a Coasean, Posnerian, Epsteinian judge would even consider such an outrageous thought. Whereas a libertarian would say, "Well, look, this is a violation of property rights. This woman owns the property rights in herself, and I don't care how much utility you get from doing this, it is just too bad. It is her body. The rapist is guilty, even though he thereby rids himself of AIDS." The only way you could get her to have sex with you—I am still assuming that as she is a virgin she could thus save your life—is to pay her. Or get her voluntary consent in any other way. If you don't get her consent, it is rape. It is a vicious, evil kind of a system, and totally unjustified, to not find you guilty of rape because utility increased thereby.

Question 3: Can I suggest a compromise? I'll explain it and see what you both think about it. Say that we prohibited all takings by the federal or the state government and this was only allowed on the local level. Perhaps this would be more like the condominium club, which makes it much easier to move into a community. I wonder if this proposal might be acceptable to both Professors Block and Epstein. We would have some sort of a takings, but you would limit the impact of it. So, what would both of you say about a system like that?

Block: This reminds me of that joke about the bathroom and the living room. If you can't tell the difference between a coercive village government and a voluntary private condo, don't come into political economy. It does not matter whether it is a world government or a state government or a national government or a town government. They are all coercive and they are all evil, and they all should be ended if we are to have justice. Whereas a condo or any other such voluntary agreement is entirely justified. So, while I am always open to compromise, I cannot see my way clear to agreeing with this one.

Epstein: That is a perfectly sensible suggestion, except that the evidence suggests that in many cases, exploitation by local governments is at least as bad and may be worse than that of national governments. (See on this Bolick, Clint. 1993. *Grassroots Tyranny: The Limits of Federalism.* Washington D.C.: Cato.) Justice is straight empirical matter. Sometimes you get small isolated minorities of one kind or another. You get a powerful zoning board and they will come up to you and say we are going to wipe you out unless you sell to one of our friends in a "voluntary" transaction. The history of the Constitution and the effort to place in this document powerful federal restraints against state expropriations after the Civil War is eloquent testimony to that phenomenon.

The other point I do want to mention is that Walter has attacked Ronald, Dick, and myself, but consider the cases in which the virgin is needed to ward off disease. This is very different from the Common Law Necessity doctrine. If you want to be fair, you have to understand what its limits are and attack it, rather than putting forth a straw man argument and then disposing of it.

This doctrine said that in times of immediate necessity, in an emergency in which you are in eminent peril of your own life, you may use somebody else's property without their consent so long as you later provide compensation for the loss thereby inflicted. It has nothing whatsoever to do with affirmative duties to give generalized aid to other individuals when there are countless numbers of individuals who are able to do it.

In the rape case, with respect to the virgin, the standard argument is that transactions costs are low and there are many different alternatives. No matter how great the need, you must go through the market instead of using coercion. So, the cases that were given are in fact cases that would receive categorical denunciation even under the traditional rules that do allow condemnation of private property for a public use. Remember, that is what we were talking about. We were not talking about private use of force for private advantage, we were talking about the eminent domain question: "nor shall private property be taken for public use without just compensation." That is the text of the relevant portions of the Fifth Amendment to the US Constitution, replicated in some form in every state constitution.

Question 4: Professor Block, how would you enforce the situation in a libertarian world where the condo or the cooperatives actually ends up taking somebody's room and turning it into a recreation room, anyway, despite the fact that it wasn't in the contract? How do you enforce that? So, how does the apartment owner, if the contract has been violated, enforce it?

Epstein: I think that's an absolutely unanswerable question.

Block: Your question was what sanctions does the condominium owner have if the condominium grabs his recreation room?

Questioner 4: Yes.

Block: And it was not in the contract?

Questioner 4: Yes.

Block: Well, in my libertarian model, he goes to the forces of law and order. This would be the private courts if there is free market anarchism or if we have limited government libertarianism or minarchism, as Richard advocates, then he goes to the government court. In either case he says to the judge, "Look, this was not part of the condominium agreement. The contract mentioned the color of the house and the color of the curtains and the type of fence, but it didn't say anything about grabbing my recreation room. They seized it anyway. I want an injunction and I want damages." So, whoever the forces of law and order are, you would appeal to them.

Epstein: But if there are forces of law and order that are not part of the condominium association, they are going to have to get their revenues through taxation. It is one thing to try to minimize the role of force in human affairs, it is quite another to pretend that you can organize them where they are never going to be used in a legitimate fashion.

Block: I disagree. There is an entire literature that Richard isn't looking at. See Murray Rothbard, Hans Hoppe, and David Friedman. These authors talk about competing defense agencies. It is at least a debatable point, but Richard dismisses this out of hand. I claim you can have competing defense agencies without a taxation system. You go to court A because court A is your court and you go on from there. If you read what Hoppe, Rothbard, and David Friedman have said about this, you understand how the competing defense agencies would work to a better effect than coercive governmental ones.

Epstein: No they would not. I have read that literature carefully. The claims made in it are farcical in my judgment. For example, suppose you are not quite sure who has been the source of aggression against you.

What you want to do is to run an investigation in the context of multiple competing defense agencies. There are 73 different agencies from whom you have to get approval in order to run any kind of investigation. The system will collapse, and then exactly what I predicted in the *Reason* article will take place: chaos. You will get bad governments instead of good governments. The reason there are 170 million people dying is because people did not follow those principles of good government I have elaborated upon. The reason why you have competition in a country like ours is although we deviate from these principles all too often, we don't deviate from them so far and so much as to allow us to descend into anarchy. And remember, the common meaning of the word anarchy (chaos) is not one which invites all sorts of exultations. Rather, it is something which seems to preach or to be aware of the prospects of immanent violence and destruction.

Block: I disagree. Etymologically, the word archy means unjustified rule. It is Kant's categorical imperative: do this, don't do that. In contrast, his hypothetical imperative would be: if you want this then do that. Archy just means arbitrary rule, and I think it is totally unjustified to rule other adult human beings without their say so. I don't oppose paternalism for three-year-old children, of course. But it is improper for adults unless they threaten or initiate violence or fraud.

In sharp contrast, "anarchy" adds the prefix "an" to "archy" and means without, or in the absence of, arbitrary rule. Critics, not advocates of free market anarchism, equate this term with chaos.

We have to put these things in perspective. If I jump up in the air right now, I am exerting a gravitational force on the earth and the earth is exerting a gravitational force on me. To put it this way would show no sense of proportion, because the gravitational force the earth places on me is way more than the gravitational force I place on it. Even so, the statement is true, that we each exert a gravitational force on the other.

My claim here is that what Richard is doing is exhibiting a similar lack of proportion. He is caviling about these stupid roads and oil wells; meanwhile, people are dying like flies under his system, a system he admits is a bad system because of errors or what have you. You know, we in New Orleans are experts on vampires. You have to stipulate this because who could deny it? We are the vampire capital of the world! To me the government resembles nothing as much as a vampire. To urge limited vampirism shows a serious lack of proportion. These vampires are out there, killing people in droves. That 170 million are people killed by their own states. In addition, governments have concocted all sorts of wars. Richard is willing to embrace this present system in order to make it a little bit easier for roadways to be built, which also kill 40,000 people a year in traffic accidents.

Epstein: I'm embracing a limited form of government. I'm not defending Idi Amin or Saddam Hussein or Stalin or Hitler. You talk about a sense of proportion (laughter). But there is a stupendous, gigantic difference between governments that allow people to essentially live out their entire lives and those that murder people in their bed when they are six years of age. What happened in all the places in which you start with anarchy is that a thug takes over and bad government results. So as Edmond Burke said, and it applies to you, Walter, all that is necessary for the forces of evil to prevail in the world is for people of goodwill to do nothing, and that is precisely what you are recommending.

Block: No, I'm not recommending doing nothing. What I'm doing is recommending getting rid of vampires, whether they are vampires that take just a little bit of blood or vampires that take gallons of blood. Here is a joke that is apropos. A man asked a woman "would you go to bed with me for a million dollars?" and she says "okay." Then he says "how about for two bucks?" and she says "what kind of woman do you think I am?" He replies: "we have already established what kind of woman you are, we are now only arguing about the price." Well, it seems to me that we have established, to my satisfaction at least, that governments are vampires and ghouls and murderers, and we are just arguing about how many people they are murdering. I don't think that's an important discussion.

Epstein: Walter, are you indifferent to living near or in Saddam Hussein's Iraq? Somehow, I very much doubt this. I think the only reason you speak as you do is that you benefit from the blessings of liberty secured by limited government. Look, Walter, let us understand one thing. When David Friedman talks about his society—I love, admire, and respect David—but this is a guy whose only example is some small obscure village in the upper mountains in Iceland in 1200 (laughter). You can't point to a single solitary real-world example of your system working successfully. All I am saying is there is something about the tradition of limited free enterprise government that makes a lot of sense. We've got to figure it out. And in your effort to repudiate this large government view, of which I am now charged with, in effect says that everything in the tradition that everybody has ever done from the beginning of time is wrong, because they don't quite understand the vampires at the gates. I'm boggled, just boggled.

Block: You say that our liberties are secured by limited government. I reply that the liberty we enjoy here is in spite of limited government, because even limited government starts off as a mafia protection racket. It goes to innocent people and says, "Look, you are going to join us whether you like it or not and you are going to pay us taxes whether you like it or not." How can an institution that starts off that way, which Richard admits starts that way, how can any good come out of an institution like that?

Epstein: Because they are not running a protection racket. If they are doing it right, they are giving services back to the people of equal or greater value than the taxes they impose.

Block: Services?

Epstein: Consider this following mental experiment. I would like to create this large national park and what we will do is we'll say that this will be Block haven, and everybody who agrees with Walter can go there. We will seal off the boundary line, and in 20 years, we will open up the gates and exhume the bodies (general laughter).

Huebert: There are only 30 seconds left.

Block: Services, schmervices. The key is not whether you give services, the key is whether they are financed on a voluntary basis or not. I could give you a piece of chalk and say that's the service for taking your wallet.

With regards to national parks, I want to ask Richard a question. Richard, where would you rather meet me tonight at three in the morning, in private enterprise Disney Land or in New York City's Central Park, which is a government park?

Epstein: Well…

Huebert: That's all we have time for. Thank you to our debaters, and thank you to the audience for coming. (General applause.)

20

Homesteading City Streets: An Exercise in Managerial Theory

This chapter is dedicated to an exploration of how city streets can best be privatized. Among the alternatives: giving them away or selling them to specific people (e.g., those who live on them, work on them, travel through them) or auctioning them off the highest bidder(s). Further, they could be disposed of piecemeal, for example, in sections of 100 feet or so, or in their entirety, for example, Broadway in Manhattan goes to one firm or, alternatively, they might be packaged in neighborhood sections, for example, all the streets in Greenwich Village end up under the control of a single commercial entity, all those in the Upper East Side to another.[1]

To most scholars, this exploration will appear as ludicrous, idiosyncratic, or even maniacal. Privatize the streets? "Under which controlled substance is a person laboring under the influence of, who would even

The author benefited from discussions with Jeff Tucker while writing this chapter; he wishes, also, to acknowledge the benefit of some very helpful suggestions made to him by two referees of this journal.

[1] I use examples from New York City since this is perhaps the most well-known locale in the world.

W. E. Block, *Property Rights*, Palgrave Studies in Classical Liberalism,
https://doi.org/10.1007/978-3-030-28353-7_20

raise such an issue, let alone attempt to soberly address it?" will be the likely reaction of most urban economists.

Nevertheless, we persist in our folly.[2] We will not here make the case for private rather than public enterprise in general. There is already a rather large extant literature on privatization.[3] It makes the Adam

[2] This is meant sarcastically. I make no apology whatsoever for attempting to apply what we have learned about the best way to supply cars and chalk and cheese and computers—namely, free enterprise—to an analogous good, roadways.

[3] Anderson, Terry L., and Peter J. Hill, "Privatizing the Commons: An Improvement," 50 S. Econ. J. 438 (1983); Anderson, Terry L. and Peter J. Hill, editors, The privatization process: a worldwide perspective, Lanham, Md.: Rowman & Littlefield Publishers, 1996; Barnett, William, "A Private Mall Becomes a Public Hall," Loyola Law Review, 1980; Benson, Bruce L., To Serve and Protect: Privatization and Community in Criminal Justice, New York, N.Y.: University Press, 1998; Block, Walter, "Drowning in Manitoba, Water Privatization in Walkerton, Ontario," http://www.lewrockwell.com/block/block4.html, August 4–5, 2001; Block, Walter, "Comment on William Stanbury's 'Privatization in Canada: Ideology, Symbolism or Substance?,'" Paul MacAvoy, William Stanbury, George Yarrow and Richard Zeckhauser, eds., Privatization and State-Owned Enterprises: Lessons for the U.K., Canada and the U.S., Boston, Kluwer, 1989, pp. 331–336; Block, Walter, "The Process of Privatization," International Privatization: Global Trends, Policies, Processes, Experiences, O. Yul Kwon, ed., Saskatchewan: Institute for Saskatchewan Enterprise, 1990, pp. 431–436; Block, Walter, "Comment on Alan Walters' 'Deregulation and Privatization: Lessons from the U.K.,'" The Law and Economics of Competition Policy, Frank Mathewson, Michael Trebilcock and Michael Walker, eds., Vancouver: The Fraser Institute, 1990, pp. 175–178; Butler, Eamonn, ed., 1988, The Mechanics of Privatization, London: Adam Smith Institute; Fitzgerald, Randall, 1989, When Government Goes Private: Successful Alternatives to Public Services, New York: Universe Books; Friedman, David, The Machinery of Freedom: Guide to a Radical Capitalism, La Salle, IL: Open Court, 2nd ed., 1989; Friedman, David, "Private Creation and Enforcement of Law: A Historical Case," Journal of Legal Studies, 8: 399–415, 1979; Hadfield, Gillian K., "Privatizing Commercial Law," Regulation, Vol. 24, No. 1, Spring 2001, pp. 40–45; Hanke, Steve H., ed., 1987, Privatization and Development, San Francisco: Institute for Contemporary Studies; Harrison, Patrick, Robert W. McGee and Walter Block, "Social Security Privatization" Commentaries on the Law of Accounting and Finance, forthcoming; Landes, William M., and Posner, Richard A., "Adjudication as a Private Good," Journal of Legal Studies, 8: 235–284, 1979; Markum Amy, Jason Bryant, Walter Block and Robert W. McGee, "Privatization of Public Schools," Commentaries on Law and Public Policy, forthcoming; Milgrom, Paul, Douglass North and Barry Weingast, "The Role of Institutions in the Revival of Trade: The Medieval Law Merchant, Private Judges and the Champagne Fairs," Economics and Politics, Vol. 2, 1990; Ohashi. T.M., T.P. Roth, Z.A. Spindler, M.L. McMillan, & K.H. Norrie, Privatization Theory & Practice, The Fraser Institute, Vancouver, B.C., 1980; Pirie, Madson, 1986, Privatization in Theory and Practice, London: Adam Smith Institute; Stringham, Edward, "Justice Without Government," Journal of Libertarian Studies, Vol. 14, No. 1, Winter 1998–1999, pp. 53–77; Roth, Gabriel, The Private Provision of Public Services in Developing Countries, Oxford: Oxford University Press, 1987; Rothbard, Murray N., For a New Liberty, Macmillan, New York, 1978; Tinsley, Patrick, "With Liberty and Justice for All: A Case for Private Police," Journal of Libertarian Studies, Vol. 14, No. 1, Winter 1998–1999, pp. 95–100; Tannehill, Morris and Linda, The Market for Liberty, New York: Laissez Faire Books, 1984; Walker, Michael A., ed., Privatization: Tactics and Techniques, The Fraser Institute, Vancouver, B.C., 1988; Woolridge, William C., Uncle Sam the Monopoly Man, New Rochelle, N.Y.: Arlington House, 1970.

Smithian[4] case that we can more effectively organize an economic system through decentralization based on private property, freely fluctuating prices, and unencumbered markets than centralization, bureaucracy, and commands.[5]

Nor will we again rehearse the arguments in favor of private rather than public roads in particular. There is already a relatively large body of work (given the admitted unpopularity of the argument) that attempts to rationalize this enterprise.[6] That is, it shows that private streets, roads,

---

[4] Smith, Adam, An Inquiry into the Nature and Causes of the Wealth of Nations, Indianapolis, IN: Liberty Fund, 1776/1979.

[5] Mises, Ludvig von, Bureaucracy, New Rochelle, N.Y.: Arlington House, 1969; Mises, Ludwig von, "Economic Calculation in the Socialist Commonwealth," in Hayek, F.A., ed., Collectivist Economic Planning, Clifton, N.J.: Kelley, 1975 (1933).

[6] Beito, David T., "From Privies to Boulevards: The Private Supply of Infrastructure in the United States during the Nineteenth Century," in Jerry Jenkins and David E. Sisk, eds., Development by Consent: The Voluntary Supply of Public Goods and Services (San Francisco, 1993): 23–48; Beito, David T. and Linda Royster Beito, "Rival Road Builders: Private Toll Roads in Nevada, 1852–1880," Nevada Historical Society Quarterly 41 (Summer 1998), 71–91; Beito, David T. "Voluntary Association and the Life of the City," Humane Studies Review, Fall 1988; Beito, David T. "Owning the Commanding Heights," Essays in Public Works History, vol. 16, 1989; Block, Walter, "Free Market Transportation: Denationalizing the Roads," Journal of Libertarian Studies: An Interdisciplinary Review, Vol. III, No. 2, Summer 1979, pp. 209–238; Block, Walter, "Congestion and Road Pricing," The Journal of Libertarian Studies: An Interdisciplinary Review, Vol. IV, No. 3, Fall 1980, pp. 299–330; Block, Walter, "Public Goods and Externalities: The Case of Roads," The Journal of Libertarian Studies: An Interdisciplinary Review, Vol. VII, No. 1, Spring 1983, pp. 1–34; Block, Walter, "Theories of Highway Safety," Transportation Research Record, #912, 1983, pp. 7–10; Block, Walter "Road Socialism," International Journal of Value-Based Management, 1996, Vol. 9, pp. 195–207; Block, Walter and Block, Matthew, "Roads, Bridges, Sunlight and Private Property Rights," Journal Des Economistes Et Des Etudes Humanes, Vol. VII, No. 2/3, June-September 1996, pp. 351–362; Block, Walter, "Roads, Bridges, Sunlight and Private Property: Reply to Gordon Tullock," Journal des Economistes et des Etudes Humaines, Vol. 8, No. 2/3, June-September 1998, pp. 315–326; Foldvary, Fred, Public Goods and Private Communities: The Market Provision of Social Services (Edward Elgar, 1994); Cadin, Michelle, and Block, Walter, (1997), "Privatize the Public Highway System," The Freeman, February, Vol. 47, No. 2., pp. 96–97; Cobin, John, M. (1999), Market Provisions of Highways: Lessons from Costanera Norte. Planning and Markets, Volume 2, Number 1; De Palma, Andre and Robin Lindsey, "Private toll roads: Competition under various ownership regimes," The Annals of Regional Science, 2000, Vol. 34, pp. 13–35; De Palma, Andre and Robin Lindsey, "A Model of Curb Rights In Private Urban Transit Markets," Canadian Transportation Research Forum, Proceedings of the 36th Annual Conference, 2001, pp. 581–596; Klein, Dan, "The Voluntary Provision of Public Goods? The Turnpike Companies of Early America," Economic Inquiry, October 1990, pp. 788–812; Klein, Dan, Majewski, J., and Baer, C., "Economy, Community and the Law: The Turnpike Movement in New York, 1797–1845," The Journal of Economic History, March 1993, pp. 106–122; Klein, Dan, Majewski, J., and Baer, C., "From Trunk to Branch: Toll Roads in New York, 1800–1860," Essays in Economic and Business History, 1993, pp. 191–209; Klein, Dan and Fielding, G.J.,

highways, bridges, tunnels, and other vehicular thoroughfares are feasible, workable, violate no scientific or ethical codes, and, actually, were the historical practice not the exception. It demonstrates benefits in terms of reduced traffic fatalities, declining automobile congestion (peak load pricing which has still eluded public sector road managers is more likely to be implemented), and more efficiency: if socialism cannot work in Cuba, North Korea, East Germany, or the USSR, why should it be supposed it would function adequately on any nation's roads or its city's streets? This literature, further, deals with issues of eminent domain, bankruptcy, encroaching (a private road owner surrounds a domicile with concrete and will not permit access or egress), monopoly, street sweeping, profiteering, policing, traffic lights, dealing with bad weather conditions, drunken motorists, and so on.

"Private Toll Roads: Learning from the Nineteenth Century," Transportation Quarterly, July 1992, pp. 321–341; Klein, Dan and Fielding, G.J., "How to Franchise Highways," Journal of Transport Economics and Policy, May 1993, pp. 113–130; Klein, Dan and Fielding, G.J., "High Occupancy/Toll Lanes: Phasing in Congestion Pricing a Lane at a Time," Policy Study, No. 170, Reason Foundation, November 1993; Lemennicier, Bertrand, "La Privatisation des rues," Journal Des Economistes Et Des Etudes Humaines, Vol. VII, No. 2/3, June-September 1996, pp 363–376; Roth, Gabriel, Paying for Roads: The Economics of Traffic Congestion, Middlesex, England: Penguin, 1967; Roth, Gabriel, The Private Provision of Public Services in Developing Countries, Oxford: Oxford University Press, 1987; Roth, Gabriel, A Self-financing Road System, London, England, The Institute of Economic Affairs, 1966; Semmens, John, "Road to Ruin," The Freeman (December, 1981); Semmens, John, "The Privatization of Highway Facilities," Transportation Research Forum, (November, 1983); Semmens, John, "Highways: Public Problems and Private Solutions," The Freeman (March, 1985); Semmens, John, "Intraurban Road Privatization," Transportation Research Record 1107 (1987); Semmens, John, "Using Competition to Break the U.S. Road Monopoly," Heritage Foundation (December 14, 1987); Semmens, John, "Privatization: Saving While Serving the Public," Goldwater Institute (April 25, 1988); Semmens, John, "Taking Over the Roads," Liberty (November 1988); Semmens, John, "Why We Need Highway Privatization," Laissez Faire Institute (March 1991); Semmens, John, "Private Highways? They're Cheaper, Better, Fairer," Phoenix Gazette (April 3, 1991); Semmens, John, "The Rationale for Toll Roads: You Get What You Pay For" Phoenix Gazette (December 16, 1992); Semmens, John, "Highway Privatization: What Are the Benefits for Arizona?," Goldwater Institute (December 1992); Semmens, John, "From Highways to Buy-Ways," Spectrum (Fall 1993); Semmens, John, "How to Solve Mandatory Auto Insurance," Goldwater Institute (July 1995); Semmens, John, "Highway Investment Analysis," Arizona Department of Transportation (December 1994); Semmens, John, "Privatize Driver's License, Registration System," Tribune (December 25, 1994); Semmens, John, "Privatizing Vehicle Registrations, Driver's Licenses and Auto Insurance," Transportation Quarterly (Fall 1995); Semmens, John, "Selling the Roads: Privatizing Transportation Systems," Liberty (1996); Semmens, John, "Goodbye, DMV," Liberty (January 1996).

It is important to realize, too, that there are numerous real-world examples of private streets which function highly effectively. These include the private streets of St. Louis, the streets internal to shopping malls and shopping centers (even the aisles of groceries and department stores may be considered for our purposes in this regard), gated communities worldwide, and the rural roads owned by associations of property owners in Finland and Sweden.[7] Contrast the private streets in Disney World with those in New York City's famous Central Park; it is no accident that the former are safe for passersby, while the latter have been the location of numerous murders and rapes.

Yes, yet another article along these lines would still have a very high marginal product, given that there are still no fully private road initiatives being undertaken at the present time.[8] On the other hand, hardly any work at all has been done on the practical issue of converting the present collectivism which earmarks road management to free enterprise. This, too, is worthy of considering, both because it can also move forward the analysis of private streets and because it can offer, as shall be seen, interesting economic insights of its own. It is to that task that we now turn.

Privatization

What, then, is the best process for converting vehicular thoroughfares from the public to the private sector, stipulating if only for the sake of argument that this is not a quixotic quest, that it can work, if it is but implemented?

There are several choices. First, let us address the issue of whether these resources should be given to the citizenry or sold to it. The case for the former seems clear: it is the people whose resources went into the creation of the roads in the first place, not that of the government. True, the state was the proximate cause of the spending, but, ultimately, the money came from the long-suffering taxpayer. Indeed, the state has no money of

[7] I owe this point to an anonymous referee of this journal.

[8] The quasi-private highways now in operation in Virginia and California are not exceptions. The goal of road privatization is to turn vehicular thoroughfares fully into the hands of private enterprise; in these cases, the state is still the ultimate owner. *See* on this (Block, 2009).

its own, over and above that mulcted from the citizenry. Further, it is the government, if we are correct in our underlying analysis, which is responsible for the problems of road socialism in the first place. It would come with particular ill-grace for the guilty institution to reap the fruits of correcting problems it itself created. The point is, if the roads are sold, the proceeds will be given to the city administration, the last group of people deserving of them.

Given, then, that we reject sales, and favor giveaways, who are the worthy recipients? Several immediately come to mind: those who travel on the streets (or otherwise use them), those who live or work in the surrounding buildings, and those who own these edifices. How can the claims of these various candidates be reconciled? How can they be ranked, so that those with greater ones are given proportionately more ownership rights than those with lesser?

Fortunately, there is a theory that can elucidate these problems. It may not give definitive answers to the nearest four decimal points, but at least it can point in a proper direction. The theory is that of libertarianism, based on private property rights and homesteading; this may be readily used as a means of determining how un-owned resources can pass from that state into human control. Again, we will not justify this perspective[9] but rather apply it to the case at hand.

How would it work? First off, if there were any case of a privately owned street seized[10] from its legitimate owners and brought into the public sector,[11] those with first claim on it would be its former owners.

---

[9] Homesteading is the process of mixing human labor with land, by farming it, or using it, or, in our present case, building a road on it. The classical justification for this form of establishing ownership over virgin territory is Locke, John, An Essay Concerning the True Origin, Extent and End of Civil Government, in E. Barker, ed., Social Contract, New York: Oxford University Press, 1948, pp. 17–18. For improvements and refinements, *see* Rothbard, Murray N., The Ethics of Liberty, Humanities Press, Atlantic Highlands, N.J., 1982; Hoppe, Hans-Hermann, *The Economics and Ethics of Private Property. Studies in Political Economy and Philosophy* (Boston: Kluwer Academic Publishers, 1993).

[10] Seized means commandeered, or taken over, by eminent domain, whether or not this taking (Epstein, Richard A., Takings: Private Property and the Power of Eminent Domain, Harvard University Press, Cambridge, Massachusetts, and London, England, 1985) was in any way compensated. (If there were full compensation, presumably there would have been no need for the state to condemn the property. City governments purchase paper, pencils, etc., on free markets every day).

[11] For example, nationalization, or, in this case, municipalization.

For example, in the New York City case, while there never were any private streets condemned by the City Council, there were two other transportation modes which were the Independent Rapid Transit Corporation (IRT) and the Brooklyn-Manhattan Transit Company (BMT). When these are privatized, they will be given back to their former owners, not to those who traveled on them, or lived next to them, or above or below them, nor, even, to those who owned such surrounding properties. Borrowing a leaf from this experience, then, the first claimants on public streets are the taxpayers who were forced to finance them. These are the real and rightful owners of the streets: those who paid for them.

Assume, however, that the identity of such persons is lost in antiquity.[12] Which other "stakeholder" would then have the next best interest in these properties?

One way to discern this is to ask, not as we are now doing, "Given the status quo, how shall we divide up the streets?," but, rather, "What would the world now look like had the city government never taken over the municipal streets, but had instead allowed this industry to develop purely under free enterprise strictures?" Had there been no government intervention, the likelihood is that the sites would have been claimed, and streets would have been built by private road companies. This, at least, was the experience during medieval European times as well as in eighteenth-

[12] Suppose, to complicate matters, that one or a few taxpayers from the eighteenth or nineteenth centuries can be identified (or, rather, their heirs), but that in total the payments owed to them were a very small proportion of the present total value of the streets. Would these few claimants be given the streets in their entirety? Not in my view. The money they paid which went toward to paving of the streets, the setting up of traffic lights, et cetera, is a very small percentage of the site value of these thoroughfares. A similar analysis applies to the case where only one heir of a slave can be found, and there is a plantation to be divided up amongst the children of the slaves and the children of the slaveholders. Does the heir of the single slave obtain the entire inheritance? Not unless it can be shown that the labor services stolen from his grandfather, plus interest, amount to all or more of the value of the plantation. If not, then the heir of the slave owns only the value that can be attributed to his ancestor. On this, *see* Block, Walter, and Guillermo Yeatts, "The Economics and Ethics of Land Reform: A Critique of the Pontifical Council for Justice and Peace's 'Toward a Better Distribution of Land: The Challenge of Agrarian Reform,'" Journal of Natural Resources and Environmental Law, Vol. 15, No. 1, 1999–2000, pp. 37–69; Raimondo, Justin, "Is Zionism Racism?," http://www.antiwar.com/justin/j080301.html, 8/3/01; Rothbard, Murray N., The Ethics of Liberty, New York: New York University Press, 1998, p. 75; Block, Walter, "On reparations to blacks for slavery," forthcoming.

century America. Who, in turn, might have invested in such companies? Although it can only be speculation, call it an educated guess, one reasonable candidate would be owners of the property alongside the street. This would be one way for the market to "internalize the externality," which might otherwise arise from different ownership of street and neighboring property. Insofar as this is true, we have another set of candidates for street ownership: those whose property abuts the street.

Would this apply, as well, to the tenants of these buildings? Not a bit of it. Tenants are not residual income claimants; they have no right to the real estate in question, per se. Their rights are limited to the *use* of these amenities, for a certain specified time. They could not possibly be entitled to the property in question, let alone ownership to it from centuries, decades, or even years ago.

What of the fact that these properties may have changed hands dozens of times throughout the years since the streets were first laid out and built? The rights survive. For the new owner(s) purchase the *entire* rights to the property, those recognized in law at the time, and, also, those that were not, for example, that ownership of contiguous property would confer a claim over the abutting street.

Another way to discern who is entitled to street ownership is based on homesteading. Again, as it would take us too far a-field to explain or justify such a procedure, we shall content ourselves with merely applying it.[13] A modicum of entitlement is automatically captured by those who "mix their labor" with an un-owned[14] piece of property. Thus, all of those who have traveled on the street by that token alone thereby obtain a claim of ownership over it.[15]

At first glance, this creates more problems than it solves. For there are many, many people who have walked, ridden cars, taxis, horse-drawn vehicles, bicycles, motorcycles, and so on, on the streets of Manhattan. It would be a real "dog's breakfast" to determine who has a legitimate claim and who does not on this basis. People don't save their bus transfers, or

[13] *See* footnote 7, supra.

[14] Or in this case, illegitimately or improperly owned (by the state).

[15] It is here that tenants of contiguous buildings can make their claim: not as tenants per se, but, rather, as commuters between their homes and places of work.

taxi-cab bills, which, even on the best of assumptions, would only be the veritable tip of the iceberg of evidence of road use. Bills for gasoline in Manhattan, or in the surrounding boroughs, would also serve as only the most indirect of evidence for use of any specific street.

Under these conditions, the most accurate assessment might well be derived through proxy. That is, we can assume that all residents of Manhattan use its streets to a certain specific degree, call it X, and those in the surrounding areas to a lesser degree, say, X/3. Or, as a rough approximation, that all of the inhabitants of the entire city (or each of the residents of all five boroughs) are the legitimate owners of all of their respective streets.

Based on these considerations, we are faced with two very different implications and thus two very different ways of distributing the thoroughfares to the people. On the one hand, the owners of the property alongside the road own it; on the other, all members of the society own one quotal share each.

But we have only begun to encounter complications. Another one concerns how the properties shall be divided up on the basis of either of these criteria. To wit, consider one long street in Manhattan, for example, Broadway, which runs the entire length of the island. Suppose there are 10,000 separate properties that abut this avenue. Does each of these 10,000 property owners assume control over 1/10,000 of the entire facility? Or do they each own that little bit of it that touches upon their property? (In this case, every real estate holder would own exactly half of Broadway affronting his property, and the other half would be given to the owner across the street).

The latter is clearly unfeasible. With 10,000 separate owners of Broadway, this avenue would quickly become impassible to traffic. Each individual[16] would be able to bring motorists to a standstill. Streets would come to resemble a Parcheesi board, and blockades could become the order of the day. This option must be rejected, but not only because of its undoubted impracticality. Fortunately, for our underlying homesteading theory, roads could never have been built in the first place in any such manner, for the same reason: initial susceptibility to blockades. Indeed,

[16] Particularly if he could get the cooperation of the man across the street.

this model serves principally as an entirely refutable objection to the whole idea of private roads.[17]

It follows, then, that no abutting real estate holder may establish such a chokehold over any street. If so, how is ownership to be divided? Clearly, the best way would be to accord with the practice of ancient road enterprises; to set up a joint stock company composed of these 1000 people, who together would control the entire venture. This in turn leads to another question: would each of the 1000 own an equal 1/1000 of a share of the corporation or would the division be unequal?

The latter is far more in keeping with the homesteading theory than the former. That is, a building that stretches along Broadway from 55th to 56th street is far more valuable than the same physical structure occupying the area between 155th and 156th. Naturally, the former would have more of a stake in Broadway than the latter. Were a road company to be set up de novo, it is inconceivable that the shares would be apportioned according to mere physical length. Based on these considerations, the ownership rights over Broadway would be distributed in a manner proportional to the assessed valuation of the property in question.

This leaves open the question of whether the stock company should own lengthwise, or in terms of geographical areas. That is, should a company own all of Broadway or 3rd avenue, or 23rd street or 42nd street (the one-dimensional format), or should one be assigned to Greenwich Village, another to Hell's Kitchen, a third to Harlem, and so on (the two-dimensional format). In terms of road management, each has advantages and disadvantages.

The main drawback of the one-dimensional model is the dispute over green light time on traffic signals. If one firm owns 3rd Avenue and another 23rd Street, and they cross at right angles, each will naturally wish to have the green light for as much time as possible, and the red for as little. In that way, traffic can flow more easily on its own property, and

[17] According to this proposal, any two owners located opposite of each other could together convert their little patch of road into a park. This would very much diminish the ability of the street to convey traffic. This is not to say that streets ought never to be converted to parks. Economic efficiency would require that this occur only when the value of the land as a park exceeds that used as a street. When one entity owns the entire length of a street, it will be in a position to internalize the externalities that might otherwise come into play.

its revenues be enhanced.[18] How, then, to settle this potential dispute? Simple. Each will bid against the other for the proportion of red and green light time. It is akin to the situation in which two ex-partners find themselves upon dissolution of the company: who keeps the firm? And the answer is, whichever of them is willing to pay more for the other's half. Presumably, the north-south artery, which in Manhattan usually serves more customers, will be able to outbid the east-west thoroughfare for the lion's share of the green light time, based upon the derived demand for these services emanating from the final consumer.

Another difficulty in this scenario will be the arrangement of staggered traffic lights; those timed in such a manner that motorists can move at a steady pace (e.g., 25 m.p.h.) without being forced to stop and wait for a red light. This will call for no mean talent of negotiation if each and every street and avenue comes under the management of a different firm.

These problems will be as nothing under two-dimensional ownership. Staggered lights and the allocation of green light time are all arranged under the aegis of one firm, so that by definition no negotiation or transactions costs need be undertaken. Instead, the practical difficulties arise when the streets of one neighborhood connect with those of another. What to do, for example, when Turtle Bay gives over to East Village? Here, similar negotiating efforts must be undertaken in terms of coordinating staggered lights and green light time.

Historical precedents can be found on each side of this debate as well. Ancient stock companies typically owned long, thin thoroughfares; this, too, was the practice of private inter-city railroads. But equally free enterprise ventures such as Disneyland, Knott's Berry Farm, and Universal Studios, and hundreds of smaller shopping malls have organized themselves into the neighborhood or two-dimensional format.

Given that there is in effect a "draw"[19] between these two models, I opt for the neighborhood format, if only because it is more modern. This

---

[18] We also eschew discussion of the monopoly problem: where the road owner jacks up the price so far as to in effect capture the property values of all adjacent property. For a discussion of this issue, *see* Block, Walter, "Free Market Transportation: Denationalizing the Roads," Journal of Libertarian Studies: An Interdisciplinary Review, Vol. III, No. 2, Summer 1979, pp. 209–238.

[19] Not of the sort that characterized the heavyweight title fight between Evander Holyfield and Lennox Lewis.

indicates that the technology of private development has migrated from one to two dimensions. Since we are privatizing in the modern era, the latter is more appropriate. If this exercise were being carried out a century or two ago, the alternative option might well have been picked.

But why choose between having your cake and eating it? Why not have both? That is, were all the roadways in Manhattan owned by a single firm, all transactions costs vanish in one fell swoop. Well, not exactly. This is somewhat of an exaggeration, as negotiations would still be necessary vis-à-vis all the tunnels and bridges connecting this borough with its three neighbors, as well as New Jersey.

Transactions Costs

It is impossible to reduce such negotiation problems[20] to zero, for wherever automobiles may travel, there will always connections between one road owner and another under any system, free enterprise or socialistic. This certainly applies under government control, where the authorities in charge of city streets, bridges, tunnels, thruways, and roads of contiguous states must all deal with one another. It might appear that transactions costs could be avoided if there were only one state authority, or one private road owner wherever highways or streets connect. But this is a mirage. The costs of coordination under such a system might be labeled management instead of transactions costs, but they would remain costs nonetheless.

It cannot be denied that such costs would still exist, even under a fully free enterprise road system. But if we have learned anything from the fall

[20] The classical statement of the relationship between transactions costs and the nature of the firm is Coase, Ronald, H., "The Nature of the Firm," Economica, November 1937, Vol. 4, pp. 386–406. *See also* his Coase, Ronald H., "The Institutional Structure of Production," American Economic Review, Vol. 82, No. 4, September 1992, pp. 713–19. Why is it that firms arise in markets, but no one firm takes over the entire economy? For Coase, this has to do with the minimization of costs within and between firms. For example, it is very expensive for the waitress to bargain with the cook, offering him a price for the meal he gives her; in order to economize on these sorts of transactions, firms are created within which markets do not occur, but rather commands; for example, the owner of the restaurant "commands" the cook to give the waitress the meal without charging her for it. However, unless there is vertical integration between the restaurant and the supplier of vegetables, for example, the former purchases these factors of production from the latter.

of the Berlin wall and the economic debacle that was the economic system of the USSR, it is that one of these systems is highly efficient, and not the other. The government system, after all, is the one that brings us the horse and buggy US Post Office. Need any more be said?

But let us posit that management within one firm is cheaper, within the relevant range, than negotiation between different street companies. Taking this idea to its ultimate logical conclusion would imply a single firm, for example, in all of North and South America, since all roads on these two continents are connected to each other.[21] Does this present any particular problem or embarrassment for the theory? Not to those[22] who maintain that the success of One Big Firm is no threat as long as it arises from, and depends solely upon, market forces.

In one sense, privatizing roads is like attempting to unscramble an egg; it is very, very complicated, because what we are trying to do in effect is bring about a situation today, which would have ensued had streets always been private. Our goal is to determine how this market would have functioned in the past and then to set up a situation, now, as close to what would have been, in this imaginary contrary to fact conditional.

[21] We pass over the "problem" of the discontinuity in Panama, given that there are bridges that enable cars to travel north and south over it. If there were none, then, instead of only one owner, there would be two, one for each of the American continents.

[22] Anderson, William, Walter Block, Thomas J. DiLorenzo, Ilana Mercer, Leon Snyman, and Christopher Westley, "The Microsoft Corporation in Collision with Antitrust Law," The Journal of Social, Political and Economic Studies, Vol. 26, No. 1, Winter 2001, pp. 287–302; Armentano, Dominick T., The Myths of Antitrust, New Rochelle, N.Y.: Arlington House, 1972; Armentano, Dominick T., Antitrust and Monopoly: Anatomy of a Policy Failure, New York, Wiley, 1982; Armentano, Dominick T., Antitrust Policy: The Case for Repeal, Washington, D.C.: The Cato Institute, 1991; Donald Armstrong, Competition versus Monopoly: Combines Policy in Perspective, Vancouver: The Fraser Institute, 1982; Block, Walter, Amending the Combines Investigation Act, Vancouver: The Fraser Institute, 1982; Block, Walter, "Austrian Monopoly Theory – a Critique," The Journal of Libertarian Studies, Vol. I, No. 4, Fall 1977, pp. 271–279; Block, Walter, "Total Repeal of Anti-trust Legislation: A Critique of Bork, Brozen and Posner, Review of Austrian Economics, Vol. 8, No. 1, 1994, pp. 35–70; DiLorenzo, Thomas J., 1997, "The Myth of Natural Monopoly," Review of Austrian Economics, Vol. 9, No. 2, pp. 43–58; Boudreaux, Donald J., and DiLorenzo, Thomas J., "The Protectionist Roots of Antitrust," Review of Austrian Economics, Vol. 6, No. 2, 1992, pp. 81–96; High, Jack, "Bork's Paradox: Static vs Dynamic Efficiency in Antitrust Analysis," Contemporary Policy Issues, Vol. 3, 1984–1985, pp. 21–34; McChesney, Fred, "Antitrust and Regulation: Chicago's Contradictory Views," Cato Journal, Vol. 10, 1991; Murray N. Rothbard, Man, Economy and State, Los Angeles, Nash, 1970; Shugart II, William F., "Don't Revise the Clayton Act, Scrap It!," 6 Cato Journal, 925, 1987; Smith, Jr., Fred L., "Why not Abolish Antitrust?," Regulation, Jan-Feb 1983, 23.

The problem is that this is essentially an entrepreneurial, or managerial, not an economic or praxeological task. For economists, it is impossible to anticipate the market. Suppose, for example, that the shoe industry had always been run under government supervision and that we were now contemplating moving it from socialism to capitalism. A whole host of questions would quickly arise, the answers to which would lie outside the realm of economics. For example, how many shoe firms would there be? What color would be the footwear? What proportion would there be between black, brown, white, tan, and other color shoes? Between shoes, runners, sneakers, and slippers? How many lace holes would there be in a shoe? Who would stitch together the shoe and its sole? How many shoe stores would be located on each block? Would there be one in every mall? How would the poor afford shoes? Would someone like Michael Jordan become a pitch-man for the product?

In like manner, it is difficult in the extreme to know, at this late date, the precise configurations of a private street and road industry, had one been allowed to be fully developed from day one. How much would the street vendors charge? Or would they provide road service for free, in a sort of super-loss leader ploy, and earn their income through billboard advertising or enhancement of real estate values (some companies are now giving away computers, gratis, which come replete with advertisements)? How would we obviate the possibility of surrounding a property owner with private roads, so that he had no means of access or egress? I speculated[23] that no one in his like mind would ever purchase a property without clearly delineated access rights, spelled out for the present and the future, but what, precisely, would be specified in contracts intended to obviate this difficulty? If road providers did charge for their services, I articulated[24] a scenario whereby this would be done by placing Universal Product Codes on the underbody of automobiles, so that their owners could be sent a monthly bill. This, of course, would set up privacy protection issues, which, in turn, have also been previously addressed.[25]

The point is though that even if a contrary-to-fact conditional society such as ours but with continuous private road ownership did indeed

[23] Block, Walter, "Free Market Transportation: Denationalizing the Roads," Journal of Libertarian Studies: An Interdisciplinary Review, Vol. III, No. 2, Summer 1979, pp. 209–238.

[24] Ibid.

[25] Ibid.

address and solve problems of this sort in this manner, it would still be a Herculean job to convert our present society into that one. Even worse, we have only our managerial-entrepreneurial speculation to buttress these suppositions, nothing more.

On the other hand, we need not be too pessimistic about this either. An imperfect privatization will be far preferable to none at all. Government streets are an administrative and safety nightmare.[26] It is inconceivable that private initiatives could do worse. In any case, the same challenge faces the privatizer of *all* industries now in government hands. Even the post office and public education, the privatization of which are far easier on theoretical grounds,[27] present complicated problems of equity, transition, and so on, as do streets.

Ordinarily, under laissez-faire capitalism, the owner of a private enterprise could charge whatever price he wished for the goods or services he supplies. If you didn't like the pricing or any other policy of McDonalds, you are free to patronize Burger King or Wendy's, or any such other emporium, or buy your burgers from the supermarket and eat them at home. It would be a bit harsh, however, to allow the new private owners of the street to engage in such an exercise of "economic freedom." This is because in the world where all streets were privatized from day one, no one would have ever built a home or a business without first contractually preventing the road owner from such unilateral behavior. Rather, there would have been an agreement preventing this, either through contract or by making the home or business owner a partner in the street enterprise. Were we now to allow the new road owners to impose their unilateral decisions on travelers, this would in effect make a gift of the entire economic value to them not only of the roads but of virtually all property within a city. Some way must be found, then, to mimic the market in streets which would have existed under free enterprise from day one, but which did not.

---

[26] Road fatality statistics are as follows:

2015	35,485
2016	37,806
2017	37,133
2018	36,750

Source: National Highway Traffic Safety Administration

[27] There are no linkages between them and virtually all other private property.

One final caveat, whether for street privatization or any other: it is important to be thorough. In many of the Eastern European countries, even including Russia and other parts of the USSR, something along the lines advocated here has been followed. Shares of stock have been created for a number of properties, collectivized farms, factories, and so on, and have been divided up widely among taxpayers, citizens, former employees, and other reasonable ownership candidates. Moreover, also much to the good, the law has allowed these shares to be traded on organized exchanges[28] so that they naturally tend to flow toward those who value them the most. The problem is, in all too many cases, the direction in which they flow is right back toward the very people responsible for the communist debacle in the first place: ex apparitchiks, goons, thugs, banking authorities, former military officers, and so on. As a result, Eastern European and former Soviet "capitalism" has come to resemble nothing so much as "free enterprise" mafia style.

It would be a shame and a pity were road privatization efforts in the United States to come to a similar sorry end. In order to obviate any such occurrence, steps must be taken to be thorough in the privatization effort, one, to ensure that vestiges of state control are eliminated, and, two, that those responsible for the present disarray do not succeed in taking any positions, let alone leadership ones, in the new regime. To wit, shares of road stock should not be given to those road managers responsible for our present astronomical level of traffic fatalities, nor should they be allowed to purchase any.[29] Indeed, the question should not be so much whether such persons should be allowed to regain control over street management as much as a debate over which criminal penalties should be imposed upon them.

As well, the state should keep its bloody hands off of the future private road, street, and highway industry. Government police should be as scarce on traffic thoroughfares as they are now on the inside of Disneyland. In the latter case, if you act obstreperously, you are sooner rather than later surrounded by a group of mice and ducks, all packing heat, who will

[28] Foreigners have been precluded from taking part, which is a shortcoming of the system.

[29] In much the same manner that those convicted of certain crimes are not allowed to own gambling establishments.

lead you away quietly from the scene of a confrontation. These private police are far better able to satisfy the requirements of consumer sovereignty than those in the public sector. After all, only the former, not the latter, can go bankrupt, because they are part of a market system. And the same holds true for bouncers in private drinking establishments. As for the "rent a cops" who serve on the Jerry Springer show, is there any doubt that they are far superior to any public alternatives when it comes to breaking up a fight at the exact point when the combatants are appropriately half undressed?

Similarly, if the death rate is to be reduced to optimal levels,[30] and traffic to be increased past horse and buggy levels, then road entrepreneurs must be able to control all aspects of highway travel, certainly including policing, pothole repair, street construction, and penalties.[31]

Conclusion

It is now time to draw this discussion to a close. I have no hard and fast conclusions as to the best way to privatize streets and highways. It is perhaps more important *that* they be privatized than *how* this task is accomplished. Once in the private sector, and these important elements of our economy will be managed in the same rational manner as all other goods and services subject to the consumer check of profits and loss.

This is not to say that there is no pattern we can use, even in broad brush strokes, to guide the privatization process: it is to imagine the contrary to fact conditional wherein city streets were always provided by private enterprise, and then to tailor the present situation to resemble that as much as possible. This, by its very nature, is difficult. Imaginary constructions cannot be relied upon without misgivings. And yet, as we have seen, there are rough shapes that may be discerned through the fog.

---

[30] Optimal levels, of course, need not be zero. The latter might be approached if the private owners imposed a 5 miles per hour speed limit, and required all autos to be of Hummer quality or above (e.g., tanks), but it is my entrepreneurial understanding that this set of rules would not maximize profits.

[31] Under the present proposal could a street owner impose the death penalty on those who drove green automobiles? Not any more than he could charge whatever price he wished.

One is that the people responsible for our present plight should be excluded from the process of privatization. Another is to as closely as possible approximate real-world private road conditions. When a thoroughfare is very long, thin, and isolated, as in the case of a private railroad, adopt that as a model: one owner for the entire avenue, for example, the one-dimension model. When the public sector amenity resembles, instead, a relatively large land holding, for example, Disneyland, then one owner might be more appropriate for an entire neighborhood of streets.

21

O.J.'s Defense: A Reductio Ad Absurdum of Coase and Posner

Even though the O.J. Simpson case has been settled, it is still much in the news. Pundits, commentators, journalists, and editorialists are still weighing in with a myriad of discussion and analysis. Should the economics profession alone remain silent on this highly charged issue when seemingly all others have entered the fray? Not a bit of it.

Even after the trial, the opinions expressed fall into two main categories.[1] One, O.J. did indeed stab his ex-wife Nicole Simpson and her

The author wishes to thank his friend and colleague David Schap of Holy Cross—who disagrees with this article practically in its entirety—for withering, but very helpful, criticisms of earlier drafts of it. Our ongoing discussions were very beneficial, encouraging me to further develop my own thinking on these issues. Needless to say, Schap is not responsible for any of the views taken therein. The author also benefitted from the comments of two anonymous referees, from presentations of earlier drafts of this paper to the economics departments of Clark University and the Amos Tuck Business School at Dartmouth College, and to the 1996 meeting of the Eastern Economics Association.

[1] It is fair to say that the O.J. Simpson murder trial was subjected to the most intensive scrutiny of any criminal case, or, indeed, any other lawsuit, in the history of American jurisprudence. Public interest in O.J. Simpson vastly outstripped other such high-profile criminal cases as Sacco and Vanzetti (Communist spies), Leopold and Loeb (the murder of a small boy), Pollard (Israeli spy), and Ethel and Julius Rosenberg (Communist spies). It is probably no exaggeration to say that this one judicial extravaganza claimed more interest than all of these others put together.

W. E. Block, *Property Rights*, Palgrave Studies in Classical Liberalism,
https://doi.org/10.1007/978-3-030-28353-7_21

companion, Ronald Goldman, and should be punished for this act, and two, he is innocent and should therefore be freed.[2] Fortunately, with the tools of modern economic analysis at our command, we are able to transcend these rather plebian alternatives. As it happens, thanks to Coasean Posnerian insights, we can have our cake and eat it too: we can defend the position that *even if* O.J. were guilty of the acts with which he is charged, he should *still* be set free. (O.J. defense team: please take note! You may wish to add the present deliberations to your repertoire when and if O.J., or anyone else like him, is next charged with murder.)[3]

The Coasean System

This is a rather tall order, so we had better begin making good on our claim. We can best do so by considering Coase (1960). According to the analytic framework developed in that work, there are two states of the

---

One reason for this is, undoubtedly, that we now live in an age of television. O.J. Simpson, moreover, an ex-professional football player, was perhaps the most famous and accomplished athlete in the history of US sports. A black man, he was married to a white woman and had a history of physically abusing her. When his wife, Nicole Simpson, was found murdered, O.J. was accused of the crime and then found innocent. If the trial was itself the focus of a media feeding frenzy, this applied to the aftermath as well. For, apart from a few exceptions, the freeing of O.J. was received with dismay on the part of whites and glee on the part of blacks; this, coupled with charges of black jury nullification (black juries are less likely to find black defendants guilty) and counter-charges of previous white jury nullification, ensures that this case will remain a highlight of US history for a long time to come.

[2] A third alternative, "jury nullification," has recently been adumbrated: O.J. is guilty, but there are now already too many black men in jail; therefore, he should go free. This exercise in affirmative action, of course, leads somewhat of a surreptitious existence. However, it may well lead, in the future, to modifications of our jury system.

[3] The present paper has little to do with the O.J. Simpson case per se. Rather, it is an attempt to create a reductio ad absurdum of the legal philosophy emanating from the University of Chicago. Almost any other lawsuit could have been selected as the vehicle for criticizing the views of legal theorists such as Coase, Posner, Demsetz, and Landes. O.J. was selected because it was in the news—it dominated the news while I was writing this paper—and because it allows for a very dramatic analysis.

My claim is the truly horrendous one that on the basis of the arguments emanating from the University of Chicago, in particular, and from the school of thought called "Law and Economics," in general, a case can actually be made for the freeing of O.J. Simpson from the charge of murder, even if he actually committed the crime! That such an abhorrent conclusion could be even contemplated, let alone be valid, I shall try to show, follows logically from errors in this philosophical system.

world. The first, for the most part, an imaginary one, is characterized by zero transactions costs. This means that one can easily and cheaply find people with whom a bargain can be struck, that no one erects artificial barriers to commercial transactions (there are no holdouts, no opportunistic behavior, etc.). States Coase (1960, p. 15):

> In order to carry out a market transaction it is necessary to discover who it is that one wishes to deal with, to inform people that one wishes to deal and on what terms, to conduct negotiations leading up to a bargain, to draw up the contract, to undertake the inspection needed to make sure that the terms of the contract are being observed, and so on.

The second, an all too real one, is earmarked by positive and/or very high transactions costs, higher, by presumption, than any possible gains which could be made by trade. Under these conditions, it is difficult or impossible to rearrange titles to property, particularly when there are numerous buyers and/or sellers potentially involved.

It is Coase's considered opinion that there should be no hard and fast property rights set up in stone prior to considerations of wealth maximization.[4] Instead, the proper function of property rights is to maximize wealth[5]; therefore, they should be defined so as to bring about this goal. Happily, for Coase, it matters not one whit how property rights disputes are settled in the zero transactions costs world. It is his belief (1960, p. 10) that:

> The judges' view that they were settling how the land was to be used would be true only in the case in which the costs of carrying out the necessary market transactions exceeded the gain which might be achieved by any rearrangement of rights.

---

[4] For critiques of Coase from a free enterprise or libertarian perspective, *see* Krecke (1992), North (1992), Block (1977), Cordato (1989, 1992a, b)—for a reply to the latter, which strengthens the case against Coase, *see* Gordon (1993).

[5] This, obviously, is a value judgment of his unsupported by any value free axiom of economic analysis. For an alternative view, *see* Arnold (1982), Benson (1989a, 1989b, 1991), Pasour (1979, 1992).

This of course is apart from considerations of equity or wealth transfer. Whether or not the judge makes an award to the person who can best maximize the value of the property, this event will occur in any case by means of a market transaction. States Coase in this regard (1960, p. 5):

> ...such an agreement would not affect the allocation of resources but would merely alter the distribution of income and wealth as between the cattle-raiser and the farmer.

But this, too, is a weakness of the Coasean system. For it is indeed a matter of importance for the contending parties, and therefore for society as a whole, how the "mere" disputation over wealth is settled. And Coase gives us no guidance as to how that issue can be justly settled.

Under the positive (e.g., prohibitively high) transactions costs assumption, the judge's decision is crucial. Given that there is now no possibility for the rearrangement of resources through side payments, whatever is determined by the member of the bench will in fact prevail.

For example, suppose that sparks from a railroad cause damage to a farmer's crops to the extent of $60, while the cost of obviating this destruction, a smoke prevention device (SPD), costs $75. Should the court find the railroad innocent of this act and force the farmer to bear the losses? Or should the court declare that the railroad has engaged in an illegitimate border crossing, or property rights violation, and, therefore, finding in favor of the farmer, compel the railroad to install the SPD?

For the old-fashioned judge, unschooled in the niceties of Coaseanism, the case is an open and shut one. The railroad trespassed on the farmer's property.[6] It should be made to stop. If the only way the railroad can continue in business without violating the farmer's rights is with a smoke prevention device, it should have to pay for this. After all, property rights are property rights, and if they are not respected, the whole society can crumble to the ground.[7]

---

[6] Under the assumption, that is, that the farmer arrived upon the scene before the railroad. Even John Locke (1955, 1960), the main intellectual opponent of Coase, would dismiss the case if the railroad had first arrived upon the scene and engaged in an act of "mixing its labor with the land." For then, it would have a legitimate title to the property.

[7] In this regard, *see* Barnett (1978), Flew (1982), Machan (1978), and Rasmussen (1980).

But for the Coasean philosophy, matters are very different. There is no such thing as property rights, that is, in a vacuum, apart from wealth maximization. Nor is it even true that the railroad is the aggressor, the farmer the victim. On the contrary, *both* parties have contributed to the altercation. If *either* of them were to disappear, or to cease and desist, the problem would be ended. Blame is entirely inappropriate in such a case. It is obvious that if the railroad stopped setting off sparks on the farmer's crops, there would be no incident to be resolved. But it is equally true, if perhaps somewhat less obvious, that if the *farmer* stopped his operations (so close to the railroad), it would be ended as well.

This is Coase's doctrine of reciprocality. In his view:

> We are dealing with a problem of a reciprocal nature. To avoid the harm to B would inflict harm on A. The real question that has to be decided is: should A be allowed to harm B or should B be allowed to harm A? The problem is to avoid the more serious harm. (Coase, 1960, p. 2)

"Who caused the smoke nuisance? The answer seems fairly clear. The smoke nuisance was caused both by the man who built the wall *and* by the man who lit the fires. Given the fires, there would have been no smoke nuisance without the wall; given the wall, there would have been no smoke nuisance without the fires. Eliminate the wall *or* the fires and the smoke nuisance would disappear. On the marginal principle it is clear that *both* were responsible and *both* should be forced to include the loss of amenity due to the smoke as a cost in deciding whether to continue the activity which gives rise to the smoke

> In the case of the cattle and the crops, it is true that there would be no crop damage without the cattle. It is equally true that there would be no crop damage without the crops. The doctor's work would not have been disturbed if the confectioner had not worked his machinery; but the machinery would have disturbed no one if the doctor had not set up his consulting room in that particular place.... If we are to discuss the problem in terms of causation, both parties cause the damage. If we are to attain an optimum allocation or resources, it is therefore desirable that both parties should take the harmful effect (the nuisance) into account in deciding their course of action. (Coase, 1960, p. 13)

Instead of determining property rights based on the old-fashioned notion of who was there first (homesteading), for Coase they depend upon wealth maximization. Moreover, it is clear that wealth can only be maximized if the railroad is allowed to prevail. If the farmer gets the nod, he will force the railroad to spend $75 in order to save only $60, a clear loss of $15. On the other hand, if the railroad is given carte blanche, it will save its $75; true, it will continue to impose costs of $60 on the farmer, much to his dismay, but at least social welfare will be maximized.[8] After all, if one business entity owned both the railroad and the farm, it would continue railroad operation; it would be counterproductive to stop it, thereby saving $60 but at the cost of $75.

Zero Transactions Costs

All this, of course, is in the world of prohibitively high transactions costs. But under the assumption of zero transactions costs, paradoxically, it matters not one whit *what* the court decides[9] in terms of who is to be the owner of the relevant property rights.[10] If the court awards them to the railroad, well and good. The farmer will not be able to bribe the railroad into installing the smoke prevention device, since the former will only take $75 or more, while the latter will offer at most slightly less than $60. On the other hand, if the farmer wins, the railroad will be able to bribe him into allowing continued pollution. For example, the railroad would be willing to offer the farmer $65, thus saving $10, compared to the SPD cost of $75. The farmer, for his part, would accept the $65, since this is more than the value of his crops (Table 21.1).

---

[8] For a critique of the use of such externalities and public goods arguments as a justification for government intervention, *see* Fox (1992), Hummel (1990), Hoppe (1989), Pasour (1981).

[9] In terms of whether or not the smoke prevention device is installed, for example, the allocation of resources. But, as we have seen, it matters very much for the relative wealth position of the farmer and the railroad.

[10] We abstract, here, from the issue of psychic income. For a treatment of this consideration, *see* Block, 1977. For an alternative view of this issue, *see* Demsetz, 1979. For a reply, *see* Block, 1995.

Table 21.1 A summary comparison of the results of the judicial decision in the hypothetical farmer versus railroad case

	Farmer wins	Railroad wins
	(1)	(2)
Zero transactions costs	no smoke prevention device (SPD) railroad (RR) bribes F \$65 Wealth F: \$65 – \$60 = \$5 Wealth RR: \$75 – \$65 = \$10 Total wealth: \$15 ("good")	no SPD no bribe economic (eco) Wealth F: –\$60 Wealth RR: +\$75 Total Wealth: +\$15 ("good")
	(3)	(4)
High transactions costs	yes, SPD no bribe (eco, t.c.) Wealth farmer (F): \$60 Wealth RR: –\$75 Total wealth: –\$15 ("bad")	no SPD no bribe total cost (t.c.) Wealth F: –\$60 Wealth RR: +\$75 Total Wealth: +\$15 ("good")

Summary of Coase's Argument

Cases 1, 2, and 4 are "good" for Coase since total wealth is maximized at +\$15; case 3 is "bad" since social wealth is minimized at –\$15. A bribe takes place in case 1 since the farmer values his crops at only \$60, while the railroad's reservation demand for the use of these crops as a sink for pollution is \$75. A bribe need not take place in case 2 for economic ("eco") reasons: the only one who can bribe is the railroad, and it need not, since it has won the verdict. Bribes cannot take place in cases 3 and 4 due to the assumption of high transactions costs ("t.c.").

The essence of the Coasean system is that private property rights are subsidiary to wealth maximization. There are indeed rights to private property for Coase, but they serve at the pleasure of wealth maximization. He states (1960, p. 9):

> The court's decision established that the doctor had the right to prevent the confectioner from using his machinery. But, of course, it would have been possible to modify the arrangements envisaged in the legal ruling by means of a bargain between the parties. The doctor would have been willing to waive his right and allow the machinery to continue in operation if the confectioner would have paid him a sum of money which was greater than

> the loss of income which he would suffer from having to move to a more costly or less convenient location or from having to curtail his activities at this location or, as was suggested as a possibility, from having to build a separate wall which would deaden the noise and vibration. The confectioner would have been willing to do this if the amount he would have to pay the doctor was less than the fall in income he would suffer if he had to change his mode of operation at this location, abandon his operation or move his confectionery business to some other location. The solution of the problem depends essentially on whether the continued use of the machinery adds more to the confectioner's income than it subtracts from the doctor's. (emphasis added)

We see, therefore, that the justification of a particular set of rights at any given time for Coase is that they maximize wealth. When they stop attaining this goal, they must be altered and abolished, and a new ownership pattern set up in their place. This is of course the reverse of the traditional theory based on the Lockean homesteading principle.[11] There, property rights are the basic bedrock of the system, and wealth maximization is predicated upon them.[12]

In the traditional outlook based on homesteading, matters are very different. Instead of placing wealth maximization front and center stage, it takes a back seat in this perspective. The key element is, who first homesteaded the given right amenity.

Does this mean that the traditional view is indifferent to wealth maximization, that Lockeans are simply unconcerned with such matters? Not at all. But for them, wealth maximization must be *predicated* upon a strong private property rights base; it cannot *determine* it. For the Lockeans, property rights are the dog, wealth maximization the tail; for the Coaseans, it is the reverse: wealth maximization is exogenous, property rights endogenous.

Suppose that the author of the present article were to punch Coase in the nose. Under the old "unsophisticated" legal dispensation, I would go

[11] *See* Locke (1955, 1960); Hoppe (1993); Rothbard (1973, 1982a, 1982b). For a critique of this view, based on wealth considerations, *see* Stroup (1988); for a reply, *see* Block (1990).

[12] To further illustrate this divergence, let us note the contrasting analysis each side offers of the law case Sturgis v Bridgeman. For the traditional view, *see* Rothbard (1982b); the alternative, of course, is Coase (1960).

to jail for assault and battery since I aggressed against him. Did I but admit the facts of the case, it would be an open and shut one.

Now consider how matters would occur under the new, more sophisticated Chicagoite legal dispensation. Here, despite an equal willingness to admit to the facts, it is no longer clear that I aggressed against him. It is equally possible that he aggressed against me by sticking his nose out at my onrushing fist! For rather than straightforward assault and battery, there is now reciprocity and mutual determination.

The way to determine not who is at fault (this is too old fashioned), but rather whether I should be allowed to go on punching him, or be made to stop and instead be punished for it, is to determine which course of action will maximize wealth. The problem with this, of course, is interpersonal comparisons of utility. Without such comparisons, it cannot objectively be determined which course of action will minimize costs.

Why do the Lockeans insist, in contrast, that the property dog wags the wealth tail? For one thing, because the alternative option implies arbitrariness. This can be seen by an examination of the illustrative numbers employed above or in any of the numerical examples offered by Coase (1960). The point is, these figures are entirely made up; they bear no relationship to reality whatsoever. Nor is the judge capable of discerning their true values. They are not objective entities, to be measured by third parties. Costs are instead subjective (Mises, 1966; Buchanan, 1969; Buchanan and Thirlby, 1981; DiLorenzo, 1990). Any finding on the part of the judge to the effect that the railroad values permission to pollute to thus and such an extent, and the farmer crops to this or that other extent must, at the bottom, be capricious. For another, the Coasean system, purposefully or not, unleashes a modicum of central planning on our society. It gives the judge powers simply not available to him in the more traditional Lockean system.[13]

Further, Coase assigns these tasks to the judge in the case of property rights under dispute. He says (1960, pp. 15, emphasis added) "The economic problem in all cases <u>of harmful effects</u> is how to maximise the value of production." However, we are a litigious people; everything,

---

[13] For a critique of socialism, no matter how unconventional its justification, *see* Mises (1969).

potentially, can come under dispute[14]—as to what is and what is not a harmful effect. This would be especially true if it became known that the judge would not look askance at those who sought to overturn ordinary property titles.[15] But if the judge can allocate property based upon his arbitrary evaluations of contending values, and if this applies to all or most property in a society, then it cannot be denied that he takes on the role of central planner.[16]

Third, it is internally contradictory to set up wealth maximization as exogenous and property rights as endogenous. Property rights are logically prior to wealth maximization. This can be seen by considering titles in one's own person, a topic discussed below at great length.

The O.J. Case

How can we apply these insights to the O.J. case? In the traditional view, matters are quite simple. On the assumption that O.J. actually killed Nicole and Ronald Goldman, things go ill for him. This is because each person is a self-owner. Murder, therefore, is akin to "stealing" one's personhood from someone else.

One would think that Coase would assent to this commonsensical (albeit awkwardly put) way of looking at matters. After all, the legitimacy of slavery is hardly a contentious issue in the modern era. Unfortunately, such a conclusion cannot be reconciled with his own position. Although he shows no signs of recognizing it, the logic of his wealth maximization philosophy compels him to adopt an altogether different stance, and a very strange one at that.

Consider the following case. O.J. values the possessions of Nicole at $100 million. She, for her part, no longer wishes to be associated with him. He is, for her, a negative value. However, assume that she is relatively poor, and/or has low self-esteem, so much so that for a mere $10 million, she will consent to whatever it is that he wishes from her.

---

[14] For the implications of altering property titles, *see* Benson (1981, 1993).

[15] The plethora of "squatters" cases is a dramatic case in point.

[16] For implications of this analysis to the area of taxation, *see* Gordon (1994). For an alternative view, *see* Buchanan (1984).

In the world of zero transactions costs, the wealth maximization solution is clear. If the judge awards O.J. the possession of his ex-wife, against her will,[17] all is well and good. "Society" gains to the tune of $90 million. He values her at $100 million worth; she loses only $10 million by being forced back into his clutches. He will only accept a bribe greater than $100 to set her free; she would be unwilling to offer more than $10 million. Even if the judge "errs" and awards Nicole her own freedom, all is still well on the wealth maximization front. For now, O.J. will bribe Nicole with some amount between $10 and $100 million—say, $40 million—and she will accede to his wishes. He will still "get" her; that is, resources will be rationally allocated.

True, O.J. will be the poorer, when the two alternative decisions are compared. In the first case, he has $100 million at his disposal, and in the second, he can call upon only $60 million ($100 million − $40 million = $60 million). On the other hand, Nicole will be richer in the second case; the only conclusion to be expected when we move from a situation where the verdict went against her to one in her favor. In the first case, her wealth position was minus $10 million; in the second, plus $30 million, a gain of $40 million to match an equal impoverishment of O.J. But for Coase this is not the essential element of the analysis.[18] Much to the contrary, Coase's aim, here, is to show that whichever decision is rendered, the aggregate wealth of society will be exactly the same, $90 million under our assumptions. In the first case, O.J. enjoys $100 million − $10 million for Nicole = $90 million; in the second, O.J. has $100 million − $40 million = $60 million, while Nicole has $40 million − $10 million = $30 million, again for a total of $90 million.

[17] We defer until the objections section the retort that it is not the business of the judge to even make a ruling in such a case; that instead it should be summarily tossed out of court.

[18] A more critical way of expressing this sentiment is to assert that the Coasean system is an unjust one; it fails to even distinguish, morally, between winning and losing. That is to say, it fails to indicate whether the judge should find in favor of the plaintiff (O.J.) or the defendant (Nicole) with regard to the justice of the resulting different wealth distributions. A Coasean might well reply that no more could be expected from a theory which is purposefully economic, for example, value free. However, this claim to vertfreiheit is invalid. After all, Coase is advising the judge regarding decision-making, surely a value-laden act. Nor is Coase's initial motivating force—wealth maximization—a value-free concept.

Summary of Coase's Argument

Cases 1, 2, and 3 are "good" for Coase since total wealth is maximized at +$90; case 4 is "bad" since social wealth is minimized at −$90. A bribe need not take place in case 1 for economic ("eco") reasons: the only one who can bribe is O.J., and he need not, since he has won the verdict. A bribe cannot take place in case 2 since Nicole values herself at only $10, while O.J.'s reservation demand for her is $100. Bribes cannot take place in cases 3 and 4 due to the assumption of very high transactions costs ("t.c.").

Now let us provide a Coasean analysis of the (very) high transactions costs scenario. Again, if the judge has the wisdom to award Nicole's person and freedom to the tender mercies of O.J., all is well and good as far as wealth maximization is concerned. O.J. benefits by possessing Nicole to the tune of $100 million, she loses only $10 million, and as a result, their combined wealth is again $90 million. However, if under the assumption of high transactions costs the judge erroneously releases Nicole under her own recognizance, wealth, horrors!, is not maximized. For in this case there is no possibility of a bribe making good the judge's oversight. By assumption, very high transactions costs render this an impossibility. Here, O.J. will have to suffer in silence. He will lose the $100 million at which he rates his ownership over her, while she will gain only $10 from having gotten rid of him. Thus, social wealth plummets from +$90 million to −$90 million, a wealth loss of $180, given the numbers we are using for illustrative purposes.

The Defense Rests

How, then, does this constitute a defense for O.J.—on the assumption that he is indeed guilty of murdering his ex-wife?[19] The reasoning is as follows: the judge *should have* awarded to O.J. the custody of Nicole. He *would* have done so had he been rational and (thus) engaged in wealth-maximizing behavior in behalf of society. Therefore, O.J. was justified in

[19] It must be conceded that even Coaseanism cannot be interpreted in such a way as to constitute a defense for O.J.'s murder of Ronald Goldman. This, at least, is beyond the ability of the present author.

seizing that which should have been awarded to him in the first place. What occurred to O.J. was simply incompatible with the Coasean system of jurisprudence.[20] His own "self-help" righted this wrong. He may have gone a bit far when he killed his ex-wife, but if so, he should not be found guilty of the crime of murder. At most, he should be held guilty of whatever level of law violation, if any, that was deemed appropriate for slave owners during the pre-civil war period who improperly killed their slaves.[21]

Let us put this in other words. A defense of O.J.'s actions can be predicated upon Coasean analysis. In that viewpoint, O.J. should have been given the rights to do with Nicole exactly as he wished. This, "unfortunately," did not occur. The actions of this aggrieved husband were compatible with the rights he would have been granted, did we but live in a Coasean world. At best, then, he should be set free; at worst, this should at least be seen as a mitigating circumstance.

Objections

There will no doubt be objections to the foregoing modest proposal. We do well then to anticipate a few of them.

1. First and foremost will be the claim that we are all self-owners and that slavery is an abomination. This is of course true but only under traditional codes of law. Coaseanism usurps all of this. For in the law and economics perspective of the University of Chicago and elsewhere, there is no such thing as starting with self-ownership or indeed with any other pattern of property rights. On the contrary, property rights—all of them, those to the person as well as those to physical goods—are the handmaiden of wealth maximization. It does not do to simply start out with the premise that anyone owns anything, even including himself. How,

---

[20] The same analysis applies to those restraining orders granted to wives whose husbands are harassing them. On the assumption that the male is richer than the female, and would have purchased the rights to her in a zero transactions costs world, no such restraints would be issued by the Coasean judge.

[21] Actually, it was legally murder (and hence illegal) to kill one's own slave in the pre-civil war US south. (I owe this point to an anonymous referee.) But as a de facto matter, such laws were in effect null and void.

after all, could such an "arbitrary" conclusion be justified? If we allowed people to simply own themselves—slavery being forbidden outright—this would amount to a market failure.[22] The state must step in, by judicially promulgating findings that are aimed at wealth maximization. This can be done, as we have seen, by ensuring that intensive would-be slave owners, such as O.J., are not balked by a high transactions costs world in their desire to own people who only have a timid, tepid, and tentative hold on themselves, such as the Nicole of our numerical example. Should O.J. be prevented from realizing his goal merely because he happens to occupy a high transactions costs world? Not at all, says Coase, certainly not when it is well within the power of the judge to right so egregious a wrong.[23]

In the traditional view of property rights, the one rejected by the new Law and Economics dispensation, the possibility of Nicole being given to O.J. as his lawful property does not even arise. In the Lockean view, each person is a self-owner, period. No one can prove, moreover, that wealth can be maximized by turning anyone over to the ownership of another. The numbers furnished in the illustration are just that, numbers. In the absence of an *agreement* between two parties, a real honest-to-goodness agreement,[24] which by stipulation did not occur in this case, there is no warrant to assume that any rearrangement of property titles will enhance social welfare or total wealth. The only way to demonstrate that a reallocation of property will indeed enhance social wealth is to observe a trade

[22] Strictly speaking, this could amount to a market failure. It would, to employ the neoclassical perspective on this, if it was indeed true that anyone would buy anyone else in a zero transactions costs world.

[23] Suppose O.J. kidnapped Nicole and kept her imprisoned for one month. Is there no scope for redress through money damages? For the Coasean, of course, there is. All a judge need do is ascertain the market value of the wages lost, plus a premium for "pain and suffering," and award this to the victim. (This is on the assumption, by no means foreordained, the kidnapping was not "justified" through considerations of wealth maximization.) But no less is true of the Lockean judge. Indeed, the very same procedure might be employed by both. But in the latter case, there would perhaps be more appreciation of the inescapable arbitrariness of the resulting numbers. Nor would there be the slightest hint of any rearrangement of property titles to the two human beings based on these numbers—as there would have to be if the Coasean judge were aware of the implications of his methodology.

[24] Not a theoretical one that would have taken place in the never-never land of zero transactions costs.

taking place. Then, we may posit, at least in the ex ante sense, that there was mutual benefit.

But nothing of the sort occurred in the O.J.–Nicole case considered above. Therefore, in the "simplistic" economics that the Law and Economic perspective is trying to replace, it is illegitimate to conclude that wealth will increase if Nicole is awarded to O.J.

2. The second objection is that in our attempt to provide a reductio ad absurdum to the Coasean system, we have made an illegitimate assumption. Coase's views, properly interpreted, have a limited application. They apply only to cases where property rights are not well-established. For example, if Sturgis v Bridgeman are having an altercation concerning noise rights, or if the Coasean farmer and the railroad cannot resolve a dispute concerning pollution, then and only then may the courts step in and resolve matters. And there, of course, the Coasean insights should be the ones applied—wealth must be maximized. But until and unless such a situation of ill-established property rights is presented to the court, it must refrain from applying the Coase theorem.

The response to this objection is that for the Coaseans, there is no such thing as well-defined property rights. *All* property rights, even the most well defined of them, whatever that might mean for a Coasean, are the handmaiden of wealth maximization. They exist only at the pleasure of the latter consideration. If anything is "well defined," it is that each person is the "sole proprietor" of himself or herself. Yet even this holds true only because, in the Coasean view, this is the way to maximize wealth. Were it ever contemplated that slavery could better lead to this goal than self-ownership, the followers of Coase would perforce have to embrace that system.

3. A third objection arises from the views of Posner, one of the preeminent Coaseans. In his (1985, p. 1196) analysis, he states:

> If I covet my neighbor's car, it is more efficient to force me to negotiate with my neighbor—to pay him his price—than it is to allow me to take his car subject to being required by a court to pay the neighbor whatever the court decides the car is worth. If I happen to have no money but want a car, it would be inefficient to let me just take a car. Indeed, unlike the first case, this transfer cannot possibly improve the allocation of resources—that is, it

> cannot move resources from a less to a more valuable employment—because value is a function of willingness to pay.

There are several problems with this attempted defense. First of all, it is incompatible with Posner's (1986, p. 440) perspective on altruism. There, he maintains that:

> …the altruist faces a free rider problem. A in our example will derive welfare from the increase in B's income whether or not A is the source of the increase. Naturally A would like to buy this increase in his welfare at the lowest possible price, so he will have an incentive to hang back in giving to charity in the hope that others will give. It might seem that regardless of what others give his contribution will add to the total amount of resources devoted to an end he values. But this is not certain. His contribution may lead others to cut back their contributions, since now a smaller contribution on their part will (in combination with A's contribution, which is new) buy the same reduction in poverty. So A will get less than a dollar benefit for every dollar he contributes, and this will lead to a lower contribution.

From whence arises the incompatibility? In the first statement above, value is (correctly) deduced by the willingness to pay. Without an agreed-upon deal which transfers resources from seller to buyer, we have no warrant to assume any wealth improvement. In the second statement, however, it is simply *assumed*, without any such warrant whatsoever, that "A will derive welfare from B" in the total absence of any such willingness or agreement. How do we know this? How *can* we, even in principle, ever know this?

Suppose that Posner were poor, and that his neighbor, the one with the car, were rich. Then, based on his views in 1986, it would be justified to take the car away from the neighbor and give it to Posner. This is logically incompatible with his 1985 writing, where, unaccountably, and surprisingly, he tries to defend traditional (e.g., non-Coasean) notions of private property. But logical consistency will not allow him to have it both ways.

Second, it is only inefficient for the neighbor to be forced to give Posner his car in a zero transactions costs world. In the very high transactions costs world[25] we have been considering, this is entirely a different matter. It is perhaps no exaggeration to say that the entire Coasean edifice is built to support the claim of Posner against his neighbor for that car under these assumptions.

Third, and most important, Posner speaks as if different people actually own things. But this (too) is incompatible with the entire Coasean (and his own!) world view. There, people own things all right, but only, and insofar as, this status lends itself to wealth maximization. How do we know that Posner's neighbor *should* own the car in the first place? What gives him the initial right to it? Homesteading? Purchase? Certainly not.[26] The problem is, Posner here too easily accepts his neighbor's ownership claim. To say the least, this failure to question the neighbor's initial property holding is very much out of keeping with his other voluminous writings. Did Posner but call this into question, he might have been as justified in seizing it, as is O.J. in appropriating the person of Nicole, his ex-wife.

4. A fourth objection also concerns the applicability of the Coasean theorem. Specifically, does it apply only to objects, to goods and services, and to capital equipment such as cows and corn, doctor's waiting rooms and confectioner's machines, airports and houses, railroads and farms, and so on, or does it pertain also to the ownership and control of people?

The force of this objection, of course, is that if it concerns only the former, and not the latter, then our attempted reductio ad absurdum fails completely. That is, if the Coasean theorem is relevant to things, not people, then there is no case at all for entertaining the notion that O.J. may own Nicole.

But this objection fails, and on three grounds. First of all, even if Coase intends that his theory be narrowly construed, we need not acquiesce. Mere intention is not enough; he would have to put forth *reasons* why considerations of wealth maximization should be compelling when it

---

[25] Who is to say whether the world, or different aspects of it, is characterized by high or low transactions costs? Given the inherent subjectivity of costs (alternatives foregone, which can, by their very nature, be known only by the economic actor in question), it would appear that anyone can maintain anything he wants.

[26] Nor even a process of trade, gifts, and so on, that Nozick (1974) calls legitimate title transfers, which, if we trace them far back enough, we arrive at the first homesteader.

comes to inanimate objects but not to human capital. This, to say the least, he has not done.

Second, there is such a thing as generalizability in (social) science; the more generalizable is a theory, other things equal, the stronger it is. This means that even if Coase gave reasons for the inapplicability of his theory to human beings—which he did not—we could still reject them, or at least give his theory lesser weight, on that ground alone.

Third, although Coase himself vouchsafed us no answer to this question on either side, followers of his have expressed themselves most forcefully on it, and in their opinion, the Law and Economics philosophy makes no distinction between the human and the non-human: it applies to both.

Let us consider Posner's views[27] on rape, since this is perhaps the closest he comes to applying the theory to people in general. Certainly, his treatment is highly relevant to our concerns regarding O.J. and Nicole in particular. In (1986, pp. 1198–1199), he defends his economic theory of the criminal law[28] against the charge that it can justify rape, on the ground that the rapist "derives extra pleasure from the coercive character of his act." He rejects this unwelcome conclusion on several grounds, one of which concerns us: "…it does not follow that he values the rape more than the victim disvalues it."

But suppose that the rapist does indeed value the rape more than the victim disvalues it.[29] The inescapable conclusion would appear to be that

[27] *See* also Demsetz (1966, 1967) for the application of the Coasean system to human beings.

[28] In the traditional view, penal and commercial law differ with regard to property rights. In penal law, the concept of property rights virtually does not exist; in contrast, in commercial law, the concern is virtually with nothing else than property rights. But this is the traditional or orthodox view.

In contrast, there is the libertarian conception, which tends to blur the line between criminal and commercial violations of law. Here, property rights is of crucial importance in not one but both cases. For further elaboration of the importance not of this distinction but of blurring it, *see* Rothbard 1982a, pp. 51–61; *see also* Epstein, 1977. I wish to acknowledge the role of an anonymous referee in bringing this point to my attention.

[29] For the Austrian skeptic, no such thing can ever be known, since interpersonal comparisons of utility are totally incompatible with the subjectivity of costs. But the Chicago-ite Coaseans are forever offering us illustrative numerical examples, of the sort mentioned above in Table 2. Let us hold them to their word, then, and ask that they accept the unwelcome implications of their analysis as well as the more tolerable ones.

Posner would have to exonerate the rapist, however unwelcome he found this position. And if the rapist, why not the murderer, again assuming that O.J. is actually guilty of this crime?[30]

Another difficulty, here, is that Posner continually writes as if it were a foregone conclusion that women should own their own bodies. Until and unless he realizes that this is the very thing in question in the (Coasean) analysis of rape,[31] he will not be acting consistently with his own premises.

Posner (1992, p. 386) revisits this question. He states:

> The rational model (this is the name Posner has chosen for his own view) has been said to imply, however, contrary to our unshakable moral intuitions, that a man who derives a special pleasure, sexual or otherwise, from the coerciveness of rape ought to be permitted to rape, provided only that he derives more pleasure from the act, over and above all substitutes (such as sex with a prostitute who will, for a price, consent to the man's abusing her physically), than the pain suffered by his victim. This example points to a familiar problem of utilitarianism—the problem of the 'utility monster,' who by virtue of having a capacity for enjoyment vastly greater than that of the average person in the society appears to stake a utilitarian moral claim to engross a disproportionate share of the society's goods. Only here the utility monster really is a monster, who by virtue of having a capacity for sadistic pleasure greater than his victim's capacity for pain stakes a moral claim to be allowed to torture, rape and kill.... (material in the first set of brackets supplied by the present author).

This is very apropos since our depiction of O.J. (in Table 21.2) is consistent with considering him to be a "utility monster" in this sense.

But Posner (1992, pp. 386–387) rejects this critique of utilitarianism:

> ...it should be plain that licensing utility monsters such as Bluebeard or de Sade to rape would not really be utility-maximizing, if only because of the

[30] It cannot be denied that there is an important distinction between the theory of law and of the law itself. One should be careful not to overlook this distinction, lest one commit the Ricardian Leap or Ricardian Vice. On this concept, *see* Schumpeter, 1954, pp. 472–473; also Rothbard, 1996, pp. 176–178. I owe this point to an anonymous referee.

[31] Or any other crime such as murder.

Table 21.2 A summary comparison of the results of the judicial decision in the hypothetical O.J. versus Nicole

	O.J. wins	Nicole wins
	(1)	(2)
Zero transactions costs	O.J. gets Nicole no bribe (eco) Wealth O.J.: \$100 Wealth Nic: −\$10 Tot wealth: \$90 ("good")	O.J. gets Nicole O.J. bribes Nicole \$40 Wealth O.J.: \$100 – \$40 = \$60 Wealth Nic: \$40 – \$10 = \$30 Tot Wealth: \$90 ("good")
	(3)	(4)
High transactions costs	O.J. gets Nicole no bribe (eco, t.c.) Wealth O.J.: \$100 Wealth Nic: −\$10 Tot wealth: \$90 ("good")	O.J. doesn't get Nicole no bribe (t.c.) Wealth O.J.: −\$100 Wealth Nic: +\$10 Tot Wealth: −\$90 ("bad")

> fear that it would engender in the community as a whole and the expense of the self-protective measures that this fear would incite.

This response, however, is highly problematic. First of all, on Posner's own grounds, there is no case for rejecting the *possibility* of the utility monster. If Coase can contemplate all sorts of possible relationships between cattleman and corn grower, between farmer and railroad, then we are entitled to construct Table 21.2 in effect depicting O.J. as a utility monster.

Second, a reprobate such as Bluebeard or de Sade is certainly not needed to illustrate our point, although it certainly is sufficient. But there are other alternatives. All we need is that there be a significant *difference* between how a man values the forced possession of a woman's body and how she rates self-ownership over her own person. One way to accomplish this is by resort to a utility monster such as Bluebeard. But this difference can *also* be attained by considering the case of a "normal" man, and a woman so lacking in self-esteem or value for her own person that it is (somehow?) determined that his value for her is greater than her own for herself. Female candidates for this position might include prostitutes, masochists, and attempted suicides. In these particular cases, using the usual Coasean Posnerian analysis, we can, while being true to the basic premises of their system, declare rape, murder, and torture to be legal, on "rational" or "economic" grounds, since the female "obviously" values herself than does the male.

Nor should we be taken in by Posner's discussion of fear and the cost of self-protective measures. Yes, with a utility monster on the loose, all women have good reason for fear and self-protection. Even in this case, Posner has failed to show that the gains enjoyed by the mad killer-rapist would be less important than those costs. But in the example of the "ordinary" killer-rapist, it simply is not true that *all* women would be in danger. On the contrary, this would apply *only* to women who have a less-than-average demand for themselves, for example, the Nicole of our numerical example. In any case, self-protective measures are likely not to amount to much, for they would be *illegal*[32] under a system strictly implied by the Posnerian analysis.

Remember, the whole issue revolves around the question of why people should be thought to own themselves. The answer emanating from the Chicago Law and Economics tradition is that this result should only obtain if it is wealth maximizing. Well, in the examples we have been considering, this would patently *not* be the case.

5. A fifth objection attacks the logical consistency of the Lockean position. The charge is that the Lockeans criticize the "arbitrariness" inherent in the Coasean judicial decisions; however, they are forced to resort to an identical procedure with regard to damages.

How would the Lockean system deal with the situation where the railroad had already destroyed some of the farmer's crops? Suppose the judge ordered compensation to the farmer in the amount of the dollar value of the crops as a redress for the trespass. For Coase, this presents no problem. Indeed, his many numerical examples highlight such behavior time and again. However, it might be claimed that for the Lockean, this is a conundrum, for any such order would of necessity have to be arbitrary.

How might the Lockean reply? If he is honest, he would have to concede that there is indeed an element of arbitrariness involved in any such juridical finding and, further, that it would be justified to make it, despite

[32] Self-protective measures should be illegal because they would reduce social wealth.

this undeniable fact. There seems to be no possible better alternative. Complex choices cannot always be made in tiny watertight compartments, no matter how highly desirable.

However, just because reality impinges with its rough edges does not mean we have to embrace it when there are alternatives. Damage awards do indeed violate economic strictures against interpersonal comparisons of utility. Who knows how much the farmer "really" suffered by his loss in crops, or the railroad, in being forced to make good on the market-based monetary equivalent. But this is no reason to employ such a method in defining property rights, especially when a preferable (Lockean homesteading) alternative exists.

By all means, say the Lockeans allow the judge to make monetary awards when he can do nothing else. But do not over-generalize from this situation and unnecessarily support Coasean considerations for the very definition of property rights when they are unnecessary and on other grounds highly problematic.

6. A sixth objection

Posner (1983, pp. 94–96) is tailor-made as a reply to our attempt at a reductio. Although rather lengthy, it is worth quoting in full lest there be any misunderstanding. He states:

> Another area in which the principle of consent and the principle of wealth maximization are potentially in conflict … is in the initial assignment of property rights, the starting point for the market system.
>
> What if A's labor is worth more to B than to A? Then it would be efficient to make A the slave of B but this result would hardly comport with the principle of consent. Such cases must be very rare. Not only will A probably have a better idea than anyone else where he could be most productively employed, but the costs of overcoming A's disincentive to work hard when the benefits of his hard work would enure exclusively to another are likely to make the net value of his labor less than if he owned it himself. If there are cases where the costs of physical coercion are so low relative to the costs of administering contracts as to make slavery a more efficient method for organizing production than any voluntary system, they either arise under such different social conditions from our own as to make ethical comparisons difficult, or involve highly unusual circumstances (e.g., military discipline) to which the term slavery is not attached.

A related problem is that where large allocative questions are involved, as in the initial assignment of rights, the very concept of wealth maximization become problematic. Since the wealth of society is the output of all tangible and intangible commodities multiplied by their market values, it is difficult to compare the wealth of two states of society in which prices are different. The prices in a social order in which one person owned all the other members of society might be different from the prices in a social order where everyone was his own master. But even here guesses may be possible. For example, if we started with a society where one person owned all the others, soon most of the others would have bought their freedom from that person because their output would be greater as free individuals than as slaves, enabling them to pay more for the right to their labor than that right was worth to the slave owner. It would be clear, then, that the slave society was inefficient, even though the prices in a slave and free society might be different for many commodities.

Consider the following example of how the initial assignment of rights might appear to have such an effect on prices that the wealth of society under alternative assignments could not be compared. Imagine that A, if a free man, would derive a lifetime market income of 100 in present value from working and a non-market income of 50 from leisure, for a total income of 150, but that if A is B's slave, A will be forced to produce an output having a market value of 110 and will obtain zero nonpecuniary income. A's wealth is higher in the free than in the slave state (150 vs zero), so that if he has the right to his labor he will not sell that right to B. Freedom is therefore wealth maximizing if A is free to begin with. But if B owns the right to A's labor, then it may seem that A will not be able to buy it back from B. How can A pay more than 100 since that is the value of his output as a free man? A's output is worth 110 to B, and A cannot use his nonpecuniary income in the free state to buy his freedom because his leisure has no value to anyone else. Therefore, it seems that slavery is wealth maximizing if the initial assignment of rights is to make A the slave of B.

But this analysis overlooks the possibility of converting non pecuniary income into pecuniary income. A's preferred mixture of work and leisure is such as to yield 100 in market income and 50 in nonpecuniary income from leisure, but A could work harder, as he does for B. Suppose by working harder (but not all the time), A could earn a market income of 120 and leisure income of 10. A could then buy his freedom from B. It is true that, having done so, A would be worse off than if he had the right to his labor

> in the first place. The point of the analysis, however, is that freedom is indeed more efficient than slavery, because by giving A his freedom in the first place we obviate the need for a transaction whereby A buys his freedom from B.
>
> Thus, while the theoretical possibility exists that efficiency might dictate slavery or some other monstrous rights assignment, it is difficult to give examples where this would actually happen. I conclude that it is possible to deduce a structure of rights congruent with our ethical intuitions from the wealth maximization premise.

This is indeed a thorough and well-thought-out defense of the wealth maximization position. Unfortunately, however, it is not without its difficulties.

To begin with, Posner (1983, p. 94) claims that there are only a few cases where it would be more efficient, for example, wealth maximizing, to allow slavery than self-ownership and freedom. All it takes, however, is one such case, to show that the Posnerian system is *not* "congruent with our ethical intuitions" (Posner, 1983, p. 96). This author is wedded to wealth maximization as a basic premise. If, through its use, we can show that even in *one* case a careful deduction from his premise leads to slavery, it casts doubt on the entire edifice.

Posner is intent, and rightly so, to maintain that his system can work based on the principle of consent. For without consent there is coercion, and no man can be free who is coerced. Given that his goal is to reconcile his system with the ordinary rejection of slavery in particular and coercion in general, he does well to start down this path. There is a problem here, though. Consent *implies* self-ownership. Logically, the issue of consent can only arise if one is a free man. In order to see this, let us consider a case of slavery where, paradoxically, our moral sense can be mobilized in *favor* of slavery.

Suppose that my son has an otherwise fatal disease for which the cure is $1 million. Assume further that:

(a) I value his life at more than $1 million.
(b) I value my freedom at less than $1 million (in effect, I value my freedom lower than I value my son's life).

(c) I do not have the requisite funds at my disposal.
(d) There is a wealthy man who is willing to pay me a million dollars for my freedom; that is, he will pay me this money as the purchase price of my total servitude.

Under these conditions, the path to wealth maximization is clear. I sell myself into slavery to this man, give the million dollars to the doctors who save my son's life. All are beneficiaries. I gain to the extent that I value my son's life more than my freedom; the doctors gain to the extent that they value the $1 million more than the costs of treatment; the rich man gains to the extent that he values me as a slave more than the cost to him of $1 million.

Now let us return to the point. I am now the legitimate slave of the rich man. Does the concept of my "consent" make any sense? Hardly. I have given up the right to engage in any such activity. The only consent that is needed to determine my actions is not "mine" but rather that of my legitimate owner.

I have given up my self-ownership rights; consent, therefore, cannot apply to me. How about the case where I *never had* ownership over myself. Can I consent to anything then? No. Consent, by its very nature, implies ownership over oneself. Here is where Posner runs into trouble. He is trying to analyze consent, as it applies to people for whom ownership rights have yet to be determined.

Let us put this in another way. Consent implies, at the very least, the use of vocal cords. But suppose we are agnostic, as Posner claims he is, about the ultimate source of self-ownership.[33] If so, how can someone legitimately "consent" to something, with clear title to a voice. Posner has constructed a circular argument: he relies on consent to establish ownership, but without ownership in the first place, there can be no consent.

---

[33] Posner, of course, is not agnostic about the procedure by which ownership over the person may properly be determined. For him, it is clearly wealth maximization. But he is agnostic about this in the sense that if the "numbers" indicate that slavery is the most efficient system of wealth maximization, he will then embrace that "curious institution." For him, ultimately, it is an empirical matter. Will slavery, or will it not, lead to greater wealth? If it will not, Posner opposes it; but if it will, then he has no alternative but to embrace it.

We are treated to the reddest of red herrings when Posner (1983, p. 95) distinguishes between a scenario where no one owns anyone else and one where a *single person* owns the entire remainder of the world. Yes, under these latter conditions, and under his (not totally unrealistic) assumptions that people will work harder on their own account than for someone else, it may well be possible that many if not most slaves will be able to buy their way out of this predicament.

This analysis, however, is predicated upon slaves being *able* to buy their freedom from their masters. And in Coase's made-up world of zero transactions costs, this is unexceptionable. But in the real world of positive and even very high transactions costs—how quickly we forget about the real world—this option is of far lesser moment.[34]

Even under these conditions, how does Posner square this situation with our intuitions about morality he is so anxious not to offend? The problem is, why should the slave have to buy his way out of anything? Under traditional ethical assumptions, freedom is the natural order. If you want to enslave someone, you may have to buy him into this situation; but you can't first enslave him, and then magnanimously allow him to purchase a manumission contract—at least not if we are operating within the bounds of conventional ethical mores.

Let us therefore eschew Posner's case of a single individual owning all others and consider some more realistic possibilities. For example, older people owning younger ones, or males owning females (to hark back to our case of O.J. and Nicole), or smarter ones owning those who are stupid. Perhaps even better yet, let us borrow a leaf from the writings of Herrnstein and Murray (1994) and consider the case of high I.Q. people ("the cognitive elite") owning the low I.Q. people (the "very dull").

Now Posner's scenario falls totally to the ground. Even without the existence of positive and very high transactions costs, it is extremely unlikely that the slaves will be able to buy their way to freedom, even

[34] Posner (1983, p. 83) states: "It would be impossible to identify, let alone negotiate for the consent of, everyone affected by a move from a price regulated to a free tomato market…" Yes, indeed, true. Transactions costs are everywhere, and they are everywhere significant. But if this is true for so picayune and unimportant a market as that for tomatoes, it holds even the more so, and much more strongly, for (potential) slave markets.

granting that "the slave would borrow against his future earnings to finance the purchase of his freedom" (Posner, 1983, p. 95).

The bedrock of Posner's (1983, pp. 95–96) numerical example is that the slave would work "harder" for himself than for his master. But working harder is merely part and parcel of the by now long-discredited labor theory of value (Bohm-Bawerk, 1959). The key isn't merely working harder but also, and even more importantly, working smarter. And if there is anything that the cognitive elite can do, it is, presumably, to wring every last bit of productivity out of their slaves at the opposite end of the IQ bell curve. How? By seeing to it that they work smarter, more so than they are capable of doing on their own. It may be true in many cases that "freedom is indeed more efficient than slavery," (Posner, 1983, p. 96) but this applies under his own assumptions, not for reasonable alternative ones such as we have specified. The point is, Posner fails to reckon with a scenario where the "cognitive elite" might be able to increase the productivity levels of those who are relatively intellectually incapacitated to greater degrees than they are able to do for themselves. On this assumption, it is possible that the productivity levels of the latter will actually be higher as slaves than as free men. If this is true, in turn, then the reasonableness of Posner's assumption must be called into question. For if such people are more productive as slaves than as free men, there will be no increase in human capital out of which to finance the manumission purchase.

Even disregarding this latter possibility, it is still not true that a positive differential between productivity as a slave and a free person will be sufficient to finance voluntary manumission. The differential will have to be greater than whatever given level of "taste for slavery" exists on the part of the slave owner. As well, it will have to overcome any desire to be controlled that may exist in the mind of the slave.

What of the slavery which occurred in the antebellum south? The fact that it existed, and long endured, and needed outside physical invasion to overturn it (Fogel and Engerman, 1974; see also Thornton, 1994) is surely evidence that it was *not* inefficient in the sense proposed by Posner.

Yet another difficulty with Posner's made-up numbers is that they fail to incorporate our analysis of O.J. and Nicole: the "will to own" other people, the "timidity" or loose link to self-ownership in one's own person. Nicole's "demand" for her own person, under our assumptions, is weaker than O.J.'s for her. The bottom line is that each of us is free to concoct any numbers we wish. Posner, undoubtedly, is a past master at creating scenarios which show wealth maximization to good effect. And he is to be congratulated upon them. But we can also create numbers showing the very opposite. And this is sufficient to override his contention that wealth maximization is necessarily compatible with traditional notions of morality.

Posner speaks of a tendency for slaves to buy their way out of this predicament. But even if this could occur, why should they have to do any such thing? Surely, a system of slavery, even with manumission written into the code as a possibility, provided that the master agrees, is an offense against ordinary notions of morality and ethics. It is also undeniable that this is one of the criteria which any theory of law must satisfy. For if it is to be acceptable, it must for one thing show a deeper understanding of the ordinary conclusions in law, and for another convince us that when it does not, that it, and not the traditional view, is somehow more in touch with basic human values.[35]

Disregarding objections about interpersonal comparisons of utility, we can perhaps agree with Posner that yes, there will be a tendency for slaves to buy their way out of their plight because of the reasonable assumption that people will be more productive on their own. If so, they can finance the purchase of their freedom with the capitalized value of the difference in the two income streams: one under slavery, the other under freedom.

However, this is only a tendency or a presumption. It need not apply in all cases. Specifically, it will not hold true given the "Herrnstein-Murray effect"; further, it will fail if the slave owner has a strong taste for slavery (Zerbe, 1994), the situation we are supposing by hypothesis to be true of O.J. Nor will it apply if the slave has a weak desire for freedom,[36] precisely our assumption for Nicole.

[35] For example, even though sales of bodily organs may well be repugnant to most sensibilities, if it can be shown that legalizing such markets will undoubtedly lead to the saving of additional lives, such a theory has satisfied the requirement that when it leads to seemingly untoward results, these, too, can be justified in terms of ordinary moral concerns.

[36] In the late Roman Empire, slaves frequently bought their freedom by credit from their masters. This might have occurred in the south had not most of the slave states passed laws prohibiting it. Firms such as the Tredegar Iron Works, which engaged in such voluntary manumission, had to conceal this fact from the authorities. (I owe this point to an anonymous referee.)

Conclusion

We have succeeded in subjecting the views of Coase and Posner to a reductio ad absurdum. If their own principles are applied to the charges against O.J. for killing Nicole, the defendant has an exculpatory "case" on the assumption that he is indeed "guilty" of killing her: in a zero transactions costs world, he would have been the owner of Nicole, with the right to do with her exactly as he pleased. In the real world of prohibitive transactions costs, he should have been granted ownership rights over her.

Too bad Lance Ito wasn't a "Coasean Judge." Were he, the world would have been in for a bit of a surprise: he would have thrown the case out before it was even heard.

References

Arnold, Roger A., 1982, "Efficiency vs. Ethics: Which Is the Proper Decision Criterion in Law Cases?," The Journal of Libertarian Studies, Vol. VI, No. 1, Winter, pp. 49–58.

Barnett, Randy E., 1978, "Toward a Theory of Legal Naturalism," The Journal of Libertarian Studies, Vol. 2, No. 2, Summer, pp. 97–108.

Benson, Bruce L., 1981, "Land Use Regulation: A Supply and Demand Analysis of Changing Property Rights," The Journal of Libertarian Studies, Vol. V, No. 4, Fall, pp. 435–451.

Benson, Bruce L., "Enforcement of Private Property Rights in Primitive Societies: Law Without Government," Journal of Libertarian Studies, 9: 1–26, 1989a.

Benson, Bruce L., 1989b, Enforcement of Private Property Rights in Primitive Societies: Law Without Government," The Journal of Libertarian Studies, Vol. IX, No. 1, Winter, pp. 1–26.

Benson, Bruce L., "An Evolutionary Contractarian View of Primitive Law: The Institutions and Incentives Arising under Customary Indian Law," The Review of Austrian Economics, Vol. 5, No. 1, 1991, pp. 41–65.

Benson, Bruce L., "The Impetus for Recognizing Private Property and Adopting Ethical Behavior in a Market Economy: Natural Law, Government Law or Evolving Self Interest," The Review of Austrian Economics, Vol. 6, No. 2, 1993, pp. 43–80.

Block, Walter, "Ethics, Efficiency, Coasian Property Rights and Psychic Income: A Reply to Demsetz," Review of Austrian Economics, Vol. 8, No. 2, 1995, pp. 61–125.

Block, Walter, "Earning Happiness Through Homesteading Unowned Land: a comment on 'Buying Misery with Federal Land' by Richard Stroup," Journal of Social Political and Economic Studies, Vol. 15, No. 2, Summer 1990, pp. 237–253.

Block, Walter, "Coase and Demsetz on Private Property Rights," The Journal of Libertarian Studies, Vol. I, No. 2, Spring 1977, pp. 111–115.

Bohm-Bawerk, Eugen, Capital and Interest, South Holland, IL: Libertarian Press, George D. Hunke and Hans F. Sennholz, trans., 1959 (1884); see particularly Part I, Chapter XII, "Exploitation Theory of Socialism-Communism."

Buchanan, James M. and G.F. Thirlby, L.S.E. Essays on Cost. New York: New York University Press, 1981.

Buchanan, James M., "The Ethical Limits of Taxation," Scandinavian Journal of Economics, 86: 102–114, 1984.

Buchanan, James M., Cost and Choice: An Inquiry into Economic Theory. Chicago: Markham, 1969.

Coase, Ronald H., "The Problem of Social Cost," Journal of Law and Economics, 3: 1–44, 1960.

Cordato, Roy E., "Subjective Value, Time Passage, and the Economics of Harmful Effects," Hamline Law Review, Vol. 12, No. 2, Spring 1989, pp. 229–244.

Cordato, Roy E., "Knowledge Problems and the Problem of Social Cost," Journal of the History of Economic Thought, 14 Fall 1992a.

Cordato, Roy E., Welfare Economics and Externalities in an Open-Ended Universe: A Modern Austrian Perspective. Boston: Kluwer, 1992b.

Demsetz, Harold, "Ethics and Efficiency in Property Rights Systems," in Time, Uncertainty and Disequilibrium: Explorations of Austrian Themes, Mario Rizzo, ed., Lexington, MA: D.C.Heath and Co., 1979.

Demsetz, Harold, "Toward a Theory of Property Rights," American Economic Review, 57: 347–359, 1967.

Demsetz, Harold, "Some Aspects of Property Rights," Journal of Law and Economics, Vol. IX, October 1966.

DiLorenzo, Thomas J., "The Subjectivist Roots of James Buchanan's Economics," The Review of Austrian Economics, Vol. 4, 1990, pp. 180–195.

Epstein, Richard, "Crime and Tort: Old Wine in Old Bottles," in Assessing the Criminal, Randy E. Barnett and John Hagel III, eds., Cambridge, MA: Ballinger, 1977.

Flew, Antony, 1982, "Could there be Universal Natural Rights?," The Journal of Libertarian Studies, Vol. VI, No. 3–4, Summer/Fall, pp. 277–288.

Fogel, Robert W., and Engerman, Stanley L., Time on the Cross: The Economics of American Negro Slavery. Ann Arbor: University of Michigan Press, 1974.

Fox, Glenn, 1992, "The Pricing of Environmental Goods: A Praxeological Critique of Contingent Valuation," Cultural Dynamics, Vol. V, No. 3, pp. 245–259.

Gordon, David, "Toward a Deconstruction of Utility and Welfare Economics," The Review of Austrian Economics, Vol. 6, No. 2, 1993, pp. 99–112.

Gordon, David, "Justice and Redistributive Taxation: James Buchanan vs. Ludwig von Mises," The Review of Austrian Economics, Vol. 8, No. 1, 1994, pp. 117–131.

Herrnstein, Richard J., and Murray, Charles, The Bell Curve: Intelligence and Class Structure in American Life, New York: The Free Press, 1994.

Hoppe, Hans-Hermann, The Economics and Ethics of Private Property: Studies in Political Economy and Philosophy. Boston: Kluwer, 1993.

Hoppe, Hans-Hermann, 1989, "Fallacies of the Public Goods Theory and the Production of Security," The Journal of Libertarian Studies, Vol. IX, No. 1, Winter, pp. 27–46.

Hummel, Jeffrey, "National Goods vs. Public Goods: Defense, Disarmament and Free Riders," The Review of Austrian Economics, Vol. IV, 1990, pp. 88–122.

Krecke, Elisabeth, "Law and the Market Order: An Austrian Critique of the Economic Analysis of Law," paper presented at the Ludwig von Mises Institute's Austrian Scholar's Conference, New York City, October 9–11, 1992.

Locke, John, An Essay Concerning the True Origin, Extent and End of Civil Government, V. 27–28, in Two Treatises of Government, P. Laslett, ed. Cambridge: Cambridge University Press, 1960.

Locke, John, Second Treatise of Civil Government. Chicago: Henry Regnery, 1955.

Machan, Tibor, 1978, "Against Nonlibertarian Natural Rights," The Journal of Libertarian Studies, Vol. 2, No. 3, Fall, pp. 233–238.

Mises, Ludwig von, Socialism, Indianapolis: Liberty Fund, 1981 (1969).

Mises, Ludwig von, Human Action. Chicago: Regnery, 1949, 1963, 1966.

North, Gary, The Coase Theorem. Tyler, TX: The Institute for Christian Economics, 1992.

Nozick, Robert, Anarchy, State and Utopia. New York: Basic Books, 1974.

Pasour, E.C., Jr. 1979, "Conservation, 'X-Inefficiency' and Efficient Use of Natural Resources," The Journal of Libertarian Studies, Vol. III, No. 4, Fall, pp. 371–390.

Pasour, E.C., Jr., 1981, "The Free Rider as a Basis for Government Intervention," The Journal of Libertarian Studies, Vol. V, No. 4, Fall, pp. 453–464.

Pasour, E.C., Jr., 1992, "Human Action and the role of the Economist in the Public Process," Cultural Dynamics, Vol. V, No. 3, pp. 303–318.

Posner, Richard, Sex and Reason. Cambridge: Harvard University Press, 1992.

Posner, Richard A., Economic Analysis of Law. 3rd ed. Boston: Little Brown, 1986.

Posner, Richard, "An Economic Theory of the Criminal Law," Columbia Law Review, Vol. 85, No. 6, October 1985.

Posner, Richard A., "The Ethical and Political Basis of the Efficiency Norm in Common Law Adjudication," in Law, Economics, and Philosophy: A Critical Introduction, with Applications to the Law of Torts, Kuperberg, Mark and Beitz, Charles, eds., New York: Rowman and Allanheld, 1983, pp. 81–101.

Rasmussen, Douglass B., 1980, "A Groundwork for Rights: Man's Natural End," The Journal of Libertarian Studies, Vol. IV, No. 1, Winter, pp. 65–76.

Rothbard, Murray N., For a New Liberty. New York: Macmillan, 1973.

Rothbard, Murray N., The Ethics of Liberty. Atlantic Highlands, NJ: Humanities Press, 1982a.

Rothbard, Murray N., "Law, Property Rights, and Air Pollution," Cato Journal, Vol. 2, No. 1, Spring, 1982b, reprinted in Economics and the Environment: A Reconciliation, Walter Block, ed., Vancouver: The Fraser Institute, 1990.

Rothbard, Murray N., "Intimidation by Rhetoric," Review of Austrian Economics, Vol. 9, No. 1, 1996, pp. 173–178.

Schumpeter, Joseph A., History of Economic Analysis. New York: Oxford University Press, 1954.

Stroup, Richard, "Buying misery with federal land," Public Choice, Vol. 57, 1988, pp. 69–77.

Thornton, Mark, "Slavery, Profitability and the Market Process," The Review of Austrian Economics, Vol. 7, No. 2, 1994, pp. 21–47.

Zerbe, Richard O., Jr., "The Law and Economics of Cannibalism: Foundations of the Economic Analysis of Normative Issues," Working Papers in Public Policy Analysis and Management, University of Washington, 1994, 94–1.

Credits

Here is the original source of chapters that comprise this book; I thank my coauthors, and the publishers of the original versions of these chapters, for reprint permissions.

Part I: Philosophy

Chapter 1. Hoppe, Hans-Hermann and Walter Block. 2002. "Property and Exploitation," *International Journal of Value-Based Management*, Vol. 15, No. 3, pp. 225–236; http://www.mises.org/etexts/propertyexploitation.pdf

Chapter 2. Block, Walter. 2001. "The Moral Dimensions of Poverty, Entitlements and Theft," *The Journal of Markets and Morality*, Vol. 4, No. 1, pp. 83–93; https://www.researchgate.net/publication/228189045_The_Moral_Dimensions_of_Poverty_Entitlements_and_Theft

Chapter 3. Block, Walter. 2002. "Ona'ah," *International Journal of Social Economics*, Vol. 29, No. 9, pp. 722–729; http://www.mises.org/etexts/ona'ah.pdf; http://www.emeraldinsight.com/Insight/viewContainer.do?containerType=Issue&containerId=18703

W. E. Block, *Property Rights*, Palgrave Studies in Classical Liberalism,
https://doi.org/10.1007/978-3-030-28353-7

Part II: Libertarian Property Rights Theory

Chapter 4. Block, Walter. 1996. "Hayek's Road to Serfdom," *Journal of Libertarian Studies: An Interdisciplinary Review*, Vol. 12, No. 2, Fall, pp. 327–350; http://www.mises.org/journals/jls/12_2/12_2_6.pdf

Chapter 5. Friedman, Milton and Walter Block. 2006. "Fanatical, Not Reasonable: A Short Correspondence Between Walter Block and Milton Friedman (on Friedrich Hayek)," *Journal of Libertarian Studies*, Vol. 20, No. 3, Summer, pp. 61–80; http://www.mises.org/journals/jls/20_3/20_3_4.pdf

Chapter 6. Block, Walter. 2002. Book Review of Pipes, Richard, *Property and Freedom: The Story of How Through the Centuries Private Ownership Has Promoted Liberty and the Rule of Law*, New York: Knopf, 2000, in *The Quarterly Journal of Austrian Economics*, Vol. 5, No. 1, Spring, pp. 97–101; http://www.mises.org/qjaedisplay.asp; http://www.mises.org/journals/qjae/pdf/qjae5_1_6.pdf

Chapter 7. Block, Walter. 1999. "Review Essay of Bethell, Tom, *The Noblest Triumph: Property and Prosperity Through the Ages*, New York: St. Martin's Press, 1998," in *The Quarterly Journal of Austrian Economics*, Vol. 2, No. 3, Fall, pp. 65–84; http://www.mises.org/journals/qjae/pdf/qjae2_3_3.pdf

Chapter 8. Block, Walter. 2002. "Radical Privatization and other Libertarian Conundrums," *The International Journal of Politics and Ethics*, Vol. 2, No. 2, pp. 165–175; http://www.walterblock.com/publications/radical_privatization.pdf

Chapter 9. Block, Walter. 2003. "Prices and Location: A Geographical and Economic Analysis," *Planning and Markets*, Vol. 6, No. 1, September; http://www-pam.usc.edu/

Part III: Reparations

Chapter 10. Block, Walter. 2002. "On Reparations to Blacks for Slavery," *Human Rights Review*, Vol. 3, No. 4, July–September, pp. 53–73; http://www.walterblock.com/publications/reparations_slavery.pdf

Chapter 11. Alston, Wilton D. and Walter Block. 2007. "Reparations, Once Again," *Human Rights Review*, December 4; http://tinyurl.com/2b75fl

Chapter 12. Block, Walter and Guillermo Yeatts. 1999–2000. "The Economics and Ethics of Land Reform: A Critique of the Pontifical Council for Justice and Peace's 'Toward a Better Distribution of Land: The Challenge of Agrarian Reform,'" *Journal of Natural Resources and Environmental Law*, Vol. 15, No. 1, pp. 37–69; http://www.walterblock.com/publications/ethics_land_reform.pdf

Note: The Journal of Natural Resources and Environmental Law has been renamed, changed to, the Kentucky Journal of Equine, Agriculture, and Natural Resources Law.

Part IV: Other Property Rights Issues

Chapter 13. Nedzel, Nadia and Walter Block. 2007. "Eminent Domain: A Legal and Economic Analysis," *Government Law and Policy Journal*, Vol. 9, No. 1, Spring, pp. 70–73; http://tinyurl.com/yw47yk

Chapter 14. Nedzel, Nadia and Walter Block. 2008. "Eminent Domain: A Legal and Economic Critique," *University of Maryland Law Journal of Race, Religion, Gender, and Class*, Vol. 7, No. 1, pp. 140–171; http://www.law.umaryland.edu/academics/journals/rrgc/current_issue.html

Chapter 15. Block Walter and Lorne Gunter. 2007. "Canadian Aboriginals: A Debate," August 16; http://www.lewrockwell.com/block/block82.html

Chapter 16. Huebert, J. H. and Walter Block. 2007. "Space Environmentalism, Property Rights, and the Law," *Memphis Law Review*, Vol. 37, No. 2, Winter, pp. 281–309

Chapter 17. Block, Walter. 2006. "Coase and *Kelo*: Ominous Parallels and Reply to Lott on Rothbard on Coase," *Whittier Law Review*, Vol. 27, No. 4, pp. 997–1022

Chapter 18. Block, Walter. 2005. "Landsburg on Crime," October 19; http://www.lewrockwell.com/block/block57.html

Chapter 19. Epstein, Richard vs. Walter Block, 2005. "Debate on Eminent Domain," *NYU Journal of Law & Liberty*, Vol. 1, No. 3, pp. 1144–1169; http://maroon.uchicago.edu/news/articles/2004/05/04/block_epstein_will_d.php (5/4/04); http://www.mises.org/blog/archives/002009.asp; http://www.nyujll.org/articles/Vol.%201%20No.%203/Vol.%201%20No.%203%20-%20Block%20and%20Epstein.pdf

Chapter 20. Block, Walter. 2002. "Homesteading City Streets; An Exercise in Managerial Theory," *Planning and Markets*, Vol. 5, No. 1, pp. 18–23; September, http://www-pam.usc.edu/; http://www-pam.usc.edu/volume5/v5i1a2s1.html; http://www-pam.usc.edu/volume5/v5i1a2sr.html

Chapter 21. Block, Walter. 1996. "O.J.'s Defense: A Reductio Ad Absurdum of the Economics of Ronald Coase and Richard Posner," *European Journal of Law and Economics*, Vol. 3, pp. 265–286; http://www.walterblock.com/publications/block_oj's-defense.pdf

I am very grateful to my co-authors and collaborators: Wilton D. Alston works as a principal research scientist in transportation safety. Milton Friedman (1912–2006) was a professor emeritus at the University of Chicago and a senior fellow at the Hoover Institution and the 1976 recipient of the Nobel Prize in economics. Lorne Gunter is a journalist with the *National Post*. Richard Epstein is a professor of law at NYU. Hans-Hermann Hoppe is a senior fellow at the Mises Institute. J.H. Huebert graduated from the University of Chicago Law School and is in private practice. Nadia Nedzel is a professor of law at Southern University. Guillermo Yeatts (1937–2018) was Chairman, D'Ordal Investments SA., and Chairman Atlas Foundation.

References

Adams, Charles. 2000. When in the Course of Human Events: Arguing the Case for Southern Secession. Lanham, MA: Rowman & Littlefield.

Alchian, Armen. 1977. *Economic Forces at Work*. Indianapolis: Liberty Fund.

Alston, Wilton. 2006a. "Where Have All the Black Libertarians Gone?" July 11.

Alston, Wilton. 2006b. "The Black Libertarian's FAQ." July 25.

America, Richard. 1993. *Paying the Social Debt: What White America Owes Black America*. New York, NY: Praeger.

Anderson, Gary M. "Welfare Programs in the Rent Seeking Society," *Southern Economic Journal* 54 (1987): 377–86.

Anderson, Martin, "Pollution," The Christian Science Monitor, January 4, 1989, p. 19, reprinted in Economics and the Environment: A Reconciliation, Walter Block, ed., Vancouver: The Fraser Institute, 1990, pp. ix–x.

Anderson, Martin. 1964. The Federal Bulldozer, Cambridge, MIT Press.

Anderson, Martin. *Welfare: The Political Economy of Welfare Reform in the United States* (Stanford: Hoover Institution Press, 1978).

Anderson, Terry L., and Leal, Donald R., Free Market Environmentalism, San Francisco: Pacific Research Institute, 1991.

Anderson, Terry, and P. J. Hill, *The Birth of the Transfer Society* (Lanham, MD: University Press of America, 1989).

Anderson, William, Walter Block, Thomas J. DiLorenzo, Ilana Mercer, Leon Snyman and Christopher Westley, "The Microsoft Corporation in Collision

W. E. Block, *Property Rights*, Palgrave Studies in Classical Liberalism,
https://doi.org/10.1007/978-3-030-28353-7

with Antitrust Law," *The Journal of Social, Political and Economic Studies*, Vol. 26, No. 1, Winter 2001, pp. 287–302.

Arceneaux, Taniecea. 2005. "Reparations for Slavery: A Cause for Reparations, A Case Against David Horowitz" *The Review of Black Political Economy*, Vol. 32, No. 3–4, Winter–Spring, pp. 141–148.

Armentano, D.T. (1972), *The Myths of Antitrust.* New Rochelle, NY: Arlington House.

Armentano, D.T. (1982), *Antitrust and Monopoly: Anatomy of a Policy Failure.* New York, NY: Wiley.

Armentano, D.T. (1991), *Antitrust Policy: The Case for Repeal.* Washington, DC: The Cato Institute.

Armstrong, D. (1982), *Competition versus Monopoly: Combines Policy in Perspective.* Vancouver: The Fraser Institute.

Arnold, Roger A., 1982, "Efficiency vs. Ethics: Which Is the Proper Decision Criterion in Law Cases?," The Journal of Libertarian Studies, Vol. VI, No. 1, Winter, pp. 49–58.

Barnett, Randy and John Hagel, eds., *Assessing the Criminal* (Cambridge, MA: Ballinger, 1977.

Barnett, Randy E. 1978. "Toward a Theory of Legal Naturalism," *The Journal of Libertarian Studies*, Vol. 2, No. 2, Summer, pp. 97–108.

Barnett, Randy E., The Structure of Liberty: Justice and the Rule of Law, Oxford: Clarendon Press, 1998a.

Barnett, Randy, 1977, "Whither anarchy? Has Robert Nozick justified the state?," The Journal of Libertarian Studies, Vol. 1, No. 1, Winter, pp. 15–22.

Barnett, Randy. "Pursuing Justice in a Free Society, Part One: Power vs. Liberty," *Criminal Justice Ethics* 4 (1985): 50–72; *The Structure of Liberty: Justice and the Rule of Law* (Oxford: Clarendon Press, 1998b).

Bastiat, Frederic. 1962. *The Law.* New York: Foundation for Economic Education.

Bauer, P.T. and Yamey, B.S. (1957), *The Economics of Underdeveloped Countries.* Chicago, IL: University of Chicago Press.

Becker, Gary. 1964. *Human Capital.* New York: National Bureau of Economic Research.

Benson, Bruce L. "An Evolutionary Contractarian View of Primitive Law: The Institutions and Incentives Arising under Customary Indian Law," *The Review of Austrian Economics* 5, 1 (1991): 41–65.

Benson, Bruce L. "Customary Law as a Social Contract: International Commercial Law," *Constitutional Political Economy* 2 (1992): 1–27.

Benson, Bruce L. "Legal Evolution in Primitive Societies," *Journal of Institutional and Theoretical Economics* 144 (1988): 772–88.

Benson, Bruce L. "The Lost Victim and Other Failures of the Public Law Experiment," *Harvard Journal of Law and Public Policy* 9 (1986): 399–427.

Benson, Bruce L. 1990. *The Enterprise of Law: Justice Without the State*. San Francisco: Pacific Research Institute.

Benson, Bruce L., "The Impetus for Recognizing Private Property and Adopting Ethical Behavior in a Market Economy: Natural Law, Government Law or Evolving Self Interest," The Review of Austrian Economics, Vol. 6, No. 2, 1993, pp. 43–80.

Benson, Bruce L., "The Spontaneous Evolution of Commercial Law," Southern Economic Journal, 55: 644–661, 1989b.

Benson, Bruce L., 1981, "Land Use Regulation: A Supply and Demand Analysis of Changing Property Rights," The Journal of Libertarian Studies, Vol. V, No. 4, Fall, pp. 435–451.

Benson, Bruce L., 1989a, Enforcement of Private Property Rights in Primitive Societies: Law Without Government," The Journal of Libertarian Studies, Vol. IX, No. 1, Winter, pp. 1–26.

Bethell, Tom, The Noblest Triumph: Property and Prosperity Through the Ages, New York: St. Martin's Press, 1998.

Bittker, Boris I. 1972. *Reparations: The Case for Black Reparations*. Boston: Beacon Press.

Block, W. (1977a), "Austrian Monopoly Theory – A Critique", *The Journal of Libertarian Studies*, Vol. I, No. 4, Fall pp. 271–9.

Block, W. (1982a),*Amending the Combines Investigation Act*. Vancouver: The Fraser Institute.

Block, W. (1994a), "Total repeal of anti-trust legislation: a critique of Bork, Brozen and Posner", *Review of Austrian Economics*, Vol. 8 No. 1, pp. 31–64.

Block, Walter and Garschina, Kenneth M., "Hayek, Business Cycles and Fractional Reserve Banking: Continuing the De-Homogenization Process," Review of Austrian Economics, Vol. 9, No. 1, 1995, pp. 77–94.

Block, Walter and Guillermo Yeatts. 1999–2000. "The Economics and Ethics of Land Reform: A Critique of the Pontifical Council for Justice and Peace's 'Toward a Better Distribution of Land: The Challenge of Agrarian Reform,'" *Journal of Natural Resources and Environmental Law*, Vol. 15, No. 1, pp. 37–69.

Block, Walter and Matthew Block. 2000. Toward a Universal Libertarian Theory of Gun (Weapon) Control," Ethics, Place and Environment, 3 (3): 289–298.

Block, Walter and Walker, Michael A., eds., Discrimination, Affirmative Action and Equal Opportunity. Vancouver: The Fraser Institute, 1982.

Block, Walter and Walter Williams, 1981, "Male-Female Earnings Differentials: A Critical Reappraisal," Journal of Labor Research, 2(2): 383–388.

Block, Walter. 1992a. 'The Economics of Discrimination,' *The Journal of Business Ethics*, Vol. 11, pp. 241–254.

Block, Walter, "Alienability, Inalienability, Paternalism and the Law: Reply to Kronman," American Journal of Criminal Law, forthcoming-b.

Block, Walter, "Coase and Demsetz on Private Property Rights," The Journal of Libertarian Studies, Vol. I, No. 2, Spring 1977b, pp. 111–115.

Block, Walter, "Congestion and Road Pricing," The Journal of Libertarian Studies, Vol. IV, No. 3, Fall 1980, pp. 299–330.

Block, Walter, "Earning Happiness Through Homesteading Unowned Land: a comment on 'Buying Misery with Federal Land' by Richard Stroup," Journal of Social Political and Economic Studies, Vol. 15, No. 2, Summer 1990a, pp. 237–253.

Block, Walter, "Ethics, Efficiency, Coasean Property Rights and Psychic Income: A Reply to Demsetz," Review of Austrian Economics, Vol. 8, No. 2, 1995, pp. 61–125.

Block, Walter, "Free Market Transportation: Denationalizing the Roads," Journal of Libertarian Studies, Vol. III, No. 2, Summer 1979, pp. 209–238.

Block, Walter, "Hayek's Road to Serfdom," Journal of Libertarian Studies: An Interdisciplinary Review, Vol. 12, No. 2, Fall 1996c, pp. 327–350.

Block, Walter, "Institutions, Property Rights and Externalities: The Case of Water Quality," Agriculture and Water Quality: Proceedings of an Interdisciplinary Symposium, Murray H. Miller, J. E. FitzGibbon, Glenn C. Fox, R.W. Gillham, and H.R. Whiteley, eds., Guelph Centre for Soil and Water Conservation, University of Guelph Press, 1992b, pp. 191–208.

Block, Walter, "O.J.'s Defense: A Reductio Ad Absurdum of the Economics of Ronald Coase and Richard Posner," European Journal of Law and Economics, 1996a, Vol. 3, pp. 265–286.

Block, Walter, "Public Goods and Externalities: The Case of Roads," The Journal of Libertarian Studies, Vol. VII, No. 1, Spring 1983a, pp. 1–34.

Block, Walter, "Road Socialism," International Journal of Value-Based Management, 1996b, Vol. 9, pp. 195–207.

Block, Walter, "The Case for De-Criminalizing Blackmail: A Reply to Lindgren and Campbell," Western State University Law Review, Vol. 24, No. 2, Spring, 1997, pp. 225–246.

Block, Walter, "The Economics of Discrimination," The Journal of Business Ethics, Vol. 11, 1992c, pp. 241–254.

Block, Walter, "Theories of Highway Safety," Transportation Research Record, #912, 1983b, pp. 7–10.

Block, Walter, "Trading Money for Silence," University of Hawaii Law Review, Vol. 8, No. 1, Spring 1986, pp. 57–73.

Block, Walter, "Epstein on Alienation: A Rejoinder," forthcoming-c.

Block, Walter, "Kuflik on Inalienability: A Rejoinder," forthcoming-d.

Block, Walter, "Market Inalienability Once Again: Reply to Radin," Thomas Jefferson Law Journal, Vol. 22, No. 1, Fall 1999a, pp. 37–88.

Block, Walter, "On Reparations to Blacks for Slavery," forthcoming-a.

Block, Walter, "Toward a Libertarian Theory of Inalienability: A Critique of Rothbard."

Barnett, Gordon, Smith, Kinsella and Epstein," Journal of Libertarian Studies, forthcoming.

Block, Walter, and Block, Matthew, "Roads, Bridges, Sunlight and Private Property Rights: Reply to Gordon Tullock," Journal Des Economistes Et Des Etudes Humanes, Vol. 8, No. 2/3, June September 1998, pp. 315–326

Block, Walter, and Gordon, David, "Extortion and the Exercise of Free Speech Rights: A Reply to Professors Posner, Epstein, Nozick and Lindgren," Loyola of Los Angeles Law Review, Vol. 19, No. 1, November 1985, pp. 37–54.

Block, Walter, Geoffrey Brennan, and Kenneth Elzinga, eds., *Morality of the Market: Religious and Economic Perspectives* (Vancouver, BC: The Fraser Institute, 1985), 495–508.

Block, Walter. "Public Goods and Externalities: The Case of Roads," *The Journal of Libertarian Studies* 7, 1 (Spring 1983): 1–33.

Block, Walter. "Total Repeal of Anti-Trust Legislation: A Critique of Bork, Brozen, and Posner," *The Review of Austrian Economics* 8, 1 (1994b): 1–64.

Block, Walter. 1976. *Defending the Undefendable*. New York: Fleet Press.

Block, Walter. 1977c. "Coase and Demsetz on Private Property Rights," The Journal of Libertarian Studies: An Interdisciplinary Review, 1 (2): 111–115. http://www.mises.org/journals/jls/1_2/1_2_4.pdf.

Block, Walter. 1982b. 'Economic Intervention, Discrimination, and Unforeseen Consequences,' in: Walter Block/Michael Walker, eds., *Discrimination, Affirmative Action and Equal Opportunity*. Vancouver: Fraser Institute.

Block, Walter. 1985. *Focus on Employment Equity: A Critique of the Abella Royal Commission on Equality in Employment* (with Michael Walker). Vancouver: Fraser Institute.

Block, Walter. 1990b. "Earning Happiness Through Homesteading Unowned Land: a comment on 'Buying Misery with Federal Land' by Richard Stroup," *Journal of Social Political and Economic Studies*, Vol. 15, No. 2, Summer, pp. 237–253.

Block, Walter. 1996. "Hayek's Road to Serfdom." *Journal of Libertarian Studies* 12, no. 2 (Fall): 339–65.

Block, Walter. 1999b. "Market Inalienability Once Again: Reply to Radin," Thomas Jefferson Law Journal, 22 (1): 37–88.

Block, Walter. 2002a. "On Reparations to Blacks for Slavery," *Human Rights Review*, Vol. 3, No. 4, July–September, pp. 53–73.

Block, Walter. 2002b. "A critique of the legal and philosophical case for rent control," Journal of Business Ethics, forthcoming.

Block, Walter. 6/10/2002c. "A Libertarian Theory of Secession and Slavery," http://www.lewrockwell.com/block/block15.html.

Block, Walter. 7/9/2002d. "Secession," http://www.lewrockwell.com/block/block18.html; reprinted: http://www.secessionist.us/secessionist_no8.htm; http://www.southernnationalist.org/secession_block.htm.

Block, Walter. 2009. *The Privatization of Roads and Highways: Human and Economic Factors*. Auburn, AL: The Mises Institute.

Boettke, P.J. (1993), *Why Perestroika Failed: The Politics and Economics of Socialist Transformation*. London: Routledge.

Böhm-Bawerk, Eugen von. *Capital and Interest*, trans. George D. Hunke and Hans F. Sennholz (South Holland, Ill.: Libertarian Press, 1959 [1884]), particularly Part I, Chapter XII, "Exploitation Theory of Socialism-Communism."

Boudreaux, D.J. and DiLorenzo, T.J. (1992), "The protectionist roots of antitrust", *Review of Austrian Economics*, Vol. 6 No. 2, pp. 81–96.

Buchanan, James M. and G.F. Thirlby, L.S.E. Essays on Cost. New York: New York University Press, 1981.

Buchanan, James M. and Gordon Tullock, *The Calculus of Consent: Logical Foundations of Constitutional Democracy* (Ann Arbor: University of Michigan Press, 1971).

Buchanan, James M. *Cost and Choice: An Inquiry into Economic Theory* (Chicago: Markham, 1969).

Buchanan, James M., "The Ethical Limits of Taxation," Scandinavian Journal of Economics, 86: 102–114, 1984.

Buchanan, James M., Robert D. Tollison, and Gordon Tullock, eds., *Toward a Theory of the Rent-Seeking Society* (College Station: Texas A&M University, 1980).

Cadin, Michelle, and Block, Walter, (1997), "Privatize the Public Highway System," The Freeman, February, Vol. 47, No. 2, pp. 96–97.

Cheung, Steven N.S., "The Contractual Nature of the Firm," Journal of Law and Economics, 26 April 1983.

Childs, Roy A., Jr., 1977, "The invisible hand strikes back," The Journal of Libertarian Studies, Vol. 1, No. 1, Winter, pp. 23–34.

Coase, Ronald H., "The Institutional Structure of Production," American Economic Review, Vol. 82, No. 4, September 1992, pp. 713–19.

Coase, Ronald. 1960. "The Problem of Social Cost," 3 Journal of Law and Economics 1–44.

Conquest, Robert (1986), The Harvest of Sorrow. NY: Oxford University Press.

Conquest, Robert (1990) The Great Terror. Edmonton, Alberta: Edmonton University Press.

Cordato, Roy E., "Subjective Value, Time Passage, and the Economics of Harmful Effects," Hamline Law Review, Vol. 12, No. 2, Spring 1989, pp. 229–244.

Cordato, Roy E., Welfare Economics and Externalities in an Open-Ended Universe: A Modern Austrian Perspective. Boston: Kluwer, 1992b.

Cordato, Roy E., "Knowledge Problems and the Problem of Social Cost," Journal of the History of Economic Thought 14 Fall 1992a.

D'Amico, Dan and Walter Block. Unpublished. "A Legal and Economic Analysis of Graffiti".

De Jasay, Anthony. *The State* (Oxford: Basil Blackwell, 1985).

Demsetz, Harold, "Ethics and Efficiency in Property Rights Systems," in Time, Uncertainty and Disequilibrium: Explorations of Austrian Themes, Mario Rizzo, ed., Lexington, MA: D.C.Heath and Co., 1979.

Demsetz, Harold, "Some Aspects of Property Rights," Journal of Law and Economics, Vol. IX, October 1966.

Demsetz, Harold, "Toward a Theory of Property Rights," American Economic Review, 57: 347–359, 1967.

DiLorenzo, T.J. (1997), "The myth of natural monopoly", *Review of Austrian Economics*, Vol. 9, No. 2, pp. 43–58.

DiLorenzo, Thomas and Block, Walter, "Critique of the Public Choice Perspective of the State," forthcoming.

DiLorenzo, Thomas J. "Competition and Political Entrepreneurship: Austrian Insights into Public Choice Theory," *The Review of Austrian Economics* 2 (1988): 59–71.

DiLorenzo, Thomas J., "The Subjectivist Roots of James Buchanan's Economics," The Review of Austrian Economics, Vol. 4, 1990, pp. 180–195.

DiLorenzo, Thomas. 2006. "Happy Secession Day." http://www.lewrockwell.com/dilorenzo/dilorenzo103.html.

Dworkin, Ronald, Taking Rights Seriously, Cambridge, MA: Harvard University Press, 1977.

Epstein, Richard A., *Forbidden Grounds: The Case against Employment Discrimination Laws*. Cambridge: Harvard University Press, 1992.

Epstein, Richard, "Crime and Tort: Old Wine in Old Bottles," in Assessing the Criminal, Randy E. Barnett and John Hagel III, eds., Cambridge, MA: Ballinger, 1977.

Evers, Williamson M., 1977, "Toward a reformulation of the law of contracts," The Journal of Libertarian Studies, Vol. 1, No. 1, Winter, pp. 3–14.

Flew, Antony, 1982, "Could there be Universal Natural Rights?," The Journal of Libertarian Studies, Vol. VI, No. 3–4, Summer/Fall, pp. 277–288.

Fogel, Robert W., and Engerman, Stanley L. 1974. *Time on the Cross: The Economics of American Negro Slavery*. Ann Arbor: University of Michigan Press.

Fox, Glenn, 1992, "The Pricing of Environmental Goods: A Praxeological Critique of Contingent Valuation," Cultural Dynamics, Vol. V, No. 3, pp. 245–259.

Friedman, David. "Private Creation and Enforcement of Law: A Historical Case," *Journal of Legal Studies* 8 (1979): 399–415.

Friedman, David. *The Machinery of Freedom: Guide to a Radical Capitalism*, 2nd ed. (La Salle, IL: Open Court, 1989).

Friedman, Milton, and Anna J. Schwartz. 1963. *A Monetary History of the U.S., 1867–1960*. New York: National Bureau of Economic Research.

Friedman, Milton, and George J. Stigler. 1946. *Roofs or Ceilings?: The Current Housing Problem*. Irvington-on-Hudson: N.Y.: Foundation for Economic Education. Reprinted in *Rent Control: Myths and Realities*. Walter Block and Edgar Olsen, eds. Vancouver, BC: Fraser Institute, 1981.

Friedman, Milton. 1962 [1996]. *Capitalism and Freedom*. Chicago: University of Chicago Press.

Gordon, David, "Justice and Redistributive Taxation: James Buchanan vs. Ludwig von Mises," The Review of Austrian Economics, Vol. 8, No. 1, 1994, pp. 117–131.

Gordon, David, "Toward a Deconstruction of Utility and Welfare Economics," The Review of Austrian Economics, Vol. 6, No. 2, 1993, pp. 99–112.

Gordon, David, ed. 1998. *Secession, State and Liberty*. New Brunswick: Transaction Publishers.

Grier, Kevin B. and Joseph P. McGarrity, "The Effect of Macroeconomic Fluctuations on the Electoral Fortunes of House Incumbents," *Journal of Law and Economics* XLI (April 1993): 143–61.

Groudine, Candace J. 1980. "Authority: H.L.A. Hart and the Problem with Legal Positivism," *The Journal of Libertarian Studies*, Vol. IV, No. 3, Summer, pp. 273–288.

Gunderson, Gerald, "Privatization and the 19th-Century Turnpike," Cato Journal, Vol. 9, No. 1, Spring/Summer 1989, pp. 191–200.

Hamowy, Ronald. 1984. *Canadian Medicine: A Study in Restricted Entry*. Vancouver: Fraser Institute.

Hayek, F.A. (1945), "The Use of Knowledge in Society", *American Economic Review*, Vol. 35, pp. 519–25.

Hayek, F.A. (1948), "Socialist calculation I, II, & III", *Individualism and Economic Order*. Chicago, IL: University of Chicago Press.

Hayek, F.A. 1944. *The Road to Serfdom*. Chicago: Chicago University Press.

Hayek, Friedrich. 1994. A Radio Discussion with Maynard C. Krueger and Charles E. Merriam. *Hayek on Hayek: An Autobiographical Dialogue*. Stephen Kresge and Leif Wenar, eds. Chicago: University of Chicago Press.

Henderson, David R. 2001. *The Joy of Freedom: An Economist's Odyssey*. Financial Times, Prentice Hall.

Herrnstein, Richard J., and Murray, Charles. 1994. The Bell Curve: Intelligence and Class Structure in American Life, New York: The Free Press.

High, J. (1984–1985), "Bork's paradox: static vs dynamic efficiency in antitrust analysis", *Contemporary Policy Issues*, Vol. 3, pp. 21–34.

High, Jack, "Bork's Paradox: Static Versus Dynamic Efficiency in Antitrust Analysis," *Contemporary Policy Issues* 3 (1984–1985): 21–34.

Hoppe, Hans-Hermann (1995), Economic Science and the Austrian Method, Auburn, AL: The Mises Institute.

Hans-Hermann Hoppe, "Marxist and Austrian Class Analysis," in *Marxism: Economics, Religion, Politics, and Philosophy*, ed. Yuri Maltsev (Boston: Dordrecht, 1992a).

Hoppe, Hans-Hermann, "Austrian Rationalism in the Age of the Decline of Positivism," Ebeling, R., ed., Austrian Economics: Perspectives on the Past and Prospects for the Future, Hillsdale, MI.: Hillsdale College Press, 1991.

Hoppe, Hans-Hermann, "The Economics and Sociology of Taxation," Rockwell. L., ed., Taxation: An Austrian View, Boston: Dordrecht, 1992b.

Hoppe, Hans-Hermann, 1989a, "Fallacies of the Public Goods Theory and the Production of Security," The Journal of Libertarian Studies, Vol. IX, No. 1, Winter, pp. 27–46.

Hoppe, Hans-Hermann, Praxeology and Economic Science. Auburn, AL: Mises Institute, Auburn University, 1988.

Hoppe, Hans-Hermann. "The Economics and Sociology of Taxation," in *Taxation: An Austrian View*, ed. L. Rockwell (Boston: Dordrecht, 1992c).

Hoppe, Hans-Hermann. 1989b. *A Theory of Socialism and Capitalism*. Boston: Kluwer Academic Publishers.

Hoppe, Hans-Hermann. 1990. 'Man, Economy, and Liberty,' *Review of Austrian Economics*, Vol. 4.

Hoppe, Hans-Hermann. 1993. *The Economics and Ethics of Private Property: Studies in Political Economy and Philosophy*. Boston: Kluwer.

Hoppe, Hans-Hermann. 2001. *Democracy – The God that Failed: The Economics and Politics of Monarchy, Democracy, and Natural Order*. Rutgers University, NJ: Transaction Publishers.

Hoppe, Hans-Hermann. *A Theory of Socialism and Capitalism: Economies, Polities, and Ethics* (Boston: Kluwer, 1989c).

Hoppe, Hans-Hermann. *A Theory of Socialism and Capitalism*; "Fallacies of the Public Goods Theory and the Production of Security," *The Journal of Libertarian Studies* IX, 1 (Winter 1989d): 27–46.

Horowitz, David. "Clarence Page's Race Problem and Mine," *Heterodoxy* (May/June 1996).

Horowitz, David. 2000. "The Latest Civil Rights Disaster: Ten Reasons Why Reparations for Slavery are a Bad Idea for Black People—And Racist Too." http://www.salon.com/news/col/horo/2000/05/30/reparations/index.html.

Horowitz, David. 2002. *Uncivil Wars: The Controversy over Reparations for Slavery*. San Francisco, CA: Encounter Books.

Horwitz, Morton, "Law and Economics: Science or Politics?," Hofstra Law Review 8 (1980).

Hummel, Jeffrey Rogers. 1996. *Emancipating Slaves, Enslaving Free Men: A History of the American Civil War*. Chicago: Open Court.

Hummell, Jeffrey Rogers. "National Goods Versus Public Goods: Defense, Disarmament, and Free Riders," *The Review of Austrian Economics* 4 (1990): 88–122.

Hutchinson, Earl Ofari, "Ten Reasons Why Reparations," http://alternet.org/story/10680/.

Jacobs, Jane. *The Death and Life of Great American Cities* (New York: Vintage, 1989).

King, J. Charles, A Rationale for Punishment, 4 J. Libertarian Stud. 151, 154 (1980).

Kinsella, Stephan N., "A Libertarian Theory of Punishment and Rights," (volume) 30 Loy. L.A. L. Rev. 607–45 (1997).

Kinsella, Stephan N., "Estoppel: A New Justification for Individual Rights," Reason Papers No. 17 (Fall 1992), p. 61.

Kinsella, Stephan N. "Punishment and Proportionality: The Estoppel Approach," 12:1 J. Libertarian Studies 51 (Spring 1996a).

Kinsella, Stephan N. "New Rationalist Directions in Libertarian Rights Theory," 12:2 J. Libertarian Studies 313–26 (Fall 1996b).

Kirzner, I.M. (1973), *Competition and Entrepreneurship*. Chicago, IL: University of Chicago Press.

Klein, Dan and Fielding, G.J., "High Occupancy/Toll Lanes: Phasing in Congestion Pricing a Lane at a Time," Policy Study, No. 170, Reason Foundation, November 1993b.

Klein, Dan and Fielding, G.J., "How to Franchise Highways," Journal of Transport Economics and Policy, May 1993a, pp. 113–130.

Klein, Dan and Fielding, G.J., "Private Toll Roads: Learning from the Nineteenth Century," Transportation Quarterly, July 1992, pp. 321–341.

Klein, Dan, "The Voluntary Provision of Public Goods? The Turnpike Companies of Early America," Economic Inquiry, October 1990, pp. 788–812.

Klein, Dan, Majewski, J., and Baer, C., "Economy, Community and the Law: The Turnpike Movement in New York, 1797–1845, The Journal of Economic History, March 1993a, pp. 106–122.

Klein, Dan, Majewski, J., and Baer, C., "From Trunk to Branch: Toll Roads in New York, 1800–1860," Essays in Economic and Business History, 1993b, pp. 191–209.

Krecke, Elisabeth, "Law and the Market Order: An Austrian Critique of the Economic Analysis of Law," paper presented at the Ludwig von Mises Institute's Austrian Scholar's Conference, New York City, October 9–11, 1992.

Kreptul, Andrei. 2003. "The Constitutional Right of Secession in Political Theory and History." *The Journal of Libertarian Studies*, Vol. 17, No. 4, Fall, pp. 30–100; http://www.mises.org/journals/jls/17_4/17_4_3.pdf.

Leff, Arthur Allen, "Economic Analysis of Law: Some Realism about Nominalism," Virginia Law Review, 60 (1974).

Levin, Michael, "Comparable Worth: The Feminist Road to Socialism," Commentary, September 1984.

Levin, Michael. 1987. *Feminism and Freedom.* New Brunswick, NJ: Transaction Books.

Levin, Michael. 1997. Why Race Matters, Westport, CT: Praeger.

Lloyd, Robert and Joseph P. McGarrity, "A Profit Analysis of the Senate Vote on Gramm-Rudman," *Public Choice* 85 (November 1995): 81–90.

Locke, John, Second Treatise of Civil Government. Chicago: Henry Regnery, 1955.

Locke, John. 1948. *An Essay Concerning the True Origin, Extent and End of Civil Government*, in E. Barker, ed., *Social Contract.* New York: Oxford University Press, pp. 17–18.

Machan, Tibor, 1978, "Against nonlibertarian natural rights," The Journal of Libertarian Studies, Vol. 2, No. 3, Fall, pp. 233–238.

Malcolm X, *Malcolm X Speaks: Selected Speeches and Statements*, ed. George Breitman (New York: Merit Publishers, 1965).

Manne, H.A. (2002), "Bring back the hostile takeover", *Wall Street Journal*, 26 June.

Manne, Henry A. 1966a. *Insider Trading and the Stock Market*, New York: Free Press.

Manne, Henry A. 1966b. 'In Defense of Insider Trading,' *Harvard Business Review*, 113, Nov./Dec.

McChesney, F. (1991a), "Antitrust and regulation: Chicago's contradictory views", *Cato Journal*, Vol. 10.

McChesney, Fred. "Antitrust and Regulation: Chicago's Contradictory Views," *Cato Journal* 10 (1991b): pp. 775–798.

McGee, Robert and Walter Block. 1989. 'Information, Privilege, Opportunity and Insider Trading,' *Northern Illinois Law Review*, December, Vol. 10, No. 1, pp. 1–35.

McGee, Robert W. 1994a. "Secession Reconsidered," *The Journal of Libertarian Studies*, Vol. 11, No. 1, Fall, pp. 11–33; http://www.mises.org/journals/jls/11_1/11_1_2.pdf.

McGee, Robert W. 1994b. "Secession as a Tool for Limiting the Growth of State and Municipal Government and Making it More Responsive: A Constitutional Proposal." *Western State University Law Review* 21. Spring.

McGee, Robert, and Block, Walter, "Pollution Trading Permits as a Form of Market Socialism, and the Search for a Real Market Solution to Environmental Pollution," Fordham University Law and Environmental Journal, Vol. VI, No. 1, Fall 1994, pp. 51–77.

McGee, Robert. "Mergers and Acquisitions: An Economic and Legal Analysis," *Creighton Law Review* 22, 3 (1989): 665–93.

Mill, John Stuart, Utilitarianism: With Critical Essays, Samuel Gorowitz, ed., New York: Bobbs-Merrill, 1971.

Mises, Ludwig von, Socialism, Indianapolis: Liberty Fund, 1981 (1969).

Mises, Ludwig von. [1949] 1966. *Human Action. A Treatise on Economics*. New Haven: Yale University Press, 1949 (3rd ed. Chicago: Regnery, 1966).

Mises, Ludwig von. [1957] 1985. *Theory and History: An Interpretation of Social and Economic Evolution*. New Haven: Yale University Press, 1957 (reprint: Auburn University, Alabama: The Ludwig von Mises Institute, 1985).

Murray, Charles. *In Pursuit: Of Happiness and Good Government* (New York: Simon & Schuster, 1990).

Murray, Charles. *Losing Ground: American Social Policy from 1950 to 1980* (New York: Basic Books, 1984).

North, Gary, The Coase Theorem. Tyler, TX: The Institute for Christian Economics, 1992.

North, Gary, Tools of Dominion: The Case Laws of Exodus. Tyler, TX: Institute for Christian Economics, 1990.

Northup, Solomon. 1997. *Twelve Years a Slave*, Academic Affairs Library, UNC-CH University of North Carolina, Chapel Hill, http://docsouth.unc.edu/northup/northup.html.

Novak, Michael, ed. 1979a. The Denigration of Capitalism. Washington, DC: American Enterprise Institute for Public Policy.

Novak, Michael, ed. 1979b. Capitalism and Socialism. Washington, DC: American Institute for Public Policy Research.

Novak, Michael. 1978. The Spirit of Democratic Capitalism. New York, NY: Simon & Schuster.

Novak, Michael. 1985. "The Liberal Society as Liberation Theology," Notre Dame Journal of Law, Ethics and Public Policy, Volume 2, No. 1.

Novak, Michael. 1986. Will it Liberate? Questions about Liberation Theology. New York: Paulist Press.

Nozick, Robert. 1974. Anarchy, State and Utopia. New York: Basic Books.

Olasky, Marvin. *The Tragedy of American Compassion* (Chicago: Regnery Gateway, 1992).

Oppenheimer, Franz. *The State* (New York: Free Life Editions, 1975 [1914]).

Osterfeld, David. "Anarchism and the Public Goods Issue: Law, Courts, and the Police," *The Journal of Libertarian Studies* 9, 1 (Winter 1989): 47–68.

Pasour, E.C., Jr., 1979, "Conservation, 'X-Inefficiency' and Efficient Use of Natural Resources," The Journal of Libertarian Studies, Vol. III, No. 4, Fall, pp. 371–390.

Pasour, E.C., Jr., 1981, "The Free Rider as a Basis for Government Intervention," The Journal of Libertarian Studies, Vol. V, No. 4, Fall, pp. 453–464.

Pasour, E.C., Jr., 1992, "Human Action and the role of the Economist in the Public Process," Cultural Dynamics, Vol. V, No. 3, pp. 303–318.

Paul, Ellen Frankel. 1987. *Property Rights and Eminent Domain*. Transaction.

Peden, Joseph R. "Property Rights in Celtic Irish Law," *The Journal of Libertarian Studies* 1, 2 (Spring 1977): 81–96.

Piven, Frances Fox and Richard A. Cloward. 1971. *Regulating the Poor: The Functions of Public Welfare*. New York: Random House.

Posner, Richard A., "The Ethical and Political Basis of the Efficiency Norm in Common Law Adjudication," in Law, Economics, and Philosophy: A Critical Introduction, with Applications to the Law of Torts, Kuperberg, Mark and Beitz, Charles, eds., New York: Rowman and Allanheld, 1983, pp. 81–101.

Posner, Richard A., Economic Analysis of Law. 3rd ed., Boston: Little Brown, 1986.

Posner, Richard, "An Economic Theory of the Criminal Law," Columbia Law Review, Vol. 85, No. 6, October 1985.

Posner, Richard, Sex and Reason, Cambridge: Harvard University Press, 1992.

Radin, Margaret Jane. 1986. "Residential Rent Control," Philosophy and Public Affairs, 15: 350–380.

Radin, Margaret Jane. 1987. "Market-Inalienability," Harvard Law Review, 100 (8): 1849–1937.

Rasmussen, Douglass B., 1980, "A Groundwork for Rights: Man's Natural End," The Journal of Libertarian Studies, Vol. IV, No. 1, Winter, pp. 65–76.

Rawls, John. 1971a. *A Theory of Justice*. Cambridge: Harvard University Press.

Rawls, John. 1971b. A Theory of Justice. Cambridge: Harvard University Press.

Robinson, Randall. 1998. *Defending the Spirit: A Black Life in America*. Middlesex, England: Penguin.

Robinson, Randall. 2000. *The Debt: What America Owes to Blacks*. New York, NY: Dutton.

Robinson, Randall. 2002. *The Reckoning*. Middlesex, England: Penguin.

Roth, Gabriel, A Self-financing Road System. London, England, The Institute of Economic Affairs, 1966.

Roth, Gabriel, Paying for Roads: The Economics of Traffic Congestion. Middlesex, England: Penguin, 1967.

Roth, Gabriel, The Private Provision of Public Services in Developing Countries. Oxford: Oxford University Press, 1987.

Rothbard, M.N. (1970a), *Man, Economy and State*. Los Angeles, CA: Nash.

Rothbard, Murray N. 1970b. *Power and Market: Government and the Economy*, Menlo Park, CA: Institute for Humane Studies.

Rothbard, Murray N. 1967. "The Principle of Secession Defended." *Colorado Springs Gazette Telegraph* (Pine Tree Column), October 3.

Rothbard, Murray N. 1973. *For a New Liberty*. New York: Macmillan, http://www.mises.org/rothbard/newliberty.asp.

Rothbard, Murray N. 1998 [1982]. *The Ethics of Liberty*. New York: New York University Press. http://www.mises.org/rothbard/ethics/ethics.asp.

Rothbard, Murray N. and Jerome Tuccille, eds., *Left and Right: Selected Essays, 1954–1965* (New York: Arno Press, 1972).

Rothbard, Murray N., "Critique of Public Choice," Logic of Action.

Rothbard, Murray N., "Intimidation by Rhetoric," Review of Austrian Economics, Vol. 9, No. 1, 1996, pp. 173–178.

Rothbard, Murray N., "Law, Property Rights, and Air Pollution," Cato Journal, Vol. 2, No. 1, Spring, 1982b, reprinted in Economics and the Environment: A Reconciliation, Walter Block, ed., Vancouver: The Fraser Institute, 1990.

Rothbard, Murray N., "Toward a Reconstruction of Utility and Welfare Economics," San Francisco: Center for Libertarian Studies, Occasional Paper #3, 1977a.

Rothbard, Murray N., 1977b, "Robert Nozick and the immaculate conception of the state, The Journal of Libertarian Studies, Vol. 1, No. 1, Winter, pp. 45–58.

Rozeff, Michael S. 2005. "Original Appropriation and Its Critics." September 1. http://www.lewrockwell.com/rozeff/rozeff18.html.

Salerno, J.T. (1990), "Ludwig von Mises as social rationalist", *Review of Austrian Economics*, Vol. 4, pp. 26–54.

Salerno, J.T. (1992), "Mises and Hayek dehomogenized", *Review of Austrian Economics*, Vol. 6, No. 2, pp. 113–46.

Salerno, J. (1995), "A final word: calculation, knowledge and appraisement", *Review of Austrian Economics*, Vol. 9 No. 1, pp. 141–2.

Salerno, Joseph T., "Ludwig von Mises's Monetary Theory in Light of Modern Monetary Thought," Review of Austrian Economics, Vol. 8, No. 1, 1994, pp. 71–115.

Sanders, John T., 1977, "The free market model versus Government: a reply to Nozick," The Journal of Libertarian Studies, Vol. 1, No. 1, Winter, pp. 35–44.

Schumpeter, Joseph A., History of Economic Analysis. New York: Oxford University Press, 1954.

Seldon, Arthur, and Harris, Ralph. 1977. "Not from Benevolence: Twenty Years of Economic Dissent." London, UK: Institute for Economic Affairs.

Shugart, W.F. II (1987), "Don't Revise the Clayton Act, Scrap It!," *Cato Journal*, Vol. 6, p. 925.

Siegan, Bernard. *Land Use without Zoning*. New York: Lexington, 1972.

Simpson, A.W.B., "Coase v. Pigou Reexamined," Journal of Legal Studies, Jan. 1996, pp. 53–97.

Simpson, A.W.B. 1987. "The Common Law & Legal Theory" & "The Survival of the Common Law System," *Legal Theory & Legal History*, Hambledon Press.

Smith, Adam. 1776/1979. An Inquiry into the Nature and Causes of the Wealth of Nations. Indianapolis, IN: Liberty Fund.

Smith, F.L. Jr (1983), "Why not Abolish Antitrust?," *Regulation*, January–February, p. 23.

Solomon, Martin M., "A Paean to Property," Liberty, June 1999, pp. 43–47.

Sowell, Thomas. 1983a. *Race and Economics*. New York: Morrow.

Sowell, Thomas. *A Conflict of Visions: Ideological Origins of Political Struggles* (New York: Morrow, 1987).

Sowell, Thomas. *Ethnic America* (New York: Basic Books, 1981).

Sowell, Thomas. *Race and Culture: A World View* (New York: Basic Books, 1994).

Sowell, Thomas. *Race and Economics* (New York: Longman, 1975).

Sowell, Thomas. *The Economics and Politics of Race: An International Perspective* (New York: Morrow, 1983b).

Sowell, Thomas. *The Vision of the Anointed* (New York: Basic Books, 1995).

Spooner, Lysander. (1966 [1870]). *No Treason*. Larkspur, CO: Ralph Myles Publisher.

Stroup, Richard, "Buying misery with federal land," Public Choice, Vol. 57, 1988, pp. 69–77.

Tannehill, Morris, and Linda Tannehill. 1984. *The Market for Liberty*. New York: Laissez-Faire Books.

Thornton, Mark, "Slavery, Profitability and the Market Process," The Review of Austrian Economics, Vol. 7, No. 2, 1994, pp. 21–47.

Tucker, William. *The Excluded Americans: Homelessness and Housing Policy*, Chicago: Regnery-Gateway, 1990.

von Mises, L. (1975), "Economic calculation in the socialist commonwealth", in Hayek, F.A. (Ed.), *Collectivist Economic Planning*, Kelley, Clifton, NJ, (first published in 1933).

von Mises, L. (1981), *Socialism*. Indianapolis , IN: Liberty Fund, (first published in 1969).

Warhaftig, I. (n.d.), "Consumer Protection: Price Fraud", *Crossroads: Halacha and the Modern World*, Vol. II, Zomet Institute, Alon Shvut-Gush Etzion, available at: http://hometown.aol.com/lazera/index2.html.

Westley, Robert. 1998. "Many Billions Gone: Is It Time to Reconsider the Case for Black Reparations?," 40 *Boston College Law Review* 429–476.

Williams, Walter E. "Good Intentions—Bad Results: The Economic Pastoral and America's Disadvantaged," *Notre Dame Journal of Law, Ethics, and Public Policy* 2, 1 (1985): pp. 179–199.

Williams, Walter E. *The State Against Blacks* (New York: McGraw-Hill, 1982).

Wilson, R. (1997), "Comparative Religious Thought on Economic Behavior and Financial Transactions", The Journal of the Association of Christian Economists, No. 23, August.

Woolridge, William C. 1970. *Uncle Sam the Monopoly Man*. New Rochelle, NY: Arlington House.

Zerbe, Richard O., Jr., "The Law and Economics of Cannibalism: Foundations of the Economic Analysis of Normative Issues," Working Papers in Public Policy Analysis and Management, University of Washington, 1994, 94–1.

The manufacturer's authorised representative in the EU is Springer Nature Customer Service Centre GmbH, Europaplatz 3, 69115 Heidelberg, Germany. If you have any concerns regarding our products, please contact ProductSafety@springernature.com

Printed and bound by CPI Group (UK) Ltd, Croydon, CR0 4YY
05/10/2026
02228125-0016